READINGS IN THE HISTORY OF PHILOSOPHY

SERIES EDITORS:

PAUL EDWARDS, The City University of New York, Brooklyn College

RICHARD H. POPKIN, University of California, San Diego

The Volumes and Their Editors:

GREEK PHILOSOPHY: THALES TO ARISTOTLE
Reginald E. Allen

GREEK AND ROMAN PHILOSOPHY AFTER ARISTOTLE
Jason L. Saunders

MEDIEVAL PHILOSOPHY: FROM
ST. AUGUSTINE TO NICHOLAS OF CUSA
John F. Wippel and Allan B. Wolter, O.F.M.

THE PHILOSOPHY OF THE SIXTEENTH AND
SEVENTEENTH CENTURIES
Richard H. Popkin

EIGHTEENTH-CENTURY PHILOSOPHY
Lewis White Beck

NINETEENTH-CENTURY PHILOSOPHY
Patrick L. Gardiner

TWENTIETH-CENTURY PHILOSOPHY:
THE ANALYTIC TRADITION
Morris Weitz

In Preparation:
TWENTIETH-CENTURY PHILOSOPHY:
THE SPECULATIVE TRADITION

Nineteenth-Century Philosophy

Edited and with an Introduction by

Patrick L. Gardiner

THE FREE PRESS
New York

PHILOSOPHERS DEPICTED ON THE COVER ARE:
UPPER LEFT, HEGEL; UPPER RIGHT, MILL;
LOWER LEFT, KIERKEGAARD; LOWER RIGHT, MARX

THE FREE PRESS
1230 Avenue of the Americas
New York, NY 10020

Manufactured in the United States of America

20 19 18 17

Library of Congress Catalog Card Number: 69-10325

ISBN 0–02–911220–6

FOREWORD

Every anthologist inevitably experiences regrets concerning the omission of authors whom he would have liked to include. In the case of nineteenth-century philosophy the complexity and diversity of the work produced makes the problem of choice an especially acute one, and I have felt it best to give prominence to certain salient themes and tendencies rather than undertake the hopeless task of trying to present every aspect of the thought of the period. Such restriction of scope has, however, meant that I have not been able to do justice to various fields in which writers of the time made significant and lasting contributions: among others, those of politics and the philosophies of art and law. I have likewise had to exclude a number of figures whose general claims to representation—whether on grounds of intrinsic importance or of influence, or of both—are high; examples are Maine de Biran, Bentham, Schelling, and Brentano. Philosophers of the pragmatist school, some of whose work appeared during the period covered, have also been omitted; these, though, are represented in another volume of the present series.

P.L.G.

CONTENTS

GENERAL
INTRODUCTION

It is a commonplace that every age is prone to interpret and evaluate the achievements of former periods in terms that are to a large extent dictated by its own particular preoccupations and interests. The history of ideas is no exception, and from this point of view there is perhaps at the present time, at any rate in the Anglo-American world, some tendency to regard the nineteenth century as constituting a curious and rather unfortunate interlude in the evolution of philosophy. Thus it may be suggested that, during the previous century, a movement of thought established itself in Europe which was comparable at least in spirit, if not in fundamental doctrine or method, with the various forms of analytical enquiry that characteristically belong to our own age. At the time of the Enlightenment (it may be argued) philosophy seemed securely set upon a course that involved the critical acceptance of certain determinate limits to human knowledge and a consequent abandonment of all its former speculative pretensions. Hume and Kant, in their different ways, had conclusively shown that it was impossible to arrive at truths concerning the nature of reality by means that transcended the procedures of ordinary empirical investigation; there existed no a priori route to an ultimate understanding of the universe, and henceforward we had no choice but to rest content with the piecemeal methods of enquiry employed and refined by the developing natural sciences. It followed that many of the issues about which philosophers had interminably debated were irresolvable in principle and that, if philosophy were to remain an activity entitled to respect, it would have to proceed along lines radically different from those it had followed in the past. The wings of traditional metaphysics had been clipped so effectively as to encourage the conjecture that it

1

would never leave the ground again. Yet, far from this being the case, the succeeding century in fact witnessed a dramatic resurgence of the metaphysical temper at its most ambitious and extravagant, resulting in the production of works that appeared to mock the labors of those thinkers who, with insight and patience, had striven to set philosophy on a new path. Only when this strange impulse had finally spent itself could lessons that had been unaccountably forgotten be learned and taken to heart once more. The gap separating Hegel's conception of the philosophical enterprise from that advanced only a few years earlier by Kant was wide and profound. And if we move from the beginning of the nineteenth century to that of the twentieth, and from Germany to England, the disparity between the approaches of Bradley and Russell must strike us no less forcibly.

Whatever its superficial plausibility, this simple picture has a number of questionable features. It seems to assume the presence of a basic homogeneity of aim and procedure among the majority of nineteenth-century writers. It implies that the type of philosophy they pursued represented a radical, even unintelligible, break with what had immediately gone before. It gives the impression that this break constituted in essentials a return to an earlier, outworn mode of philosophizing, not that it initiated anything in the nature of a new departure. And so far as twentieth-century developments are concerned, it suggests that these should primarily be understood as exemplifying a reaction against preceding trends rather than as illustrating significant continuities or affinities with them. All such claims are, however, open to challenge.

To see why, let us begin by briefly recalling the background to the period, starting with some of its more general aspects. Philosophical ideas do not originate in a vacuum, and their initial stimulus is frequently to be found in circumstances that lie outside the domain of philosophy itself, in such spheres as scientific investigation, moral or religious belief, political and social change. The nineteenth century witnessed revolutionary upheavals in all these areas. On the one hand, there were vast transformations in the life of society, deriving in part from the spread of industrialism and monopoly capitalism, in part from the impact of powerful nationalist and democratic ideologies. On the other, there were important shifts at the level of thought and knowledge. Crucial discoveries in the natural sciences—undertaken by men like Faraday and Maxwell, Schwann and Darwin, and involving (among other things) the development of atomic and radiation theory in physics, the introduction of cell theory and the formulation of evolutionary hyptheses in biology—not only led to revised conceptions of the world and of man's place within it; they also had repercussions in other departments of opinion, such as ethics and (even more critically) religion, where the difficulty of reconciling theological dogma with scientific findings became, for many minds, acute. Nor was this all. Further problems arose in the latter region from the growth of biblical criticism, itself but one manifestation of advances, parallel to those in the physical sciences, which overtook the historical studies at this time and gave to history a prestige never before attained. As Nietzsche once put it, "For modern men 'education' and 'historical education' seem to mean the same thing, with the difference that the one phrase is longer."*

Given—as many nineteenth-century writers believed†—that it is part of the philosopher's task to reflect and interpret contemporary movements in thought and behavior, it would be natural to expect originality and imagination, rather than a tired nostalgia for old ways, to characterize the philosophical work produced during such a period : we should expect, too, that it would exhibit diversity and variety, as opposed to monolithic conformity to some single pattern or program. And these expectations are, as a matter of fact, fulfilled. If we set beside one another outstanding figures of the age—for example, Hegel and Comte, Kierkegaard and Marx, Mill and Bradley—it is not so much their similarities as their differences that immediately impress us, differences which often involve deep-rooted divergences of outlook and principle. Nor could it plausibly be maintained that such men were regressive thinkers, anxious to restore philosophy to the character accorded it by (say) the seventeenth-century rationalists; on the contrary, they were in general extremely suspicious of the categories and presuppositions that underlay the constructions of earlier system-builders. This is not to deny that there was an abundance of speculation, much of which could be said to be "metaphysical" in the sense in which that term is now (frequently with pejorative overtones) applied; it is also true that a great deal of what was written appears, from a modern point of view, to làck the robust sense of reality Russell has extolled, easily becoming lost in mystification and obscure paradox. But here two points should be borne in mind.

First, the speculative tendencies inherent in the Idealist metaphysics of the period were not without their critics. Moreover, in writers like Comte, Mill, and Mach, hostility toward transcendent theorizing was combined with a profound respect for, and preoccupation with, the methods of the natural sciences; the deflationary tradition of empiricism, associated in the first instance with Hume, was far from quiescent. Secondly, the Idealist conception of philosophy was itself a highly

---

* *The Use and Abuse of History*, § IV.
†Cf. Hegel's remark (*Philosophy of Right*, Preface) that "philosophy is *its own time expressed in thoughts*."

complex intellectual phenomenon, which branched out in unexpected directions and which often, even in the hands of its central exponents, presented aspects oddly at variance with the other-worldly aspirations commonly attributed to them. The concept of the Absolute, as variously employed by Fichte, Schelling, Hegel, and (later) Bradley, is no doubt a puzzling enough idea; even so, it would be misleading to suggest that it was used by all these philosophers to designate, at least in any straightforward sense, some supra-mundane entity, set apart from or above the world of ordinary experience. Nor should the fact be over-looked that some Idealist thinkers, in the course of arriving at their apparently very remote and abstract conclusions, displayed a penetrating insight into the concrete particularity and detail of reality as it is experienced at the level of our everyday consciousness. This was especially true of Hegel. Intensely aware of the circumstances that made the age in which he wrote one of significant change and transition, he was at the same time—as the Preface to his *Phenomenology of Spirit* shows—opposed to philosophical attempts to reduce the diversified content of experience to the terms of a bare and empty formalism that would hurl "what is determinate and distinct" into the "abyss of vacuity."

Nineteenth-century Idealism, in other words, presents a paradoxical aspect. From one point of view its adherents seem to endorse the claims of unrestricted speculation, while from another they often appear peculiarly sensitive to the empirical contingencies of situation and circumstance and to the limitations these impose upon the exercise of pure reason. This paradox finds a partial explanation in the relation of the Idealists to the Kantian philosophy, and it will therefore be necessary to glance briefly at some of Kant's own ideas.

According to Kant, the world as we know and comprehend it is in an essential way dependent upon the interpretative apparatus of the human mind. It is through the mind's activity in imposing order upon the raw material of sensation that we are presented with an objective world of phenomena; a world, moreover, that conforms to certain universal principles which render it intelligible to rational enquiry. Thus it can be asserted a priori of our experience that there are propositions—such, for instance, as the statement that every event has a cause —which are valid without exception throughout its entire range. But though Kant considered that the structural character of empirical reality was due to the operation of the human intellect, he by no means wished to suggest that the world was a mere creation of our own minds. The sensory material, which we interpret so as to form a unitary system of objective things and events, is itself given to us from without, having its ultimate ground in a realm of what Kant called *noumena* or "things in themselves." He claimed, however, that we are necessarily ignorant of the nature of these inexperienceable entities. The categories and principles that constitute the framework of our knowledge of phenomena are inapplicable to whatever lies beyond the reach of possible experience, and it was Kant's precise objection to the theories of "dogmatic" metaphysicians that they had sought to employ these categories in a manner that transcended the limits within which they could legitimately be used. At the same time, this was not to say that metaphysical conceptions were themselves devoid of value or that they served no important function in our lives. If, for example, we moved from the sphere of theoretical knowledge and certainty to that of practical choice and conviction, it could be seen (Kant claimed) that such notions as God, freedom, and immortality have a crucial role to play as postulates of the moral consciousness, ideas like those of ultimate responsibility and desert being indispensable elements in our picture of the moral life. In Kant's ethical philosophy, indeed, the general distinction already drawn at the theoretical level between phenomena and noumena acquired a more specific, and (it might be argued) very different, dimension of meaning. For it now emerged as providing a scheme in terms of which the notion of man as a moral agent might be elucidated and understood. Each individual was to be regarded as belonging to two separate domains or "worlds," one phenomenal and empirical, the other noumenal or "intelligible." And in the light of this duality—perhaps as radical as any proposed in the history of ethics—Kant was led to interpret the moral life as necessarily involving a conflict between transcendent will and natural inclination. On the one side, there were the demands of duty, conceived as having their source in man's nature as a rational self-determining being; on the other, there were the various desires and aversions attributable to him as a merely physical and psychological phenomenon.

In some of these ideas it is possible to discern the germs of what later became full-fledged speculative theses. Kant had insisted upon the role of reason as active, creative; the mind was not to be envisaged as a kind of mirror, passively reflecting an independently given reality, but as a legislative productive agency. A similar view of mind permeated subsequent Idealist thinking; here, however, it was combined with a repudiation of the Kantian doctrine of inexperienceable "things in themselves," the latter being treated as an unwarranted departure from Kant's own teachings concerning knowledge and meaning. And from this attitude of partial acceptance and partial rejection of the Kantian position a number of consequences flowed.

In the first place, it inevitably led to a concentration upon the subject of knowledge as opposed to its object. In all the major Idealist philosophies of the time problems relating to the self and to the nature of self-consciousness became the focus of attention; and while Kant himself had made striking and original contributions to these topics, in the works of his successors what he had said about them underwent important transformations and extensions. To start with, the operations of the human intellect in constructing an objective empirical world were no longer considered as fully intelligible if treated in abstraction from other facets of human life and activity. Already, in the eighteenth century, J. G. Herder had criticized the philosophical tendency to separate the personality into water-tight compartments, and with Fichte this criticism finds more determinate expression : the volitional aspects of thought and knowledge are emphasized, and stress is laid upon the relations between the criteria we adopt in interpreting our experience and our status as active purposive beings in the world—"Will," he wrote in his *Naturrecht,* "is in a special sense the essence of reason." In Fichte's case, moreover, the conception he propounded of an active striving ego was infused with notions that stemmed from his view of man's ultimate destiny as a moral being. Thus it could be said that his system also represents an attempt to overcome the division, apparent in Kant's philosophy, between the cognitive and moral dimensions of the self : the autonomy Kant assigned to the moral agent takes on a wider significance when it is claimed that our fundamental epistemological presuppositions need to be seen in a context which exhibits them as "posits" requisite to the fulfillment of our potentialities as members of an all-embracing moral order. Fichte's particular ethical preoccupations are suggestive, too, of another important feature of post-Kantian thought. In earlier philosophies (and this was to some extent true of Kant as well) human nature tended to be conceived along individualistic lines, and in a static nontemporal fashion that took no account of development. It was characteristic of nineteenth-century Idealism, on the other hand, to underline the social aspects of knowledge and self-consciousness : the standards and critieria implicit in our ways of approaching and understanding reality were the products of men as communal beings, with shared aims and objectives; further, the individual's awareness and conception of himself presupposed, and was intimately dependent upon, the existence of other persons to whom he stood in determinate relations. But to speak of society and of the institutions and cultural bonds it implies was to speak of something in a continual process of change and evolution; and this, among other considerations, lent support to the belief that the adequate analysis of mind and its categories could only be undertaken within a perspective of historical development. In Hegel, whose philosophy was throughout imbued with a profoundly historical consciousness, such a view found a powerful and formidable advocate.

However penetrating and influential their insights in these areas may have been, it would nonetheless be wrong to suppose that the Idealists conceived themselves to be merely propounding new theories of man and society. The elimination of the Kantian postulate of a noumenal realm beyond the reach of mind opened the way to doctrines according to which everything must ultimately be conceived as being mental or "spiritual" in character. Thus the priority accorded to the human subject was inseparably connected with a wider vision in which it could be said that reality as a whole was comprehended in subjective terms, the Kantian conception of philosophy as reflection upon the manner in which the human mind structures experience being transformed into a metaphysic wherein the rational categories to be investigated were regarded as in some sense constituting the innermost essence of the world itself. This line of thought is discernible in both Fichte and Schelling, at least at certain stages of their somewhat variegated intellectual careers; but it was again Hegel (in any case a far more impressive thinker than either of the other two) who followed out its implications most fully, developing a system in which a number of familiar divisions—for instance, between concept and object, thought and existence, epistemology and ontology—often seem to dissolve or else lose their hold.

The Hegelian philosophy is of a bewildering complexity and many-sidedness, and its innumerable interpreters have differed as widely in their views of its content and significance as they have in their judgments of its value. But one or two general points, bearing upon its subsequent influence and repercussions, may be made about it here. First, it should be realized that Hegel's idealism did not include the claim that the world depends for its existence upon the finite individual conciousness. Rather, the concept basic to his system was the metaphysical one of *absolute* mind, or spirit (*Geist*). Spirit, so understood, comprehends all that there is, and in its outward manifestations, comprising both material nature and human history, it confronts the finite intelligence as an objective reality. This, however, raises further considerations. Spirit, according to Hegel, is essentially creative and involved in a constant process of self-development and self-expression; from this point of view, the history of the world can be seen as the history of the various forms spirit assumes in the course of externalizing itself so as to realize its inherent nature. Fundamentally the movement reflects the unfolding of logical categories which it is the function of philosophical enquiry to uncover; nevertheless, it is not one of smooth transition from one phase to the next, but proceeds instead through conflict and contradiction : each stage gives rise to its opposite in a continual pattern of transcendence leading toward higher unities. The series thereby generated was described by Hegel as "dialectical," this idea of dialectical development, with its emphasis upon opposition and division, being in turn related to another important Hegelian conception. For, in Hegel's view, both man and nature were embodiments of spirit, different modes in which it expressed its essence. It followed that the division between man as conscious subject and the objective world that surrounded him was, when properly interpreted, a division within spirit itself. In Hegelian terminology, it represented spirit's "self-alienation" (*Selbstentfremdung*) : what confronted the subject as if it were irreducibly "other" was in fact itself a product of reason, and, as such, its external and foreign character was apparent only. Hegel suggested that the removal of this illusion was achieved through knowledge, or by what might be termed the "internalization" of the object by systematic understanding; the aim of such understanding was to dispel the deceptive alienation, so that (as he put it) we may "divest the objective world that stands opposed to us of its strangeness and . . . find ourselves at home in it." The final goal of spirit could thus be said to be the attainment, through the medium of human knowledge, of a total consciousness and comprehension of itself. The world would present itself as a wholly intelligible system, dynamically interrelated in all its parts, and idea and reality would be reconciled.

Hegel's notion of spirit's struggle to overcome self-alienation in the course of realizing its "Ideal being" has been treated by some commentators as partly deriving from the conception of inner conflict implicit in Kant's analysis of moral experience : if the Kantian individual is replaced by the "world-self" of Idealist philosophy we have (it is suggested) the basic elements of the Hegelian theory. Others have regarded it as primarily religious in inspiration, an attempt to give philosophical expression to ideas mythically portrayed in the Christian doctrines of creation, fall, and redemption. Certainly Hegel himself stressed the religious implications of his system, contending that it was in mode of representation rather than in essential content that religion and philosophy diverged; and it is also true that his teachings were gratefully accepted in some theological quarters as a way of bringing the claims of universal reason into harmony with the demands of religious faith. But—as a glance at developments subsequent to Hegel's death shows—this was by no means a general response. By the 1840s a reaction had already set in, leading to the disintegration of the synthesis he had so impressively proclaimed.

How did this come about? In part it can be said to have been due to ambiguities inherent in the system itself, some of Hegel's key ideas proving susceptible to interpretations that resulted in a radical transformation of his original scheme. Thus, in the works of thinkers like Feuerbach, Stirner, and (above all) Marx and Engels, familiar Hegelian themes reappear; they do so, however, in a different guise and in a vastly altered context. Where Hegel had spoken at times of the underlying identity of philosophy and religion, these men pictured belief in God as a form of alienation which it was the task of philosophy to reveal and help to overcome : man had projected his essence, his attributes and powers, upon a mythical being outside himself, thereby depriving himself of a true sense of his own worth and possibilities. Again, they claimed that Hegel, by setting pure thought or spirit at the center of his system, had reduced all actual existents, including man himself, to the status of mere attributes or "predicates" of a wholly ideal subject; against this, it was urged that being is necessarily prior to thought, and that man, conceived as the inhabitant of a substantial empirical world, must be substituted for the mystical *Geist* of Hegelian metaphysics. Herein lies the source of the Marxian claim to have "demystified" Hegel, turning him the right way up. Marx himself was greatly influenced by the social theories of British and French radicals, particularly by those of Saint-Simon; even so, his ideas initially took shape within a Hegelian framework, and it is fascinating to observe how, in his earlier and more philosophical writings, he systematically transposed and reinterpreted Hegel's cardinal conceptions in the course of formulating his own doctrines. Thus the notions of self-externalization and self-realization, which Hegel ascribed to spirit, are also prominent in Marx. But for the latter it was man—"a human natural subject, with eyes and ears"—who was the true creative agency, "objectifying" himself and his powers in the manipulation of nature and the construction of his world. Like Hegel, too, Marx came to envisage historical development in terms of a dialectical movement; it was, however, treated by him as operating at the level of economic activity and class struggle rather than on the plane of autonomous categories and incarnate ideas. Similarly, he thought that alienation indubitably occurred; but it was flesh-and-blood humanity, not Hegelian absolute spirit, that suffered it, the institutions of men and the products of their labor appearing before them as independent forces with the power to control their actions and dehumanize their lives. Nor could such alienation (exemplified for Marx in the industrial

society of his time) be overcome by mere understanding and philosophical reflection, since that would leave everything as before. The
solution lay in action, not in thought; only through the reappropriation
of a world grown "alien and hostile"—a reappropriation involving the
total transformation of society—would men at last be able to realize
themselves and fulfill their potentialities as free rational beings.

The fundamental change in emphasis and direction which Marx
imposed upon the Hegelian philosophy was symptomatic of a wider
revulsion. The original appeal of that philosophy had partly lain in its
apparent ability to unify and render intelligible every aspect of thought
and experience as elements of a dynamic interdependent system. And
it had also held attractions from a practical standpoint. For it was
interpreted as implying that, in the moral and political spheres, it was
necessary to comply with the prevailing institutions and practices of
one's society and culture—a doctrine comforting to a generation
shocked by the French Revolution and its turbulent aftermath. As the
century wore on, though, objections multiplied. Could thought and
reality be reconciled, let alone identified? What justified the confident
assertions that reason was "sovereign of the world" and that history
was a "rational process"? How valid was the suggestion that, in the
final analysis, God and the world were one? What exactly was the
status of the human intellect, and how were its credentials as an instrument for probing the secrets of reality to be assessed? And what room
had been left for the individual, regarded as a source and center of
value in his own right, within the Hegelian edifice? These were among
the questions raised by critics of a variety of persuasions, ranging from
Schopenhauer and Kierkegaard to Nietzsche and (despite his Hegelian
affiliations) Bradley. In pursuing them, such men not only reopened
and accentuated divisions Hegelian Idealism had sought metaphysically
to overcome. They also furthered the exploration of a topic which—
as we saw earlier—had never in fact been far from the foreground of
the Idealists' own concern, notwithstanding their preoccupation with
more general and rarefied issues. This topic was the nature of man.

It is, indeed, in its attitude toward human nature that nineteenth-
century thought offers some of its most striking contrasts with the
speculation of the preceding period. By and large, eighteenth-century
philosophers had assumed that the contents and operations of the
psyche lay wholly open to inspection, the results of introspective investigation being such as to afford a paradigm of certain knowledge. They
had been deeply impressed, too, by the methods and achievements of
the advancing physical sciences, exemplified above all in the work of
Newton; in consequence these tended to supply the frame of reference

in terms of which they constructed their accounts of the human mind and character. Behind their labors lay the hope and prospect of founding a universal "science of man," whereby human motivation and behavior could be explained and the future of society rationally predicted and controlled. But these were assumptions which a number of nineteenth-century thinkers were strenuously concerned to deny. Both Fichte's "activist" conception of the personality (comparable in some respects to the ideas propounded by his French contemporary Maine de Biran) and Hegel's dialectical view of the development of consciousness can be regarded as initiating, in different ways, protests against earlier, scientifically inspired, modes of interpreting the life of the mind. Nevertheless, it was in the work of later writers that the tendency to reject Enlightenment presuppositions in favor of new categories and models became most apparent; the pictures of mental activity presented by Schopenhauer, Nietzsche, and Kierkegaard (to cite three important examples) are worlds away from anything to be found in the pages of, say, Hume or Condillac.

It would be impossible to delineate in a short space the various complex elements involved in this profound shift of perspective; Kierkegaard's contribution, in particular, raises special problems originating in his personal situation as a thinker of somewhat idiosyncratic religious convictions. So far as Schopenhauer and Nietzsche are concerned, however, certain salient factors stand out. One corollary of earlier views was a proneness to envisage the mind as if it were a clear transparent pool, wherein discrete "particles of consciousness"—sensations, impressions, ideas, and so forth—could be observed to move and coalesce according to discoverable patterns and regularities. The most famous interpretative device used in this connection—the venerable "law of association of ideas"—survived into the middle of the nineteenth century through its continued propagation at the hands of English empiricists like J. S. Mill; and it was precisely to theorists of this school that Nietzsche alluded when he contemptuously critized attempts to found human psychology upon something "purely passive, automatic, reflexive, molecular, and, moreover, profoundly stupid."* In contrast with all such approaches Nietzsche, like Schopenhauer before him, tended to portray each individual as a center of powerful inner drives and forces of whose operation the man himself might be partly or wholly unaware; if the human mind was to be compared to a pool, it could only be to one that was dark and opaque, perturbations on its surface offering no more than a clue to what was happening in

_____
*Genealogy of Morals, I, § I.

its remote depths. Again, both writers stressed the intimate relations subsisting between the intellectual, volitional, and physical sides of our natures, and underlined the need to look at human beings in a manner that acknowledged their status as biological organisms, actively engaged in preserving and asserting themselves in the world. In Schopenhauer's case, the attention he paid to the last point was obscured by his having chosen to develop his thought in the form of a system which, while rivaling Hegel's in scope and comprehensiveness, was based on the notion of metaphysical nonrational will instead of that of cosmic reason; as a result he sometimes presented what he had to say in a puzzling and paradoxical fashion. Nonetheless, this did not prevent him from formulating a host of important insights, not least of which was the claim that the authoritative position traditionally ascribed to the intellect, whether as a source of incontrovertible truth or as an ultimate determinant of action, constituted a gross distortion of the facts. Far from playing the independent and masterful role attributed to it, it should (Schopenhauer contended) primarily be seen as the instrument or servant of biological needs and deep-rooted urges, the influence of which it was in general unable to withstand and whose true significance it frequently failed to comprehend. As expanded and elaborated by Nietzsche, such suggestions assumed a startling and revolutionary character, having far-reaching epistemological and ethical implications as well as their more obvious psychological ones. Thus they issued in a ruthlessly sceptical analysis, not merely of the concepts and beliefs implicit in the everyday or commonsense view of the world, but also of the moral and religious assumptions underlying pervasive social norms and attitudes; an analysis which, in Nietzsche's view, had liberating consequences—"perhaps there has never been so open a sea."* Thought, language, and behavior were, he held, permeated by myths and rationalizations of all kinds; and these, while being on the whole conducive to the interests of human life and survival, possessed no claim to objective validity or final truth.† Nor were the theoretical structures of philosophers exempt from his destructive critique. He was no friend of systematizers—"The will to system," he wrote, "is a lack of integrity"—and he lavished scorn upon those who professed to detect a nonsensory "real" world beneath the merely

* *The Gay Science*, § 343.
†Much of Nietzsche's thinking about man and society was imbued with evolutionary ideas. But it would be a mistake to regard him as an exponent of some form of "social Darwinism," such as one finds, for example, in the writings of Herbert Spencer. Capacity for survival through adaptation to circumstances was not, for Nietzsche, an infallible sign of worth or merit: on the contrary, he often implied the reverse.

"apparent" one of ordinary experience. Though given at times to speculative flights of his own, he was from this point of view a profoundly antimetaphysical writer, and it is interesting to notice how closely he often approaches the position of thinkers associated with a philosophical tradition quite different from that to which he is usually thought to belong. In his respect for experiential data, as in his sensitivity to the role of convention in human thinking and to the dangers of illicit reification, he frequently resembles Ernst Mach, who was a considerable influence in the development of twentieth-century logical empiricism.

Unlike Nietzsche, however, Mach was a notable mathematician and physicist. And here, with Mach's name in mind, it is worth recalling that the contributions of the more spectacular representatives of nineteenth-century thought by no means exhaust the significance of the period as a whole. Few of the writers so far considered paid much attention to problems relating to scientific method and procedure, and when they did so their references tended, not infrequently, to be colored by a certain suspicion and even hostility. In part, this may have been due to the belief—already alluded to—that accepted scientific models of explanation could not be extended uncritically to all areas of enquiry; it is also true that the metaphysical idiom some of them favored was scarcely one which a strict observance of the canons of scientific reasoning would appear to justify. But, whatever its grounds, such an attitude was in any event far from being universally shared by the philosophers of the time.

Thus, quite early in the century, Auguste Comte, originally a disciple of Saint-Simon, founded a philosophy explicitly based on the principle that no statement or theory was worthy of acceptance if it did not satisfy the standards embodied in the notions of scientific justification and inference. It followed that all claims to knowledge of a theological or metaphysical character must be rejected. At first sight such a thesis might seem a long way from anything advanced by the Idealists and their successors; yet there existed, in fact, analogies as well as differences between the two approaches. For example, Comte (like Hegel) formulated his ideas within a comprehensive historical framework: the evolution of human consciousness conformed to a progressive pattern of development, theological and metaphysical modes of thought giving way to scientific ones at every level of enquiry; this was the essence of the famous Comtean "law of the three stages." Again, it was the need to understand man as a social being that provided Comte with the chief inspiration of his work. On the other hand, his conception of what such understanding would amount to was very much his own. Despite inevitable differences entailed by variations in subject matter, the methods to be employed were basically the same as those used in other branches of scientific investigation, and involved the establishment of laws and generalizations verifiable by appeal to the facts of experience. Comte was, moreover, insistent upon the importance of public standards of test and confirmation; he had no patience with theories which relied upon the "interior observation" of private mental data, and regarded physiology and sociology as between them covering the entire field of human behavior—there was no place for an intermediate "psychological" science based on purely introspective data.

Comte's views met with a rather mixed reception. Thus Marx, who came to them after he had worked out his own sociological and economic doctrines, was not impressed. By contrast, they met with a sympathetic response in J. S. Mill, who was in agreement with Comte's general approach and at the same time saw in his ideas a useful corrective to some of the crudities of the Utilitarian social theory he had inherited from his father and from Bentham. Even so, Mill's reaction was not one of unqualified approval, as his essay, *Auguste Comte and Positivism,* made clear. He objected, for instance, to Comte's attempt to reduce the study of psychological states and processes to physiological terms, and he was also highly critical of the authoritarian nature of the French philosopher's practical recommendations. Furthermore, in his own *System of Logic* he undertook to provide a much more detailed and thorough investigation of the character of scientific thinking than any Comte himself had produced. Comte's conception of science and the manner in which he pictured the relation between scientific hypotheses and experience was, indeed, somewhat lacking in subtlety; for this reason, among others, the connection between his philosophy and that associated with the twentieth-century "Vienna Circle" is rather more tenuous than the common label of "positivism" might suggest. The emphatic claims he made on behalf of the scientific attitude did, however, act as a powerful stimulus, helping to promote a far more sophisticated and searching philosophical analysis of scientific method and terminology than had previously been undertaken. Mill and his brilliant critic, Whewell, in the first half of the century; Clifford, Pearson, and Mach in the second half : these were among the men whose genius and perception laid the foundations of present-day philosophy of science. Nor were the effects of what they wrote confined to the field within which many of their chief contributions were made. For through their endeavors to elucidate, in a sober and cautious spirit of enquiry, the structure and concepts of scientific theories, they also played an important part in directing attention to those wider problems of linguistic meaning and significance which have, to such a marked degree, come to occupy philosophers in more recent years.

Enough has perhaps been said, though in a very brief and summary fashion, to illustrate the variety and originality displayed by thinkers of the period with this collection of readings is concerned. It is quite often suggested that the philosophy of the past may to a large extent be understood as prefiguring, in schematic or speculative terms, lines of investigation which later find concrete application in specific empirical disciplines. The nineteenth century affords ample confirmation of such a view, at any rate in the sphere of the human studies; the interest of much that was then written consists partly in its anticipation of the diverse anthropological, sociological, and psychological enquiries that have achieved stature in our own age. And this is connected with a further feature of the period, namely, the spirit of critical self-consciousness that pervaded it. As we saw, the immediate point of departure was the survey of thought and knowledge undertaken by Kant : the nature and range of human reason, both theoretically and practically considered, had been subjected to a scrutiny of hitherto unprecedented comprehensiveness and rigor. Despite what is sometimes supposed, the significance of this appraisal was not in fact lost upon nineteenth-century writers, several of whom may be said to have deepened and extended its implications in crucial ways. Theories were admittedly propounded that appear to involve an evident breach of Kantian principles; but even where that is so, it is often possible to read the message they contain in more than one sense. The speculative systems of the time have, indeed, a Janus-like quality; what, from one standpoint, may look like an effort to delineate the structure of ultimate reality, from another may present itself rather as an attempt to acquire a clearer understanding of ourselves as conscious and reflective participants in the world. Nor should it be forgotten that those who set most store by abstract metaphysical argument frequently adopted a highly critical approach when it was a matter of assessing common forms of thinking and reasoning; Bradley's destructive analysis, which eventually led him to treat the final truth of things as beyond the reach of the discursive understanding, is a case in point. It is true that Bradley's conclusions, like those of many of his contemporaries, subsequently found little favor; yet, in repudiating them, his successors were themselves caused to revise certain traditional doctrines of logic and meaning, with consequences that proved momentous. Such radical evaluation and re-evaluation of basic assumptions, resulting at times in the subversion of established beliefs and attitudes, has classically been considered an essential function of philosophy. The nineteenth century was rich in examples of its influence and power.

I

FICHTE

JOHANN GOTTLIEB FICHTE (1762-1814) was born at Rammenau in Saxony. His family was a poor one, and he owed his education largely to the benevolence of a local landed proprietor. In 1780 he attended the University of Jena as a theology student, subsequently continuing his studies at Wittenberg and Leipzig. The philosopher whose work originally impressed him was Spinoza, but he later fell under the influence of Kant and in 1792 published anonymously his *Essay towards a Critique of All Revelation* which was at first thought to be by Kant himself. The error proved advantageous to Fichte, since Kant, in pointing out the confusion, warmly praised the work that had occasioned it. Fichte's reputation was consequently enhanced, and within two years he was appointed to a professorship at Jena. Here, however, his career progressed less smoothly. He was known at this time for radical opinions (he had expressed fervent support for the French Revolution), and he gave initial expression to his reformist enthusiasm by boldly attacking the student fraternities; the intense unpopularity this incurred led to his having to withdraw from the town for some months in 1795. Worse was to follow. Three years later, in a journal of which he was coeditor, he published two articles concerning the nature of religious belief, one by F. K. Forberg (1770-1848) and the other by himself. Fichte's contribution, *On the Foundation of Our Belief in a Divine Government of the Universe*, contains in a succinct form certain cardinal tenets of his philosophical position. Nevertheless, it was ill-received. Charges of atheism were leveled, and the rancorous controversy that ensued finally resulted in Fichte's dismissal; nor was he helped during this difficult period by Kant, who went out of his way to dissociate his philosophy from the ideas of his embarrassing follower. The last ten years of Fichte's life witnessed a revival of his fortunes. In 1804 he was nominated to a chair at Erlangen; in 1807-08, during the period of the Napoleonic occupation, he was in Berlin, giving his impassioned *Addresses to the German Nation;* and in 1810 he was made dean of the philosophical faculty at the newly founded university in that city. Yet there persisted in Fichte's personality a strain of dogmatic aggressiveness which antagonized others, and his relations with both colleagues and pupils at Berlin were far from easy. "For the smallest fault," wrote one of the former (Solger), "he treats the students as if they were imps of hell."

The majority of Fichte's important philosophical books—epistemological, ethical, and political—were written in his thirties, when he was still very much under the influence of Kant and regarded his system as the natural continuation and fulfillment of the Kantian program. They included *Basis of the Entire Theory of Science* (1794), *Basis of Natural Right* (1796), *The System of Ethics* (1798), and *The Closed Commercial State* (1800). Owing to the use of a forbiddingly abstract technical vocabulary and a failure to provide examples, Fichte's writing tends to be tortuous and obscure. He did, however, make various efforts to render his thought intelligible to a wider public, one such attempt being his essay *The Vocation of Man* (1800). Though not conspicuous for elegance, this work is interesting as expressing some of Fichte's main preoccupations and themes, with their affinities to later pragmatist and existentialist doctrines; it is also develops ideas already implicit in the article that led to his dismissal from Jena, and marks the beginning of the transition from his earlier philosophy of mind, in which he was chiefly concerned to elicit the presuppositions of consciousness, to the later, more overtly metaphysical stage of his thinking, when the conception of an all-embracing absolute spirit, comprehending the whole of reality, was increasingly stressed. In the first section of the book Fichte expounds a deterministic theory, with mind depicted as a mere product of an objective natural order; in the second he presents a form of subjective idealism, everything being reduced to mental pictures or representations. Both views raise difficulties, and the third section —entitled "Faith"—points to a fresh approach. As the extract reproduced here shows, Fichte suggests that the interpretations we put upon experience are not, in the last analysis, susceptible to a purely theoretical justification or demonstration, and he emphasizes the primacy of practical interest and moral commitment in determining the outlook we adopt upon the world.

On the Foundation of Our Belief in a Divine Government of the Universe*

The author of the present essay has for some time recognized it as his duty to set before a larger public the results of his philosophical work on the above subject. Hitherto this has been made available only to the auditors of his academic lectures. He had intended to present his ideas on this subject with the definiteness and precision that is appropriate to the sanctity which it possesses for so many honorable persons. Unfortunately the author's time was occupied with other tasks and the execution of his plan had to be repeatedly postponed.

As coeditor of the present journal, the author is obliged to put before the public the following essay of an excellent philosopher† and this has facilitated the execution of the plan just mentioned. The [Forberg's] essay coincides on many points with the present author's own convictions and hence he can on several matters simply refer the reader to it as an exposition of his own position as well. In other respects, however, the [Forberg's] essay, although not exactly opposed to the present author's views, has not quite reached the latter's position; and this makes it imperative to make the present writer's position publicly known, especially since he believes that his special intellectual approach involves more basic issues than those usually raised by philosophers. However, for the time being nothing more is attempted than a sketch of this approach. A more elaborate treatment will have to wait for another occasion.

The tendency to treat the so-called moral proof or any of the other arguments for the existence of God as genuine proofs has been

---

*Originally published as "Über der Grund unsers Glaubens an eine Göttliche Weltregierung" in the *Philosophisches Journal*, Vol. VIII (1798). The present translation is by Paul Edwards and is here published for the first time.

†Fichte here refers to Forberg's "Entwickelung des Begriffs der Religion" ("The Development of the Concept of Religion") which was published in the same issue of the *Philosophisches Journal*.

a source of almost universal confusion and is likely to remain so for a long time. The assumption is apparently made that belief in God was for the first time given to the human race by means of such argumentation. Poor philosophy! I should like to know how your representatives who, after all, are also only human beings obtain what they wish to give us by means of their proofs; or if these representatives are in fact beings of a higher nature, one wonders how they can count on obtaining acceptance and understanding in us others without presupposing something analogous to their belief. No, this is not how things stand. Philosophy can explain facts—it cannot bring them into existence except for the one fact of philosophy itself. As little as it will occur to the philosopher to persuade mankind to believe from now on in the existence of material objects in space or to treat the changes of these objects as successive events in time, so little should he be inclined to persuade mankind to believe in a divine government of the world. All of this happens without any persuasion on the philosopher's part and he accepts these facts without question. It is the business of the philosopher to deduce these facts as necessarily implied in the essence of rational beings as such. Hence our procedure must not be regarded as a conversion of the unbeliever but as a deduction of the believer's conviction. Our only task is to deal with the causal question, "How does man arrive at his belief?"

In dealing with this question it is essential to realize that this belief must not be represented as an arbitrary assumption which a human being may make or not make as he sees fit—as a freely chosen decision to take as true what the heart desires and because the heart desires it and as a supplement or substitute for the insufficiency of the available logical arguments. What is founded in reason is absolutely necessary; and what is not necessary is therefore a violation of reason. A person who regards the latter as fact is a deluded dreamer, however pious his attitude may be.

Where now will the philosopher, who presupposes belief in God, search for the necessary ground which he is supposed to furnish? Should he base himself on the alleged necessity with which the existence or the nature of the world of the senses implies a rational author? The answer must be an emphatic "no." For he knows only too well that such an inference is totally unwarranted, although misguided thinkers have made such a claim in their embarrassment to explain something whose existence they cannot deny but whose true ground is hidden from them. The original understanding, which is placed under the guardianship of reason and the direction of its mechanism, is incapable of such a step. One may regard the world of the senses either from the point of view of commonsense which is also that of the natural sciences or else from the transcendental standpoint. In the former case reason is required to stop at the existence of the world as something absolute : the world exists simply because it does and it is the way it is simply because it is that way. From this point of view something absolute is accepted and this absolute being simply is the universe : the two are identical. The universe is regarded as a whole which is grounded in itself and complete by itself. From this point of view, the world is an organized and organizing whole containing the ground of all phenomena within itself and its immanent laws. If, while occupying the standpoint of the pure natural sciences, we demand an explanation of the existence and nature of the universe in terms of an intelligent cause, our demand is total nonsense. Moreover, the assertion that an intelligent being is the author of the world of the senses does not help us in the least—it is not really an intelligible pronouncement and what we get are a few empty words instead of a genuine answer to a question that should not have been raised in the first place. An intelligent being is unquestionably constituted by thoughts; and the first intelligible word has yet to be spoken on the subject of how, in the monstrous system of a creation out of nothing, thoughts can be transmuted into matter, or how, in a system that is hardly more rational, the world can become what it is as the result of the action of thoughts upon self-sufficient eternal matter.

It may be admitted that these difficulties vanish if we adopt the transcendental standpoint. There is then no longer an independent world : everything is now simply a reflection of our inner activity. However, one cannot inquire into the ground of something that does not exist and we cannot thus assume something outside of it in terms of which it is to be explained.

We cannot start from the world of the senses in order to climb to the notion of a moral world order so long, that is, as we really start with the sense-world and do not surreptitiously introduce a moral order into it.

Our belief in a moral world order must be based on the concept of a supersensible world.

There is such a concept. I find myself free from any influence of the sense-world, absolutely active in and through myself, and hence I am a power transcending all that is sensuous. This freedom is not, however, indefinite: it has its purpose, and this is not a purpose received from the outside but rather one posited by the free self from its inner nature. My own self and my necessary goal are the supersensible reality.

I cannot doubt this freedom or its nature without giving up my own self.

I cannot doubt this, I say—I cannot even think of the possibility that things are not this way, that this inner voice might deceive me and that it requires to be authorized and justified by reference to something external. Concerning this insight I cannot engage in any further rationalizations, interpretations, or explanations. It is what is absolutely positive and categorical.

I cannot transcend this insight unless I decide to destroy my inner nature—I cannot question it because I cannot *will* to question it. Here is the limit to the otherwise untamed flight of reason—here we find the voice that constrains the intellect because it also constrains the heart. Here is the point where thinking and willing are united and where harmony is brought into my being. I could indeed question the insight concerning my freedom if I wanted to fall into contradiction with my own self, for there is no immanent limitation confining the reasoning faculty : it freely advances into the infinite and must be able to do this since I am free in all my utterances and only I myself can set a limit to myself through my own will. Our moral vocation is therefore itself the outcome of a moral attitude and it is identical with our faith. One is thus quite right in maintaining that faith is the basis of all certainty. This is how it must be; since morality, if it is really morality, can be constructed only out of itself and not out of any logically coercive argumentation.

I could question the insight of my moral freedom if I were ready to plunge into a bottomless abyss (if only in a theoretical fashion); if I were ready to forego absolutely any firm point of reference; if I were prepared to do without that certainty that accompanies all my thinking and without which I could not even set out on speculative inquiries. For there is no firm point of reference except the one indicated here : it is founded in the moral sentiment and not in logic; if our rational faculty does not get to it or else proceeds beyond it, the result is that we find ourselves in an unbounded ocean in which each wave is pushed along by some other wave.

By adopting the goal set before me by my own nature, and by making it the purpose of my real activity, I ipso facto posit the possibility of achieving this purpose through my actions. The two statements are identical—to adopt something as my purpose means that I posit it as something real at some future time; if something is posited as real, its possibility is thereby necessarily implied. I must, if I am not to deny my own nature, first set myself the execution of this goal : and I must, secondly assume that it can be realized. There are in fact absolutely identical : they are not two acts but the one indivisible act dictated by the moral sentiment.

One should note the absolute necessity of what has here been shown. (The reader is requested to grant me for the moment that the possibility of realizing the ultimate moral goal has been demonstrated.) We are not dealing with a wish, a hope, a piece of reflection and consideration, of grounds pro and con, a free decision to assume something whose opposite one also regards as possible. Given the decision to obey the laws of one's inner nature, the assumption is strictly necessary : it is immediately contained in the decision; it is in fact that decision.

One should also observe the logical sequence of the ideas here presented. The inference is not from possibility to reality, but the other way around. Our contention is not : I ought since I can; it is rather : I can since I ought. That I ought and what I ought to do comes first and is most immediately evident. It requires no further explanation, justification, or authorization. It is intrinsically true and evident. It is not based on or conditioned by any other truth, but on the contrary all other truths are conditioned by it. This logical order has frequently been overlooked. A person who maintains that I must first know whether I can do something before I can judge that I ought to do it, is thereby, if he is making a practical judgment, negating the primacy of the moral law and hence the moral law itself, while, if he is making a theoretical judgment, he thereby totally misconstrues the original sequence of our rational processes.

To say that I must simply adopt the goal of morality, that its realization is possible and possible through me, means that every action which I ought to perform and the circumstances that condition such an action are means to my adopted goal. It is in the light of this that my existence, the existence of other moral beings and of the world of the senses as our common stage receive their relation to morality. A wholly new order is thus brought into being and the sense-world with all its immanent laws is no more than the support underlying this order. The world of the senses proceeds in its course according to its eternal laws in order to provide freedom with a sphere of operation, but it does not have the slightest influence on morality or immorality, it does not in any way control a free being. The latter soars above all nature in self-sufficiency and independence. The realization of the purpose of reason can be accomplished only through the efforts of free beings, but because of a higher law this purpose will unquestionably be attained. It is possible to do what is right and every situation is geared to this through the higher law just mentioned : because of this law the moral deed succeeds infallibly and the immoral deed fails just as certainly.

The entire universe now exhibits a totally different appearance to us.

This change in appearance will be further illuminated if we raise ourselves to the transcendental viewpoint. Transcendental theory teaches that the world is nothing but the sensuous appearance, given according to intelligible rational laws, of our own inner activity, our own intelligence operating within boundaries that must remain incomprehensible; and a human being cannot be blamed if he has an uncanny feeling when faced with the total disappearance of the ground underneath him. The boundaries just mentioned are admittedly beyond our understanding as far as their origin is concerned. However, practical philosophy teaches that this does not significantly affect anything of practical importance. The boundaries are the clearest and most certain of all things—they determine our fixed position in the moral arrangement of things. What you perceive as a consequence of your position in this moral order has reality and, moreover, the only reality that concerns you : it is the permanent interpretation of the injunction of your duty, the living expression of what you ought to do simply because you ought to do it. Our world is the sensualized material of our duty; the latter is the truly real in things, the genuine primal stuff of all appearances. The compulsion with which our belief in things is forced upon us is a moral compulsion—the only one that can be exerted upon a free being. Nobody can, without destruction of his nature, surrender his moral calling to such a degree that it cannot preserve him, within the limits previously mentioned, for a higher and nobler future state. Considered as the result of a moral world order, this belief in the reality of the sense-world can even be regarded as a kind of revelation. It is our duty that is revealed in the world of the senses.

This is the true faith : this moral order is *the Divine* which we accept. It is constituted by acting rightly. This is the only possible confession of faith : to do what duty prescribes and to do this gaily and naturally, without doubt or calculation of consequences. As a result, this Divine becomes alive and real in us; every one of our deeds is performed in the light of this presupposition and all their consequences will be preserved in the Divine.

True atheism, unbelief and godlessness in the real sense, consists in calculation of consequences, in refusing to obey the voice of one's conscience until one thinks one can foresee the success of one's actions and in thus elevating one's own judgment above that of God and in making oneself into God. He who wills to do evil in order to produce good is a godless person. Under a moral government of the world good cannot come out of evil; and as certainly as one believes in the former, so one cannot believe the latter. You must not lie even, as a result, the world were to collapse and become a heap of ruins. But this last is only a manner of speaking : if you were permitted to believe seriously that the world would collapse, then at the very least your own nature would be self-contradictory and self-destroying. In fact you do not believe this, you cannot believe it, and you are not even permitted to believe it : you know that the plan of the world's preservation does not contain a lie.

The faith just stated is the whole and complete faith. This living and effective moral order is identical with God. We do not and cannot grasp any other God. There is no rational justification for going beyond this moral world order and for inferring the existence of a separate entity as its cause. Our original reason certainly does not make any such inference and it does not know any such separate entity—only a philosophy that misunderstands its own nature draws such an inference. Is this moral world order no more than a contingent entity, something that might not be, that might be as it is or otherwise so that its existence and nature requires to be explained in terms of a cause, so that belief in it requires to be legitimized by showing its ground? If you will stop listening to the demands of a worthless system and if instead you will consult your own inner nature, then you will find that the moral world order is the absolute beginning of all objective knowledge (just as your freedom and your moral vocation are the absolute beginning of all subjective knowledge) and all other objective knowledge must be founded and conditioned by it, while the moral world order itself cannot be conditioned by anything else, since outside of it there is nothing else. You cannot even attempt the explanation [of the moral order] without falsifying and endangering the nature of the original assumption. The assumption of a moral world order is such that it is absolutely self-evident and it does not tolerate any supporting arguments. Yet you wish to make the assumption dependent on such argumentation.

And this ratiocination, how can you succeed with it? After you have undermined the immediate conviction, how do you then proceed to fortify it? Indeed, it does not stand well with your faith if you can embrace it only on condition that it has an external source and if it collapses in the absence of such a support.

Even if one were to permit you to draw this inference and, as a consequence, to conclude that an author of the moral world order exists, what would that conclusion amount to? This entity is supposed to be distinct from you and from the world, it is supposed to engage in activities in the world in accordance with its plans and must therefore be capable of having ideas, of having personality and consciousness. But what do you mean by "personality" and "consciousness"? It is plain that when you use these words, you refer to what you have found and come to know in yourself under these labels. The least attention to these notions will teach you that they can be properly employed only if what they refer to is limited and finite. You therefore make the entity to which you apply these predicates into something finite. You have not, as you intended to, succeeded in thinking about God— you have merely multiplied yourself in your thoughts. You can no more explain the moral world order by reference to this entity than by reference to yourself : the moral world order remains unexplained and absolute as before. Indeed, in talking the way you do, you have not engaged in any genuine thinking at all, but you have merely disturbed the air with empty sounds. You could have predicted this outcome without difficulty. You are a finite being and how can that which is finite grasp and understand the infinite?

If faith keeps to what is immediately given, it remains firm and unshakable; if it is made dependent on the concept [of the personal God just discussed] then it becomes shaky, for the concept is impossible and full of contradictions.

It is therefore a misunderstanding to maintain that it is doubtful whether or not there is a God. On the contrary, that there is a moral world order, that in this order a definite position has been assigned to every rational individual and that his work counts, that the destiny of every person (unless it is the consequence of his own conduct) is derived from this plan, that without this plan no hair drops from a head, nor a sparrow from a roof, that every good deed succeeds while every evil one fails and that everything must go well for those who love only the good—all this is not doubtful at all but the most certain thing in the world and the basis of all other certainty, in fact the only truth that is objectively absolutely valid. On the other side, any- body who reflects just a moment and who is candid about the outcome of this reflection cannot doubt that the concept of God as a separate substance is impossible and contradictory. It is permissible to say this openly and put down the idle chatter of the schools in order to elevate the true religion of joyful morality.

The Vocation of Man*

—I demand something beyond a mere presentation or conception; something that is, has been, and will be, even if the presentation
were not; and which the presentation only records, without producing
it, or in the smallest degree changing it. A mere presentation I now
see to be a deceptive show; my presentations must have a meaning
beneath them, and if my entire knowledge revealed to me nothing but
knowledge, I would be defrauded of my whole life. That there is nothing whatever but my presentations or conceptions, is, to the natural
sense of mankind, a silly and ridiculous conceit which no man can
seriously entertain, and which requires no refutation. To the better-
informed judgment, which knows the deep, and, *by mere reasoning,*
irrefragable grounds for this assertion, it is a prostrating, annihilating
thought.

And what is, then, this something lying beyond all presentation,
towards which I stretch forward with such ardent longing? What is the
power with which it draws me towards it? What is the central point
in my soul to which it is attached, and with which only it can be effaced?

"Not merely TO KNOW, but according to thy knowledge TO DO, is thy
vocation" :—thus is it loudly proclaimed in the innermost depths of
my soul, as soon as I recollect myself for a moment, and turn my observation upon myself. "Not for idle contemplation of thyself, not for
brooding over devout sensations;—no, for action art thou here; thine
action, and thine action alone, determines thy worth."

This voice leads me from presentation, from mere cognition, to
something which lies beyond it, and is entirely opposed to it; to something which is greater and higher than all knowledge, and which contains within itself the end and object of all knowledge. When I act, I
doubtless know that I act, and how I act; but this knowledge is not the
act itself, but only the observation of it. This voice thus announces to me

---

*From Book III of *The Vocation of Man* (trans. William Smith), in *The Popular
Works of J. G. Fichte* (London, 1848), Vol. I, pp. 469-489.

precisely that which I sought; a something lying beyond mere knowledge, and, in its nature, wholly independent of it.

Thus it is, I know it immediately. But having once entered within the domain of speculation, the doubt which has been awakened within me, will secretly endure, and will continue to disturb me. Since I have placed myself in this position, I can obtain no complete satisfaction until everything which I accept is justified before the tribunal of speculation. I have thus to ask myself,—how is it thus? Whence arises that voice in my soul which directs me to something beyond mere presentation and knowledge?

There is within me an impulse to absolute, independent self-activity. Nothing is more insupportable to me, than to be merely by another, for another, and through another; I must be something for myself and by myself alone. This impulse I feel along with the perception of my own existence, it is inseparably united to my consciousness of myself.

I explain this feeling to myself, by reflection; and add to this blind impulse the power of sight, by thought. According to this impulse I must act as an absolutely independent being :—thus I understand and translate the impulse. I must be independent. Who am I? Subject and object in one,—the conscious being and that of which I am conscious, gifted with intuitive knowledge and myself revealed in that intuition, the thinking mind and myself the object of the thought—inseparable, and ever present to each other. As both, must I be what I am, absolutely by myself alone;—by myself originate conceptions,—by myself produce a condition of things lying beyond these conceptions. But how is the latter possible? To nothing I cannot unite any being whatever; from nothing there can never arise something; my objective thought is necessarily mediative only. But any being which is united to another being, does thereby, by means of this other being, become dependent;—it is no longer a primary, original, and genetic, but only a secondary and derived being. I am constrained to unite myself to something;—to another being I cannot unite myself, without losing that independence which is the condition of my own existence.

My conception and origination of a purpose, however, is, by its very nature, absolutely free,—producing something out of nothing. To such a conception I must unite my activity, in order that it may be possible to regard it as free, and as proceeding absolutely from myself alone.

In the following manner, therefore, do I conceive of my independence as *I*. I ascribe to myself the power of originating a conception simply because I originate it, of originating *this* conception simply because I originate *this* one,—by the absolute sovereignty of myself as an intelligence. I further ascribe to myself the power of manifesting this conception beyond itself by means of an action;—ascribe to myself a real, active power, capable of producing something beyond itself,— a power which is entirely different from the mere power of conception. These conceptions, which are called conceptions of design, or purposes, are not, like the conceptions of mere knowledge, copies of something already given, but rather types of something yet to be produced; the real power lies beyond them, and is *in itself* independent of them;— it only receives from them its immediate determinations, which are apprehended by knowledge. Such an independent power it is that, in consequence of this impulse, I ascribe to myself.

Here then, it appears, is the point to which the consciousness of all reality unites itself;—the real efficiency of my conception, and the real power of action which, in consequence of it, I am compelled to ascribe to myself, is this point. Let it be as it may with the reality of a sensible world beyond me; I possess reality and comprehend it,—it lies within my own being, it is native to myself.

I conceive this, my real power of action, in thought, but I do not create it by thought. The immediate feeling of my impulse to independent activity lies at the foundation of this thought; the thought does no more than portray this feeling, and accept it in its own form,—the form of thought. This procedure may, I think, be vindicated before the tribunal of speculation.

What! Shall I, once more, knowingly and intentionally deceive myself? This procedure can by no means be justified before that strict tribunal.

I feel within me an impulse and an effort towards outward activity; this appears to be true, and to be the only truth which belongs to the matter. Since it is I who feel this impulse, and since I cannot pass beyond myself, either with my whole consciousness, or in particular with my capacity of sensation,—since this *I* itself is the last point at which I feel this impulse, therefore it certainly appears to me as an impulse founded in myself, to an activity also founded in myself. Might it not be however that this impulse, although unperceived by me, is in reality the impulse of a foreign power invisible to me, and that notion of independence merely a delusion, arising from my sphere of vision being limited to myself alone? I have no reason to assume this, but just as little reason to deny it. I must confess that I absolutely know nothing, and can know nothing, about it.

Do I then indeed *feel* that real power of free action, which, strangely enough, I ascribe to myself without knowing anything of it? By no means;—it is merely the *determinable* element, which, by the well-known laws of thought whereby all capacities and all powers arise, we are compelled to add in imagination to the *determinate* element—the real action, which itself is, in like manner, only an assumption.

Is that procession, from the mere conception to an imaginary realization of it, anything more than the usual and well-known procedure of all objective thought, which always strives to be, not mere thought, but something more? By what dishonesty can this procedure be made of more value here than in any other case?—can it possess any deeper significance, when to the conception of a thought it adds a realization of this thought, than when to the conception of this table it adds an actual and present table? "The conception of a purpose, a particular determination of events in me, appears in a double shape,—partly as *subjective*—a Thought; partly as *objective*—an Action." What reason, which would not unquestionably itself stand in need of a genetic deduction, could I adduce against this explanation?

I say that I feel this impulse :—it is therefore I myself who say so, and think so while I say it? Do I then really feel, or only think that I feel? Is not all which I call feeling only a presentation produced by my objective process of thought, and indeed the first transition point of all objectivity? And then again, do I really think, or do I merely think that I think? And do I think that I really think, or merely that I possess the idea of thinking? What can hinder speculation from raising such questions, and continuing to raise them without end? What can I answer, and where is there a point at which I can command such questionings to cease? I know, and must admit, that each definite act of consciousness may be made the subject of reflection, and a new consciousness of the first consciousness may thus be created; and that thereby the immediate consciousness is raised a step higher, and the first consciousness darkened and made doubtful; and that to this ladder there is no highest step. I know that all scepticism rests upon this process, and that the system which has so violently prostrated me is founded on the adoption and the clear consciousness of it.

I know that if I am not merely to play another perplexing game with this system, but intend really and practically to adopt it, I must refuse obedience to that voice within me. I cannot *will* to act, for according to that system I cannot *know* whether I can really act or not :—I can never believe that I truly act; that which seems to be my action must appear to me as entirely without meaning, as a mere delusive picture. All earnestness and all interest is withdrawn from my life; and life, as well as thought, is transformed into a mere play, which proceeds from nothing and tends to nothing.

Shall I then refuse obedience to that inward voice? I will not do so. I will freely accept the vocation which this impulse assigns to me, and in this resolution I will lay hold at once of thought, in all its reality and truthfulness, and on the reality of all things which are pre-supposed therein. I will restrict myself to the position of natural thought in which this impulse places me, and cast from me all those over-refined and subtle inquiries which alone could make me doubtful of its truth.

I understand thee now, sublime Spirit! I have found the organ by which to apprehend this reality, and, with this, probably all other reality. Knowledge is not this organ :—no knowledge can be its own foundation, its own proof; every knowledge pre-supposes another higher knowledge on which it is founded, and to this ascent there is no end. It is FAITH, that voluntary acquiesence in the view which is natur-ally presented to us, because only through this view we can fulfil our vocation;—this it is, which first lends a sanction to knowledge, and raises to certainty and conviction that which without it might be mere delusion. It is not knowledge, but a resolution of the will to admit the validity of knowledge.

Let me hold fast for ever by this doctrine, which is no mere verbal distinction, but a true and deep one, bearing with it the most important consequences for my whole existence and character. All my conviction is but faith; and it proceeds from the character, not from the under-standing. Knowing this, I will enter upon no disputation, because I foresee that thereby nothing can be gained; I will not suffer myself to be perplexed by it, for the source of my conviction lies higher than all disputation; I will not suffer myself to entertain the desire of press-ing this conviction on others by reasoning, and I will not be surprised if such an undertaking should fail. I have adopted my mode of thinking first of all for myself, not for others, and before myself only will I justify it. He who possesses the honest, upright purpose of which I am conscious, will also attain a similar conviction; but without that, this conviction can in no way be attained. Now that I know this, I also know from what point all culture of myself and others must proceed; from the will, not from the understanding. If the former be only fixedly and honestly directed towards the Good, the latter will of itself apprehend the True. Should the latter only be exercised, whilst the former remains neglected, there can arise nothing whatever but a dexterity in groping after vain and empty refinements, throughout the absolute void inane. Now that I know this, I am able to confute all false knowledge that may rise in opposition to my faith. I know that every pretended truth, produced by mere speculative thought, and not founded upon faith, is assuredly false and surreptitious; for mere knowledge, thus produced, leads only to the conviction that we can know nothing. I know that such false knowledge never can discover anything but what it has previously placed in its premises through faith, from which it probably draws conclusions which are wholly false. Now that I know this, I possess the touchstone of all truth and of all conviction. Conscience alone is the root of all truth : whatever is opposed to conscience, or stands in the way of the fulfilment of her behests, is assuredly false; and it is impossible for me to arrive at a conviction of its truth, even if I should be unable to discover the fallacies by which it is produced.

So has it been with all men who have ever seen the light of this world. Without being conscious of it, they apprehend all the reality which has an existence for them, through faith alone; and this faith forces itself on them simultaneously with their existence;—it is born with them. How could it be otherwise? If in mere knowledge, in mere perception and reflection, there is no ground for regarding our mental presentations as more than mere pictures which necessarily pass before our view, why do we yet regard all of them as more than this, and assume, as their foundation, something which exists independently of all presentation? If we all possess the capacity and the instinct to proceed beyond our first natural view of things, why do so few actually go beyond it, and why do we even defend ourselves, with a sort of bitterness, from every motive by which others try to persuade us to this course? What is it which holds us confined within this first natural belief? Not inferences of reason, for there are none such; it is the interest we have in a reality which we desire to produce;—the good, absolutely for its own sake,—the common and sensuous, for the sake of the enjoyment they afford. No one who lives can divest himself of this interest, and just as little can he cast off the faith which this interest brings with it. We are all born in faith;—he who is blind, follows blindly the secret and irresistible impulse; he who sees, follows by sight, and believes because he resolves to believe.

What unity and completeness does this view present—what dignity does it confer on human nature! Our thought is not founded on itself alone, independently of our impulses and affections;—man does not consist of two independent and separate elements; he is absolutely one. All our thought is founded on our impulses—as a man's affections are, so is his knowledge. These impulses compel us to a certain mode of thought only so long as we do not perceive the constraint; the constraint vanishes the moment it is perceived; and it is then no longer the impulse by itself, but we ourselves, according to our impulse, who form our own system of thought.

But I shall open my eyes; shall learn thoroughly to know myself; shall discover that constraint;—this is my vocation. I shall thus, and under that supposition I shall necessarily, form my own mode of thought. Then shall I stand absolutely independent, thoroughly equipt and perfected through my own act and deed. The primitive source of all my other thought and of my life itself, that from which everything proceeds which can have an existence in me, for me, or through me, the innermost spirit of my spirit,—is no longer a foreign power, but it is, in the strictest possible sense, the product of my own will. I am wholly my own creation. I might have followed blindly the leading of my spiritual nature. But I would not be a work of Nature but of myself, and I have become so even by means of this resolution. By endless subtleties I might have made the natural conviction of my own mind dark and doubtful. But I have accepted it with freedom, simply because I resolved to accept it. I have chosen the system which I have now adopted with settled purpose and deliberation from among other possible modes of thought, because I have recognized in it the only one consistent with my dignity and my vocation. With freedom and consciousness I have returned to the point at which Nature had left me. I accept that which she announces;—but I do not accept it because I must; I believe it because I will.

The exalted vocation of my understanding fills me with reverence. It is no longer the deceptive mirror which reflects a series of empty pictures, proceeding from nothing and tending to nothing; it is bestowed upon me for a great purpose. Its cultivation for this purpose is entrusted to me; it is placed in my hands, and at my hands it will be required.—It is placed in my hands. I know immediately—and here my faith accepts the testimony of my consciousness without farther criticism—I know that I am not placed under the necessity of allowing my thoughts to float about without direction or purpose, but that I can voluntarily arouse and direct my attention to one object, turn it away again towards another;—know that it is neither a blind necessity which compels me to a certain mode of thought, nor an empty chance which runs riot with my thoughts; but that it is I who think, and that I can think of that whereof I determine to think. Thus by reflection I have discovered something more; I have discovered that I myself, by my own act alone, produce my whole system of thought, and the particular view which I take of truth in general; since it remains with me either to deprive myself of all sense of truth by means of over-refinement, or to yield myself to this view with faithful obedience. My whole mode of thought, and the cultivation which my understanding receives, as well as the objects to which I direct it, depend entirely on myself. True insight is merit;—the perversion of my capacity for knowledge, thoughtlessness, obscurity, error, and unbelief, are guilt.

There is but one point towards which I have unceasingly to direct all my attention,—namely what I ought to do, and how I may most suitably fulfil the obligation which binds me to do it. All my thoughts must have a bearing on my actions, and must be capable of being considered as means, however remote, to this end; otherwise they are an idle and aimless show, a mere waste of time and strength, and the perversion of noble power, which is entrusted to me for a very different end.

I dare hope, I dare surely promise myself, to follow out this undertaking with good results. The Nature on which I have to act is not a foreign element, called into existence without reference to me, into which I cannot penetrate. It is moulded by my own laws of thought, and must be in harmony with them; it must be thoroughly transparent, knowable and penetrable to me, even to its inmost recesses. In all its phenomena it expresses nothing but the connexions and relations of my own being to myself, and as surely as I may hope to know myself, so surely may I expect to comprehend it. Let me seek only that which I ought to seek, and I shall find; let me ask only that which I ought to ask, and I shall receive an answer.

That voice within my soul in which I believe, and on account of which I believe in every other thing to which I attach credence, does not merely command me to act *in general*. This is impossible; all these general principles are formed only through my own voluntary observation and reflection, applied to many individual facts; but never in themselves express any fact whatever. This voice of my conscience announces to me precisely what I ought to do, and what leave undone, in every particular situation of life; it accompanies me, if I will but listen to it with attention, through all the events of my life, and never refuses me my reward where I am called upon to act. It carries with it immediate conviction, and irresistibly compels my assent to its behests :—it is impossible for me to contend against it.

To listen to it, to obey it honestly and unreservedly, without fear or equivocation,—this is my true vocation, the whole end and purpose of my existence. My life ceases to be an empty play without truth or significance. There is something that must absolutely be done for its own sake alone;—that which conscience demands of me in this particular situation of life it is mine to do, for this only am I here;—to know it, I have understanding; to perform it, I have power. Through this edict of conscience alone, truth and reality are introduced into my conceptions. I cannot refuse them my attention and my obedience without thereby surrendering the very purpose of my own existence.

Hence I cannot withhold my belief from the reality which they announce, without at the same time renouncing my vocation. It is absolutely true, without farther proof or confirmation,—nay, it is the first truth, and the foundation of all other truth and certainty, that this voice must be obeyed; and therefore everything becomes to me true and certain, the truth and certainty of which is assumed in the possibility of such an obedience.

There appear before me in space, certain phenomena, to which I transfer the idea of myself;—I conceive of them as beings like myself. Speculation, when carried out to its last results, has indeed taught me, or would teach me, that these supposed rational beings out of myself are but the products of my own presentative power; that, according to certain laws of my thought, I am compelled to represent out of myself my conception of myself; and that, according to the same laws, I can only transfer this conception to certain definite intuitions. But the voice of my conscience thus speaks :—"Whatever these beings may be in and for themselves, thou shall act towards them as self-existent, free, substantive beings, wholly independent of thee. Assume it as already known, that they can give a purpose to their own being wholly by themselves, and quite independently of thee; never interrupt the accomplishment of this purpose, but rather further it to the utmost of thy power. Honour their freedom, lovingly take up their purposes as if they were thine own." Thus ought I to act :—by this course of action *ought* all my thought to be guided,—nay, it *shall* and *must* necessarily be so, if I have resolved to obey the voice of my conscience. I shall therefore always regard these beings as in possession of an existence for themselves wholly independent of mine, as capable of forming and carrying out their own purposes;—from this point of view, I shall never be able to regard them otherwise, and my previous speculations shall vanish from before me like an empty dream.—I *think* of them as beings like myself, I have said; but strictly speaking, it is not mere thought by which they are first presented to me as such. It is by the voice of my conscience,—the command :—"Here set a limit to thy freedom; here recognize and reverence purposes which are not thine own." This it is which is first translated into the thought, "Here, certainly and truly, are beings like myself, free and independent." To view them otherwise, I must in action renounce, and in speculation disregard, the voice of my conscience.

Other phenomena present themselves before me which I do not

regard as beings like myself, but as things irrational. Speculation finds no difficulty in showing how the conception of such things is developed solely from my own presentative faculty, and its necessary modes of activity. But I apprehend these things, also, through want, desire, and enjoyment. Not by the mental conception, but by hunger, thirst, and their satisfaction, does anything become for me food and drink. I am necessitated to believe in the reality of that which threatens my sensuous existence, or in that which alone is able to maintain it. Conscience enters the field in order that it may at once sanctify and restrain this natural impulse. "Thou shalt maintain, exercise, and strengthen thyself and thy physical powers, for they have been counted upon in the plans of reason. But thou canst only maintain them by using them in a legitimate manner, comformable to the inward nature of such things. There are also, besides thee, many other beings like thyself, whose powers have been counted upon like thine own, and can only be maintained in the same way as thine own. Concede to them the same privilege that has been allowed to thee. Respect what belongs to them, as their possession;—use what belongs to thee, legitimately as thine own." Thus ought I to act,—according to this course of action must I think. I am compelled to regard these things as standing under their own natural laws, independent of, though perceivable by, me; and therefore to ascribe to them an independent existence. I am compelled to believe in such laws; the task of investigating them is set before me, and that empty speculation vanishes like a mist when the genial sun appears.

In short, there is for me absolutely no such thing as an existence which has no relation to myself, and which I contemplate merely for the sake of contemplating it;—whatever has an existence for me, has it only through its relation to myself. But there is, in the highest sense, only one relation to me possible, all others are but subordinate forms of this :—my vocation to moral activity. My world is the object and sphere of my duties, and absolutely nothing more; there is no other world for me, and no other qualities of my world than what are implied in this;—my whole united capacity, all finite capacity, is insufficient to comprehend any other. Whatever possesses an existence for me, can bring its existence and reality into contact with me only through this relation, and only through this relation do I comprehend it :—for any other existence than this I have no organ whatever.

To the question, whether, in deed and in fact, such a world exists as that which I represent to myself, I can give no answer more fundamental, more raised above all doubt, than this :—I have, most certainly and truly, these determinate duties, which announce themselves to me as duties towards certain objects, to be fulfilled by means of certain materials;—duties which I cannot otherwise conceive of, and cannot otherwise fulfil, than within such a world as I represent to myself. Even to one who had never meditated on his own moral vocation, if there could be such a one, or who, if he had given it some general consideration, had, at least, never entertained the slightest purpose of fulfilling it at any time within an indefinite futurity,—even for him, his sensuous world, and his belief in its reality, arises in other manner than from his ideas of a moral world. If he do not apprehend it by the thought of his duties, he certainly does so by the demand for his rights. What he perhaps never requires of himself, he does certainly exact from others in their conduct towards him,—that they should treat him with propriety, consideration, and respect, not as an irrational thing, but as a free and independent being;—and thus, in supposing in them an ability to comply with his own demands, he is compelled also to regard them as themselves considerate, free, and independent of the dominion of mere natural power. Should he never propose to himself any other purpose in his use and enjoyment of surrounding objects, but simply that of enjoying them, he at least demands this enjoyment as a right, in the possession of which he must be left undisturbed by others; and thus he apprehends even the irrational world of sense, by means of a moral idea. These claims of respect for his rationality, independence, and preservation, no one can resign who possesses a conscious existence; and with these claims, at least, there is united in his soul, earnestness, renunciation of doubt, and faith in a reality, even if they be not associated with the recognition of a moral law within him. Take the man who denies his own moral vocation, and thy existence, and the existence of a material world, except as a mere futile effort in which speculation tries her strength,—approach him practically, introduce his own principles into life, and act as if either he had no existence at all, or were merely a portion of rude matter,—he will soon lay aside his scornful indifference, and indignantly complain of thee; earnestly call thy attention to thy conduct towards him; maintain that thou oughtst not and darest not so to act; and thus prove to thee, by deeds, that thou art assuredly capable of acting upon him; that *he is*, and that *thou art,*— that there is a medium by which thou canst influence him, and that thou, at least, hast duties to perform towards him.

Thus, it is not the operation of supposed external objects, which indeed exist for us, and we for them, only in so far as we already know of them; and just as little an empty vision evoked by our own imagination and thought, the products of which must, like itself, be mere empty pictures;—it is not these, but the necessary faith in our own freedom and power, in our own real activity and in the definite laws of human action, which lies at the root of all our consciousness of a reality external to ourselves;—a consciousness which is itself but faith, since it is founded on another faith, of which however it is a necessary consequence. We are compelled to believe that we act, and that we ought to act in a certain manner; we are compelled to assume a certain sphere for this action; this sphere is the real, actually present world, such as we find it;—and on the other hand, the world is absolutely nothing more than this sphere, and cannot, in any other way, extend itself beyond it. From this necessity of action proceeds the consciousness of the actual world; and not the reverse way, from the consciousness of the actual world the necessity of action :—this, not that, is the first; the former is derived from the latter. We do not act because we know, but we know because we are called upon to act :—the practical reason is the root of all reason. The laws of action for rational beings are *immediately certain*; their world is only certain through that previous certainty. We cannot deny these laws without plunging the world, and ourselves with it, into absolute annihilation;—we raise ourselves from this abyss, and maintain ourselves above it, solely by our moral activity.

There is something which I am called upon to do, simply in order that it may be done; something to avoid doing, solely that it may be left undone. But can I act without having an end in view beyond the action itself, without directing my attention to something which can become possible through my action, and only through that? Can I will, without having something which I will? No :—this would entirely contradict the nature of my mind. To every action there is united in my thought, immediately and by the laws of thought itself, a condition of things placed in futurity, to which my action is related as the efficient cause to the effect produced. But this purpose or end of my action must not be given to me for its own sake,—perhaps through some necessity of Nature,—and then my course of action determined according to this end; I must not have an end assigned to me, and then inquire how I must act in order to attain this end; my action must not be dependent on the end; but I must act in a certain manner, simply because I ought so to act;—this is the first point. That a result will follow from this course of action, is proclaimed by the voice within me. This result necessarily becomes an end to me, since I am bound to perform the action which brings it, and it alone, to pass. I will that something shall come to pass, because I must act so that it may come to pass;—thus as I do not hunger because food is before me, but a thing becomes food for me because I hunger; so I do not act as I do because a certain end is to be attained, but the end becomes mine because I am bound to act in the particular manner by which it may be attained. I have not first in view the point towards which I am to draw my line, and then, by its position, determine the direction of my line, and the angle that it shall make; but I draw my line absolutely in a right angle, and thereby the points are determined through which my line must pass. The end does not determine the commandment; but, on the contrary, the primitive purport of the commandment determines the end.

I say, it is the law which commands me to act that of itself assigns an end to my action; the same inward voice that compels me to think that I ought to act thus, compels me also to believe that from my action some result will arise; it opens to my spiritual vision a prospect into another world,—which is really a world, a state, namely, and not an action,—but another and better world than that which is present to the physical eye; it makes me aspire after this better world, embrace it with every impulse, long for its realization, live only in it, and in it alone find satisfaction. The law itself is my guarantee for the certain attainment of this end. The same resolution by which I devote my whole thought and life to the fulfilment of this law, and determine to see nothing beyond it, brings with it the indestructible conviction, that the promise it implies is likewise true and certain, and renders it impossible for me to conceive the possibility of the opposite. As I live in obedience to it, I live also in the contemplation of its end; live in that better world which it promises to me. . . .

II

HEGEL

GEORG WILHELM FRIEDRICH HEGEL (1770-1831) was born at Stuttgart. In 1788 he enrolled at the University of Tübingen, studying theology, philology, and philosophy; it was at Tübingen, too, that he became a friend of Schelling and of the poet Hölderlin, both of whom shared his early enthusiasm for the French Revolution. Hegel's development as a philosopher was slow and laborious; he made little impression upon his teachers, and for several years after leaving Tübingen he earned his living by taking tutorial posts, first in Berne and later at Frankfurt. While engaged in this somewhat unrewarding work he wrote various papers, mainly on theological subjects; though these are of considerable interest from the point of view of his subsequent thought, he published none of them. In 1801 he obtained a position at the University of Jena, and, after producing a piece on the philosophies of Schelling and Fichte, embarked on the "voyage of discovery" which was to issue in his own masterpiece, *The Phenomenology of Spirit* (1807). The Battle of Jena, on the eve of which he completed the book, led to the closure of the university, and Hegel had to look for other employment. A short period during which he edited a newspaper at Bamberg was followed by his appointment as rector of a gymnasium at Nuremberg; here he wrote his *Science of Logic* (1812-16). His reputation as an important and original philosopher was now established. From 1816 to 1818 he occupied a chair at Heidelberg, where he published his *Encyclopaedia of the Philosophical Sciences*, and he then moved to Berlin, remaining there as professor of philosophy until his death from cholera in 1831. His *Outlines of the Philosophy of Right* appeared in 1821, to be succeeded by new editions of the *Encyclopaedia* in 1827 and 1830. Hegel's lectures on the history of philosophy and on the philosophies of art, religion, and history, which he delivered while in Berlin, were all published posthumously.

40

The range and sweep of Hegel's thinking, and the cumbrous and often repellent manner in which he chose to express it, combine to make him a philosopher of exceptional difficulty. This is true above all of his *Phenomenology*, called by Marx "the true birthplace and secret of the Hegelian philosophy": it represents a kind of imaginative reconstruction, supplemented by historical allusions, of the different outlooks and attitudes which men, as embodiments of "spirit," adopt at successive stages of their development toward complete knowledge of themselves and their world. The selections from the *Phenomenology* presented here comprise one of its most arresting and influential discussions; apart from anything else, there are interesting connections with ideas later put forward by Feuerbach and Marx. Like Fichte before him, Hegel held that developed self-consciousness presupposed an awareness, not merely of a phenomenal world, but also of the presence of other conscious beings within that world: the individual can achieve adequate confirmation of his self-identity only through the medium of other persons, in whom he sees himself reflected and from whom he demands recognition. Yet, at the same time, his drive to assert his own freedom and independence causes him in the first instance to seek the destruction of the other, who confronts him as a rival existence. In this way there is engendered, as a kind of unstable compromise, the famous dialectic of master and servant which Hegel analyzes with a wealth of pregnant suggestion and which he also regards as giving rise to further forms of mental and social attitude: stoicism, scepticism, and what is called the "unhappy consciousness." If the first two of these constitute attempts by the unsatisfied subject to attain self-sufficiency through rejecting the world and withdrawing into the inner sanctum of himself, the third involves, by contrast, an explicit recognition of the contradictions that inevitably beset all such efforts. The individual is now aware of himself as a divided personality, in which his changeless ideal nature seems to stand opposed to what he finds when he considers his inescapable entanglement in the shifting conditions of his actual existence in the world. Thus the master-servant situation, originally portrayed as a relationship between separate persons, returns once more; now, however, it takes the form of a duality haunting the consciousness of a single self—a duality which (Hegel further suggests) obtains mythical expression at a certain stage of religious experience, in the notion of a gulf dividing God from man.

The next selection is from *The Science of Logic*. In the *Phenomenology* Hegel claimed to show how spirit, after surmounting a series of partial or incomplete views, finally achieved "absolute knowledge" of itself: the antithesis between subjective consciousness and objective truth was overcome, and thought and reality were seen to coincide. Some of the implications of this became clear in his Introduction to the *Logic*. Logic, for Hegel, is not a purely formal discipline, indifferent to content, and he accords it a function very dissimilar to that traditionally assigned to it. As the science of thought, it can at the same time be said to treat of reality, for the categories of pure thought in their dialectical development cannot legitimately be distinguished from the inner truth and movement of existence itself.

If logic in one sense deals with the ultimate character of the world, the philosophies of nature and of history are each concerned with different aspects of its concrete or external manifestation. In the concluding selections, taken from his *Philosophy of History*, Hegel speaks of the relations between them, and discusses the manner in which the course of human history can be said to represent a rational process which conforms to a determinate pattern. To avoid confusion, it should be noted that he uses the term "spirit" here in a narrower sense than he does in some other contexts, restricting it to cover the sphere of human thought and behavior which he opposes to that of physical nature or "matter."

Master and Servant*

Self-consciousness exists in itself and for itself, in that, and by the fact that it exists for another self-consciousness; that is to say, it *is* only by being acknowledged or "recognized". The conception of this its unity in its duplication, of infinitude realizing itself in self-consciousness, has many sides to it and encloses within it elements of varied significance. Thus its moments must on the one hand be strictly kept apart in detailed distinctiveness, and, on the other, in this distinction must, at the same time, also be taken as not distinguished, or must always be accepted and understood in their opposite sense. This double meaning of what is distinguished lies in the nature of self-consciousness :—of its being infinite, or directly the opposite of the determinateness in which it is fixed. The detailed exposition of the notion of this spiritual unity in its duplication will bring before us the process of Recognition.

Self-consciousness has before it another self-consciousness; it has come outside itself. This has a double significance. First it has lost its own self, since it finds itself as an *other* being; secondly, it has thereby sublated that other, for it does not regard the other as essentially real, but sees its own self in the other.

It must cancel this its other. To do so is the sublation of that first double meaning, and is therefore a second double meaning. First, it must set itself to sublate the other independent being, in order thereby to become certain of itself as true being, secondly, it thereupon proceeds to sublate its own self, for this other is itself.

This sublation in a double sense of its otherness in a double sense is at the same time a return in a double sense into its self. For, firstly, through sublation, it gets back itself, because it becomes one with itself again through the cancelling of *its* otherness; but secondly, it likewise gives otherness back again to the other self-consciousness, for it was

*From *The Phenomenology of Mind* (trans. J. Baillie; London, George Allen & Unwin Ltd., 1964), pp. 229-240.

43

aware of being in the other, it cancels this its own being in the other and thus lets the other again go free.

This process of self-consciousness in relation to another self-consciousness has in this manner been represented as the action of one alone. But this action on the part of the one has itself the double significance of being at once its own action and the action of that other as well. For the other is likewise independent, shut up within itself, and there is nothing in it which is not there through itself. The first does not have the object before it only in the passive form characteristic primarily of the object of desire, but as an object existing independently for itself, over which therefore it has no power to do anything for its own behoof, if that object does not *per se* do what the first does to it. The process then is absolutely the double process of both self-consciousnesses. Each sees the other do the same as itself; each itself does what it demands on the part of the other, and for that reason does what it does, only so far as the other does the same. Action from one side only would be useless, because what is to happen can only be brought about by means of both.

The action has then a *double entente* not only in the sense that it is an act done to itself as well as to the other, but also in the sense that the act *simpliciter* is the act of one as well as of the other regardless of their distinction.

In this movement we see the process repeated which came before us as the play of forces; in the present case, however, it is found in consciousness. What in the former had effect only for us [contemplating experience], holds here for the terms themselves. The middle term is self-consciousness which breaks itself up into the extremes; and each extreme is this interchange of its own determinateness, and complete transition into the opposite. While *qua* consciousness, it no doubt comes outside itself, still, in being outside itself, it is at the same time restrained within itself, it exists for itself, and its self-externalization for consciousness. *Consciousness* finds that it immediately is and is not another consciousness, as also that this other is for itself only when it cancels itself as existing for itself, and has self-existence only in the self-existence of the other. Each is the mediating term to the other, through which each mediates and unites itself with itself; and each is to itself and to the other an immediate self-existing reality, which, at the same time, exists thus for itself only through this mediation. They recognize themselves as mutually recognizing one another.

This pure conception of recognition, of duplication of self-consciousness within its unity, we must now consider in the way its process appears for self-consciousness. It will, in the first place, present the aspect of the disparity of the two, or the break-up of the middle term into the extremes, which, *qua* extremes, are opposed to one another, and of which one is merely recognized, while the other only recognizes.

Self-consciousness is primarily simple existence for self, self-identity by exclusion of every other from itself. It takes its essential nature and absolute object to be Ego; and in this immediacy, in this bare fact of its self-existence, it is individual. That which for it is other stands as unessential object, as object with the impress and character of negation. But the other is also a self-consciousness; an individual makes its appearance in antithesis to an individual. Appearing thus in their immediacy, they are for each other in the manner of ordinary objects. They are independent individual forms, modes of consciousness that have not risen above the bare level of life (for the existent object here has been determined as life). They are, moreover, forms of consciousness which have not yet accomplished for one another the process of absolute abstraction, of uprooting all immediate existence, and of being merely the bare, negative fact of self-identical consciousness; or, in other words, have not yet revealed themselves to each other as existing purely for themselves, i.e., as self-consciousness. Each is indeed certain of its own self, but not of the other, and hence its own certainty of itself is still without truth. For its truth would be merely that its own individual existence for itself would be shown to it to be an independent object, or, which is the same thing, that the object would be exhibited as this pure certainty of itself. By the notion of recognition, however, this is not possible, except in the form that as the other is for it, so it is for the other; each in its self through its own action and again through the action of the other achieves this pure abstraction of existence for self.

The presentation of itself, however, as pure abstraction of self-consciousness consists in showing itself as a pure negation of its objective form, or in showing that it is fettered to no determinate existence, that it is not bound at all by the particularity everywhere characteristic of existence as such, and is *not* tied up with life. The process of bringing all this out involves a twofold action—action on the part of the other and action on the part of itself. In so far as it is the other's action, each aims at the destruction and death of the other. But in this there is implicated also the second kind of action, self-activity; for the former implies that it risks its own life. The relation of both self-consciousnesses is in this way so constituted that they prove themselves and each other through a life-and-death struggle. They must enter into this struggle, for they must bring their certainty of themselves, the certainty of being for themselves, to the level of objective truth, and make this a fact both

in the case of the other and in their own case as well. And it is solely by
risking life that freedom is obtained; only thus is it tried and proved
that the essential nature of self-consciousness is not bare existence, is not
the merely immediate form in which it at first makes its appearance, is
not its mere absorption in the expanse of life. Rather it is thereby
guaranteed that there is nothing present but what might be taken as
a vanishing moment—that self-consciousness is merely pure self-existence, being-for-self. The individual, who has not staked his life, may,
no doubt, be recognized as a Person; but he has not attained the truth
of this recognition as an independent self-consciousness. In the same
way each must aim at the death of the other, as it risks its own life
thereby; for that other is to it of no more worth than itself; the other's
reality is presented to the former as an external other, as outside itself;
it must cancel that externality. The other is a purely existent consciousness and entangled in manifold ways; it must view its otherness as
pure existence for itself or as absolute negation.

This trial by death, however, cancels both the truth which was to
result from it, and therewith the certainty of self altogether. For just
as life is the natural "position" of consciousness, independence without
absolute negativity, so death is the natural "negation" of consciousness,
negation without independence, which thus remains without the requisite significance of actual recognition. Through death, doubtless, there
has arisen the certainty that both did stake their life, and held it lightly
both in their own case and in the case of the other; but that is not for
those who underwent this struggle. They cancel their consciousness
which had its place in this alien element of natural existence; in other
words, they cancel themselves and are sublated as terms or extremes
seeking to have existence on their own account. But along with this
there vanishes from the play of change the essential moment, viz. that
of breaking up into extremes with opposite characteristics; and the
middle term collapses into a lifeless unity which is broken up into
lifeless extremes, merely existent and not opposed. And the two do
not mutually give and receive one another back from each other through
consciousness; they let one another go quite indifferently, like things.
Their act is abstract negation, not the negation characteristic of consciousness, which cancels in such a way that it preserves and maintains
what is sublated, and thereby survives its being sublated.

In this experience self-consciousness becomes aware that *life* is as
essential to it as pure self-consciousness. In immediate self-consciousness the simple ego is absolute object, which, however, is for us or in
itself absolute mediation, and has as its essential moment substantial
and solid independence. The dissolution of that simple unity is the

result of the first experience; through this there is posited a pure self-consciousness, and a consciousness which is not purely for itself, but for another, i.e. as an existent consciousness, consciousness in the form and shape of thinghood. Both moments are essential, since, in the first instance, they are unlike and opposed, and their reflexion into unity has not yet come to light, they stand as two opposed forms or modes of consciousness. The one is independent, and its essential nature is to be for itself; the other is dependent, and its essence is life or existence for another. The former is the Master or Lord, the latter the Servant.*

The master is the consciousness that exists *for itself*; but no longer merely the general notion of existence for self. Rather, it is a consciousness existing on its own account which is mediated with itself through another consciousness, i.e. through another whose very nature implies that it is bound up with an independent being or with thinghood in general. The master brings himself into relation to both these moments, to a thing as such, the object of desire, and to the consciousness whose essential character is thinghood. And since the master, (a) *qua* notion of self-consciousness, an immediate relation of self-existence, but (b) is now moreover at the same time mediation, or a being-for-self which is for itself only through an other—he [the master] stands in relation (a) immediately to both (b) mediately to each through the other. The master relates himself to the servant mediately through independent existence, for that is precisely what keeps the servant in thrall; it is his chain, from which he could not in the struggle get away, and for that reason he proved himself to be dependent, to have his independence in the shape of thinghood. The master, however, is the power controlling this state of existence, for he has shown in the struggle that he holds it to be merely something negative. Since he is the power dominating existence, while this existence again is the power controlling the other [the servant], the master holds, *par consequence,* this other in subordination. In the same way the master relates himself to the thing mediately through the servant. The servant being a self-consciousness in the the broad sense, also takes up a negative attitude to things and cancels them; but the thing is, at the same time, independent for him, and, in consequence, he cannot, with all his negating get so far as to annihilate it outright and be done with it; that is to say, he merely works on it. To the master, on the other hand, by means of this mediating process, belongs the immediate relation, in the sense of the pure negation of it, in other words he gets the enjoyment. What mere desire did not attain, he now succeeds in attaining, viz. to have done with the thing, and find satisfaction in enjoyment. Desire alone

*Translated as *Bondsman* in the original.

did not get the length of this, because of the independence of the thing. The master however, who has interposed the servant between it and himself, thereby relates himself merely to the dependence of the thing, and enjoys it without qualification and without reserve. The aspect of its independence he leaves to the servant, who labours upon it.

In these two moments, the master gets his recognition through another consciousness, for in them the latter affirms itself as unessential, both by working upon the thing, and, on the other hand, by the fact of being dependent on a determinate existence; in neither case can this other get the mastery over existence, and succeed in absolutely negating it. We have thus here this moment of recognition, viz. that the other consciousness cancels itself as self-existent, and, *ipso facto,* itself does what the first does to it. In the same way we have the other moment, that this action on the part of the second is the action proper of the first; for what is done by the servant is properly an action on the part of the master. The latter exists only for himself, that is his essential nature; he is the negative power without qualification, a power to which the thing is naught. And he is thus the absolutely essential act in this situation, while the servant is not so, he is an unessential activity. But for recognition proper there is needed the moment that what the master does to the other he should also do to himself, and what the servant does to himself, he should do to the other also. On that account a form of recognition has arisen that is one sided and unequal.

In all this, the unessential consciousness is, for the master, the object which embodies the truth of his certainty of himself. But it is evident that this object does not correspond to its notion; for, just where the master has effectively achieved lordship, he really finds that something has come about quite different from an independent consciousness. It is not an independent, but rather a dependent consciousness that he has achieved. He is thus not assured of self-existence as his truth; he finds that his truth is rather the unessential consciousness, and the fortuitous unessential action of that consciousness.

The truth of the independent consciousness is accordingly the consciousness of the servant. This doubtless appears in the first instance outside itself, and not as the truth of self-consciousness. But just as lordship showed its essential nature to be the reverse of what it wants to be, so, too, bondage will, when completed, pass into the opposite of what it immediately is: being a consciousness repressed within itself, it will enter into itself, and change round into real and true independence.

We have seen what bondage is only in relation to lordship. But it is a self-consciousness, and we have now to consider what it is, in this regard, in and for itself. In the first instance, the master is taken to be the essential reality for the state of bondage; hence, for it, the truth is the independent consciousness existing for itself, although this truth is not taken yet as inherent in bondage itself. Still, it does in fact contain within itself this truth of pure negativity and self-existence, because it has experienced this reality within it. For this consciousness was not in peril and fear for this element or that, nor for this or that moment of time, it was afraid for its entire being; it felt the fear of death, the sovereign master. It has been in that experience melted to its inmost soul, has trembled throughout its every fibre, and all that was fixed and steadfast has quaked within it. This complete perturbation of its entire substance, this absolute dissolution of all its stability into fluent continuity, is, however, the simple, ultimate nature of self-consciousness, absolute negativity, pure self-referent existence, which consequently is involved in this type of consciousness. This moment of pure self-existence is moreover a fact for it; for in the master it finds this as its object. Further, this servant's consciousness is not only this total dissolution in a general way; in serving and toiling the servant actually carries this out. By serving he cancels in every particular aspect his dependence on and attachment to natural existence, and by his work removes this existence away.

The feeling of absolute power, however, realized both in general and in the particular form of service, is only dissolution implicitly; and albeit the fear of the lord is the beginning of wisdom, consciousness is not therein aware of being self-existent. Through work and labour, however, this consciousness of the servant comes to itself. In the moment which corresponds to desire in the case of the master's consciousness, the aspect of the non-essential relation to the thing seemed to fall to the lot of the servant, since the thing there retained its independence. Desire has reserved to itself the pure negating of the object and thereby unalloyed feeling of self. This satisfaction, however, just for that reason is itself only a state of evanescence, for it lacks objectivity or subsistence. Labour, on the other hand, is desire restrained and checked, evanescence delayed and postponed; in other words, labour shapes and fashions the thing. The negative relation to the object passes into the *form* of the object, into something that is permanent and remains; because it is just for the labourer that the object has independence. This negative mediating agency, this activity giving shape and form, is at the same time the individual existence, the pure self-existence of that consciousness, which now in the work it does is externalized and passes into the condition of permanence. The consciousness that toils and serves accordingly attains by this means the direct apprehension of that independent being as its self.

But again, shaping or forming the object has not only the positive significance that the servant becomes thereby aware of himself as factually and objectively self-existent; this type of consciousness has also a negative import, in contrast with its first moment, the element of fear. For in shaping the thing it only becomes aware of its own proper negativity, its existence on its own account, as an object, through the fact that it cancels the actual form confronting it. But this objective negative element is precisely the alien, external reality, before which it trembled. Now, however, it destroys this extraneous alien negative, affirms and sets itself up as a negative in the element of permanence, and thereby becomes for itself a self-existent being. In the master, the servant feels self-existence to be something external, an objective fact; in fear self-existence is present within himself; in fashioning the thing, self-existence comes to be felt explicitly as his own proper being, and he attains the consciousness that he himself exists in its own right and on its own account (*an und für sich*). By the fact that the form is objectified, it does not become something other than the consciousness moulding the thing through work; for just that form is his pure self-existence, which therein becomes truly realized. Thus precisely in labour where there seemed to be merely some outsider's mind and ideas involved, the servant becomes aware, through this re-discovery of himself by himself, of having and being a "mind of his own".

For this reflexion of self into self the two moments, fear and service in general, as also that of formative activity, are necessary : and at the same time both must exist in a universal manner. Without the discipline of service and obedience, fear remains formal and does not spread over the whole known reality of existence. Without the formative activity shaping the thing, fear remains inward and mute, and consciousness does not become objective for itself. Should consciousness shape and form the thing without the initial state of absolute fear, then it has a merely vain and futile "mind of its own"; for its form or negativity is not negativity *per se,* and hence its formative activity cannot furnish the consciousness of itself as essentially real. If it has endured not absolute fear, but merely some slight anxiety, the negative reality has remained external to it, its substance has not been through and through infected thereby. Since the entire content of its natural consciousness has not tottered and shaken, it is still inherently a determinate mode of being; having a "mind of its own" (*der eigene Sinn*) is simply stubbornness (*Eigensinn*), a type of freedom which does not get beyond the attitude of bondage. As little as the pure form can become its essential nature, so little is that form, considered as extending over particulars, a universal formative activity, an absolute notion; it is rather a piece of cleverness which has mastery within a certain range, but not over the universal power nor over the entire objective reality.

Stoicism: Scepticism: The Unhappy Consciousness*

Independent self-consciousness partly finds its essential reality in the bare abstraction of Ego. On the other hand, when this abstract ego develops further and forms distinctions of its own, this differentiation does not become an objective inherently real content for that self-consciousness. Hence this self-consciousness does not become an ego which truly differentiates itself in its abstract simplicity, or one which remains identical with itself in this absolute differentiation. The repressed and subordinated type of consciousness, on the other hand, becomes, in the formative activity of work, an object to itself, in the sense that the form, given to the thing when shaped and moulded, is his object; he sees in the master, at the same time, self-existence as a real mode of consciousness. But the subservient consciousness as such finds these two moments fall apart—the moment of itself as independent object, and the moment of this object as a mode of consciousness, and so its own proper reality. Since, however, the form and the self-existence are for us, or objectively in themselves, one and the same, and since in the notion of independent consciousness the inherent reality is consciousness, the phase of inherent existence (*Ansichsein*) or thinghood, which received its shape and form through labour, is no other substance than consciousness. In this way, we have a new attitude or mode of consciousness brought about : a type of consciousness which takes on the form of infinitude, or one whose essence consists in unimpeded movement of consciousness. It is one which *thinks* or is free self-consciousness. For thinking does not mean being an abstract ego, but an ego which has at the same time the significance of inherently existing in itself; it means being object to itself or relating itself to objective reality in such a way that this connotes the self-existence of that consciousness for which it is an object. The object does not for

*Ibid., pp. 242-253.

thinking proceed by way of presentations or figures, but of notions, conceptions, i.e. of a differentiated reality or essence, which, being an immediate content of consciousness, is nothing distinct from it. What is presented, shaped and constructed, and existent as such, has the form of being something other than consciousness. A notion, however, is at the same time an existent, and this distinction, so far as it falls in consciousness itself, is its determinate content. But in that this content is, at the same time, a conceptually constituted, a comprehended (*begriffener*) content, consciousness remains immediately aware within itself of its unity with this determinate existent so distinguished; not as in the case of a presentation, where consciousness from the first has to take special note that this is its idea; on the contrary, the notion is for me *eo ipso* and at once *my* notion. In thinking I am free, because I am not in an other, but remain simply and solely in touch with myself; and the object which for me is my essential reality, is an undivided unity my self-existence; and my procedure in dealing with notions is a process within myself.

It is essential, however, in this determination of the above attitude of self-consciousness to keep hold of the fact that this attitude is thinking consciousness in general, that its object is immediate unity of the self's implicit, inherent existence, and of its existence explicitly for self. The self-same consciousness which repels itself from itself, becomes aware of being an element existing in itself. But to itself it is this element to begin with only as universal reality in general, and not as this essential reality appears when developed in all the manifold details it contains, when the process of its being brings out all its fullness of content.

This freedom of self-consciousness, as is well known, has been called *Stoicism*, in so far as it has appeared as a phenomenon conscious of itself in the course of the history of man's spirit. Its principle is that consciousness is essentially that which thinks, is a thinking reality, and that anything is really essential for consciousness, or is true and good, only when consciousness in dealing with it adopts the attitude of a thinking being.

The manifold, self-differentiating expanse of life, with all its individualization and complication, is the object upon which desire and labour operate. This varied activity has now contracted itself into the simple distinction which is found in the pure process of thought. What has still essential reality is not a distinction in the sense of a determinate thing, or in the shape of a consciousness of a determinate kind of natural existence, in the shape of a feeling, or again in the form of desire and its specific purpose, whether that purpose be set up by the consciousness desiring or by an extraneous consciousness. What has still essential significance here is solely that distinction which is a thought-constituted distinction, or which, when made, is not distinguished from me. This consciousness in consequence takes a negative attitude towards the relation of lordship and bondage. Its action, in the case of the master, results in his not simply having his truth in and through the bondsman; and, in that of the bondsman, in not finding his truth in the will of his master and in service. The essence of this consciousness is to be free, on the throne as well as in fetters, throughout all the dependence that attaches to its individual existence, and to maintain that stolid lifeless unconcern which persistently withdraws from the movement of existence, from effective activity as well as from passive endurance, into the simple essentiality of thought. Stubbornness is that freedom which makes itself secure in a solid singleness, and keeps *within* the sphere of bondage. Stoicism, on the other hand, is the freedom which ever comes directly out of that sphere, and returns back into the pure universality of thought. It is a freedom which can come on the scene as a general form of the world's spirit only in a time of universal fear and bondage, a time, too, when mental cultivation is universal, and has elevated culture to the level of thought.

Now while this self-consciousness finds its essential reality to be neither something other than itself, nor the pure abstraction of ego, but ego which has within it otherness—otherness in the sense of a thought-constituted distinction—so that this ego in its otherness is turned back directly into itself; yet this essential nature is, at the same time, only an abstract reality. The freedom of self-consciousness is indifferent towards natural existence, and has, therefore, let this latter go and remain free. The reflexion is thus duplicated. Freedom of thought takes only pure thought as its truth, and this lacks the concrete filling of life. It is, therefore, merely the notion of freedom, not living freedom itself; for it is, to begin with, only thinking in general that is its essence, the form as such, which has turned away from the independence of things and gone back into itself. Since, however, individuality when acting should show itself to be alive, or when thinking should grasp the living world as a system of thought, there ought to lie in thought itself a content to supply the sphere of the ego, in the former case with what is good, and, in the latter, true, in order that there should throughout be no other ingredient in what consciousness has to deal with, except the notion which is the real essence. But here, by the way in which the notion as an abstraction cuts itself off from the multiplicity of things, the notion has *no content in itself*; the content is a datum, is given. Consciousness, no doubt, abolishes the content as an external, a foreign existent, by the fact that it thinks it, but the notion is a determinate notion, and this *determinateness* of the notion is the alien element the notion contains within it. Stoicism, therefore, got embarrassed, when, as the expression went, it was asked for the criterion of truth in general, i.e. properly speaking, for a *content* of thought itself. To the question what is good and true, it responded by giving again the abstract, contentless thought; the true and good are to consist in reasonableness. But this self identity of thought is simply once more pure form, in which nothing is determinate. The general terms true and good, wisdom and virtue, with which Stoicism has to stop short, are, therefore, in a general way, doubtless elevating; but seeing that they cannot actually and in fact reach any expanse of content, they soon begin to get wearisome.

This thinking consciousness, in the way in which it is thus constituted, as abstract freedom, is therefore only incomplete negation of otherness. Withdrawn from existence solely into itself, it has not there fully vindicated itself as the absolute negation of this existence. The content is held indeed to be only thought, but is thereby also taken to be determinate thought, and at the same time determinateness as such.

Scepticism is the realization of that of which Stoicism is merely the notion, and is the actual experience of what freedom of thought is; it is in itself and essentially the negative, and must so exhibit itself. With the reflexion of self-consciousness into the simple, pure thought of itself, independent existence or permanent determinateness has, in contrast to that reflexion, dropped as a matter of fact out of the infinitude of thought. In Scepticism, the entire unessentiality and unsubstantiality of this "other" becomes a reality for consciousness. Thought becomes thinking which wholly annihilates the being of the world with its manifold determinateness, and the negativity of free self-consciousness becomes aware of attaining, in these manifold forms which life assumes, real negativity.

It is clear from the foregoing that, just as Stoicism answers to the *notion* of independent consciousness, which appeared as a relation of lordship and bondage, Scepticism, on its side, corresponds to its *realization,* to the negative attitude towards otherness, to desire and labour. But if desire and work could not carry out for self-consciousness the process of negation, this polemical attitude towards the manifold substantiality of things will, on the other hand, be successful, because it turns against them as a free self-consciousness, and one complete within itself beforehand; or, expressed more definitely, because it has inherent in itself thought or the principle of infinitude, where the independent elements in their distinction from one another are held to be merely vanishing qualities. The differences, which, in the pure thinking of self are only the *abstraction* of differences, become here the whole of the differences; and every differentiated existent becomes a difference of self-consciousness.

With this we get determined the action of Scepticism in general, as also its mode and nature. It shows the dialectic movement, which is sense-certainty, perception, and understanding. It shows, too, the unessentiality of that which holds good in the relation of master and servant, and which for abstract thought itself passes as determinate. That relation involves, at the same time, a determinate situation, in which there are found even moral laws, as commands of the sovereign lord. The determinations in abstract thought, however, are scientific notions, into which formal contentless thought expands itself, attaching the notion, as a matter of fact in merely an external fashion, to the existence independent of it, and holding as valid only determinate notions, albeit they are still pure abstractions.

Dialectic as a negative process, taken immediately as it stands, appears to consciousness, in the first instance, as something at the mercy of which it is, and which does not exist through consciousness itself. In Scepticism, on the other hand, this negative process is a moment of self-consciousness, which does not simply find its truth and its reality vanish, without self-consciousness knowing how, but rather which in the certainty of its own freedom, itself makes this other, so claiming to be real, vanish. Self-consciousness here not only makes the objective as such to disappear before the negations of Scepticism but also its own function in relation to the object, where the object is held to be objective and made good—i.e. its function of perceiving as also its process of securing what is in danger of being lost, viz. sophistry and *its* self-constituted and self-established truth. By means of this self-conscious negation, self-consciousness procures for itself the certainty of its own freedom, brings about the experience of that freedom, and thereby raises it into the truth. What vanishes is what is determinate, the difference which, no matter what its nature or whence it comes, sets up to be fixed and unchangeable. The difference has nothing permanent in it, and must vanish before thought because to be differentiated just means not to have being in itself, but to have its essential nature solely in an other. Thinking, however, is the insight into this character of what is differentiated; it is the negative function in its simple, ultimate form.

Sceptical self-consciousness thus discovers, in the flux and alternation of all that would stand secure in its presence, its own freedom, as given by and received from its own self. It is aware of being this ἀταραξία of self-thinking thought, the unalterable and genuine certainty of its self. This certainty does not arise as a result out of something extraneous and foreign which stowed away inside itself its whole complex development; a result which would thus leave behind the process by which it came to be. Rather consciousness itself is thoroughgoing dialectical restlessness, this mêlée of presentations derived from sense and thought, whose differences collapse into oneness, and whose identity is similarly again resolved and dissolved—for this identity is itself determinateness as contrasted with non-identity. This consciousness, however, as a matter of fact, instead of being a self-same consciousness, is here neither more nor less than an absolutely fortuitous embroglio, the giddy whirl of a perpetually self-creating disorder. This is what it takes itself to be; for itself maintains and produces this self-impelling confusion. Hence it even confesses the fact; it owns to being an entirely fortuitous *individual* consciousness—a consciousness which is empirical, which is directed upon what admittedly has no reality for it, which obeys what, in its regard, has no essential being, which realizes and does what it knows to have no truth. But while it passes in this manner for an individual, isolated, contingent, in fact animal life, and a lost self-consciousness, it also, on the contrary, again turns itself into universal self-sameness; for it is the negativity of all singleness and all difference. From this self-identity, or rather within its very self, it falls back once more into that contingency and confusion, for this very self-directed process of negation has to do solely with what is single and individual, and is occupied with what is fortuitous. This form of consciousness is, therefore, the aimless fickleness and instability of going to and fro, hither and thither, from one extreme of self-same self-consciousness, to the other contingent, confused and confusing consciousness. It does not itself bring these two thoughts of itself together. It finds its freedom, at one time, in the form of elevation above all the whirling complexity and all the contingency of mere existence, and again, at another time, likewise confesses to falling back upon what is unessential, and to being taken up with that. It lets the unessential content in its thought vanish; but in that very act it is the consciousness of something unessential. It announces absolute disappearance but the announcement *is,* and this consciousness is the evanescence expressly announced. It announces the nullity of seeing, hearing, and so on, yet *itself* sees and hears. It proclaims the nothingness of essential ethical principles, and makes those very truths the sinews of its own conduct. Its deeds and its words belie each other continually; and itself, too, has the doubled contradictory consciousness of immutability and sameness, and of utter contingency and non-identity with itself. But it keeps asunder the poles of this contradiction within itself; and bears itself towards the contradiction as it does in its purely negative process in general. If sameness is shown to it, it points out unlikeness, non-identity; and when the latter, which it has expressly mentioned the moment before, is held up to it, it passes on to indicate sameness and identity. Its talk, in fact, is like a squabble among self-willed children, one of whom says A when the other says B, and again B, when the other says A, and who, through being in contradiction with themselves, procure the joy of remaining in contradiction with one another.

In Scepticism consciousness gets, in truth, to know itself as a consciousness containing contradiction within itself. From the experience of this proceeds a new attitude which brings together the two thoughts which Scepticism holds apart. The want of intelligence which Scepticism manifests regarding itself is bound to vanish, because it is in fact *one* consciousness which possesses these two modes within it. This new attitude consequently is one which is *aware* of being the double consciousness of itself as self-liberating, unalterable, self-identical, and as utterly self-confounding, self-perverting; and this new attitude is the consciousness of this contradiction within itself.

In Stoicism, self-consciousness is the bare and simple freedom of itself. In Scepticism, it realizes itself, negates the other side of determinate existence, but, in so doing, really doubles itself, and is itself now a duality. In this way the duplication, which previously was divided between two individuals, the lord and the servant, is concentrated into one. Thus we have here that dualizing of self-consciousness within itself, which lies essentially in the notion of mind; but the unity of the two elements is not yet present. Hence the *Unhappy Consciousness,* the Alienated Soul which is the consciousness of self as a divided nature, a doubled and merely contradictory being.

This unhappy consciousness, divided and at variance within itself, must, because this contradiction of its essential nature is felt to be a single consciousness, always have in the one consciousness the other also; and thus must be straightway driven out of each in turn, when it thinks it has therein attained to the victory and rest of unity. Its true return into itself, or reconciliation with itself, will, however, display the notion of mind endowed with a life and existence of its own, because it implicitly involves the fact that, while being an undivided consciousness, it is a double-consciousness. It is itself the gazing of one self-consciousness into another, and itself is both, and the unity of both is also its own essence; but objectively and consciously it is not yet this essence itself—is not yet the unity of both.

Since, in the first instance, it is the immediate, the implicit unity of both, while for it they are not one and the same, but opposed, it takes one, namely, the simple unalterable as essential, the other, the manifold and changeable as the unessential. For it, both are realities foreign to each other. Itself, because consciousness of this contradiction, assumes the aspect of changeable consciousness and is to itself the unessential; but as consciousness of unchangeableness, of the ultimate essence, it must, at the same time, proceed to free itself from the unessential, i.e. to liberate itself from itself. For though in its own view it is indeed only the changeable, and the unchangeable is foreign and extraneous to it, yet itself is simple, and therefore unchangeable consciousness, of which consequently it is conscious as its essence, but still in such wise that itself is again in its own regard not this essence. The position, which it assigns to both, cannot, therefore, be an indifference of one to the other, i.e. cannot be an indifference of itself towards the unchangeable. Rather it is immediately both itself; and the relation of both assumes for it the form of a relation of essence to the non-essential, so that this latter has to be cancelled; but since both are to it equally essential and are contradictory, it is only the conflicting contradictory process in which opposite does not come to rest in its own opposite, but produces itself therein afresh merely as an opposite.

Here, then, there is a struggle against an enemy, victory over whom really means being worsted, where to have attained one result is really to lose it in the opposite. Consciousness of life, of its existence and action, is merely pain and sorrow over this existence and activity; for therein consciousness finds only consciousness of its opposite as its essence—and of its own nothingness. Elevating itself beyond this, it passes to the unchangeable. But this elevation is itself this same consciousness. It is, therefore, immediately consciousness of the opposite, viz. of itself as single, individual, particular. The unchangeable, which comes to consciousness, is in that very fact at the same time affected by particularity, and is only present with this latter. Instead of particularity having been abolished in the consciousness of immutability, it only continues to appear there still.

In this process, however, consciousness experiences just this appearance of particularity in the unchangeable, and of the unchangeable in particularity. Consciousness becomes aware of particularity *in general* in the immutable essence, and at the same time it there finds its own particularity. For the truth of this process is precisely that the double consciousness is one and single. This unity becomes a fact to it, but in the first instance the unity is one in which the diversity of both factors is still the dominant feature. Owing to this, consciousness has before it the threefold way in which particularity is connected with unchangeableness. In one form it comes before itself as opposed to the unchangeable essence, and is thrown back to the beginning of that struggle, which is, from first to last, the principle constituting the entire situation. At another time it finds the unchangeable appearing in the form of particularity; so that the latter is an embodiment of unchangeableness, into which, in consequence, the entire form of existence passes. In the third case, it discovers *itself* to be this particular fact in the unchangeable. The first unchangeable is taken to be merely the alien, external Being,[1] which passes sentence on particular existence; since the second unchangeable is a form or mode of particularity like itself,[2] it, i.e. the consciousness, becomes in the third place spirit (*Geist*), has the joy of finding itself therein, and becomes aware within itself that its particularity has been reconciled with the universal. . . .[3]

1. God as Judge [Tr.].
2. Christ [Tr.].
3. The religious communion [Tr.].

General Concept of Logic*

The need to begin with the subject itself, without preliminary observations, is felt nowhere more strongly than in the Science of Logic. In every other science, the Subject dealt with, and the Method of the Science, are distinguished from one another; and further the subject is not absolutely original, but depends upon other concepts, and is connected in all directions with other material. It is therefore granted to these other sciences to regard both their Principles (with the connexions of these) and also their Method, as starting from assumptions—to begin with applying forms of Definition and so on, which are presupposed as known and accepted, and to make use of familiar forms of reasoning for the establishment of their general concepts and fundamental determinations.

Logic on the other hand cannot take for granted any of these forms of reflection or rules and laws of thought, for these are part of the very fabric of Logic, and must be demonstrated within the boundaries of the science itself. But not only the scheme of philosophic method, but also the very concept of philosophy in general belongs to the content of Logic and in fact constitutes its final result; what Logic is, cannot be set out beforehand—on the contrary this knowledge of what Logic is can only be reached as the end and consummation of the whole treatment of the subject. Moreover the subject of Logic (Thinking, or more precisely Conceptual Thinking) is really treated of within the boundaries of the science itself; the Concept of this Thinking is engendered in the course of development of the Science, and therefore cannot precede it. Therefore what is set forth in a preliminary way in this Introduction does not aim at establishing the concept of Logic at all, or at justifying beforehand its substance and method scientifically, but—by help of some reasoned and historical explanations and reflections—at bringing

*From *The Science of Logic* (trans. W. H. Johnston and L. G. Struthers; London George Allen & Unwin Ltd., 1929), Vol. I, pp. 53-70.

more clearly before the mind the point of view from which this science is to be regarded.

When Logic is taken as the science of Thinking in general, it is understood that this Thinking constitutes the *bare form* of cognition, that Logic abstracts from all *content,* and that the (so-called) other *constituent* of a cognition—that is, its *Matter,*—must come from a different source; that thus Logic—as something of which this Matter is wholly and entirely independent—can provide only the formal conditions of true knowledge, and cannot, in and by itself, contain real truth, nor even be the path to real truth, because just that which is the essence of truth,—that is, its content—lies outside Logic.

But in the first place it is most inept to say that Logic abstracts from all *Content,* that it teaches only the rules of Thinking without going into what is thought or being able to consider its nature. For since Thinking and Rules of Thinking are the subject of Logic, Logic has directly in them its own peculiar content;—has in them the second constituent of cognition—its Matter—about the structure of which it concerns itself.

But secondly, the ideas upon which the concept of Logic has hitherto rested have partly died out already, and, for the rest, it is time that they should disappear altogether, and that this science should be taken from a higher point of view, and should receive an entirely different structure.

The hitherto accepted concept of Logic rests upon the assumed separation of the *Content* of knowledge and the *Form* of knowledge (or *Truth* and *Certainty*)—a separation that it assumed once for all in ordinary consciousness. First, it is assumed that the material of knowledge is present in and for itself in the shape of a finished world apart from Thinking, that Thinking is in itself empty, and comes to that world from outside as Form to Matter, fills itself therewith, and only thus gets a content, and thereby becomes real knowing.

Next, these two constituents—for it is supposed that they have the reciprocal relation of constituents, and Cognition is constructed out of them in a mechanical or at best a chemical fashion—these constituents are placed in an order of merit in which the object is regarded as something in itself finished and complete, something which, as far as its reality is concerned, could entirely dispense with thought, while on the other hand, Thought is something incomplete which has to seek completion by means of some material, and indeed has to adapt itself to its material as if it were a form in itself pliable and undetermined. Truth is supposed to be the agreement of Thought with its object, and in order to bring about this agreement (for the agreement is not there by itself) thinking must accommodate and adapt itself to its object.

Thirdly, when the difference of Matter and Form, of Object and Thought, is not left thus nebulous and undetermined, but is taken more definitely, each is regarded as a sphere separated from the other. Thus Thought in its reception and formation of material is supposed not to go beyond itself—its reception of material and accommodation thereto is still regarded as a modification of self by which Thought is not transformed into its Other; moreover, self-conscious determination is held to belong to Thought alone; thus Thought in its relation to the Object of Thought does not go out of itself to the Object, while the Object, as a thing-in-itself, simply remains a something beyond Thought.

These views concerning the relation to one another of Subject and Object express the determinations which constitute the nature of our ordinary consciousness just as it appears; but these prejudices, translated into the sphere of Reason—as if the same relationship held there or had any truth by itself—are errors, the refutation of which throughout all departments of the spiritual and physical world is Philosophy itself; or rather, since these errors bar the way, they must be renounced at the very threshold of Philosophy.

The older Metaphysic had in this respect a loftier conception of Thought than that which has become current in more modern times. For the older Metaphysic laid down as fundamental that that which by thinking is known of and in things, that alone is what is really true in them; that what is really true is not things in their immediacy, but only things when they have been taken up into the Form of Thought, as conceptions. Thus this older Metaphysic stands for the view that thinking and the determinations of thinking are not something foreign to the objects of thought, but are rather of the very essence of those objects; in other words that *Things* and the *Thinking* of them are in harmony in and for themselves,—indeed language itself expresses an affinity between them,—that thought in its immanent determinations, and the true nature of things, are one and the same content.

But *reflective* Understanding assumed possession of Philosophy. We must learn precisely what is meant by this expression, which indeed is frequently used as a catch-word; by it is to be understood generally the abstracting and separating intelligence which clings tenaciously to the separations which it has made. Directed against Reason, this intelligence behaves as *crude Common Sense* and maintains the view that Truth rests upon sense-reality, that thoughts are *only* thoughts, meaning that it is sense-perception that first endows them with substance and reality, that Reason—in as far as it is merely Reason—can spin nothing but idle fancies. In this renunciation of Reason by itself, the concept of Truth is lost; it is restricted to the cognition of merely subjective Truth, of mere appearance, of something to which the nature of the thing itself does not correspond; *knowing* falls back into *opinion*.

But this turn which Cognition takes, and which has the air of being a loss and a retrogression, has something deeper behind it—something upon which the uplifting of Reason to the loftier spirit of the newer Philosophy chiefly depends. That is, the ground of this now everywhere prevalent idea is to be sought in a perception of the *necessary conflict* with each other of the determinations of Understanding. The reflection already mentioned is this, that the immediate concrete must be transcended, and must undergo determination and abstraction. But reflection must, just as much, transcend these its own separative determinations, and forthwith relate them to each other. Then at the standpoint of this relating, the conflict emerges. This relating activity of reflection belongs in itself to Reason; that transcending of these determinations which attains to a perception of their conflict, is the great negative step towards the true concept of Reason. But this perception, being merely partial, falls into the error of fancying that it is Reason which is in contradiction with itself, and does not recognize that the contradiction is just the lifting of Reason above the limitations of Understanding, and the dissolution of these. Instead of starting from this point to make the final step upwards, knowledge, recognizing the unsatisfactory nature of the determinations of Understanding, flies straight back to sensible existence, thinking to find therein stability and unity. But on the other hand, since this knowledge knows itself to be knowledge only of appearances, its insufficiency is confessed, yet at the same time it is supposed that things, though not rightly known in themselves, still are rightly known within the sphere of appearances; as though only the *kinds of objects* were different, and the one kind, namely Things in themselves, did not fall within knowledge, and the other kind, namely Appearances, did so fall. It is as though accurate perception were attributed to a man, with the proviso that he yet could not perceive Truth but only untruth. Absurd as this would be, a true knowledge which did not know the object of knowledge as it is in itself, would be equally absurd.

The *criticism of the Forms of Common Understanding* has had the result (mentioned above) that these Forms have no *applicability to things in themselves*. This can have no other meaning than that the Forms are in themselves something untrue. But if they are allowed to remain as valid for subjective Reason and for experience, then criticism has made no change in them, but leaves them in the same attitude towards the Subject of knowledge, as they formerly had towards the Object of knowledge. But if they do not suffice for the Thing in itself, then still less should common understanding, to which they are supposed to belong, put up with them and be content with them. If they cannot be determinations of the *Thing in itself,* they can still less be determinations of Understanding, to which we must allow at the very least the dignity of a Thing in itself. The determinations of Finite and Infinite are similarly in conflict—whether they are applied to the world, to time and space, or are determinations within the mind; just as black and white produce grey whether they are mixed on a canvas or the palette; so if our World-representation is dissolved by having the determinations of Finite and Infinite transferred to it, still more must the Mind itself, which contains them both, be something self-contradictory and self-dissolving. It is not the constitution of the Matter or Object to which they are applied or in which they occur, that can make the difference, for the Object contains the contradiction only through these determinations and in accordance with them.

Thus this Criticism has only separated the forms of objective Thinking from the Thing, and left them, as it found them, in the Subject of Thought. For in doing so, it has not regarded these Forms in and for themselves, according to their characteristic content, but has simply taken them up as a corollary from subjective Logic; so that it was not a question of the deduction of them in themselves, nor of a deduction of them as subjective-logical Forms, and still less a question of the dialectical consideration of them.

Transcendental Idealism, carried more consistently to its logical conclusion, has recognized the emptiness of that spectre of the *Thing-in-itself* which the critical philosophy left over—an abstract shadow, detached from all content—and had it in view to demolish it altogether. Also this philosophy made a beginning of letting Reason produce its own determinations out of itself. But the subjective attitude of this attempt did not admit of its being carried to completion. Henceforth this attitude—and with it that beginning, and the development of pure philosophy—was given up.

But that which has commonly been understood by Logic is considered without any reference to metaphysical import. In its present condition, this Science has indeed no Content of such a kind that it can be regarded by ordinary consciousness as reality and truth. But Logic is not on this account a mere formal science, destitute of significant truth. In any case, the province of truth is not to be looked for in that subject-matter which is lacking in Logic, and to the want of which the inadequacy of the Science is commonly attributed: the emptiness and worthlessness of the logical forms reside solely in the way in which they have been considered and treated. Whilst as fixed determinations they fall apart and cannot he held together in organic unity, they are mere dead forms, and have not dwelling in them the spirit which is their living concrete unity. Thus they are destitute of solid content and substantial filling. The content which we miss in the logical forms, is nothing other than a solid foundation and concreting of those abstract forms, and it is customary to seek this substantial essence for them, from outside. But it is just logical Reason which is that substantial or real, which holds together in itself all abstract determinations, and is their solid absolutely concrete unity. Thus we do not need to seek far afield for what is usually regarded as a filling or content; it is not the fault of the subject-matter of Logic if it is supposed to be without content or filling, but of the way in which Logic is conceived.

This reflection leads us nearer to the problem of the point of view from which Logic is to be regarded; how it is distinguished from the mode of treatment which this science has hitherto received, and to what extent it is the only true point of view upon which Logic is in the future to be permanently based.

In the *Phenomenology of Spirit* (Bamberg and Würzburg, 1807) I have set forth the movement of consciousness, from the first crude opposition between itself and the Object, up to absolute knowledge. This process goes through all the forms of the *relation of thought to its object,* and reaches the *Concept of Science* as its result. Thus this concept (apart from the fact that it arises within the boundaries of Logic) needs here no justification, having already received its justification in that place; the concept is incapable of any other justification than just this production by consciousness; for to consciousness, all its forms are resolved into this concept, as into the truth. A reasoned deduction or elucidation of the concept of science can at best render this service, that by it the concept is presented to the mind, and a historical knowledge of it is produced; but a definition of science, or—more precisely—of logic, has its evidence solely in the inevitableness (already referred to) of its origin. The definition with which any science makes an absolute beginning can contain nothing other than the precise and correct expression of that which is presented to one's mind *as the accepted and recognized* subject-matter and purpose of the science. That exactly this or that is thus presented is a historical asseveration, in respect of which one may indeed appeal to certain facts as commonly accepted; or rather the request can be made that certain facts may be granted as accepted. And still we find that one man here and another there will bring forward, here a case and there an instance, according to which something more and other is to be understood by various expressions, into the definition of which therefore a narrower or more general determination is to be admitted, and in accordance with which the science is to be arranged. It further depends upon argument *what* should be admitted or excluded, and within what limit and scope; and there stand open to argument the most manifold and varied opinions, among which only arbitrary choice can make a fixed and final decision. In this mode of procedure, of beginning a science with its definition, nothing is said of the need that the *inevitableness* of the *subject-matter*, and therefore of the Science itself, should be demonstrated.

The concept of pure Science, and the Deduction of it, are assumed in the present treatise so far as this, that the *Phenomenology of Spirit* is nothing other than the Deduction of this concept. Absolute Knowledge is the *Truth* of all modes of Consciousness, because according to the process of knowledge, it is only when absolute knowledge has been reached that the separation of the *Object of Knowledge* from *Subjective Certainty* is completely resolved, and Truth equated to this Certainty, and this Certainty equated to Truth.

So pure Science presupposes deliverance from the opposition of Consciousness. Pure Science includes *Thought in so far as it is just as much the Thing in itself as it is Thought, or the Thing in itself in so far as it is just as much pure Thought as it is the Thing in itself.* Truth, as *Science*, is pure Self-Consciousness unfolding itself, and it has the form of Self in that what exists in and for itself is the known concept, while the Concept as such is that which exists in and for itself.

This objective thinking is then the content of the pure science. Hence Logic is so little merely formal, so little destitute of the matter necessary for real and true knowledge, that on the contrary its Content is the only Absolutely True, or (if we wish still to employ the word *matter*) is the true genuine matter—a Matter, however, to which Form is not external, since this Matter is in fact Pure Thought, and thus Absolute Form itself. Logic is consequently to be understood as the System of Pure Reason, as the Realm of Pure Thought. *This realm is the Truth as it is, without husk in and for itself.* One may therefore express it thus : that this content *shows forth God as he is in his eternal essence before the creation of Nature and of a Finite Spirit.*

Anaxagoras is praised as the man who first gave voice to the idea that we ought to lay down, as the World-principle, Nous, that is Thought, and Thought as the World-essence. He thus laid the foundation of an intellectual view of the Universe, and of this view

Logic must be the pure form. In it we are not concerned with thinking *about* something lying outside thought, as the basis of thought, nor with Forms which serve merely as *signs* of Truth; on the contrary, the necessary Forms and characteristic determinations of thought are the Content and the Supreme Truth itself.

In order that we may at least envisage this we must put aside the opinion that Truth is something tangible. Such tangibility has for example been imported even into the Platonic Ideas, which are in the thought of God, as though they were things existing, but existing in a world or region outside the world of Reality, a world other than that of those Ideas, and only having real Substantiality in virtue of this otherness. The Platonic Idea is nothing other than the Universal, or more precisely the Concept of an Object of Thought; it is only in its concept that anything has actuality; in so far as it is other than its concept, it ceases to be actual and is a non-entity; the aspect of tangibility and of sensuous externality to self belongs to that non-entical aspect.—From the other side, however, one can refer to the characteristic ideas of ordinary Logic; for it is assumed that, for instance, Definitions comprise not determinations which belong only to the cognizing Subject, but determinations which belong to the Object, and constitute its most essential and inmost nature. Again, when from given determinations we conclude to others, it is assumed that what is concluded is not something external to the Object and foreign to it, but that it belongs to the object,—that Being corresponds to Thought.—Speaking generally, it lies at the very basis of our use of the Forms of Concept, Judgment, Inference, Definition, Division, and so on, that they are Forms not merely of self-conscious Thinking but also of the objective understanding.—*To think* is an expression which attributes specially to Consciousness the determination which it contains. But in as far as it is allowed that *Understanding, and Reason, are of the World of Objects,* that Spirit and Nature have General Laws in accordance with which their life and their mutations are governed, in so far is it admitted that the determinations of Thought also have objective validity and existence.

The Critical Philosophy has indeed turned Metaphysics into Logic, but—as already mentioned—like the later idealism it shied at the Object, and gave to logical determinations an essentially subjective signification; thus both the Critical Philosophy and the later idealism remained saddled with the Object which they shunned, and for Kant a "Thing-in-itself," for Fichte an abiding "Resistance-principle," was left over as an unconquerable Other. But that freedom from the opposition of consciousness which Logic must be able to assume, lifts these thought-determinations above such a timid and incomplete point of view, and requires that those determinations should be considered not with any such limitation and reference, but as they are in and for themselves, as Logic, as Pure Reason.

Kant considers that Logic—that is, the aggregate of Definitions and Propositions which are called Logic in the ordinary sense—is fortunate in that it has fallen to its lot to attain so early to completion, before the other sciences; for Logic has not taken any step backwards since Aristotle,—but also it has taken no step forwards—the latter because to all appearance it was already finished and complete.—If Logic has undergone no change since Aristotle—and in fact when one looks at modern compendiums of Logic the changes consist to a large extent merely in omissions—what is rather to be inferred from this is, that Logic is all the more in need of a thorough overhaul; for when Spirit has worked on for two thousand years, it must have reached a better reflective consciousness of its own thought and its own unadulterated essence. A comparison of the forms to which Spirit has risen in the worlds of Practice and Religion, and of Science in every department of knowledge Positive and Speculative,—a comparison of these with the form which Logic—that is, Spirit's knowledge of its own pure essence—has attained, shows such a glaring discrepancy that it cannot fail to strike the most superficial observer that the latter is inadequate to the lofty development of the former, and unworthy of it.

As a matter of fact the need of a transformation of Logic has long been felt. It may be said that, both in Form and in Content, as exhibited in text-books, Logic has become contemptible. It is still trailed along rather with a feeling that one cannot do without Logic altogether, and from a surviving adherence to the tradition of its importance, than from any conviction that that familiar content, and occupation with those empty forms, can be valuable and useful.

The additions—psychological, educational, even physiological—which Logic received during a certain period were, later, almost universally recognized as disfigurements. In themselves, a great part of these psychological, educational, and physiological observations, laws, and rules, must appear very trivial and futile, whether they occur in Logic or anywhere else. Besides, such rules as for instance that one should think out and test what one reads in books or hears by word of mouth, that when one does not see well, one should use spectacles to help one's eyes—rules which in text-books on so-called Applied Logic are put forward with great seriousness and formality to help us to attain to truth—these must appear to all the world to be superfluous—except

indeed to the writer or teacher who is at his wits' end to know how
to piece out the inadequate lifeless content of his Logic. [1]

As to this content, we have given above the reason why it is so
empty and lifeless. Its determinations are assumed to stand immovably
rigid and are brought into a merely external relation with one another.
Because in the operations of judgment and syllogism it is chiefly their
quantitative element that is referred to and built upon, everything rests
on an external difference, on mere comparison, and becomes a wholly
analytic procedure, a matter of merely mechanical calculation. The
deduction of the so-called rules and laws (especially of Syllogism) is not
much better than a manipulation of rods of unequal length in order
to sort and arrange them according to size—like the child's game of
trying to fit into their right places the various pieces of a picture-puzzle.
Not without reason, therefore, has this Thinking been identified with
Reckoning, and Reckoning with this Thinking. In Arithmetic the
numbers are taken as non-significant, as something that, except for
equality or inequality—that is, except for quite external relations—
has no significance,—that contains no Thought, either in itself or in
its relations. When it is worked out in a mechanical way that three-
fourths multiplied by two-thirds make a half, this operation involves
about as much or as little thought as the calculation whether in any
Figure of Syllogism this or that Mood is admissible.

In order that these dead bones of Logic may be re-vivified by
Mind, and endowed with content and coherence, its Method must be
that by means of which alone Logic is capable of becoming a Pure
Science. In the present condition of Logic, hardly a suspicion of scientific Method is to be recognized. It has very nearly the structure of
merely Empirical Science. For attaining their purpose, empirical
sciences have hit upon a characteristic Method of defining and classi-
fying their material as best they can. Pure Mathematics again has
its own Method, which suits its abstract objects and the quantitative
determinations with which alone it is concerned. I have in the Preface
to the *Phenomenology of Spirit* said what is essential concerning this
Method and especially concerning the subordinate nature of such
Science as can find a place in Mathematics; but it will also be more
closely considered within the bounds of Logic itself. Spinoza, Wolf,
and others, have allowed themselves to be misled into applying this

1. *Observation in first edition.* A work on this science which has recently appeared,
System of Logic by Fries, returns to the anthropological foundations. The ideas and
opinions on which it is based are so shallow in themselves and in their development
that I am saved the trouble of having to take any notice of this insignificant performance.

method in Philosophy, and identifying the external process of concept-less quantity with the conceptual process, which is self-contradictory. Hitherto Philosophy had not discovered its own method; it regarded with an envious eye the systematic structure of Mathematics and, as already remarked, borrowed this, or sought help in the method of Sciences which are only a medley of given material and empirical maxims and ideas—or took refuge in a crude rejection of all Method. But the exposition of that which alone is capable of being the true Method of philosophic Science belongs to Logic itself; since method is the consciousness of the form taken by the inner spontaneous move-ment of the content of Logic. In the *Phenomenology of Spirit* I have set out an example of this Method as applied to a more concrete object, namely to Consciousness.[2] We have here modes of consciousness each of which in realizing itself abolishes itself, has its own negation as its result,—and thus passes over into a higher mode. The one and only thing *for securing scientific progress* (and for quite *simple* insight into which, it is essential to strive)—is knowledge of the logical precept that Negation is just as much Affirmation as Negation, or that what is self-contradictory resolves itself not into nullity, into abstract Noth-ingness, but essentially only into the negation of its *particular* content, that such negation is not an all-embracing Negation, but is *the negation of a definite somewhat* which abolishes itself, and thus is a definite negation; and that thus the result contains in essence that from which it results—which is indeed a tautology, for otherwise it would be some-thing immediate and not a result. Since what results, the negation, is a *definite* negation, it has a *content*. It is a new concept, but a higher, richer concept than that which preceded; for it has been enriched by the negation or opposite of that preceding concept, and thus contains it, but contains also more than it, and is the unity of it and its opposite. —On these lines the system of Concepts has broadly to be constructed, and to go on to completion in a resistless course, free from all foreign elements, admitting nothing from outside.

I could not of course imagine that the Method which in this System of Logic I have followed—or rather which this System follows of itself—is not capable of much improvement, of much elaboration in detail, but at the same time I know that it is the only true Method. This is already evident from the fact that the Method is no-ways different from its object and content;—for it is the content in itself, *the Dialectic which it has in itself*, that moves it on. It is clear that no expositions

2. And later as applied to other concrete objects, and corresponding departments of Philosophy.

can be regarded as scientific which do not follow the course of this Method, and which are not conformable to its simple rhythm, for that is the course of the thing itself. . . .

That by means of which the Concepts forges ahead is the above-mentioned Negative which it carries within itself; it is this that constitutes the genuine dialectical procedure. *Dialectic*—which has been regarded as an isolated part of Logic, and which as regards its purpose and standpoint has, one may aver, been entirely misunderstood—is thus put in quite a different position.—The Platonic Dialectic too, even in the *Parmenides* (and still more directly in other places), is sometimes intended merely to dispose of and to refute through themselves limited assertions, and sometimes again has nullity for its result. Dialectic is generally regarded as an external and negative procedure, that does not pertain to the subject-matter, that is based on a mere idle subjective craving to disturb and unsettle what is fixed and true, or that at best leads to nothing except the futility of the dialectically treated matter.

Kant set Dialectic higher, and this part of his work is among the greatest of his merits,—for he freed Dialectic from the semblance of arbitrariness attributed to it in ordinary thought, and set it forth as *a necessary procedure of Reason*. Since Dialectic was regarded merely as the art of producing deceptions and bringing about illusions, it was straightway assumed that it played a cheating game, and that its whole power depended solely on concealment of the fraud; that its results were reached surreptitiously, and were a mere subjective illusion. When Kant's dialectical expositions in the *Antinomies of Pure Reason* are looked at closely (as they will be more at large in the course of this work) it will be seen that they are not indeed deserving of any great praise; but the general idea upon which he builds and which he has vindicated, is the *Objectivity of Appearance* and the *Necessity of Contradiction* which belongs to the very nature of thought-determinations; primarily indeed in so far as these determinations are applied by Reason to *Things in themselves*; but further, just what these determinations are *in Reason* and *in respect of that which is self-existent,*—just this it is which is their own nature. This result, *grasped on its positive side*, is nothing other than the inherent *Negativity* of these thought-determinations, their self-moving soul, the principle of all physical and spiritual life. But if people stop short at the abstract-negative aspect of the Dialectic, they reach only the familiar result that Reason is incapable of cognition of the Infinite;—a strange result, for —since the Infinite is the Reasonable—it amounts to saying that Reason is incapable of cognizing that which is Reasonable.

It is in this Dialectic (as here understood) and in the comprehension of the Unity of Opposites, or of the Positive in the Negative, that *Speculative knowledge* consists. This is the most important aspect of the Dialectic, but for thought that is as yet unpractised and unfree, it is the most difficult. If thought is still in the process of cutting itself loose from concrete sense-presentation and from syllogizing (*Räsonnieren*), it must first practice abstract thinking, and learn to hold fast concepts in their definiteness and to recognize by means of them. An exposition of Logic with this in view must, in its Method, follow the division above mentioned, and with regard to the more detailed content must hold to the determinations of the particular concepts without embarking upon the Dialectic. As far as external structure is concerned, this Logic would be similar to the usual presentation of the science, but as regards content would be distinct from it, and still would serve for practice in abstract thinking, though not in speculative thinking (a purpose which could not be in any degree fulfilled by the Logic which has become popular by means of psychological and anthropological trappings). It would present to the mind the picture of a methodically ordered whole, although the soul of the structure, the Method itself (which lives in Dialectic), would not be apparent in it.

As regards *education and the relation of the individual to Logic*, I observe in conclusion that this Science, like grammar, has two different aspects or values. It is one thing to him who approaches Logic and the Sciences in general for the first time, and another thing to him who comes back from the Sciences to Logic. He who begins to learn grammar, finds in its Forms and Laws dry abstractions, contingent rules, briefly an isolated multitude of determinations which only indicate the worth and significance of their face-value. At first, knowledge recognizes in them nothing whatever but barely themselves. On the other hand, if anyone has mastered a language, and has also a comparative knowledge of other languages, he and he only is capable of discerning the spirit and the culture of a people in the grammar of their language. Those same dry Rules and Forms have now for him a full and living value. Through grammar he can recognize the expression of mind in general—that is, Logic. Thus he who approaches Logic finds in the science at first an isolated system of abstractions that is self-contained and does not reach out to other knowledges and sciences. On the contrary, contrasted with the wealth of our world-presentations and the apparently real content of the other sciences, and compared with the promise of absolute Science to unfold the essential character of this wealth, the *inner nature* of Spirit and of the world, and to unveil *the Truth*, this science—in its abstract form, in the colourless cold simplicity of its purely formal determinations—looks, rather, as if the last thing to be expected from it were the fulfilment of such a promise, and as if it would stand empty in face of that wealth. On a first acquaintance, the significance of Logic is limited to itself; its content is regarded as only an isolated occupation with thought-determinations, *alongside of* which other scientific activities have their own material and their own intrinsic worth, upon which Logic may perhaps have some formal influence which it seems to exercise spontaneously, and for which logical structure and logical study can certainly be dispensed with, at need. The other Sciences have mostly rejected the regular Method, of a connected series of Definitions, Axioms, Theorems and their Proofs, and so forth; while so-called Natural Logic plays its part automatically in such series, and works of its own motion, without any special knowledge having Thought itself for its object. Above all the matter and content of these sciences keeps entirely independent of Logic, and altogether makes its appeal more to our senses, feeling, impressions, and practical interests.

Thus then Logic must certainly be learnt, at first, as something of which one has indeed perception and understanding, but which seems at the beginning to lack scope, profundity, and wider significance. It is only through a profounder acquaintance with other sciences that Logic discovers itself to subjective thought as not a mere abstract Universal, but as a Universal which comprises in itself the full wealth of Particulars;—just as a proverb, in the mouth of a youth who understands it quite accurately, yet fails of the significance and scope which it has in the mind of a man of years and experience, for whom it expresses the full force of its content. Thus the value of Logic only receives due appreciation when it is seen to result from knowledge of the particulars sciences; so regarded, it presents itself to the mind as Universal Truth, not as a *particular* department of knowledge *alongside of* other departments and other realities, but as the very essence of all these other Contents.

Now though when one begins to study it, Logic is not present to the mind in all this recognized power, yet none the less the mind of the student conceives from it a power which will lead him into all truth. The System of Logic is the realm of shades, a world of simple essentialities freed from all concretion of sense. To study this Science, to dwell and labour in this shadow-realm, is a perfect training and discipline of consciousness. In this realm the mind carries on a business which is far removed from the intuitions and aims of sense, from emotions, from ideas which are a mere matter of opinion. Regarded on its negative side, the work consists in holding at bay the accidentals of syllogizing thought and the arbitrary preference and acceptance from among opposing arguments.

But above all, Thought wins thus self-reliance and independence. It becomes at home in the region of the abstract and in progression by means of concept which have no substratum of sensation, it develops an unconscious power of taking up into the forms of Reason the multiplicity of all other knowledge and science, comprehending and holding fast what is essential therein, stripping off externalities and in this way extracting what is logical,—or, which is the same thing, filling with the content of all truth the abstract outline of Logic acquired by study, and giving it the value of a Universal, which no longer appears as a Particular side by side with other Particulars, but reaches out beyond all this, and is the essential nature thereof,—that is, the Absolute Truth.

Philosophical History*

The only Thought which Philosophy brings with it to the contemplation of History, is the simple conception of *Reason*; that Reason is the Sovereign of the World; that the history of the world, therefore, presents us with a rational process. This conviction and intuition is a hypothesis in the domain of history as such. In that of Philosophy it is no hypothesis. It is there provided by speculative cognition, that Reason —and this term may here suffice us, without investigation the relation sustained by the Universe to the Divine Being—is *Substance,* as well as *Infinite Power;* its own *Infinite Material* underlying all the natural and spiritual life which it originates, as also the *Infinite Form*—that which sets this Material in motion. On the one hand, Reason is the *substance* of the Universe; viz., that by which and in which all reality has its being and subsistence. On the other hand, it is the *Infinite Energy* of the Universe; since Reason is not so powerless as to be incapable of producing anything but a mere ideal, a mere intention—having its place outside reality, nobody knows where; something separate and abstract, in the heads of certain human beings. It is *the Infinite complex of things,* their entire Essence and Truth. It is its own material which it commits to its own Active Energy to work up; not needing, as finite action does, the conditions of an external material of given means from which it may obtain its support, and the objects of its activity. It supplies its own nourishment, and is the object of its own operations. While it is exclusively its own basis of existence, and absolute final aim, it is also the energizing power realizing this aim; developing it not only the phenomena of the Natural, but also of the Spiritual Universe—the History of the World. That this "Idea" or "Reason" is the *True,* the *Eternal,* the absolutely *powerful* essence; that it reveals itself in the World, and that in that World nothing else is revealed but this and its honor and glory—is the thesis which, as we have said, has been proved in Philosophy, and is here regarded as demonstrated. . . .

*From *The Philosophy of History* (trans. J. Sibree; New York, 1944), pp. 9-20.

It must be observed at the outset, that the phenomenon we investigate—Universal History—belongs to the realm of *Spirit*. The term *"World,"* includes both physical and psychical Nature. Physical Nature also plays its part in the World's History, and attention will have to be paid to the fundamental natural relations thus involved. But, Spirit, and the course of its development, is our substantial object. Our task does not require us to contemplate Nature as a Rational System in itself—though in its own proper domain it proves itself such —but simply in its relation to *Spirit*. On the stage on which we are observing it—Universal History—Spirit displays itself in its most concrete reality. Notwithstanding this (or rather for the very purpose of comprehending the *general* principles which this, its form of *concrete reality*, embodies) we must premise some abstract character-istics of the *nature of Spirit*. Such an explanation, however, cannot be given here under any other form than that of bare assertion. The present is not the occasion for unfolding the idea of Spirit speculatively; for whatever has a place in an Introduction, must, as already observed, be taken as simply historical; something assumed as having been ex-plained and proved elsewhere; or whose demonstration awaits the sequel of the Science of History itself. . . .

The nature of Spirit may be understood by a glance at its direct opposite—*Matter*. As the essence of Matter is Gravity, so, on the other hand, we may affirm that the substance, the essence of Spirit is Freedom. All will readily assent to the doctrine that Spirit, among other properties, is also endowed with Freedom; but philosophy teaches that all the qualities of Spirit exist only through Freedom; that all are but means for attaining Freedom; that all seek and produce this and this alone. It is a result of speculative Philosophy, that Freedom is the sole truth of Spirit. Matter possesses gravity in virtue of its tendency toward a central point. It is essentially composite; consisting of parts that *exclude* each other. It seeks its Unity; and therefore exhibits itself as self-destructive, as verging toward its opposite [an indivisible point]. If it could attain this, it would be Matter no longer, it would have perished. It strives after the realization of its Idea; for in Unity it exists *ideally*. Spirit, on the contrary, may be defined as that which has its centre in itself. It has not a unity outside itself, but has already found it; it exists *in* and *with itself*. Matter has its essence out of itself; Spirit is *self-contained existence* (Bei-sich-selbst-sein). Now this is Freedom, exactly. For if I am dependent, my being is referred to something else which I am not; I cannot exist independently of some-thing external. I am free, on the contrary, when my existence depends upon myself. This self-contained existence of Spirit is none other than self-consciousness—consciousness of one's own being. Two things must be distinguished in consciousness; first, the fact *that I know;* secondly, *what I know.* In *self* consciousness these are merged in one; for Spirit *knows itself.* It involves an appreciation of its own nature, as also an energy enabling it to realize itself; to make itself *actually* that which it is *potentially.* According to this abstract definition it may be said of Universal History, that it is the exhibition of Spirit in the process of working out the knowledge of that which it is potentially. And as the germ bears in itself the whole nature of the tree, and the taste and form of its fruits, so do the first traces of Spirit virtually contains the whole of that History. The Orientals have not attained the knowledge that Spirit—Man *as such*—is free; and because they do not know this, they are not free. They only know that *one is free.* But on this very account, the freedom of that one is only caprice; ferocity—brutal recklessness of passion, or a mildness and tameness of the desires, which is itself only an accident of Nature—mere caprice like the former.—That *one* is therefore only a Despot; not a *free man.* The consciousness of Freedom first arose among the Greeks, and therefore they were free; but they, and the Romans likewise, knew only that *some* are free—not man as such. Even Plato and Aristotle did not know this. The Greeks, there-therefore, had slaves; and their whole life and the maintenance of their splendid liberty, was implicated with the institution of slavery : a fact moreover, which made that liberty on the one hand only an accidental, transient and limited growth; on the other hand, constituted it a rigorous thraldom of our common nature—of the Human. The German nations, under the influence of Christianity, were the first to attain the consciousness, that man, as man, is free : that is the *free-dom* of Spirit which constitutes its essence. This consciousness arose first in religion, the inmost region of Spirit; but to introduce the prin-ciple into the various relations of the actual world, involves a more extensive problem than its simple implanation; a problem whose solution and application require a severe and lengthened process of culture. In proof of this, we may note that slavery did not cease immediately on the reception of Christianity. Still less did liberty predominate in States; or Governments and Constitutions adopt a rational organization, or recognize freedom as their basis. That applica-tion of the principle to political relations; the thorough moulding and interpenetration of the constitution of society by it, is a process identical with history itself. I have already directed attention to the distinction here involved, between a principle as such, and its *application; i.e.,* its introduction and carrying out in the actual phenomena of Spirit and Life. This is a point of fundamental importance in our science, and one which must be constantly respected as essential. And in the same way as this distinction has attracted attention in view of the *Christian* principle of self-consciousness—Freedom; it also shows itself as an essential one, in view of the principle of Freedom *generally.* The History of the world is none other than the progress of the consciousness of Freedom; a progress whose development according to the necessity of its nature, it is our business to investigate.

The general statement given above, of the various grades in the consciousness of Freedom—and which we applied in the first instance to the fact that the Eastern nations knew only that *one* is free; the Greek and Roman world only that *some* are free; while *we* know that all men absolutely (man *as man*) are free—supplies us with the natural division of Universal History, and suggests the mode of its discussion. This is remarked, however, only incidentally and anticipatively; some other ideas must be first explained.

The destiny of the spiritual World, and—since this is the *substantial World,* while the physical remains subordinate to it, or, in the language of speculation, has no truth *as against* the spiritual—*the final cause of the World at large,* we allege to be the *consciousness* of its own freedom on the part of Spirit, and *ipso facto,* the *reality* of that freedom. But that this term "Freedom," without further qualification, is an indefinite, and incalculable ambiguous term; and that while that which it represents is the *ne plus ultra* of attainment, it is liable to an infinity of misunderstandings, confusions and errors, and to become the occasion for all imaginable excesses—has never been more clearly known and felt than in modern times. Yet for the present, we must content ourselves with the term itself without further definition. Attention was also directed to the importance of the infinite difference between a principle in the abstract, and its realization in the concrete. In the process before us, the essential nature of freedom—which involves in it absolute necessity—is to be displayed as coming to a consciousness of itself (for it is in its very nature, self-consciousness) and thereby realizing its existence. Itself is its own object of attainment, and the sole aim of Spirit. This result it is, at which the process of the World's History has been continually aiming; and to which the sacrifices that have ever and anon been laid on the vast altar of the earth, through the long lapse of ages, have been offered. This is the only aim that sees itself realized and fulfilled; the only pole of repose amid the

ceaseless change of events and conditions, and the sole efficient principle that pervades them. This final aim is God's purpose with the
world; but God is the absolutely perfect Being, and can, therefore,
will nothing other than himself—his own Will. The Nature of His
Will—that is, His Nature itself—is what we here call the Idea of
Freedom; translating the language of Religion into that of Thought.

The Nature of Historical Change*

History in general is therefore the development of Spirit in *Time,* as Nature is the development of the Idea in *Space.*

If then we cast a glance over the World's-History generally, we see a vast picture of changes and transactions; of infinitely manifold forms of peoples, states, individuals, in unresting succession. Everything that can enter into and interest the soul of man—all our sensibility to *goodness, beauty, and greatness*—is called into play. On every hand aims are adopted and pursued, which we recognize, whose accomplishment we desire—we hope and fear for them. In all these occurrences and changes we behold human action and suffering predominant; everywhere something akin to ourselves, and therefore everywhere something that excites our interest for or against. Sometimes it attracts us by beauty, freedom, and rich variety, sometimes by energy such as enables even vice to make itself interesting. Sometimes we see the more comprehensive mass of some general interest advancing with comparative slowness, and subsequently sacrificed to an infinite complication of trifling circumstances, and so dissipated into atoms. Then, again, with a vast expenditure of power a trivial result is produced; while from what appears unimportant a tremendous issue proceeds. On every hand there is the motliest throng of events drawing us within the circle of its interest, and when one combination vanishes another immediately appears in its place.

The general thought—the category which first presents itself in this restless mutation of individuals and peoples, existing for a time and then vanishing—is that of *change* at large. The sight of the ruins of some ancient sovereignty directly leads us to contemplate this thought of change in its negative aspect. What traveller among the ruins of Carthage, of Palmyra, Persepolis, or Rome, has not been stimulated to reflections on the transiency of kingdoms and men, and to sadness at the thought of a vigorous and rich life now departed—a sadness which

*Ibid., pp. 72-79.

does not expend itself on personal losses and the uncertainty of one's own undertakings, but is a disinterested sorrow at the decay of a splendid and highly cultured national life! But the next consideration which allies itself with that of change, is that change while it imports dissolution, involves at the same time the rise of a *new life*—that while death is the issue of life, life is also the issue of death. This is a grand conception; one which the Oriental thinkers attained, and which is perhaps the highest in their metaphysics. In the idea of *Metempsychosis* we find it evolved in its relation to individual existence; but a myth more generally known, is that of the *Phœnix* as a type of the Life of *Nature*; eternally preparing for itself its funeral pile, and consuming itself upon it; but so that from its ashes is produced the new, renovated, fresh life. But this image is only Asiatic; oriental not occidental. Spirit—consuming the envelope of its existence—does not merely pass into another envelope, nor rise rejuvenescent from the ashes of its previous form; it comes forth exalted, glorified, a purer spirit. It certainly makes war upon itself—consumes its own existence; but in this very destruction it works up that existence into a new form, and each successive phase becomes in its turn a material, working on which it exalts itself to a new grade.

If we consider Spirit in this aspect—regarding its changes not merely as rejuvenescent transitions, *i.e.*, returns to the same form, but rather as manipulations of itself, by which it multiplies the material for future endeavors—we see it exerting itself in a variety of modes and directions; developing its powers and gratifying its desires in a variety which is inexhaustible; because every one of its creations, in which it has already found gratification, meets it anew as material, and is a new stimulus to plastic activity. The abstract conception of mere change gives place to the thought of Spirit manifesting, developing, and perfecting its powers in every direction which its manifold nature can follow. What powers it inherently possesses we learn from the variety of products and formations which it originates. In this pleasurable activity, it has to do only with itself. As involved with the conditions of mere nature—internal and external—it will indeed meet in these not only opposition and hindrance, but will often see its endeavors thereby fail; often sink under the complications in which it is entangled either by Nature or by itself. But in such case it perishes in fulfilling its own destiny and proper function, and even thus exhibits the spectacle of self-demonstration as spiritual activity.

The very essence of Spirit is activity; it realizes its potentiality— makes itself its own deed, its own work—and thus it becomes an object to itself; contemplates itself as an objective existence. Thus is it with

the Spirit of a people : it is a Spirit having strictly defined characteristics, which erects itself into an objective world, that exists and persists
in a particular religious form of worship, customs, constitution, and
political laws—in the whole complex of its institutions—in the events
and transactions that make up its history. That is its work—that is what
this particular Nation *is*. Nations are what their deeds are. Every
Englishman will say : We are the men who navigate the ocean, and
have the commerce of the world; to whom the East Indies belong and
their riches; who have a parliament, juries, etc.—The relation of the
individual to that Spirit is that he appropriates to himself this substantial existence; that it becomes his character and capability, enabling
him to have a definite place in the world—to be *something*. For he
finds the being of the people to which he belongs an already established,
firm world—objectively present to him—with which he has to incorporate himself. In this its work, therefore—its world—the Spirit of the
people enjoys its existence and finds its satisfaction.—A Nation is moral
—virtuous—vigorous—while it is engaged in realizing its grand objects,
and defends its work against external violence during the process of
giving to its purposes an objective existence. The contradiction between
its potential, subjective being—its inner aim and life—and its *actual*
being is removed; it has attained full reality, has itself objectively
present to it. But this having been attained, the activity displayed by
the Spirit of the people in question is no longer needed; it has its desire.
The Nation can still accomplish much in war and peace at home and
abroad; but the living substantial soul itself may be said to have ceased
its activity. The essential, supreme interest has consequently vanished
from its life, for interest is present only where there is opposition. The
nation lives the same kind of life as the individual when passing from
maturity to old age—in the enjoyment of itself—in the satisfaction
of being exactly what it desired and was able to attain. Although its
imagination might have transcended that limit, it nevertheless abandoned any such aspirations as objects of *actual endeavor,* if the real
world was less than favorable to their attainment—and restricted its
aim by the conditions thus imposed. This mere *customary life* (the
watch wound up and going on of itself) is that which brings on natural
death. Custom is activity without opposition, for which there remains
only a formal duration; in which the fulness and zest that originally
characterized the aim of life are out of the question—a merely external
sensuous existence which has ceased to throw itself enthusiastically into
its object. Thus perish individuals, thus perish peoples by a natural
death; and though the latter may continue in being, it is an existence
without intellect or vitality; having no need of its institutions, because

the need for them is satisfied—a political nullity and tedium. In order that a truly universal interest may arise, the Spirit of a People must advance to the adoption of some new purpose; but whence can this new purpose originate? It would be a higher, more comprehensive conception of itself—a transcending of its principle—but this very act would involve a principle of a new order, a new National Spirit.

Such a new principle does in fact enter into the Spirit of a people that has arrived at full development and self-realization; it dies not a simple natural death—for it is not a mere single individual, but a spiritual, generic life; in its case natural death appears to imply destruction through its own agency. The reason of this difference from the single natural individual, is that the Spirit of a people exists as a *genus,* and consequently carries within it its own negation, in the very generality which characterizes it. A people can only die a violent death when it has become naturally dead in itself, as, *e.g.,* the German Imperial Cities, the German Imperial Constitution.

It is not of the nature of the all pervading Spirit to die this merely natural death; it does not simply sink into the senile life of mere custom, but—as being a National Spirit belonging to Universal History—attains to the consciousness of what its work is; it attains to a conception of itself. In fact it is world-historical only in so far as a *universal principle* has lain in its fundamental element—in its grand aim : only so far is the work which such a spirit produces, a moral, political organization. If it be mere desires that impel nations to activity, such deeds pass over without leaving a trace; or their traces are only ruin and destruction. Thus, it was first Chronos—Time—that ruled; the Golden Age, without moral products; and what was produced—the offspring of that Chronos—was devoured by it. It was Jupiter—from whose head Minerva sprang, and to whose circle of divinities being Apollo and the Muses—that first put a constraint upon Time, and set a bound to its principle of decadence. He is the Political god, who produced a moral work—the State.

In the very element of an achievement the quality of generality, of thought, is contained; without thought it has no objectivity; that is its basis. The highest point in the development of a people in this—to have gained a conception of its life and condition—to have reduced its laws, its ideas of justice and morality to a science; for in this unity [of the objective and subjective] lies the most intimate unity that Spirit can attain to in and with itself. In its work it is employed in rendering itself an object of its own contemplation; but it cannot develop itself objectively in its essential nature, except in *thinking* itself.

At this point, then, Spirit is acquainted with its principles—the general character of its acts. But at the same time, in virtue of its very generality, this work of thought is different in point of form from the actual achievements of the national genius, and from the vital agency by which those achievements have been performed. We have then before us a *real* and an *ideal* existence of the Spirit of the Nation. If we wish to gain the general idea and conception of what the Greeks were, we find it in Sophocles and Aristophanes, in Thucydides and Plato. In these individuals the Greek spirit conceived and thought itself. This is the profounder kind of satisfaction which the Spirit of a people attains; but it is "ideal," and distinct from its "real" activity.

At such a time, therefore, we are sure to see a people finding satisfaction in the *idea* of virtue; putting *talk* about virtue partly side by side with actual virtue, but partly in the place of it. On the other hand pure, universal thought, since its nature is universality, is apt to bring the Special and Spontaneous—Belief, Trust, Customary Morality—to reflect upon itself, and its primitive simplicity; to show up the limitation with which it is fettered—partly suggesting reasons for renouncing duties, partly itself *demanding reasons,* and the connection of such requirements with Universal Thought; and not finding that connection, seeking to impeach the authority of duty generally, as destitute of a sound foundation.

At the same time the isolation of individuals from each other and from the Whole makes its appearance; their aggressive selfishness and vanity; their seeking personal advantage and consulting this at the expense of the State at large. That inward principle in transcending its outward manifestations is subjective also in *form*—viz., selfishness and corruption in the unbound passions and egotistic interests of men.

Zeus, therefore, who is represented as having put a limit to the devouring agency of Time, and stayed this transiency by having established something inherently and independently durable—Zeus and his race are themselves swallowed up, and that by the very power that produced them—the principle of thought, perception, reasoning, insight derived from rational grounds, and the requirement of such grounds.

Time is the negative element in the sensuous world. Thought is the same negativity, but it is the deepest, the infinite form of it, in which therefore all existence generally is dissolved; first *finite* existence—*determinate,* limited form : but existence *generally,* in its objective character, is limited; it appears therefore as a mere datum—something immediate—authority;—and is either intrinsically finite and limited, or presents itself as a limit for the thinking subject, and its infinite reflection on itself [unlimited abstraction].

But first we must observe how the life which proceeds from death, is itself, on the other hand, only individual life; so that, regarding the species as the real and substantial in this vicissitude, the perishing of the individual is a regress of the species into individuality. The perpetuation of the race is, therefore, none other than the monotonous repetition of the same kind of existence. Further, we must remark how perception—the comprehension of being by thought—is the source and birthplace of a new, and in fact higher form, in a principle which while it preserves, dignifies its material. For Thought is that *Universal*—that *Species* which is immortal, which preserves identity with itself. The particular form of Spirit not merely passes away in the world by natural causes in Time, but is annulled in the automatic self-mirroring activity of consciousness. Because this annulling is an activity of Thought, it is at the same time conservative and elevating in its operation. While then, on the one side, Spirit annuls the reality, the permanence of that which it *is*, it gains on the other side, the essence, the Thought, the Universal element of that which *it only was* [its transient conditions]. Its principle is no longer that immediate import and aim which it was previously, but the *essence* of that import and aim.

The result of this process is then that Spirit, in rendering itself objective and making this its being an object of thought, on the one hand destroys the determinate form of its being, on the other hand gains a comprehension of the universal element which it involves, and thereby gives a new form to its inherent principle. In virtue of this, the substantial character of the National Spirit has been altered—that is, its principle has risen into another, and in fact a higher principle.

It is of the highest importance in apprehending and comprehending History to have and to understand the thought involved in this transition. The individual traverses as a unity various grades of development, and remains the same individual; in like manner also does a people, till the Spirit which it embodies reaches the grade of universality. In this point lies the fundamental, the Ideal necessity of transition. This is the soul—the essential consideration—of the philosophical comprehension of History.

Spirit is essentially the result of its own activity: its activity is the transcending of immediate, simple, unreflected existence—the negation of that existence, and the returning into itself. We may compare it with the seed; for with this the plant begins, yet it is also the result of the plant's entire life. But the weak side of life is exhibited in the fact that the commencement and the result are disjoined from each other. Thus also is it in the life of individuals and peoples. The life of a people ripens a certain fruit; its activity aims at the complete manifestation of the principle which it embodies. But this fruit does not fall back into the bosom of the people that produced and matured it; on the contrary, it becomes a poison-draught to it. That poison-draught it cannot let alone, for it has an insatiable thirst for it : the taste of the draught is its annihilation, though at the same time the rise of a new principle.

We have already discussed the final aim of this progression. The principles of the successive phases of Spirit that animate the Nations in a necessitated gradation, are themselves only steps in the development of the one universal Spirit, which through them elevates and completes itself to a self-comprehending *totality*.

While we are thus concerned exclusively with the Idea of Spirit, and in the History of the World regard everything as only its manifestation, we have, in traversing the past—however extensive its periods—only to do with what is *present;* for philosophy, as occupying itself with the True, has to do with the *eternally present*. Nothing in the past is lost for it, for the Idea is ever present; Spirit is immortal; with it there is no past, no future, but an essential *now*. This necessarily implies that the present form of Spirit comprehends within it all earlier steps. These have indeed unfolded themselves in succession independently; but what Spirit is it has always been essentially; distinctions are only the development of this essential nature. The life of the ever present Spirit is a circle of progressive embodiments, which looked at in one aspect still exist beside each other, and only as looked at from another point of view appear as past. The grades which Spirit seems to have left behind it, it still possesses in the depths of its present.

III

SCHOPENHAUER

ARTHUR SCHOPENHAUER (1788-1860) was the son of a Danzig businessman. In 1809 he enrolled at the University of Göttingen, starting as a medical student but later turning to philosophy. After working for a time under G. E. Schulze, with whom he studied Plato and Kant, he transferred to Berlin were he attended the lectures of Fichte and Schleiermacher; despite the contempt Schopenhauer expressed for Fichte in his own writings, there is no doubt that some of the latter's ideas exercised a formative influence upon the development of his philosophy. In 1813 he completed and published his doctoral dissertation, *On the Fourfold Root of the Principle of Sufficient Reason*, and this was followed, five years later, by the appearance of his principal work, *The World as Will and Idea*. Schopenhauer secured a lecturing post in Berlin in 1820, but his doctrines made little headway against the prevailing Hegelian philosophy and he eventually retired into private life, devoting himself to writing. In 1836 he published *On the Will in Nature* and in 1841 a volume containing two separate essays, one on the freedom of the will and the other on the basis of morality, which he entitled *The Two Fundamental Problems of Ethics*. He also produced a new edition of his main work (1844), vastly expanded by the addition of fifty supplementary chapters; but it was not until the eighteen fifties, when a collection of his essays called *Parerga and Paralipomena* appeared, that he began to receive wide recognition. During the last few years of his life lectures on his system were given in leading German universities, and he was the subject of articles in various foreign periodicals.

The popularity Schopenhauer ultimately achieved was in part due to his reputation as an uncompromising opponent of Hegelianism, the influence of which was by mid-century in decline; and it is true that the virulence of his attacks was matched only by those of his admirer, Kierkegaard. Retrospectively, however, these appear of minor significance when set beside his work as a whole; it is important, too, not to overlook the affinities that existed between some of his preoccupations and those of his Idealist contemporaries whom he so strenuously criticized. Like Fichte, for instance, he stressed the pragmatic dimension of ordinary human thought and knowledge; he shared Schelling's concern for the emerging biological studies, as opposed to "mechanical" sciences like physics and chemistry; in common with Hegel himself, he was deeply interested in the phenomena of art and religion, seeing in these expressions of human experience which deserved more serious philosophical investigation than they had received at the hands of typical Enlightenment theorists. Yet at the same time his work remained profoundly different in general tenor and tone. Schopenhauer was scornful of attempts to reconcile philosophy with Christian theology; he emphasized both the nonrational amoral character of ultimate reality and the limits of human understanding, and all his thinking is imbued with a pervasive pessimism regarding the value of life and existence. The conclusion to which his philosophy leads is the negation of the world in self-denial, not—as Nietzsche's was to do—its affirmation in activity.

Adapting to his own purposes the Kantian division between phenomena and noumena, Schopenhauer distinguished between the world as it presents itself to the perceiving consciousness, where it appears as "idea" or "representation" (*Vorstellung*), and the world as it is in its innermost essence, characterizable as "will" and recognizable by each man in his own inner experience.* As his remarks about the scope of what he called the "principle of sufficient reason" make clear, it is only at the level of the world as idea that everyday categories of thought and explanation have application, Schopenhauer insisting upon the purely practical purposes these are designed to serve. Within this metaphysical framework, he succeeded in providing a highly imaginative and individual picture of the nature and situation of human beings in the world, a picture that often seems to anticipate not only Freudian theories of unconscious motivation, but also—in its rejection of Cartesian intellectualism and its assertion of the identity of body and will—various recent approaches in the philosophy of mind. It is worth noting, too, that his views on ethics,

*Compare Nietzsche's comments, pp. 337-340 below.

and the mysticism with which his philosophy ends, exercised an important
influence upon Wittgenstein.

The following selections are from Books II and IV of Schopenhauer's
main work, apart from the last, which is drawn from Chapter 19 of the supplements to the 1844 edition. They concern different aspects of the world as will.
Books I and III, to which references occur in the text, concern the world as idea
or representation; in the case of the first it is considered as the object of empirical knowledge, in the case of the second as the object of art.

The Will as Thing-in-Itself*

17

In the first book we considered the representation only as such, and hence only according to the general form. It is true that, so far as the abstract representation, the concept, is concerned, we also obtained a knowledge of it according to its content, in so far as it has all content and meaning only through its relation to the representation of perception, without which it would be worthless and empty. Therefore, directing our attention entirely to the representation of perception, we shall endeavour to arrive at a knowledge of its content, its more precise determinations, and the forms it presents to us. It will be of special interest for us to obtain information about its real significance, that significance, otherwise merely felt, by virtue of which these pictures or images do not march past us strange and meaningless, as they would otherwise inevitably do, but speak to us directly, are understood, and acquire an interest that engrosses our whole nature. . . .

18

In fact, the meaning that I am looking for of the world that stands before me simply as my representation, or the transition from it as mere representation of the knowing subject to whatever it may be besides this, could never be found if the investigator himself were nothing more than the purely knowing subject (a winged cherub without a body). But he himself is rooted in that world; and thus he finds himself in it as an *individual,* in other words, his knowledge, which is the conditional supporter of the whole world as representation, is nevertheless given entirely through the medium of a body, and the affections of this body are, as we have shown, the starting-point for the under-

*From Vol. I of *The World as Will and Representation* (trans. E. F. J. Payne; Dover Publications, Inc., New York, 1966), pp. 95-119. Reprinted through permission of the publisher.

standing in its perception of this world. For the purely knowing subject as such, this body is a representation like any other, an object among objects. Its movements and actions are so far known to him in just the same way as the changes of all other objects of perception; and they would be equally strange and incomprehensible to him, if their meaning were not unravelled for him in an entirely different way. Otherwise, he would see his conduct follow on presented motives with the constancy of a law of nature, just as the changes of other objects follow upon causes, stimuli, and motives. But he would be no nearer to understanding the influence of the motives than he is to understanding the connexion with its cause of any other effect that appears before him. He would then also call the inner, to him incomprehensible, nature of those manifestations and actions of his body a force, a quality, or a character, just as he pleased, but he would have no further insight into it. All this, however, is not the case; on the contrary, the answer to the riddle is given to the subject of knowledge appearing as individual, and this answer is given in the word *Will*. This and this alone gives him the key to his own phenomenon, reveals to him the significance and shows him the inner mechanism of his being, his actions, his movements. To the subject of knowing, who appears as an individual only through his identity with the body, this body is given in two entirely different ways. It is given in intelligent perception as representation, as an object among objects, liable to the laws of these objects. But it is also given in quite a different way, namely as what is known immediately to everyone, and is denoted by the word *will*. Every true act of his will is also at once and inevitably a movement of his body; he cannot actually will the act without at the same time being aware that it appears as a movement of the body. The act of will and the action of the body are not two different states objectively known, connected by the bond of causality; they do not stand in the relation of cause and effect, but are one and the same thing, though given in two entirely different ways, first quite directly, and then in perception for the understanding. The action of the body is nothing but the act of will objectified, i.e., translated into perception. Later on we shall see that this applies to every movement of the body, not merely to movement following on motives, but also to involuntary movement following on mere stimuli; indeed, that the whole body is nothing but the objectified will, i.e., will that has become representation. All this will follow and become clear in the course of our discussion. Therefore the body, which in the previous book and in the essay *On the Principle of Sufficient Reason* I called the *immediate object,* according to the one-sided viewpoint deliberately taken there (namely that of the representation), will here from another point of view be called the *objectivity of the will*. Therefore, in a certain sense, it can also be said that the will is knowledge *a priori* of the body, and that the body is knowledge *a posteriori* of the will. Resolutions of the will relating to the future are mere deliberations of reason about what will be willed at some time, not real acts of will. Only the carrying out stamps the resolve; till then, it is always a mere intention that can be altered; it exists only in reason, in the abstract. Only in reflection are willing and acting different; in reality they are one. Every true, genuine, immediate act of the will is also at once and directly a manifest act of the body; and correspondingly, on the other hand, every impression on the body is also at once and directly an impression on the will.

The identity of the will and of the body, provisionally explained, can be demonstrated only as is done here, and that for the first time, and as will be done more and more in the further course of our discussion. In other words, it can be raised from immediate consciousness, from knowledge in the concrete, to rational knowledge of reason, or be carried over into knowledge in the abstract. On the other hand, by its nature it can never be demonstrated, that is to say, deduced as indirect knowledge from some other more direct knowledge, for the very reason that it is itself the most direct knowledge. If we do not apprehend it and stick to it as such, in vain shall we expect to obtain it again in some indirect way as derived knowledge. It is a knowledge of quite a peculiar nature, whose truth cannot therefore really be brought under one of the four headings by which I have divided all truth in the essay *On the Principle of Sufficient Reason,* § 29 *seqq.,* namely, logical, empirical, transcendental, and metalogical. For it is not, like all these, the reference of an abstract representation to another representation, or to the necessary form of intuitive or of abstract representing, but it is the reference of a judgement to the relation that a representation of perception, namely the body, has to that which is not a representation at all, but is *toto genere* different therefrom, namely will. I should therefore like to distinguish this truth from every other, and call it *philosophical truth* κατ' ἐξοχήν. We can turn the expression of this truth in different ways and say : My body and my will are one; or, What as representation of perception I call my body, I call my will in so far as I am conscious of it in an entirely different way comparable with no other; or, My body is the objectivity of my will; or, Apart from the fact that my body is my representation, it is still my will, and so on.

19

Whereas in the first book we were reluctantly forced to declare our own body to be mere representation of the knowing subject, like all the other objects of this world of perception, it has now become clear to us that something in the consciousness of everyone distinguishes the representation of his own body from all others that are in other respects quite like it. This is that the body occurs in consciousness in quite another way, *toto genere* different, that is denoted by the word *will*. It is just this double knowledge of our own body which gives us information about that body itself, about its action and movement following on motives, as well as about its suffering through outside impressions, in a word, about what it is, not as representation, but as something over and above this, and hence what it is *in itself*. We do not have such immediate information about the nature, action, and suffering of any other real objects.

The knowing subject is an individual precisely by reason of this special relation to the one body which, considered apart from this, is for him only a representation like all other representations. But the relation by virtue of which the knowing subject is an *individual*, subsists for that very reason only between him and one particular representation among all his representations. He is therefore conscious of this particular representation not merely as such, but at the same time in a quite different way, namely as a will. But if he abstracts from that special relation, from that twofold and completely heterogeneous knowledge of one and the same thing, then that one thing, the body, is a representation like all others. Therefore, in order to understand where he is in this matter, the knowing individual must either assume that the distinctive feature of that one representation is to be found merely in the fact that his knowledge stands in this double reference only to that one representation; that only into this one object of perception is an insight in two ways at the same time open to him; and that this is to be explained not by a difference of this object from all others, but only by a difference between the relation of his knowledge to this one object and its relation to all others. Or he must assume that this one object is essentially different from all others; that it alone among all objects is at the same time will and representation, the rest, on the other hand, being mere representation, i.e., mere phantoms. Thus, he must assume that his body is the only real individual in the world, i.e., the only phenomenon of will, and the only immediate object of the subject. That the other objects, considered as mere *representations,* are like his body, in other words, like this body fill space (itself perhaps existing only as representation), and also, like this body, operate in space—this, I say, is demonstrably certain from the law of causality, which is *a priori* certain for representations, and admits of no effect without a cause. But apart from the fact that we can infer from the effect only a cause in general, not a similar cause, we are still always in the realm of the mere representation, for which alone the law of causality is valid, and beyond which it can never lead us. But whether the objects known to the individual only as representations are yet, like his own body, phenomena of a will, is, as stated in the previous book, the proper meaning of the question as to the reality of the external world. To deny this is the meaning of *theoretical egoism*, which in this way regards as phantoms all phenomena outside its own will, just as practical egoism does in a practical respect; thus in it a man regards and treats only his own person as a real person, and all others as mere phantoms. Theoretical egoism, of course, can never be refuted by proofs, yet in philosophy it has never been positively used otherwise than as a sceptical sophism, i.e., for the sake of appearance. As a serious conviction, on the other hand, it could be found only in a madhouse; as such it would then need not so much a refutation as a cure. Therefore we do not go into it any further, but regard it as the last stronghold of scepticism, which is always polemical. Thus our knowledge, bound always to individuality and having its limitation in this very fact, necessarily means that everyone can *be* only one thing, whereas he can *know* everything else, and it is this very limitation that really creates the need for philosophy. Therefore we, who for this very reason are endeavouring to extend the limits of our knowledge through philosophy, shall regard this sceptical argument of theoretical egoism, which here confronts us, as a small frontier fortress. Admittedly the fortress is impregnable, but the garrison can never sally forth from it, and therefore we can pass it by and leave it in our rear without danger.

The double knowledge which we have of the nature and action of our own body, and which is given in two completely different ways, has now been clearly brought out. Accordingly, we shall use it further as a key to the inner being of every phenomenon in nature. We shall judge all objects which are not our own body, and therefore are given to our consciousness not in the double way, but only as representations, according to the analogy of this body. We shall therefore assume that as, on the one hand, they are representation, just like our body, and are in this respect homogeneous with it, so on the other hand, if we set aside their existence as the subject's representation, what still remains over must be, according to its inner nature, the same as what in ourselves we call *will*. For what other kind of existence or reality could we attribute to the rest of the material world? From what source could we take the elements out of which we construct such a world? Besides the will and the representation, there is absolutely nothing known or conceivable for us. If we wish to attribute the greatest known reality to the material world, which immediately exists only in our representation, then we give it that reality which our own body has for each of us, for to each of us this is the most real of things. But if now we analyse the reality of this body and its actions, then, beyond the fact that it is our representation, we find nothing in it but the will; with this even its reality is exhausted. Therefore we can nowhere find another kind of reality to attribute to the material world. If, therefore, the material world is to be something more than our mere representation, we must say that, besides being the representation, and hence in itself and of its inmost nature, it is what we find immediately in ourselves as will. . . .

21

From all these considerations the reader has now gained in the abstract, and hence in clear and certain terms, a knowledge which everyone possesses directly in the concrete, namely as feeling. This is the knowledge that the inner nature of his own phenomenon, which manifests itself to him as representation both through his actions and through the permanent substratum of these his body, is his *will*. This will constitutes what is most immediate in his consciousness, but as such it has not wholly entered into the form of the representation, in which object and subject stand over against each other; on the contrary, it makes itself known in an immediate way in which subject and object are not quite clearly distinguished, yet it becomes known to the individual himself not as a whole, but only in its particular acts. The reader who with me has gained this conviction, will find that of itself it will become the key to the knowledge of the innermost being of the whole of nature, since he now transfers it to all those phenomena that are given to him, not like his own phenomenon both in direct and in indirect knowledge, but in the latter solely, and hence merely in a one-sided way, as *representation* alone. He will recognize that same will not only in those phenomena that are quite similar to his own, in men and animals, as their innermost nature, but continued reflection will lead him to recognize the force that shoots and vegetates in the plant, indeed the force by which the crystal is formed, the force that turns the magnet to the North Pole, the force whose shock he encounters from the contact of metals of different kinds, the force that appears in the elective affinities of matter as repulsion and attraction, separation and union, and finally even gravitation, which acts so powerfully in all matter, pulling the stone to the earth and the earth to the sun; all these he will recognize as different only in the phenomenon, but the same according to their inner nature. He will recognize them all as that which is immediately known to him so intimately and better than everything else, and where it appears most distinctly is called *will*. It is only this application of reflection which no longer lets us stop at the phenomenon, but leads us on to the *thing-in-itself*. Phenomenon means representation and nothing more. All representation, be it of whatever kind it may, all *object*, is *phenomenon*. But only the *will* is *thing-in-itself*; as such it is not representation at all, but *toto genere* different therefrom. It is that of which all representation, all object, is the phenomenon, the visibility, the *objectivity*. It is the innermost essence, the kernel, of every particular thing and also of the whole. It appears in every blindly acting force of nature, and also in the deliberate conduct of man, and the great difference between the two concerns only the degree of the manifestation, not the inner nature of what is manifested.

22

Now, if this *thing-in-itself* (we will retain the Kantian expression as a standing formula)—which as such is never object, since all object is its mere appearance or phenomenon, and not it itself—is to be thought of objectively, then we must borrow its name and concept from an object, from something in some way objectively given, and therefore from one of its phenomena. But in order to serve as a point of explanation, this can be none other than the most complete of all its phenomena, i.e., the most distinct, the most developed, the most directly enlightened by knowledge; but this is precisely man's *will*. We have to observe, however, that here of course we use only a *denominatio a potiori,* by which the concept of will therefore receives a greater extension than it has hitherto had. Knowledge of the identical in different phenomena and of the different in similar phenomena is, as Plato so often remarks, the condition for philosophy. But hitherto the identity of the inner essence of any striving and operating force in nature with the will has not been recognized, and therefore the many kinds of phenomena that are only different species of the same genus were not regarded as such; they were considered as being heterogeneous. Consequently, no word could exist to describe the concept of this genus. I therefore name the genus after its most important species, the direct knowledge of which lies nearest to us, and leads to the indirect knowledge of all the others. But anyone who is incapable of carrying out the required extension of the concept will remain involved in a permanent misunderstanding. For by the word *will,* he will always understand only that species of it hitherto exclusively described by the term, that is to say, the will guided by knowledge, strictly according to motives, indeed only to abstract motives, thus manifesting itself under the guidance of the faculty of reason. This, as we have said, is only the most distinct phenomenon or appearance of the will. We must now clearly separate out in our thoughts the innermost essence of this phenomenon, known to us directly, and then transfer it to all the weaker, less distinct phenomena of the same essence, and by so doing achieve the desired extension of the concept of will. From the opposite point of view, I should be misunderstood by anyone who thought that ultimately it was all the same whether we expressed this essence-in-itself of all phenomena by the word will or by any other word. This would be the case if this thing-in-itself were something whose existence we merely *inferred,* and thus knew only indirectly and merely in the abstract. Then certainly we could call it what we liked; the name would stand merely as the symbol of an unknown quantity. But the word *will,* which, like a magic word, is to reveal to us the innermost essence of everything in nature, by no means expresses an unknown quantity, something reached by inferences and syllogisms, but something known absolutely and immediately, and that so well that we know and understand what will is better than anything else, be it what it may. Hitherto, the concept of *will* has been subsumed under the concept of *force*; I, on the other hand, do exactly the reverse, and intend every force in nature to be conceived as will. We must not imagine that this is a dispute about words or a matter of no consequence; on the contrary, it is of the very highest significance and importance. For at the root of the concept of *force,* as of all other concepts, lies knowledge of the objective world through perception, in other words, the phenomenon, the representation, from which the concept is drawn. It is abstracted from the province where cause and effect reign, that is, from the representation of perception, and it signifies just the causal nature of the cause at the point where this causal nature is etiologically no longer explicable at all, but is the necessary presupposition of all etiological explanation. On the other hand, the concept of *will* is of all possible concepts the only one that has its origin *not* in the phenomenon, *not* in the mere representation of perception, but which comes from within, and proceeds from the most immediate consciousness of everyone. In this consciousness each one knows and at the same time is himself his own individuality according to its nature immediately, without any form, even the form of subject and object, for here knower and known coincide. Therefore, if we refer the concept of *force* to that of *will*, we have in fact referred something more unknown to something infinitely better known, indeed to the one thing really known to us immediately and completely; and we have very greatly extended our knowledge. If, on the other hand, we subsume the concept of *will* under that of *force,* as has been done hitherto, we renounce the only immediate knowledge of the inner nature of the world that we have, since we let it disappear in a concept abstracted from the phenomenon, with which therefore we can never pass beyond the phenomenon.

23

The *will* as thing-in-itself is quite different from its phenomenon, and is entirely free from all the forms of the phenomenon into which it first passes when it appears, and which therefore concern only its *objectivity,* and are foreign to the will itself. Even the most universal form of all representation, that of object for subject, does not concern it, still less the forms that are subordinate to this and collectively have their common expression in the principle of sufficient reason. As we know, time and space belong to this principle, and consequently plurality as well, which exists and has become possible only through them. In this last respect I shall call time and space the *principium individuationis,* an expression borrowed from the old scholasticism, and I beg the reader to bear this in mind once and for all. For it is only by means of time and space that something which is one and the same according to its nature and the concept appears as different, as a plurality of coexistent and successive things. Consequently, time and space are the *principium individuationis,* the subject of so many subtleties and disputes among the scholastics which are found collected in Suarez (*Disp. 5,* sect. 3). It is apparent from what has been said that the will as thing-in-itself lies outside the province of the principle of sufficient reason in all its forms, and is consequently completely groundless, although each of its phenomena is entirely subject to that principle. Further, it is free from all *plurality,* although its phenomena in time and space are innumerable. It is itself one, yet not as an object is one, for the unity of an object is known only in contrast to possible plurality. Again, the will is one not as a concept is one, for a concept originates only through abstraction from plurality; but it is one as that which lies outside time and space, outside the *principium individuationis,* that is to say, outside the possibility of plurality. Only when all this has become quite clear to us through the following consideration of phenomena and of the different manifestations of the will, can we fully understand the meaning of the Kantian doctrine that time, space, and causality do not belong to the thing-in-itself, but are only the forms of our knowing.

The groundlessness of the will has actually been recognized where it manifests itself most distinctly, that is, as the will of man; and this has been called free and independent. But as to the groundlessness of the will itself, the necessity to which its phenomenon is everywhere liable has been overlooked, and actions have been declared to be free, which they are not. For every individual action follows with strict necessity from the effect of the motive on the character. As we have already said, all necessity is the relation of the consequent to the ground, and nothing else whatever. The principle of sufficient reason is the universal form of every phenomenon, and man in his action, like every other phenomenon, must be subordinated to it. But because in self-consciousness the will is known directly and in itself, there also lies in this consciousness the consciousness of freedom. But the fact is over-looked that the individual, the person, is not will as thing-in-itself, but is *phenomenon* of the will, is as such determined, and has entered the form of the phenomenon, the principle of sufficient reason. Hence we get the strange fact that everyone considers himself to be *a priori* quite free, even in his individual actions, and imagines he can at any moment enter upon a different way of life, which is equivalent to saying that he can become a different person. But *a posteriori* through experience, he finds to his astonishment that he is not free, but liable to necessity; that notwithstanding all his resolutions and reflections he does not change his conduct, and that from the beginning to the end of his life he must bear the same character that he himself condemns, and, as it were, must play to the end the part he has taken upon himself. I cannot pursue this discussion any further here, for, being ethical, it belongs to another part of this work. Meanwhile, I wish to point out here only that the *phenomenon* of the will, in itself groundless, is yet subject as such to the law of necessity, that is to say, to the principle of sufficient reason, so that in the necessity with which the phenomena of nature ensue, we may not find anything to prevent us from recognizing in them the manifestations of the will.

Hitherto we have regarded as phenomena of the will only those changes that have no other ground than a motive, i.e., a representation. Therefore in nature a will has been attributed only to man, or at most to animals, because, as I have already mentioned elsewhere, knowing or representing is of course the genuine and exclusive characteristic of the animal kingdom. But we see at once from the instinct and mechanical skill of animals that the will is also active where it is not guided by any knowledge. That they have representations and knowledge is of no account at all here, for the end towards which they work as definitely as if it were a known motive remains entirely unknown to them. Therefore, their action here takes place without motive, is not guided by the representation, and shows us first and most distinctly how the will is active even without any knowledge. The one-year-old bird has no notion of the eggs for which it builds a nest; the young spider has no idea of the prey for which it spins a web; the ant-lion has no notion of the ant for which it digs a cavity for the first time. The larva of the stag-beetle gnaws the hole in the wood, where it will undergo its metamorphosis, twice as large if it is to become a male beetle as if it is to become a female, in order in the former case to have room for the horns, though as yet it has no idea of these. In the actions of such animals the will is obviously at work as in the rest of their activities, but is in blind activity, which is accompanied, indeed, by knowledge, but not guided by it. Now if we have once gained insight into the fact that representation as motive is not a necessary and essential condition of the will's activity, we shall more easily recognize the action of the will in cases where it is less evident. For example, we shall no more ascribe the house of the snail to a will foreign to the snail itself but guided by knowledge, than we shall say that the house we ourselves build comes into existence through a will other than our own. On the contrary, we shall recognize both houses as works of the will objectifying itself in the two phenomena, working in us on the basis of motives, but in the snail blindly as formative impulse directed outwards. Even in us the same will in many ways acts blindly; as in all those functions of our body which are not guided by knowledge, in all its vital and vegetative processes, digestion, circulation, secretion, growth, and reproduction. Not only the actions of the body, but the whole body itself, as was shown above, is phenomenon of the will, objectified will, concrete will. All that occurs in it must therefore occur through will, though here this will is not guided by knowledge, not determined according to motives, but acts blindly according to causes, called in this case *stimuli.* . . .

It only remains for us to take the final step, namely that of extending our method of consideration to all those forces in nature which act according to universal, immutable laws, in conformity with which there take place the movements of all those bodies, such bodies being entirely without organs, and having no susceptibility to stimulus and no knowledge of motive. We must therefore also apply the key for an understanding of the inner nature of things, a key that only the immediate knowledge of our inner nature could give us, to these phenomena of the inorganic world, which are the most remote of all from us. Now let us consider attentively and observe the powerful, irresistible impulse with which masses of water rush downwards, the persistence and determination with which the magnet always turns back to the North Pole, the keen desire with which iron flies to the magnet, the vehemence with which the poles of the electric current strive for reunion, and which, like the vehemence of human desires, is increased by obstacles. Let us look at the crystal being rapidly and suddenly formed with such regularity of configuration; it is obvious that this is only a perfectly definite and precisely determined striving in different directions constrained and held firm by coagulation. Let us observe the choice with which bodies repel and attract one another, unite and separate, when set free in the fluid state and released from the bonds of rigidity. Finally, we feel directly and immediately how a burden, which hampers our body by its gravitation towards the earth, incessantly presses and squeezes this body in pursuit of its one tendency. If we observe all this, it will not cost us a great effort of the imagination to recognize once more our own inner nature, even at so great a distance. It is that which in us pursues its ends by the light of knowledge, but here, in the feeblest of its phenomena, only strives blindly in a dull, one-sided, and unalterable manner. Yet, because it is everywhere one and the same—just as the first morning dawn shares the name of sunlight with the rays of the full midday sun—it must in either case bear the name of *will*. For this word indicates that which is the being-in-itself of every thing in the world, and is the sole kernel of every phenomenon.

However, the remoteness, in fact the appearance of a complete difference between the phenomena of inorganic nature and the will, perceived by us as the inner reality of our own being, arises principally from the contrast between the wholly determined conformity to law in the one species of phenomenon, and the apparently irregular arbitrariness in the other. For in a man individuality stands out powerfully; everyone has a character of his own, and hence the same motive does not have the same influence on all, and a thousand minor circumstances, finding scope in one individual's wide sphere of knowledge but remaining unknown to others, modify its effect. For this reason an action cannot be predetermined from the motive alone, since the other factor, namely an exact acquaintance with the individual character, and with the knowledge accompanying that character, is wanting. On the other hand, the phenomena of the forces of nature show the other extreme in this respect. They operate according to universal laws, without deviation, without individuality, in accordance with openly manifest circumstances, subject to the most precise predetermination; and the same force of nature manifests itself in its million phenomena in exactly the same way. . . .

Character and Motivation*

55

That the will as such is *free,* follows already from the fact that, according to our view, it is the thing-in-itself, the content of all phenomena. The phenomenon, on the other hand, we recognize as absolutely subordinate to the principle of sufficient reason in its four forms. As we know that necessity is absolutely identical with consequent from a given ground, and that the two are convertible concepts, all that belong to the phenomenon, in other words all that is object for the subject that knows as an individual, is on the one hand ground or reason, on the other consequent, and in this last capacity is determined with absolute necessity; thus it cannot be in any respect other than it is. The whole content of nature, the sum-total of her phenomena, is absolutely necessary, and the necessity of every part, every phenomenon, every event, can always be demonstrated, since it must be possible to find the ground or reason on which it depends as consequent. This admits of no exception; it follows from the unrestricted and absolute validity of the principle of sufficient reason. But on the other hand, this same world in all its phenomena is for us objectivity of the will. As the will itself is not phenomenon, not representation or object, but thing-in-itself, it is also not subordinate to the principle of sufficient reason, the form of all object. Thus it is not determined as consequent by a reason or ground, and so it knows no necessity; in other words, it is *free.* The concept of freedom is therefore really a negative one, since its content is merely the denial of necessity, in other words, the denial of the relation of consequent to its ground according to the principle of sufficient reason. Now here we have before us most clearly the point of unity of that great contrast, namely the union of freedom with necessity, which in recent times has often been discussed, yet never, so far as I know, clearly and adequately. Everything as phenomenon, as

Ibid., pp. 286-298.

object, is absolutely necessary; *in itself* it is will, and this is perfectly free to all eternity. The phenomenon, the object, is necessarily and unalterably determined in the concatenation of grounds and consequents which cannot have any discontinuity. But the existence of this object in general and the manner of its existing, that is to say, the Idea which reveals itself in it, or in other words its character, is directly phenomenon of the will. Hence, in conformity with the freedom of this will, the object might not exist at all, or might be something originally and essentially quite different. In that case, however, the whole chain of which the object is a link, and which is itself phenomenon of the same will, would also be quite different. But once there and existent, the object has entered the series of grounds and consequents, is always necessarily determined therein, and accordingly cannot either become another thing, i.e., change itself, or withdraw from the series, i.e., vanish. Like every other part of nature, man is objectivity of the will; therefore all that we have said holds good of him also. Just as everything in nature has its forces and qualities that definitely react to a definite impression, and constitute its character, so man also has his *character,* from which the motives call forth his actions with necessity. In this way of acting his empirical character reveals itself, but in this again is revealed his intelligible character, i.e., the will in itself, of which he is the determined phenomenon. Man, however, is the most complete phenomenon of the will, and, as was shown in the second book, in order to exist, this phenomenon had to be illuminated by so high a degree of knowledge that even a perfectly adequate repetition of the inner nature of the world under the form of the representation became possible in it. This is the apprehension of the Ideas, the pure mirror of the world, as we have come to know them in the third book. Therefore in man the will can reach full self-consciousness, distinct and exhaustive knowledge of its own inner nature, as reflected in the whole world. As we saw in the preceding book, art results from the actual presence and existence of the degree of knowledge. At the end of our whole discussion it will also be seen that, through the same knowledge, an elimination and self-denial of the will in its most perfect phenomenon is possible, by the will's relating such knowledge to itself. Thus the freedom which in other respects, as belonging to the thing-in-itself, can never show itself in the phenomenon, in such a case appears in this phenomenon; and by abolishing the essential nature at the root of the phenomenon, whilst the phenomenon itself still continues to exist in time, it brings about a contradiction of the phenomenon with itself. In just this way, it exhibits the phenomena of holiness and self-denial. All this, however, will be fully understood only at the end of this book.

Meanwhile, all this indicates only in a general way how man is distinguished from all the other phenomena of the will by the fact that freedom, i.e., independence of the principle of sufficient reason, which belongs only to the will as thing-in-itself and contradicts the phenomenon, may yet in his case possibly appear even in the phenomenon, where it is then, however, necessarily exhibited as a contradiction of the phenomenon with itself. In this sense not only the will in itself, but even man can certainly be called free, and can thus be distinguished from all other things. But how this is to be understood can become clear only through all that follows, and for the present we must wholly disregard it. For in the first place we must beware of making the mistake of thinking that the action of the particular, definite man is not subject to any necessity, in other words that the force of the motive is less certain than the force of the cause, or than the following of the conclusion from the premises. If we leave aside the above-mentioned case, which, as we have said, relates only to an exception, the freedom of the will as thing-in-itself by no means extends directly to its phenomenon, not even where this reaches the highest grade of visibility, namely in the rational animal with individual character, in other words, the man. This man is never free, although he is the phenomenon of a free will, for he is the already determined phenomenon of this will's free willing; and since he enters into the form of all objects, the principle of sufficient reason, he develops the unity of that will into a plurality of actions. But since the unity of that will in itself lies outside time, this plurality exhibits itself with the conformity to law of a force of nature. Since, however, it is that free willing which becomes visible in the man and in his whole conduct, and is related to this as the concept to the definition, every particular deed of the man is to be ascribed to the free will, and directly proclaims itself as such to consciousness. Therefore, as we said in the second book, everyone considers himself *a priori* (i.e., according to his original feeling) free, even in his particular actions, in the sense that in every given case any action is possible to him, and only *a posteriori*, from experience and reflection thereon, does he recognize that his conduct follows with absolute necessity from the coincidence of the character with the motives. Hence it arises that any coarse and uncultured person, following his feelings, most vigorously defends complete freedom in individual actions, whereas the great thinkers of all ages, and the more profound religious teachings, have denied it. But the person who has come to see clearly that man's whole inner nature is will, and that man himself is only phenomenon of this will, but that such phenomenon has the principle of sufficient reason as its necessary form, knowable even from the subject, and appearing in this case as the law of motivation; to such a person a doubt as to the inevitability of the deed, when the motive is presented to the given character, seems like doubting that the three angles of a triangle are equal to two right angles. In his *Doctrine of Philosophical Necessity,* Priestley has very adequately demonstrated the necessity of the individual action. Kant, however, whose merit in this regard is specially great, was the first to demonstrate the coexistence of this necessity with the freedom of the will in itself, i.e., outside the phenomenon, for he established the difference between the intelligible and empirical characters. I wholly support this distinction, for the former is the will as thing-in-itself, in so far as it appears in a definite individual in a definite degree, while the latter is this phenomenon itself as it manifests itself in the mode of action according to time, and in the physical structure according to space. To make the relation between the two clear, the best expression is that already used in the introductory essay, namely that the intelligible character of every man is to be regarded as an act of will outside time, and thus indivisible and unalterable. The phenomenon of this act of will, developed and drawn out in time, space, and all the forms of the principle of sufficient reason, is the empirical character as it exhibits itself for experience in the man's whole manner of action and course of life. The whole tree is only the constantly repeated phenomenon of one and the same impulse that manifests itself most simply in the fibre, and is repeated and easily recognizable in the construction of leaf, stem, branch, and trunk. In the same way, all man's deeds are only the constantly repeated manifestation, varying somewhat in form, of his intelligible character, and the induction resulting from the sum of these gives us his empirical character. However, I shall not repeat Kant's masterly exposition here, but shall presuppose that it is already known. . . .

Apart from the fact that the will, as the true thing-in-itself, is something actually original and independent, and that in self-consciousness the feeling of originality and arbitrariness must accompany its acts, though these are already determined; apart from this, there arises the semblance of an empirical freedom of the will (instead of the transcendental freedom which alone is to be attributed to it). Thus there arises the appearance of a freedom of the individual acts from the attitude of the intellect towards the will which is explained, separated out, and subordinated in the nineteenth chapter of the second volume, under No. 3.* The intellect gets to know the conclusions of the will only *a posteriori* and empirically. Accordingly, where a choice is presented to it, it has no datum as to how the will is going to decide. For the intelligible character, by virtue of which with the given motives only

*See pp. 126-130 below.

one decision is possible, which is accordingly a necessary decision, the intelligible character, I say, does not come into the knowledge of the intellect; the empirical character only is successively known to it through its individual acts. Therefore it seems to be the knowing consciousness (intellect) that two opposite decisions are equally possible to the will in a given case. But this is just the same as if we were to say in the case of a vertical pole, thrown off its balance and hesitating which way to fall, that "it can topple over to the right or to the left." Yet this *"can"* has only a subjective significance, and really means "in view of the data known to us." For objectively, the direction of the fall is necessarily determined as soon as the hesitation takes place. Accordingly, the decision of one's own will is undetermined only for its spectator, one's own intellect, and therefore only relatively and subjectively, namely for the subject of knowing. In itself and objectively, on the other hand, the decision is at once determined and necessary in the case of every choice presented to it. But this determination enters consciousness only through the ensuing decision. We even have an empirical proof of this when some difficult and important choice lies before us, yet only under a condition that has not yet appeared but is merely awaited, so that for the time being we can do nothing, but must maintain a passive attitude. We then reflect on how we shall decide when the circumstances that allow us freedom of activity and decision have made their appearance. It is often the case that far-seeing, rational deliberation speaks rather in support of one of the resolves, while direct inclination leans rather to the other. As long as we remain passive and under compulsion, the side of reason apparently tries to keep the upper hand, but we see in advance how strongly the other side will draw us when the opportunity for action comes. Till then, we are eagerly concerned to place the motives of the two sides in the clearest light by coolly meditating on the *pro et contra*, so that each motive can influence the will with all its force when the moment arrives, and so that some mistake on the part of the intellect will not mislead the will into deciding otherwise than it would do if everything exerted an equal influence. This distinct unfolding of the motives on both sides is all that the intellect can do in connexion with the choice. It awaits the real decision just as passively and with the same excited curiosity as it would that of a foreign will. Therefore, from its point of view, both decisions must seem to it equally possible. Now it is just this that is the semblance of the will's empirical freedom. Of course, the decision enters the sphere of the intellect quite empirically as the final conclusion of the matter. Yet this decision proceeded from the inner nature, the intelligible character, of the individual will in its conflict with given motives, and hence came about with complete necessity. The intellect can do nothing more here than clearly examine the nature of the motives from every point of view. It is unable to determine the will itself, for the will is wholly inaccessible to it, and, as we have seen, is for it inscrutable and impenetrable.

If, under the same conditions, a man could act now in one way, now in another, then in the meantime his will itself would have had to be changed, and thus would have to reside in time, for only in time is change possible. But then either the will would have to be a mere phenomenon, or time would have to be a determination of the thing-in-itself. Accordingly, the dispute as to the freedom of the individual action, as to the *liberum arbitrium indifferentiae*, really turns on the question whether the will resides in time or not. If, as Kant's teaching as well as the whole of my system makes necessary, the will as thing-in-itself is outside time and outside every form of the principle of sufficient reason, then not only must the individual act in the same way in the same situation, and not only must every bad deed be the sure guarantee of innumerable others that the individual *must* do and *cannot* leave undone, but, as Kant says, if only the empirical character and the motives were completely given, a man's future actions could be calculated like an eclipse of the sun or moon. Just as nature is consistent, so also is the character; every individual action must come about in accordance with the character, just as every phenomenon comes about in accordance with a law of nature. The cause in the latter case and the motive in the former are only the occasional causes, as was shown in the second book. The will, whose phenomenon is the whole being and life of man, cannot deny itself in the particular case, and the man also will always will in the particular what he wills on the whole.

The maintenance of an empirical freedom of will, a *liberum arbitrium indifferentiae*, is very closely connected with the assertion that places man's inner nature in a *soul* that is originally a *knowing*, indeed really an abstract *thinking* entity, and only in consequence thereof a *willing* entity. Such a view, therefore, regarded the will as of a secondary nature, instead of knowledge, which is really secondary. The will was even regarded as an act of thought, and was identified with the judgement, especially by Descartes and Spinoza. According to this, every man would have become what he is only in consequence of his *knowledge.* He would come into the world as a moral cipher, would know the things in it, and would then determine to be this or that, to act in this or that way. He could, in consequence of new knowledge, choose a new course of action, and thus become another person. Further, he would then first know a thing to be *good*, and in consequence will it, instead of first *willing* it, and in consequence calling it *good*. According to the whole of my fundamental view, all this is a reversal of the true relation. The will is first and original; knowledge is merely added to it as an instrument belonging to the phenomenon of the will. Therefore every man is what he is through his will, and his character is original, for willing is the basis of his inner being. Through the knowledge added to it, he gets to know in the course of experience *what* he is; in other words, he becomes acquainted with his character. Therefore he *knows* himself in consequence of, and in accordance with, the nature of his will, instead of *willing* in consequence of, and according to, his knowing, as in the old view. According to this view, he need only consider *how* he would best like to be, and he would be so; this is its freedom of the will. It therefore consists in man's being his own work in the light of knowledge. I, on the other hand, say that he is his own work prior to all knowledge, and knowledge is merely added to illuminate it. Therefore he cannot decide to be this or that; also he cannot become another person, but he *is* once for all, and subsequently knows *what* he is. With those other thinkrs, he *wills* what he knows; with me he *knows* what he wills. . . .

The motives determining the phenomenon or appearance of the character, or determining conduct, influence the character through the medium of knowledge. Knowledge, however, is changeable, and often vacillates between error and truth; yet, as a rule, in the course of life it is rectified more and more, naturally in very different degrees. Thus a man's manner of acting can be noticeably changed without our being justified in inferring from this a change in his character. What the man really and generally wills, the tendency of his innermost nature, and the goal he pursues in accordance therewith—these we can never change by influencing him from without, by instructing him, otherwise we should be able to create him anew. Seneca says admirably: *velle non discitur;*[1] in this he prefers truth to his Stoic philosophers, who taught: διδακτὴν εἶναι τὴν ἀρετήν (*doceri posse virtutem*).[2] From without, the will can be affected only by motives; but these can never change the will itself, for they have power over it only on the presupposition that it is precisely such as it is. All that the motives can do, therefore, is to alter the direction of the will's effort, in other words to make it possible for it to seek what it invariably seeks by a path different from the one it previously followed. Therefore instruc-

1. "Willing cannot be taught." [*Epist.* 81, 14. Tr.]
2. "Virtue can be taught." [Diogenes Laërtius, Vii, 91, Tr.]

tion, improved knowledge, and thus influence from without, can indeed teach the will that it erred in the means it employed. Accordingly, outside influence can bring it about that the will pursues the goal to which it aspires once for all in accordance with its inner nature, by quite a different path, and even in an entirely different object, from what it did previously. But such an influence can never bring it about that the will wills something actually different from what it has willed hitherto. This remains unalterable, for the will is precisely this willing itself, which would otherwise have to be abolished. However, the former, the ability to modify knowledge, and through this to modify action, goes so far that the will seeks to attain its ever unalterable end, for example, Mohammed's paradise, at one time in the world of reality, at another in the world of imagination, adapting the means thereto, and so applying prudence, force, and fraud in the one case, abstinence, justice, righteousness, alms, and pilgrimage to Mecca in the other. But the tendency and endeavour of the will have not themselves been changed on that account, still less the will itself. Therefore, although its action certainly manifests itself differently at different times, its willing has nevertheless remained exactly the same. *Velle non discitur.*

For motives to be effective, it is necessary for them to be not only present but known; for according to a very good saying of the scholastics, which we have already mentioned, *causa finalis movet non secundum suum esse reale, sed secundum esse cognitum.*[3] For example, in order that the relation which exists in a given man between egoism and sympathy may appear, it is not enough that he possesses some wealth and sees the misery of others; he must also know what can be done with wealth both for himself and for others. Not only must another's suffering present itself to him, but he must also know what suffering is, and indeed what pleasure is. Perhaps on a first occasion he did not know all this so well as on a second; and if now on a similar occasion he acts differently, this is due simply to the circumstances being really different, namely as regards that part of them which depends on his knowledge of them, although they appear to be the same. Just as not to know actually existing circumstances deprives them of their effectiveness, so, on the other hand, entirely imaginary circumstances can act like real ones, not only in the case of a particular deception, but also in general and for some length of time. For example, if a man is firmly persuaded that every good deed is repaid to him a hundredfold in a future life, then such a conviction is valid and effective in precisely the same way as a safe bill of exchange at a very long date, and he can give from

3. "The final cause operates not according to its real being, but only according to its being as that is known." [Tr.]

egoism just as, from another point of view, he would take from egoism. He himself has not changed : *velle non discitur.* In virtue of this great influence of knowledge on conduct, with an unalterable will, it comes about that the character develops and its different features appear only gradually. It therefore appears different at each period of life, and an impetuous, wild youth can be followed by a staid, sober, manly age. In particular, what is bad in the character will come out more and more powerfully with time; but sometimes passions to which a man gave way in his youth are later voluntarily restrained, merely because the opposite motives have only then come into knowledge. Hence we are all innocent to begin with, and this merely means that neither we nor others know the evil of our own nature. This appears only in the motives, and only in the course of time do the motives appear in knowledge. Ultimately we become acquainted with ourselves as quite different from what *a priori* we considered ourselves to be; and then we are often alarmed at ourselves.

Repentance never results from the fact that the will has changed —this is impossible—but from a change of knowledge. I must still continue to will the essential and real element of what I have always willed; for I am myself this will, that lies outside time and change. Therefore I can never repent of what I have willed, though I can repent of what I have done, when, guided by false concepts, I did something different from what was in accordance with my will. *Repentance* is the insight into this with more accurate knowledge. It extends not merely to worldly wisdom, the choice of means, and judging the appropriateness of the end to my will proper, but also to what is properly ethical. Thus, for example, it is possible for me to have acted more egoistically than is in accordance with my character, carried away by exaggerated notions of the need in which I myself stood, or even by the cunning, falseness, and wickedness of others, or again by the fact that I was in too much of a hurry; in other words, I acted without deliberation, determined not by motives distinctly known in the abstract, but by motives of mere perception, the impression of the present moment, and the emotion it excited. This emotion was so strong that I really did not have the use of my faculty of reason. But here also the return of reflection is only corrected knowledge, and from this repentance can result, which always proclaims itself by making amends for what has happened, so far as that is possible. But it is to be noted that, in order to deceive themselves, men prearrange apparent instances of precipitancy which are really secretly considered actions. For by such fine tricks we deceive and flatter no one but ourselves. The reverse case to what we have mentioned can also occur. I can be misled by too great confidence in others, or by not knowing the relative value of the good things of life, or by some abstract dogma in which I have now lost faith. Thus I act less egoistically than is in accordance with my character, and in this way prepare for myself repentance of another kind. Thus repentance is always corrected knowledge of the relation of the deed to the real intention. In so far as the will reveals its Ideas in space alone, that is to say, through mere form, the matter already controlled and ruled by other Ideas, in this case natural forces, resists the will, and seldom allows the form that was striving for visibility to appear in perfect purity and distinctness, i.e., in perfect beauty. This will, revealing itself in time alone, i.e., through actions, finds an analogous hindrance in the knowledge that rarely gives it the data quite correctly; and in this way the deed does not turn out wholly and entirely in keeping with the will, and therefore leads to repentance. Thus repentance always results from corrected knowledge, not from change in the will, which is impossible. Pangs of conscience over past deeds are anything but repentance; they are pain at the knowledge of oneself in one's own nature, in other words, as will. They rest precisely on the certainty that we always have the same will. If the will were changed, and thus the pangs of conscience were mere repentance, these would be abolished; for then the past could no longer cause any distress, as it would exhibit the manifestations of a will that was no longer that of the repentant person. We shall discuss in detail the significance of pangs of conscience later on.

The influence exerted by knowledge as the medium of motives, not indeed on the will itself, but on its manifestation in actions, is also the basis of the chief difference between the actions of men and those of animals, since the methods of cognition of the two are different. The animal has only knowledge of perception, but man through the faculty of reason has also abstract representations, concepts. Now, although animal and man are determined by motives with equal necessity, man nevertheless has the advantage over the animal of a complete *elective decision (Wahlentscheidung)*. This has often been regarded as a freedom of the will in individual actions, although it is nothing but the possibility of a conflict, thoroughly fought out, between several motives, the strongest of which then determines the will with necessity. For this purpose the motives must have assumed the form of abstract thoughts, since only by means of these is real deliberation, in other words, a weighing of opposed grounds for conduct, possible. With the animal a choice can take place only between motives of perception actually present; hence this choice is restricted to the narrow sphere of its present apprehension of perception. Therefore the necessity of the determination of the will by motives, like that of the effect by the cause, can be exhibited in perception and directly only in the case of the animals, since here the spectator has the motives just as directly before his eyes as he has their effect. In the case of man, however, the motives are almost always abstract representations; these are not shared by the spectator, and the necessity of their effect is concealed behind their conflict even from the person himself who acts. For only *in abstracto* can several representations lie beside one another in consciousness as judgements and chains of conclusions, and then, free from all determination of time, work against one another, until the strongest overpowers the rest, and determines the will. This is the complete *elective decision* or faculty of deliberation which man has as an advantage over the animal, and on account of which freedom of will has been attributed to him, in the belief that this willing was a mere result of the operation of his intellect, without a definite tendency to serve as its basis. The truth is, however, that motivation works only on the basis and assumption of his definite tendency, that is in his case individual, in other words, a character. . . .

Virtue and Renunciation*

Morality without argumentation and reasoning, that is, mere moralizing, cannot have any effect, because it does not motivate. But a morality that *does* motivate can do so only by acting on self-love. Now what springs from this has no moral worth. From this it follows that no genuine virtue can be brought about through morality and abstract knowledge in general, but that such virtue must spring from the intuitive knowledge that recognizes in another's individuality the same inner nature as in one's own.

For virtue does indeed result from knowledge, but not from abstract knowledge communicable through words. If this were so, virtue could be taught, and by expressing here in the abstract its real nature and the knowledge at its foundation, we should have ethically improved everyone who comprehended this. But this is by no means the case. On the contary, we are as little able to produce a virtuous person by ethical discourses or sermons as all the systems of aesthetics from Aristotle's downwards have ever been able to produce a poet. For the concept is unfruitful for the real inner nature of virtue, just as it is for art; and only in a wholly subordinate position can it serve as an instrument in elaborating and preserving what has been ascertained and inferred in other ways. *Velle non discitur.*[4] In fact, abstract dogmas are without influence on virtue, i.e., on goodness of disposition; false dogmas do not disturb it, and true ones hardly support it. Actually it would be a bad business if the principal thing in a man's life, his ethical worth that counts for eternity, depended on something whose attainment was so very much subject to chance as are dogmas, religious teachings, and philosophical arguments. For morality dogmas have merely the value that the man who is virtuous from another kind of knowledge shortly to be discussed has in them a scheme or formula. According to this, he renders to his own faculty of reason an account,

Ibid., pp. 367-396.
4. "Willing cannot be taught." [Tr.]

for the most part only fictitious, of his non-egoistical actions, the nature of which it, in other words he himself, does not *comprehend.* With such an account he has been accustomed to rest content.

Dogmas can of course have a powerful influence on *conduct,* on outward actions, and so can custom and example (the latter, because the ordinary man does not trust his judgment, of whose weakness he is conscious, but follows only his own or someone else's experience); but the disposition is not altered in this way.[5] All abstract knowledge gives only motives, but, as was shown above, motives can alter only the direction of the will, never the will itself. But all communicable knowledge can affect the will as motive only; therefore, however the will is guided by dogmas, what a person really and generally wills still remains the same. He has obtained different ideas merely of the ways in which it is to be attained, and imaginary motives guide him like real ones. Thus, for instance, it is immaterial, as regards his ethical worth, whether he makes donations to the destitute, firmly persuaded that he will receive everything back tenfold in a future life, or spends the same sum on improving an estate that will bear interest, late certainly, but all the more secure and substantial. And the man who, for the sake of orthodoxy, commits the heretic to the flames, is just as much a murderer as the bandit who earns a reward by killing; indeed, as regards inner circumstances, so also is he who massacres the Turks in the Promised Land, if, like the burner of heretics, he really does it because he imagines he will thus earn a place in heaven. For these are anxious only about themselves, about their egoism, just like the bandit, from whom they differ only in the absurdity of their means. As we have already said, the will can be reached from outside only through motives; but these alter merely the way in which it manifests itself, never the will itself. *Velle non discitur.*

In the case of good deeds, however, the doer of which appeals to dogmas, we must always distinguish whether these dogmas are really the motive for them, or whether, as I said above, they are nothing more than the delusive account by which he tries to satisfy his own faculty of reason about a good deed that flows from quite a different source. He performs such a deed because he is *good,* but he does not understand how to explain it properly, since he is not a philosopher, and yet he would like to think something with regard to it. But the distinction is very hard to find, since it lies in the very depths of our inner nature. Therefore we can hardly ever pronounce a correct moral judgement on the actions of others, and rarely on our own. The deeds

5. The Church would say they are mere *opera operata,* that are of no avail unless grace gives the faith leading to regeneration; but of this later on.

and ways of acting of the individual and of a nation can be very much modified by dogmas, example, and custom. In themselves, however, all deeds (*opera operata*) are merely empty figures, and only the disposition that leads to them gives them moral significance. But this disposition can be actually quite the same, in spite of a very different external phenomenon. With an equal degree of wickedness one person can die on the wheel, and another peacefully in the bosom of his family. It can be the same degree of wickedness that expresses itself in one nation in the crude characteristics of murder and cannibalism, and in another finely and delicately in miniature, in court intrigues, oppressions, and subtle machinations of every kind; the inner nature remains the same. It is conceivable that a perfect State, or even perhaps a complete dogma of rewards and punishments after death firmly believed in, might prevent every crime. Politically much would be gained in this way; morally, absolutely nothing; on the contrary, only the mirroring of the will through life would be checked.

Genuine goodness of disposition, disinterested virtue, and pure nobleness of mind, therefore, do not come from abstract knowledge; yet they do come from knowledge. But it is a direct and intuitive knowledge that cannot be reasoned away or arrived at by reasoning; a knowledge that, just because it is not abstract, cannot be communicated, but must dawn on each of us. It therefore finds its real and adequate expression not in words, but simply and solely in deeds, in conduct, in the course of a man's life. We who are here looking for the theory of virtue, and who thus have to express in abstract terms the inner nature of the knowledge lying at its foundation, shall nevertheless be unable to furnish that knowledge itself in this expression, but only the concept of that knowledge. We thus always start from conduct, in which alone it becomes visible, and refer to such conduct as its only adequate expression. We only interpret and explain this expression, in other words, express in the abstract what really takes place in it.

Now before we speak of the *good* proper, in contrast to the *bad* that has been described, we must touch on the mere negation of the bad as an intermediate stage; this is *justice*. We have adequately explained above what right and wrong are; therefore we can briefly say here that the man who voluntarily recognizes and accepts that merely moral boundary between wrong and right, even where no State or other authority guarantees it, and who consequently, according to our explanation, never in the affirmation of his own will goes to the length of denying the will that manifests itself in another individual, is *just*. Therefore, in order to increase his own well-being, he will not inflict suffering on others; that is to say, he will not commit any crime; he will respect the rights and property of everyone. We now see that for such a just man the *principium individuationis* is no longer an absolute partition as it is for the bad; that he does not, like the bad man, affirm merely his own phenomenon of will and deny all others; that others are not for him mere masks, whose inner nature is quite different from his. On the contrary, he shows by his way of acting that he *again recognizes* his own inner being, namely the will-to-live as thing-in-itself, in the phenomenon of another given to him merely as representation. Thus he finds himself again in that phenomenon up to a certain degree, namely that of doing no wrong, i.e., of not injuring. Now in precisely this degree he sees through the *principium individuationis,* the veil of Maya. To this extent he treats the inner being outside himself like his own; he does not injure it. . . .

We have found that voluntary justice has its innermost origin in a certain degree of seeing through the *principium individuationis,* while the unjust man remains entirely involved in this principle. This seeing through can take place not only in the degree required for justice, but also in the higher degree that urges a man to positive benevolence and well-doing, to philanthropy. Moreover, this can happen however strong and energetic the will that appears in such an individual may be in itself. Knowledge can always counterbalance it, can teach a man to resist the temptation to do wrong, and can even produce every degree of goodness, indeed of resignation. Therefore the good man is in no way to be regarded as an originally weaker phenomenon of will than the bad, but it is knowledge that masters in him the blind craving of will. Certainly there are individuals who merely seem to be good-natured on account of the weakness of the will that appears in them; but what they are soon shows itself in the fact that they are not capable of any considerable self-conquest, in order to perform a just or good deed.

Now if, as a rare exception, we come across a man who possesses a considerable income, but uses only a little of it for himself, and gives all the rest to persons in distress, whilst he himself forgoes many pleasures and comforts, and we try to make clear to ourselves the action of this man, we shall find, quite apart from the dogmas by which he himself will make his action intelligible to his faculty of reason, the simplest general expression and the essential character of his way of acting to be that he *makes less distinction than is usually made between himself and others.* The very distinction is in the eyes of many so great, that the suffering of another is a direct pleasure for the wicked, and a welcome means to their own well-being for the unjust. The merely just person is content not to cause it; and generally most people know and are acquainted with innumerable sufferings of others in their vicinity, but do not decide to alleviate them, because to do so they would have to undergo some privation. Thus a strong distinction seems to prevail in each of all these between his own ego and another's. On the other hand, to the noble person, whom we have in mind, this distinction is not so significant. The *principium individuationis,* the form of the phenomenon, no longer holds him so firmly in its grasp, but the suffering he sees in others touches him almost as closely as does his own. He therefore tries to strike a balance between the two, denies himself pleasures, undergoes privations, in order to alleviate another's suffering. He perceives that the distinction between himself and others, which to the wicked man is so great a gulf, belongs only to a fleeting, deceptive phenomenon. He recognizes immediately and without reasons or arguments, that the in-itself of his own phenomenon is also that of others, namely that will-to-live which constitutes the inner nature of everything, and lives in all; in fact, he recognizes that this extends even to the animals and to the whole of nature; he will therefore not cause suffering even to an animal.[6]

He is now just as little able to let others starve, while he himself has enough and to spare, as anyone would one day be on short commons, in order on the following day to have more than he can enjoy. For the veil of Maya has become transparent for the person who performs works of love, and the deception of the *principium individuationis* has left him. Himself, his will, he recognizes in every creature, and hence in the sufferer also. He is free from the perversity with which the will-to-live, failing to recognize itself, here in one individual enjoys fleeting and delusive pleasures, and there in another individual suffers and starves in return for these. Thus this will inflicts misery and endures misery, not knowing that, like Thyestes, it is eagerly devouring its own flesh. Then it here laments its unmerited suffering, and there commits an outrage without the least fear of Nemesis, always merely because it

6. Man's right over the life and power of animals rests on the fact that, since with the enhanced clearness of consciousness suffering increases in like measure, the pain that the animal suffers through death or work is still not so great as that which man would suffer through merely being deprived of the animal's flesh or strength. Therefore in the affirmation of his own existence, man can go so far as to deny the existence of the animal. In this way, the will-to-live as a whole endures less suffering than if the opposite course were adopted. At the same time, this determines the extent to which man may, without wrong, make use of the powers of animals. This limit, however, is often exceeded, especially in the case of beasts of burden, and of hounds used in hunting. The activities of societies for the prevention of cruelty to animals are therefore directed especially against these. In my opinion, that right does not extend to vivesection, particularly of the higher animals. On the other hand, the insect does not suffer through its death as much as man suffers through its sting. The Hindus do not see this.

fails to recognize itself in the phenomenon of another, and thus does
not perceive eternal justice, involved as it is in the *principium individuationis,* and so generally in that kind of knowledge which is governed
by the principle of sufficient reason. To be cured of this delusion and
deception of Maya and to do works of love are one and the
same thing; but the latter is the inevitable and infallible symptom
of the knowledge.

The opposite of the sting of conscience, whose origin and significance were explained above, is the *good conscience,* the satisfaction
we feel after every disinterested deed. It springs from the fact that
such a deed, as arising from the direct recognition of our own inner
being-in-itself in the phenomenon of another, again affords us the
verification of this knowledge, of the knowledge that our true self exists
not only in our own person, in this particular phenomenon, but in
everything that lives. In this way, the heart feels itself enlarged, just
as by egoism it feels contracted. For just as egoism concentrates our
interest on the particular phenomenon of our own individuality, and
then knowledge always presents us with the innumerable perils that
continually threaten this phenomenon, whereby anxiety and care
become the keynote of our disposition, so the knowledge that every
living thing is just as much our own inner being-in-itself as is our own
person, extends our interest to all that lives; and in this way the heart
is enlarged. Thus through the reduced interest in our own self, the
anxious care for that self is attacked and restricted at its root; hence
the calm and confident serenity afforded by a virtuous disposition and a
good conscience, and the more distinct appearance of this with every
good deed, since this proves to ourselves the depth of that disposition.
The egoist feels himself surrounded by strange and hostile phenomena,
and all his hope rests on his own well-being. The good person lives in
a world of friendly phenomena; the well-being of any of these in his
own well-being. Therefore, although the knowledge of the lot of man
generally does not make his disposition a cheerful one, the permanent
knowledge of his own inner nature in everything that lives nevertheless
gives him a certain uniformity and even serenity of disposition. For
the interest extended over innumerable phenomena cannot cause such
anxiety as that which is concentrated on one phenomenon. The accidents that concern the totality of individuals equalize themselves, while
those that befall the individual entail good or bad fortune.

Therefore, although others have laid down moral principles which
they gave out as precepts for virtue and laws necessarily to be observed,
I cannot do this, as I have said already, because I have no "ought"
or law to hold before the eternally free will. On the other hand, in

reference to my discussion, what corresponds and is analogous to that undertaking is that purely theoretical truth, and the whole of my argument can be regarded as a mere elaboration thereof, namely that the will is the in-itself of every phenomenon, but itself as such is free from the forms of that phenomenon, and so from plurality. In reference to conduct, I do not know how this truth can be more worthily expressed than by the formula of the *Veda* already quoted. *Tat tvam asi* ("This art thou!"). Whoever is able to declare this to himself with clear knowledge and firm inward conviction about every creature with whom he comes in contact, is certain of all virtue and bliss, and is on the direct path to salvation. . . .

68

. . . Just as previously we saw hatred and wickedness conditioned by egoism, and this depending on knowledge being entangled in the *principium individuationis,* so we found as the source and essence of justice, and, when carried farther to the highest degrees, of love and magnanimity, that penetration of the *principium individuationis.* This penetration alone, by abolishing the distinction between our own individuality and that of others, makes possible and explains perfect goodness of disposition, extending to the most disinterested love, and the most generous self-sacrifice for others.

Now, if seeing through the *principium individuationis,* if this direct knowledge of the identity of the will in all its phenomena, is present in a high degree of distinctness, it will at once show an influence on the will which goes still farther. If that veil of Maya, the *principium individuationis,* is lifted from the eyes of a man to such an extent that he no longer makes the egoistical distinction between himself and the person of others, but takes as much interest in the sufferings of other individuals as in his own, and thus is not only benevolent and charitable in the highest degree, but even ready to sacrifice his own individuality whenever several others can be saved thereby, then it follows automatically that such a man, recognizing in all beings his own true and innermost self, must also regard the endless sufferings of all that lives as his own, and thus take upon himself the pain of the whole world. No suffering is any longer strange or foreign to him. All the miseries of others, which he sees and is so seldom able to alleviate, all the miseries of which he has indirect knowledge, and even those he recognizes merely as possible, affect his mind just as do his own. It is no longer the changing weal and woe of his person that he has in view, as is the case with the man still involved in egoism, but, as he sees through the *principium individuationis,* everything lies equally near to him. He knows the whole, comprehends its inner nature, and finds it involved in a constant passing away, a vain striving, an inward conflict, and a continual suffering. Wherever he looks, he sees suffering humanity and the suffering animal world, and a world that passes away. Now all this lies just as near to him as only his own person lies to the egoist. Now how could he, with such knowledge of the world, affirm this very life through constant acts of will, and precisely in this way bind himself more and more firmly to it, press himself to it more and more closely? Thus, whoever is still involved in the *principium individuationis,* in egoism, knows only particular things and their relation to his own person, and these then become ever renewed *motives* of his willing. On the other hand, that knowledge of the whole, of the inner nature of the thing-in-itself, which has been described, becomes the *quieter* of all and every willing. The will now turns away from life; it shudders at the pleasures in which it recognizes the affirmation of life. Man attains to the state of voluntary renunciation, resignation, true composure, and complete will-lessness. . . .

True salvation, deliverance from life and suffering, cannot even be imagined without complete denial of the will. Till then, everyone is nothing but this will itself, whose phenomenon is an evanescent existence, an always vain and constantly frustrated striving, and the world full of suffering as we have described it. All belong to this irrevocably and in like manner. For we found previously that life is always certain to the will-to-live, and its sole actual form is the present from which they never escape, since birth and death rule in the phenomenon. The Indian myth expresses this by saying that "they are born again." The great ethical difference of characters means that the bad man is infinitely remote from attaining that knowledge, whose result is the denial of the will, and is therefore in truth *actually* abandoned to all the miseries which appear in life as *possible.* For even the present fortunate state of his person is only a phenomenon brought about by the *principium individuationis,* and the illusion of Maya, the happy dream of a beggar. The sufferings that in the vehemence and passion of his pressing will he inflicts on others are the measure of the sufferings, the experience of which in his own person cannot break his will and lead to final denial. On the other hand, all true and pure affection, and even all free justice, result from seeing through the *principium individuationis;* when this penetration occurs in all its force, it produces perfect sanctification and salvation, the phenomenon of which are the state of resignation previously described, the unshakable peace accompanying this, and the highest joy and delight in death. . . .

The Incommunicable*

In now bringing to a conclusion the main points of ethics, and with these the whole development of that one idea the imparting of which was my object, I do not wish by any means to conceal an objection concerning this last part of the discussion. On the contrary, I want to show that this objection lies in the nature of the case, and that it is quite impossible to remedy it. This objection is that, after our observations have finally brought us to the point where we have before our eyes in perfect saintliness the denial and surrender of all willing, and thus a deliverance from a world whose whole existence presented itself to us as suffering, this now appears to us as a transition into empty *nothingness....*

What is universally assumed as positive, what we call *being,* the negation of which is expressed by the concept *nothing* in its most general significance, is exactly the world as representation, which I have shown to be the objectivity, the mirror, of the will. We ourselves are also this will and this world, and to it belongs the representation in general as one aspect of it. The form of this representation is space and time; and so, for this point of view, everything that exists must be in some place and at some time. Then the concept, the material of philosophy, and finally the word, the sign of the concept, also belong to the representation. Denial, abolition, turning of the will are also abolition and disappearance of the world, of its mirror. If we no longer perceive the will in this mirror, we ask in vain in what direction it has turned, and then, because it no longer has any *where* and any *when,* we complain that it is lost in nothingness.

If a contrary point of view were possible for us, it would cause the signs to be changed, and would show what exists for us as nothing, and this nothing as that which exists. But so long as we ourselves are

Ibid., pp. 408-412.

the will-to-live, this last, namely the nothing as that which exists, can be known and expressed by us only negatively, since the old saying of Empedocles, that like can be known only by like, deprives us here of all knowledge, just as, conversely, on it ultimately rests the possibility of all our actual knowledge, in other words, the world as representation, or the objectivity of the will; for the world is the self-knowledge of the will.

If, however, it should be absolutely insisted on that somehow a positive knowledge is to be acquired of what philosophy can express only negatively as denial of the will, nothing would be left but to refer to that state which is experienced by all who have attained to complete denial of the will, and which is denoted by the names ecstasy, rapture, illumination, union with God, and so on. But such a state cannot really be called knowledge, since it no longer has the form of subject and object; moreover, it is accessible only to one's own experience that cannot be further communicated.

We, however, who consistently occupy the standpoint of philosophy, must be satisfied here with negative knowledge, content to have reached the final landmark of the positive. If, therefore, we have recognized the inner nature of the world as will, and have seen in all its phenomena only the objectivity of the will; and if we have followed these from the unconscious impulse of obscure natural forces up to the most conscious action of man, we shall by no means evade the consequence that, with the free denial, the surrender, of the will, all those phenomena also are now abolished. The constant pressure and effort, without aim and without rest, at all grades of objectivity in which and through which the world exists; the multifarious forms succeeding one another in gradation; the whole phenomenon of the will; finally, the universal forms of this phenomenon, time and space, and also the last fundamental form of these, subject and object; all these are abolished with the will. No will : no representation, no world.

Before us there is certainly left only nothing; but that which struggles against this flowing away into nothing, namely our nature, is indeed just the will-to-live which we ourselves are, just as it is our world. That we abhor nothingness so much is simply another way of saying that we will life so much, and that we are nothing but this will and know nothing but it alone. But we now turn our glance from our own needy and perplexed nature to those who have overcome the world, in whom the will, having reached complete self-knowledge, has found itself again in everything, and then freely denied itself, and who then merely wait to see the last trace of the will vanish with the body that is animated by that trace. Then, instead of the restless pressure and effort; instead of the constant transition from desire to apprehension and from joy to sorrow; instead of the never-satisfied and never-dying hope that constitutes the life-dream of the man who wills, we see that peace that is higher than all reason, that ocean-like calmness of the spirit, that deep tranquillity, that unshakable confidence and serenity, whose mere reflection in the countenance, as depicted by Raphael and Correggio, is a complete and certain gospel. Only knowledge remains; the will has vanished. We then look with deep and painful yearning at that state, beside which the miserable and desperate nature of our own appears in the clearest light by the contrast. Yet this consideration is the only one that can permanently console us, when, on the one hand, we have recognized incurable suffering and endless misery as essential to the phenomenon of the will, to the world, and on the other see the world melt away with the abolished will, and retain before us only empty nothingness. In this way, therefore, by contemplating the life and conduct of saints, to meet with whom is of course rarely granted to us in our own experience, but who are brought to our notice by their recorded history, and, vouched for with the stamp of truth by art, we have to banish the dark impression of that nothingness, which as the final goal hovers behind all virtue and holiness, and which we fear as children fear darkness. We must not even evade it, as the Indians do, by myths and meaningless words, such as reabsorption in *Brahman,* or the *Nirvana* of the Buddhists. On the contrary, we freely acknowledge that what remains after the complete abolition of the will is, for all who are still full of the will, assuredly nothing. But also conversely, to those in whom the will has turned and denied itself, this very real world of ours with all its suns and galaxies, is—nothing.

On the Primacy of the Will in Self-Consciousness*

The will, as the thing-in-itself, constitutes the inner, true, and indestructible nature of man, yet in itself it is without consciousness. For consciousness is conditioned by the intellect, and the intellect is a mere accident of our being, for it is a function of the brain. The brain, together with the nerves and spinal cord attached to it, is a mere fruit, a product, in fact a parasite, of the rest of the organism, in so far as it is not directly geared to the organism's inner working, but serves the purpose of self-preservation by regulating its relations with the external world. On the other hand, the organism itself is the visibility, the objectivity, of the individual will, its image, as this image presents itself in that very brain (which in the first book we learned to recognize as the condition of the objective world in general). Therefore, this image is brought about by the brain's forms of knowledge, namely space, time, and causality; consequently it presents itself as something extended, successively acting, and material, in other words, operative or effective. The parts of the body are both directly felt and perceived by means of the senses only in the brain. In consequence of this, it can be said that the intellect is the secondary phenomenon, the organism the primary, that is, the immediate phenomenal appearance of the will; the will is metaphysical, the intellect physical; the intellect, like its objects, is mere phenomenon, the will alone is thing-in-itself. Then, in a more and more *figurative* sense, and so by way of comparison, it can be said that the will is the substance of man, the intellect the accident; the will is the matter, the intellect the form; the will is heat, the intellect light. . . .

This fundamentally different nature of the will and the intellect, the simplicity and originality essential in the former in contrast to the complicated and secondary character of the latter, becomes even clearer to us when we observe their strange interplay within us, and see in a

*From Vol. II, pp. 201-211.

particular case how the images and ideas arising in the intellect set the will in motion, and how entirely separated and different are the roles of the two. Now it is true that we can already observe this in the case of actual events that vividly excite the will, whereas primarily and in themselves they are merely objects of the intellect. But, to some extent, it is not so obvious here that this reality as such primarily exists only in the intellect; and again, the change generally does not occur as rapidly as is necessary, if the thing is to be easily seen at a glance, and thus really comprehensible. On the other hand, both these are the case if it is mere ideas and fantasies that we allow to act on the will. If, for example, we are alone, and think over our personal affairs, and then vividly picture to ourselves, say, the menace of an actually present danger, and the possibility of an unfortunate outcome, anxiety at once compresses the heart, and the blood ceases to flow. But if the intellect then passes to the possibility of the opposite outcome, and allows the imagination to picture the happiness long hoped-for as thereby attained, all the pulses at once quicken with joy, and the heart feels as light as a feather, until the intellect wakens up from its dream. But then let some occasion lead the memory to an insult or injury suffered long ago, and anger and resentment at once storm through the breast that a moment before was at peace. Then let the image of a long-lost love arise, called up by accident, with which is connected a whole romance with its magic scenes, and this anger will at once give place to profound longing and sadness. Finally, if there occur to us some former humiliating incident, we shrivel up, would like to be swallowed up, blush with shame, and often try to divert and distract ourselves forcibly from it by some loud exclamation, scaring away evil spirits as it were. We see that the intellect strikes up the tune, and the will must dance to it; in fact, the intellect causes it to play the part of a child whom its nurse at her pleasure puts into the most different moods by chatter and tales alternating between pleasant and melancholy things. This is due to the fact that the will in itself is without knowledge, but the understanding associated with it is without will. Therefore the will behaves like a body that is moved, the understanding like the causes that set it in motion, for it is the medium of motives. Yet with all this, the primacy of the will becomes clear again when this will, that becomes, as we have shown, the sport of the intellect as soon as it allows the intellect to control it, once makes its supremacy felt in the last resort. This it does by prohibiting the intellect from having certain representations, by absolutely preventing certain trains of thought from arising, because it knows, or in other words experiences from the self-same intellect, that they would arouse in it any one of the emotions

previously described. It then curbs and restrains the intellect, and forces
it to turn to other things. However difficult this often is, it is bound to
succeed the moment the will is in earnest about it; for the resistance then
comes not from the intellect, which always remains indifferent, but
from the will itself; and the will has an inclination in one respect for a
representation it abhors in another. Thus the representation is in itself
interesting to the will, just because it excites it. At the same time, however, abstract knowledge tells the will that this representation will
cause it a shock of painful and unworthy emotion to no purpose. The
will then decides in accordance with this last knowledge, and forces
the intellect to obey. This is called "being master of oneself"; here
obviously the master is the will, the servant the intellect, for in the last
instance the will is always in command, and therefore constitutes the
real core, the being-in-itself, of man. In this respect 'Ηγεμονικόν[1]
would be a fitting title for the *will;* yet again this title seems to apply to
the *intellect,* in so far as that is the guide and leader, like the footman
who walks in front of the stranger. In truth, however, the most striking
figure for the relation of the two is that of the strong blind man carrying the sighted lame man on his shoulders.

The relation of the will to the intellect here described can further
be recognized in the fact that the intellect is originally quite foreign
to the decisions of the will. It furnishes the will with motives; but only
subsequently, and thus wholly *a posteriori,* does it learn how these have
acted, just as a man making a chemical experiment applies the reagents,
and then waits for the result. In fact, the intellect remains so much
excluded from the real resolutions and secret decisions of its own will
that sometimes it can only get to know them, like those of a stranger,
by spying out and taking unawares; and it must surprise the will in the
act of expressing itself, in order merely to discover its real intentions.
For example, I have devised a plan, but I still have some scruple
regarding it; on the other hand, the feasibility of the plan, as regards
its possibility, is completely uncertain, since it depends on external
circumstances that are still undecided. Therefore at all events it is
unnecessary for the present to come to a decision about it, and so for
the time being I let the matter rest. Now I often do not know how
firmly I am already attached in secret to this plan, and how I desire
that it be carried into effect, in spite of the scruple; in other words, my
intellect does not know this. But only let a favourable report reach me
as to its feasibility, and at once there arises within me a jubilant, irresistible gladness, diffused over my whole being and taking permanent

1. "The principal faculty" (a Stoic term). [Tr.]

possession of it, to my own astonishment. For only now does my intellect learn how firmly my will had already laid hold of the plan, and how entirely it was in agreement therewith, whereas the intellect had still regarded it as entirely problematical and hardly a match for that scruple. Or in another case, I have entered very eagerly into a mutual obligation that I believe to be very much in accordance with my wishes. As the matter progresses, the disadvantages and hardships make themselves felt, and I begin to suspect that I even repent of what I pursued so eagerly. However, I rid myself of this suspicion by assuring myself that, even if I were not bound, I should continue on the same course. But then the obligation is unexpectedly broken and dissolved by the other party, and I observe with astonishment that this happens to my great joy and relief. We often do not know what we desire or fear. For years we can have a desire without admitting it to ourselves or even letting it come to clear consciousness, because the intellect is not to know anything about it, since the good opinion we have of ourselves would inevitably suffer thereby. But if the wish is fulfilled, we get to know from our joy, not without a feeling of shame, that this is what we desired; for example, the death of a near relation whose heir we are. Sometimes we do not know what we really fear, because we lack the courage to bring it to clear consciousness. In fact, we are often entirely mistaken as to the real motive from which we do or omit to do something, till finally some accident discloses the secret to us, and we know that our real motive was not what we thought of it as being, but some other that we were unwilling to admit to ourselves, because it was by no means in keeping with our good opinion of ourselves. For example, as we imagine we omit to do something for purely moral reasons; yet we learn subsequently that we were deterred merely by fear, since we do it as soon as all danger is removed. In individual cases this may go so far that a man does not even guess the real motive of his action, in fact does not regard himself as capable of being influenced by such a motive; yet it is the real motive of his action. Incidentally, we have in all this a confirmation and illustration of the rule of La Rochefoucauld : *"L'amour-propre est plus habile que le plus habile homme du monde,"*[2] in fact even a commentary on the Delphic γνῶθι σαυτόν[3] and its difficulty. Now if, on the other hand, as all philosophers imagine, the intellect constituted our true inner nature, and the decisions of the will were a mere result of knowledge, then precisely *that* motive alone, from which we *imagined* we acted, would necessarily be decisive for our moral worth, on the analogy that the

2. "Self-esteem is cleverer than the cleverest man of the world." [Tr.]
3. "Know yourself." [Tr.]

intention, not the result, is decisive in this respect. But then the distinction between imagined and actual motive would really be impossible. Therefore, all cases described here, and moreover the analogous cases which anyone who is attentive can observe in himself, enable us to see how the intellect is such a stranger to the will that occasionally it is even mystified thereby. For it is true that it furnishes the will with motives; but it does not penetrate into the secret workshop of the will's decisions. It is, of course, a confidant of the will, yet a confidant that does not get to know everything. A confirmation of this is also afforded by the fact that occasionally the intellect does not really trust the will; and at some time or other almost everyone will have an opportunity of observing this in himself. Thus, if we have formed some great and bold resolution—which, however, as such is only a promise given by the will to the intellect—there often remains within us a slight, unconfessed doubt whether we are quite in earnest about it, whether, in carrying it out, we shall not waver or flinch, but shall have firmness and determination enough to carry it through. It therefore requires the deed to convince us of the sincerity of the resolve.

All these facts are evidence of the complete difference between the will and the intellect, and demonstrate the former's primacy and the latter's subordinate position.

IV

COMTE

Auguste Comte (1798-1857) was born at Montpellier, in the south of France; his father, a tax collector, was a royalist in politics and a Catholic in religion. His early interests were mathematical, and he spent two years at the École Polytechnique in Paris before being expelled, in 1816, for taking part in a student revolt. In the following year he became Saint-Simon's secretary and the ensuing partnership, lasting seven years, was of immense consequence for the development of Comte's views on history and social theory. His first important work—*Plan of the Scientific Works Necessary for the Reorganisation of Society* (1822), in which many of the ideas germane to his later thought were originally propounded—was published during this period. In 1826, after quarrelling with Saint-Simon and trying to make his living by tutoring and journalism, he embarked upon a series of public lectures, expounding his "positive philosophy"; he was forced, however, to abandon these as a result of the onset of a psychological disorder, and in the following year he even attempted suicide. The first volume of his principal work, the *Cours de philosophie positive,* appeared in 1830, and it was succeeded by five further volumes, the last being published in 1842. In the latter year he also separated from his wife, shortly afterward becoming involved in a relationship with another woman—Clothilde de Vaux—who seems to have played some part in influencing the direction his thinking took in the last decade of his life. For in his *General View of Positivism* (1848) and his more comprehensive *System of Positive Polity* (1852-54), Comte supplemented his conception of a scientifically ordered society by introducing the notion of a "religion of humanity"; this was envisaged as acting as an inspiring and unifying social force and was portrayed as retaining much of the ritual, though none of the supernatural dogma, of the theological institutions it was designed to supersede.

131

Comte regarded himself as the founder of sociology, and his philosophical ideas are integrally bound up with his theories of scientific and social progress. In the introductory chapters of his main work, extracts from which are reproduced here, he provided a general conspectus of his system and method, together with an indication of his epistemological presuppositions. Though his views on knowledge were in some ways continuous with those advanced by British and French empiricists in the eighteenth century, Comte was distinctive in his firm adherence to scientific criteria of verifiability and in his refusal to countenance the procedures of introspective psychology. Some of his objections to what he termed "the pretended psychological method" appear in the last selection, which is also of interest in the stress there laid upon the emotional, as opposed to the intellectual, aspects of human life and behavior.

The Nature of the Positive Philosophy*

A general statement of any system of philosophy may be either a sketch of a doctrine to be established, or a summary of a doctrine already established. If greater value belongs to the last, the first is still important, as characterizing from its origin the subject to be treated. In a case like the present, where the proposed study is vast and hitherto indeterminate, it is especially important that the field of research should be marked out with all possible accuracy. For this purpose, I will glance at the considerations which have originated this work, and which will be fully elaborated in the course of it.

In order to understand the true value and character of the Positive Philosophy, we must take a brief general view of the progressive course of the human mind, regarded as a whole; for no conception can be understood otherwise than through its history.

From the study of the development of human intelligence, in all directions, and through all times, the discovery arises of a great fundamental law, to which it is necessarily subject, and which has a solid foundation of proof, both in the facts of our organization and in our historical experience. The law is this :—that each of our leading conceptions,—each branch of our knowledge,—passes successively through three different theoretical conditions : the Theological, or fictitious; the Metaphysical, or abstract; and the Scientific, or positive. In other words, the human mind, by its nature, employs in its progress three methods of philosophizing, the character of which is essentially different, and even radically opposed : viz., the theological method, the metaphysical, and the positive. Hence arise three philosophies, or general systems of conceptions on the aggregate of phenomena, each of which excludes the others. The first is the necessary point of departure of the human understanding; and the third is its fixed and definitive state. The second is merely a state of transition.

*From *The Positive Philosophy of Auguste Comte* (trans. Harriet Martineau; London, 1853), Vol. I, pp. 1-17.

In the theological state, the human mind, seeking the essential nature of beings, the first and final causes (the origin and purpose) of all effects,—in short, Absolute knowledge,—supposes all phenomena to be produced by the immediate action of supernatural beings.

In the metaphysical state, which is only a modification of the first, the mind supposes, instead of supernatural beings, abstract forces, veritable entities (that is, personified abstractions) inherent in all beings, and capable of producing all phenomena. What is called the explanation of phenomena is, in this stage, a mere reference of each to its proper entity.

In the final, the positive state, the mind has given over the vain search after Absolute notions, the origin and destination of the universe, and the causes of phenomena, and applies itself to the study of their laws,—that is, their invariable relations of succession and resemblance. Reasoning and observation, duly combined, are the means of this knowledge. What is now understood when we speak of an explanation of facts is simply the establishment of a connection between single phenomena and some general facts, the number of which continually diminishes with the progress of science.

The Theological system arrived at the highest perfection of which it is capable when it substituted the providential action of a single Being for the varied operations of the numerous divinities which had been before imagined. In the same way, in the last stage of the Metaphysical system, men substitute one great entity (Nature) as the cause of all phenomena, instead of the multitude of entities as first supposed. In the same way, again, the ultimate perfection of the Positive system would be (if such perfection could be hoped for) to represent all phenomena as particular aspects of a single general fact;—such as Gravitation, for instance.

The importance of the working of this general law will be established hereafter. At present, it must suffice to point out some of the grounds of it.

There is no science which, having attained the positive stage, does not bear marks of having passed through the others. Some time since it was (whatever it might be) composed, as we can now perceive, of metaphysical abstractions; and, further back in the course of time, it took its form from theological conceptions. We shall have only too much occasion to see, as we proceed, that our most advanced sciences still bear very evident marks of the two earlier periods through which they have passed.

The progress of the individual mind is not only an illustration, but an indirect evidence of that of the general mind. The point of departure of the individual and of the race being the same, the phases of the mind of a man correspond to the epochs of the mind of the race. Now, each of us is aware, if he looks back upon his own history, that he was a theologian in his childhood, a metaphysician in his youth, and a natural philosopher in his manhood. All men who are up to their age can verify this for themselves.

Besides the observation of facts, we have theoretical reasons in support of this law.

The most important of these reasons arises from the necessity that always exists for some theory to which to refer our facts, combined with the clear impossibility that, at the outset of human knowledge, men could have formed theories out of the observation of facts. All good intellects have repeated, since Bacon's time, that there can be no real knowledge but that which is based on observed facts. This is incontestable, in our present advanced stage; but, if we look back to the primitive stage of human knowledge, we shall see that it must have been otherwise then. If it is true that every theory must be based upon observed facts, it is equally true that facts cannot be observed without the guidance of some theory. Without such guidance, our facts would be desultory and fruitless; we could not retain them : for the most part we could not even perceive them.

Thus, between the necessity of observing facts in order to form a theory, and having a theory in order to observe facts, the human mind would have been entangled in a vicious circle, but for the natural opening afforded by Theological conceptions. This is the fundamental reason for the theological character of the primitive philosophy. This necessity is confirmed by the perfect suitability of the theological philosophy to the earliest researches of the human mind. It is remarkable that the most inaccessible questions,—those of the nature of beings, and the origin and purpose of phenomena,—should be the first to occur in a primitive state, while those which are really within our reach are regarded as almost unworthy of serious study. The reason is evident enough :—that experience alone can teach us the measure of our powers; and if men had not begun by an exaggerated estimate of what they can do, they would never have done all that they are capable of. Our organization requires this. At such a period there could have been no reception of a positive philosophy, whose function is to discover the laws of phenomena, and whose leading characteristic is to regard as interdicted to human reason those sublime mysteries which theology explains, even to their minutest details, with the most attractive facility. It is just so under a practical view of the nature of the researches with which men first occupied themselves. Such inquiries offered the powerful charm of unlimited empire over the external world,—a world destined wholly for our use, and involved in every way with our existence. The theological philosophy, presenting this view, administered exactly the stimulus necessary to incite the human mind to the irksome labour without which it could make no progress. We can now scarcely conceive of such a state of things, our reason having become sufficiently mature to enter upon laborious scientific researches, without needing any such stimulus as wrought upon the imaginations of astrologers and alchemists. We have motive enough in the hope of discovering the laws of phenomena, with a view to the confirmation or rejection of a theory. But it could not be so in the earliest days; and it is to the chimeras of astrology and alchemy that we owe the long series of observations and experiments on which our positive science is based. Kepler felt this on behalf of astronomy, and Berthollet on behalf of chemistry. Thus was a spontaneous philosophy, the theological, the only possible beginning, method, and provisional system, out of which the Positive Philosophy could grow. It is easy, after this, to perceive how Metaphysical methods and doctrines must have afforded the means of transition from the one to the other.

The human understanding, slow in its advance, could not step at once from the theological into the positive philosophy. The two are so radically opposed, that an intermediate system of conceptions has been necessary to render the transition possible. It is only in doing this, that Metaphysical conceptions have any utility whatever. In contemplating phenomena, men substitute for supernatural direction a corresponding entity. This entity may have been supposed to be derived from the supernatural action : but it is more easily lost sight of, leaving attention free for the facts themselves, till, at length, metaphysical agents have ceased to be anything more than the abstract names of phenomena. It is not easy to say by what other process than this our minds could have passed from supernatural considerations to natural; from the theological system to the positve.

The Law of human development being thus established, let us consider what is the proper nature of the Positive Philosophy.

As we have seen, the first characteristic of the Positive Philosophy is that it regards all phenomena as subjected to invariable natural *Laws*. Our business is,—seeing how vain is any research into what are called *Causes*, whether first or final,—to pursue an accurate discovery of these Laws, with a view to reducing them to the smallest possible number. By speculating upon causes, we could solve no difficulty about origin and purpose. Our real business is to analyse accurately the circumstances of phenomena, and to connect them by the natural relations of succession and resemblance. The best illustration of this is the case of the doctrine of Gravitation. We say that the general phenomena of the universe are *explained* by it, because it connects under one head the whole immense variety of astronomical facts; exhibiting the constant tendency of atoms towards each other in direct proportion to their masses, and in inverse proportion to the squares of their distances; whilst the general fact itself is a mere extension of one which is perfectly familiar to us, and which we therefore say that we know;—the weight of bodies on the surface of the earth. As to what weight and attraction are, we have nothing to do with that, for it is not a matter of knowledge at all. Theologians and metaphysicians may imagine and refine about such questions; but Positive Philosophy rejects them. When any attempt has been made to explain them, it has ended only in saying that attraction is universal weight, and that weight is terrestrial attraction : that is, that the two orders of phenomena are identical; which is the point from which the question set out. Again, M. Fourier, in his fine series of researches on Heat, has given us all the most important and precise laws of the phenomena of heat, and many large and new truths, without once inquiring into its nature, as his predecessors had done when they disputed about calorific matter and the action of an universal ether. In treating his subject in the Positive method, he finds inexhaustible material for all his activity of research, without betaking himself to insoluble questions.

Before ascertaining the stage which the Positive Philosophy has reached, we must bear in mind that the different kinds of our knowledge have passed through the three stages of progress at different rates, and have not therefore arrived at the same time. The rate of advance depends on the nature of the knowledge in question, so distinctly that, as we shall see hereafter, this consideration constitutes an accessary to the fundamental law of progress. Any kind of knowledge reaches the positive stage early in proportion to its generality, simplicity, and independence of other departments. Astronomical science, which is above all made up of facts that are general, simple, and independent of other sciences, arrived first; then terrestrial Physics; then Chemistry; and, at length, Physiology. . . .

In mentioning just now the four principal categories of phenomena,—astronomical, physical, chemical, and physiological,—there was an omission which will have been noticed. Nothing was said of Social phenomena. Though involved with the physiological, Social phenomena demand a distinct classification, both on account of their importance and of their difficulty. They are the most individual, the most complicated, the most dependent on all others; and therefore they must be the latest,—even if they had no special obstacle to encounter. This branch of science has not hitherto entered into the domain of Positive Philosophy. Theological and metaphysical methods, exploded in other departments, are as yet exclusively applied, both in the way of inquiry and discussion, in all treatment of Social subjects, though the best minds are heartily weary of eternal disputes about divine right and the sovereignty of the people. This is the great, while it is evidently the only gap which has to be filled, to constitute, solid and entire, the Positive Philosophy. Now that the human mind has grasped celestial and terrestrial physics,—mechanical and chemical; organic physics, both vegetable and animal,—there remains one science, to fill up the series of sciences of observation,—Social physics. This is what men have now most need of : and this it is the principal aim of the present work to establish.

It would be absurd to pretend to offer this new science at once in a complete state. Others, less new, are in very unequal conditions of forwardness. But the same character of positivity which is impressed on all the others will be shown to belong to this. This once done, the philosophical system of the moderns will be in fact complete, as there will then be no phenomenon which does not naturally enter into some one of the five great categories. All our fundamental conceptions having become homogeneous, the Positive state will be fully established. It can never again change its character, though it will be for ever in course of development by additions of new knowledge. Having acquired the character of universality which has hitherto been the only advantage resting with the two preceding systems, it will supersede them by its natural superiority, and leave to them only an historical existence.

We have stated the special aim of this work. Its secondary and general aim is this :—to review what has been effected in the Sciences, in order to show that they are not radically separate, but all branches from the same trunk. If we had confined ourselves to the first and special object of the work, we should have produced merely a study of Social physics : whereas, in introducing the second and general, we offer a study of Positive Philosophy, passing in review all the positive sciences already formed. . . .

The study of the Positive Philosophy affords the only rational means of exhibiting the logical laws of the human mind, which have hitherto been sought by unfit methods. To explain what is meant by this, we may refer to a saying of M. de Blainville, in his work on Comparative Anatomy, that every active, and especially every living being, may be regarded under two relations—the Statical and the Dynamical; that is, under conditions or in action. It is clear that all considerations range themselves under the one or the other of these heads. Let us apply this classification to the intellectual functions.

If we regard these functions under their Statical aspect—that is, if we consider the conditions under which they exist—we must determine the organic circumstances of the case, which inquiry involves it with anatomy and physiology. If we look at the Dynamic aspect, we have to study simply the exercise and results of the intellectual powers of the human race, which is neither more nor less than the general object of the Positive Philosophy. In short, looking at all scientific theories as so many great logical facts, it is only by the thorough observation of these facts that we can arrive at the knowledge of logical laws. These being the only means of knowledge of intellectual phenomena, the illusory psychology, which is the last phase of theology, is excluded. It pretends to accomplish the discovery of the laws of the human mind by contemplating it in itself; that is, by separating it from causes and effects. Such an attempt, made in defiance of the physiological study of our intellectual organs, and of the observation of rational methods of procedure, cannot succeed at this time of day.

The Positive Philosophy, which has been rising since the time of Bacon, has now secured such a preponderance, that the metaphysicians themselves profess to ground their pretended science on an observation of facts. They talk of external and internal facts, and say that their business is with the latter. This is much like saying that vision is explained by luminous objects painting their images upon the retina. To this the physiologists reply that another eye would be needed to see the image. In the same manner, the mind may observe all phenomena but its own. It may be said that a man's intellect may observe his passions, the seat of the reason being somewhat apart from that of the emotions in the brain; but there can be nothing like scientific observation of the passions, except from without, as the stir of the emotions disturbs the observing faculties more or less. It is yet more out of the question to make an intellectual observation of intellectual processes. The observing and observed organ are here the same, and its action cannot be pure and natural. In order to observe, your intellect must pause from activity; yet it is this very activity that you want to observe. If you cannot effect the pause, you cannot observe : if you do effect it, there is nothing to observe. The results of such a method are in proportion to its absurdity. After two thousand years of psychological pursuit, no one proposition is established to the satisfaction of its followers. They are divided, to this day, into a multitude of schools, still disputing about the very elements of their doctrine. This interior observation gives birth to almost as many theories as there are observers. We ask in vain for any one discovery, great or small, which has been made under this method. The psychologists have done some good in keeping up the activity of our understandings, when there was no better work for our faculties to do; and they may have added something to our stock of knowledge. If they have done so, it is by practising the Positive method—by observing the progress of the human mind in the light of science; that is, by ceasing, for the moment, to be psychologists.

The view just given in relation to logical Science becomes yet more striking when we consider the logical Art.

The Positive method can be judged of only in action. It cannot be looked at by itself, apart from the work on which it is employed. At all events, such a contemplation would be only a dead study, which could produce nothing in the mind which loses time upon it. We may talk for ever about the method, and state it in terms very wisely, without knowing half so much about it as the man who has once put it in practice upon a single particular of actual research, even without any philosophical intention. Thus it is that psychologists, by dint of reading the precepts of Bacon and the discourses of Descartes, have mistaken their own dreams for science.

Without saying whether it will ever be possible to establish *a priori* a true method of investigation, independent of a philosophical study of the sciences, it is clear that the thing has never been done yet, and that we are not capable of doing it now. We cannot as yet explain the great logical procedures, apart from their applications. If we ever do, it will remain as necessary then as now to form good intellectual habits by studying the regular application of the scientific methods which we shall have attained.

This, then, is the first great result of the Positive Philosophy—the manifestation by experiment of the laws which rule the Intellect in the investigation of truth; and, as a consequence the knowledge of the general rules suitable for that object. . . .

The Positive Philosophy offers the only solid basis for that Social Reorganization which must succeed the critical condition in which the most civilized nations are now living.

It cannot be necessary to prove to anybody who reads this work that Ideas govern the world, or throw it into chaos; in other words, that all social mechanism rests upon Opinions. The great political and moral crisis that societies are now undergoing is shown by a rigid analysis to arise out of intellectual anarchy. While stability in fundamental maxims is the first condition of genuine social order, we are suffering under an utter disagreement which may be called universal. Till a certain number of general ideas can be acknowledged as a rallying-point of social doctrine, the nations will remain in a revolutionary state, whatever palliatives may be devised; and their institutions can be only provisional. But whenever the necessary agreement on first principles can be obtained, appropriate institutions will issue from them, without shock or resistance; for the causes of disorder will have been arrested by the mere fact of the agreement. It is in this direction that those must look who desire a natural and regular, a normal state of society.

Now, the existing disorder is abundantly accounted for by the existence, all at once, of three incompatible philosophies,—the theological, the metaphysical, and the positive. Any one of these might alone secure some sort of social order; but while the three co-exist, it is impossible for us to understand one another upon any essential point whatever. If this is true, we have only to ascertain which of the philosophies must, in the nature of things, prevail; and, this ascertained, every man, whatever may have been his former views, cannot but concur in its triumph. The problem once recognized cannot remain long unsolved; for all considerations whatever point to the Positive Philosophy as the one destined to prevail. It alone has been advancing during a course of centuries, throughout which the others have been declining. The fact is incontestable. Some may deplore it, but none can destroy it, nor therefore neglect it but under penalty of being betrayed by illusory speculations. This general revolution of the human mind is nearly accomplished. We have only to complete the Positive Philosophy by bringing Social phenomena within its comprehension, and afterwards consolidating the whole into one body of homogeneous doctrine. The marked preference which almost all minds, from the highest to the commonest, accord to positive knowledge over vague and mystical conceptions, is a pledge of what the reception of this philosophy will be when it has acquired the only quality that it now wants— a character of due generality. When it has become complete, its supremacy will take place spontaneously, and will re-establish order throughout society. There is, at present, no conflict but between the theological and metaphysical philosophies. They are contending for the task of reorganizing society; but it is a work too mighty for either of them. The Positive Philosophy has hitherto intervened only to examine both, and both are abundantly discredited by the process. It is time now to be doing something more effective, without wasting our forces in needless controversy. It is time to complete the vast intellectual operation begun by Bacon, Descartes, and Galileo, by constructing the system of general ideas which must henceforth prevail among the human race. This is the way to put an end to the revolutionary crisis which is tormenting the civilized nations of the world. . . .

Because it is proposed to consolidate the whole of our acquired knowledge into one body of homogeneous doctrine, it must not be supposed that we are going to study this vast variety as proceeding from a single principle, and as subjected to a single law. There is something so chimerical in attempts at universal explanation by a single law, that it may be as well to secure this Work at once from any imputation of the kind, though its development will show how undeserved such an imputation would be. Our intellectual resources are too narrow, and the universe is too complex, to leave any hope that it will ever be within our power to carry scientific perfection to its last degree of simplicity. Moreover, it appears as if the value of such an attainment, supposing it possible, were greatly overrated. The only way, for instance, in which we could achieve the business, would be by connecting all natural phenomena with the most general law we know,—which is that of Gravitation, by which astronomical phenomena are already connected with a portion of terrestrial physics. Laplace has indicated that chemical phenomena may be regarded as simple atomic effects of the Newtonian attraction, modified by the form and mutual position of the atoms. But supposing this view provable (which it cannot be while we are without data about the constitution of bodies), the difficulty of its application would doubtless be found so great that we must still maintain the existing division between astronomy and chemistry, with the difference that we now regard as natural that division which we should then call artificial. Laplace himself presented his idea only as a philosophic device, incapable of exercising any useful influence over the progress of chemical science. Moreover, supposing this insuperable difficulty overcome, we should be no nearer to scientific unity, since we then should still have to connect the whole of physiological phenomena with the same law, which certainly would not be the least difficult part of the enterprise. Yet, all things considered, the hypothesis we have glanced at would be the most favourable to the desired unity.

The consideration of all phenomena as referable to a single origin is by no means necessary to the systematic formation of science, any more than to the realization of the great and happy consequences that we anticipate from the Positive Philosophy. The only necessary unity is that of Method, which is already in great part established. As for the doctrine, it need not be *one;* it is enough that it should be *homogeneous.* It is, then, under the double aspect of unity of method and homogeneousness of doctrine that we shall consider the different classes of positive theories in this work. While pursuing the philosophical aim of all science, the lessening of the number of general laws requisite for the explanation of natural phenomena, we shall regard as presumptuous every attempt, in all future time, to reduce them rigorously to one. . . . .

The Hierarchy of the Sciences*

We propose to classify the fundamental sciences. They are six, as we shall soon see. We cannot make them less; and most scientific men would reckon them as more. Six objects admit of 720 different dispositions, or, in popular languages, changes. Thus we have to choose the one right order (and there can be but one right) out of 720 possible ones. Very few of these have ever been proposed; yet we might venture to say that there is probably not one in favour of which some plausible reason might not be assigned; for we see the wildest divergences among the schemes which have been proposed,—the sciences which are placed by some at the head of the scale being sent by others to the further extremity. Our problem is, then, to find the one rational order, among a host of possible systems.

Now we must remember that we have to look for the principle of classification in the comparison of the different orders of phenomena, through which science discovers the laws which are her object. What we have to determine is the real dependence of scientific studies. Now, this dependence can result only from that of the corresponding phenomena. All observable phenomena may be included within a very few natural categories, so arranged as that the study of each category may be grounded on the principal laws of the preceding, and serve as the basis of the next ensuing. This order is determined by the degree of simplicity, or, what comes to the same thing, of generality of their phenomena. Hence results their successive dependence, and the greater or lesser facility for being studied.

It is clear, *a priori,* that the most simple phenomena must be the most general; for whatever is observed in the greatest number of cases is of course the most disengaged from the incidents of particular cases. We must begin then with the study of the most general or simple phenomena, going on successively to the more particular or complex. This must be the most methodical way, for this order of generality or

*Ibid., pp. 24-33.

simplicity fixes the degree of facility in the study of phenomena, while it determines the necessary connection of the sciences by the successive dependence of their phenomena. It is worthy of remark in this place that the most general and simple phenomena are the furthest removed from Man's ordinary sphere, and must thereby be studied in a calmer and more rational frame of mind than those in which he is more nearly implicated; and this constitutes a new ground for the corresponding sciences being developed more rapidly.

We have now obtained our rule. Next we proceed to our classification.

We are first struck by the clear division of all natural phenomena into two classes—of inorganic and of organic bodies. The organized are evidently, in fact, more complex and less general than the inorganic, and depend upon them, instead of being depended on by them. Therefore it is that physiological study should begin with inorganic phenomena; since the organic include all the qualities belonging to them, with a special order added, viz. the vital phenomena, which belong to organization. We have not to investigate the nature of either; for the Positive Philosophy does not inquire into natures. Whether their nature be supposed different or the same, it is evidently necessary to separate the two studies of inorganic matter and of living bodies. Our classification will stand through any future decision as to the way in which living bodies are to be regarded; for, on any supposition, the general laws of inorganic physics must be established before we can proceed with success to the examination of a dependent class of phenomena.

Each of these great halves of natural philosophy has subdivisions. Inorganic physics must, in accordance with our rule of generality and the order of dependence of phenomena, be divided into two sections—of celestial and terrestrial phenomena. Thus we have Astronomy, geometrical and mechanical, and Terrestrial Physics. The necessity of this division is exactly the same as in the former case.

Astronomical phenomena are the most general, simple, and abstract of all; and therefore the study of natural philosophy must clearly begin with them. They are themselves independent, while the laws to which they are subject influence all others whatsoever. The general effects of gravitation preponderate, in all terrestrial phenomena, over all effects which may be peculiar to them, and modify the original ones. It follows that the analysis of the simplest terrestrial phenomenon, not only chemical, but even purely mechanical, presents a greater complication than the most compound astronomical phenomenon. The most difficult astronomical question involves less intricacy than the simple movement of even a solid body, when the determining circumstances are to be computed. Thus we see that we must separate these two studies, and proceed to the second only through the first, from which it is derived.

In the same manner, we find a natural division of Terrestrial Physics into two, according as we regard bodies in their mechanical or their chemical character. Hence we have Physics, properly so called, and Chemistry. Again, the second class must be studied through the first. Chemical phenomena are more complicated than mechanical, and depend upon them, without influencing them in return. Every one knows that all chemical action is first submitted to the influence of weight, heat, electricity, etc., and presents moreover something which modifies all these. Thus, while it follows Physics, it presents itself as a distinct science.

Such are the divisions of the sciences relating to inorganic matter. An analogous division arises in the other half of Natural Philosophy— the science of organized bodies.

Here we find ourselves presented with two orders of phenomena; those which relate to the individual, and those which relate to the species, especially when it is gregarious. With regard to Man, especially, this distinction is fundamental. The last order of phenomena is evidently dependent on the first, and is more complex. Hence we have two great sections in organic physics—Physiology, properly so called, and Social Physics, which is dependent on it. In all Social phenomena we perceive the working of the physiological laws of the individual; and moreover something which modifies their effects, and which belongs to the influence of individuals over each other—singularly complicated in the case of the human race by the influence of generations on their successors. Thus it is clear that our social science must issue from that which relates to the life of the individual. On the other hand, there is no occasion to suppose, as some eminent physiologists have done, that Social Physics is only an appendage to physiology. The phenomena of the two are not identical, though they are homogeneous; and it is of high importance to hold the two sciences separate. As social conditions modify the operation of physiological laws, Social Physics must have a set of observations of its own. . . .

Thus we have before us five fundamental Sciences in successive dependence,—Astronomy, Physics, Chemistry, Physiology, and finally Social Physics. The first considers the most general, simple, abstract, and remote phenomena known to us, and those which affect all others without being affected by them. The last considers the most particular, compound, concrete phenomena, and those which are the most interesting to Man. Between these two, the degrees of speciality, of complexity, and individuality are in regular proportion to the place of the respective sciences in the scale exhibited. This—casting out everything arbitrary—we must regard as the true filiation of the sciences; and in it we find the plan of this work. . . .

This gradation is in essential conformity with the order which has spontaneously taken place among the branches of natural philosophy, when pursued separately, and without any purpose of establishing such order. Such an accordance is a strong presumption that the arrangement is natural. Again, it coincides with the actual development of natural philosophy. If no leading science can be effectually pursued otherwise than through those which precede it in the scale, it is evident that no vast development of any science could take place prior to the great astronomical discoveries to which we owe the impulse given to the whole. The progression may since have been simultaneous; but it has taken place in the order we have recognized.

This consideration is so important that it is difficult to understand without it the history of the human mind. The general law which governs this history, as we have already seen, cannot be verified, unless we combine it with the scientific gradation just laid down : for it is according to this gradation that the different human theories have attained in succession the theological state, the metaphysical, and finally the positive. If we do not bear in mind the law which governs progression, we shall encounter insurmountable difficulties : for it is clear that the theological or metaphysical state of some fundamental theories must have temporarily coincided with the positive state of others which precede them in our established gradation, and actually have at times coincided with them; and this must involve the law itself in an obscurity which can be cleared up only by the classification we have proposed.

Again, this classification marks, with precision, the relative perfection of the different sciences, which consists in the degree of precision of knowledge, and in the relation of its different branches. It is easy to see that the more general, simple, and abstract any phenomena are, the less they depend on others, and the more precise they are in themselves, and the more clear in their relations with each other. Thus, organic phenomena are less exact and systematic than inorganic; and of these again terrestrial are less exact and systematic than those of astronomy. This fact is completely accounted for by the gradation we have laid down; and we shall see as we proceed, that the possibility of applying mathematical analysis to the study of phenomena is exactly in proportion to the rank which they hold in the scale of the whole.

There is one liability to be guarded against, which we may mention here. We must beware of confounding the degree of precision which we are able to attain in regard to any science, with the certainty of the science itself. The certainty of science, and our precision in the knowledge of it, are two very different things, which have been too often confounded; and are so still, though less than formerly. A very absurd proposition may be very precise; as if we should say, for instance, that the sum of the angles of a triangle is equal to three right angles; and a very certain proposition may be wanting in precision in our statement of it; as, for instance, when we assert that every man will die. If the different sciences offer to us a varying degree of precision, it is from no want of certainty in themselves, but of our mastery of their phenomena.

The most interesting property of our formula of gradation is its effect on education, both general and scientific. This is its direct and unquestionable result. It will be more and more evident as we proceed, that no science can be effectually pursued without the preparation of a competent knowledge of the anterior sciences on which it depends. Physical philosophers cannot understand Physics without at least a general knowledge of Astronomy; nor Chemists, without Physics and Astronomy; nor Physiologists, without Chemistry, Physics, and Astronomy; nor, above all, the students of Social philosophy, without a general knowledge of all the anterior sciences. . . .

Such is the operation of our great law upon scientific education through its effect on Doctrine. We cannot appreciate it duly without seeing how it affects Method.

As the phenomena which are homogeneous have been classed under one science, while those which belong to other sciences are heterogeneous, it follows that the Positive Method must be constantly modified in a uniform manner in the range of the same fundamental science, and will undergo modifications, different and more and more compound, in passing from one science to another. Thus, under the scale laid down, we shall meet with it in all its varieties; which could not happen if we were to adopt a scale which should not fulfil the conditions we have admitted. This is an all-important consideration; for if, as we have already seen, we cannot understand the positive method in the abstract, but only by its application, it is clear that we can have no adequate conception of it but by studying it in its varieties of application. No one science, however well chosen, could exhibit it. Though the Method is always the same, its procedure is varied. For instance, it should be Observation with regard to one kind of phenomena, and Experiment with regard to another; and different kinds of experiment, according to the case. In the same way, a general precept, derived from one fundamental science, however applicable to another, must have its spirit preserved by a reference to its origin; as in the case of the theory of Classifications. The best idea of the Positive Method would, of course, be obtained by the study of the most primitive and exalted of the sciences, if we were confined to one; but this isolated view would give no idea of its capacity of application to others in a modified form. Each science has its own proper advantages; and without some knowledge of them all, no conception can be formed of the power of the Method.

One more consideration must be briefly adverted to. It is necessary, not only to have a general knowledge of all the sciences, but to study them in their order. What can come of a study of complicated phenomena, if the student have not learned, by the contemplation of the simpler, what a Law is, what it is to Observe; what a Positive conception is; and even what a chain of reasoning is? Yet this is the way our young physiologists proceed every day,—plunging into the study of living bodies, without any other preparation than a knowledge of a dead language or two, or at most a superficial acquaintance with Physics and Chemistry, acquired without any philosophical method, or reference to any true point of departure in Natural philosophy. In the same way, with regard to Social phenomena, which are yet more complicated, what can be effected but by the rectification of the intellectual instrument, through an adequate study of the range of anterior phenomena? There are many who admit this : but they do not see how to set about the work, nor understand the Method itself, for want of the preparatory study; and thus, the admission remains barren, and social theories abide in the theological or metaphysical state, in spite of the efforts of those who believe themselves positive reformers.

These, then, are the four points of view under which we have recognized the importance of a Rational and Positive Classification.

It cannot but have been observed that in our enumeration of the sciences there is a prodigious omission. We have said nothing of Mathematical science. The omission was intentional; and the reason is no other than the vast importance of mathematics. This science will be the first of which we shall treat. Meantime, in order not to omit from our sketch a department so prominent, we may indicate here the general results of the study we are about to enter upon.

In the present state of our knowledge we must regard Mathematics less as a constituent part of natural philosophy than as having been, since the time of Descartes and Newton, the true basis of the whole of natural philosophy; though it is, exactly speaking, both the one and the other. To us it is of less value for the knowledge of which it consists, substantial and valuable as that knowledge is, than as being the most powerful instrument that the human mind can employ in the investigation of the laws of natural phenomena.

In due precision, Mathematics must be divided into two great sciences, quite distinct from each other—Abstract Mathematics, or the Calculus (taking the word in its most extended sense), and Concrete Mathematics, which is composed of General Geometry and of Rational Mechanics. The Concrete part is necessarily founded on the Abstract, and it becomes in its turn the basis of all natural philosophy; all the phenomena of the universe being regarded, as far as possible, as geometrical or mechanical.

The Abstract portion is the only one which is purely instrumental, it being simply an immense extension of natural logic to a certain order of deductions. Geometry and mechanics must, on the contrary, be regarded as true natural sciences, founded, like all others, on observation, though, by the extreme simplicity of their phenomena, they can be systematized to much greater perfection. It is this capacity which has caused the experimental character of their first principles to be too much lost sight of. But these two physical sciences have this peculiarity, that they are now, and will be more and more, employed rather as method than as doctrine. . . .

We have now considered, in the form of a philosophical problem, the rational plan of the study of the Positive Philosophy. The order that results is this; an order which of all possible arrangements is the only one that accords with the natural manifestation of all phenomena. MATHEMATICS, ASTRONOMY, PHYSICS, CHEMISTRY, PHYSIOLOGY, SOCIAL PHYSICS.

Intellectual and Moral Phenomena[*]

While Descartes was rendering to the world the glorious service of instituting a complete system of Positive Philosophy, the reformer, with all his bold energy, was unable to raise himself so far above his age as to give its complete logical extension to his own theory by comprehending in it the part of physiology that relates to intellectual and moral phenomena. After having instituted a vast mechanical hypothesis upon the fundamental theory of the most simple and universal phenomena, he extended in succession the same philosophical spirit to the different elementary notions relating to the inorganic world; and finally subordinated to it the study of the chief physical functions of the animal organism. But, when he arrived at the functions of the affections and the intellect, he stopped abruptly, and expressly constituted from them a special study, as an appurtenance of the meta-physico-theological philosophy, to which he thus endeavoured to give a kind of new life, after having wrought far more successfully in sapping its scientific foundations. We have an unquestionable evidence of the state of his mind in his celebrated paradox about the intelligence and instincts of animals. He called brutes automata, rather than allow the application of the old philosophy to them. Being unable to pursue this method with Man, he delivered him over expressly to the domain of metaphysics and theology. It is difficult to see how he could have done otherwise, in the then existing state of knowledge : and we owe to his strange hypothesis, which the physiologists went to work to confute, the clearing away of the partition which he set up between the study of animals and that of Man, and consequently, the entire elimination among the higher order of investigators, of theological and metaphysical philosophy. What the first contradictory constitution of the modern philosophy was, we may see in the great work of Malebranche, who was the chief interpreter of Descartes, and who shows how his philosophy continued to apply to the most complex parts of the intellectual system

[*] *Ibid.*, pp. 458-466.

the same methods which had been shown to be necessarily futile with regard to the simplest subjects. It is necessary to indicate this state of things because it has remained essentially unaltered during the last two centuries, notwithstanding the vast progress of positive science, which has all the while been gradually preparing for its inevitable transformation. The school of Boerhaave left Descartes's division of subjects as they found it : and if they, the successors of Descartes in physiology, abandoned this department of it to the metaphysical method, it can be no wonder that intellectual and moral phenomena remained, till this century, entirely excluded from the great scientific movement originated and guided by the impulse of Descartes. The growing action of the positive spirit has been, during the whole succeeding interval, merely critical,—attacking the inefficacy of metaphysical studies,—exhibiting the perpetual reconciliation of the naturalists on points of genuine doctrine, in contrast to the incessant disputes of various metaphysicians, arguing still, as from Plato downwards, about the very elements of their pretended science : this criticism itself relating only to results, and still offering no objection to the supremacy of metaphysical philosophy, in the study of Man, in his intellectual and moral aspects. It was not till our own time that modern science, with the illustrious Gall for its organ, drove the old philosophy from this last portion of its domain, and passed on in the inevitable course from the critical to the organic state, striving in its turn to treat in its own way the general theory of the highest vital functions. However imperfect the first attempts, the thing is done. Subjected for half a century to the most decisive tests, this new doctrine has clearly manifested all the indications which can guarantee the indestructible vitality of scientific conceptions. Neither enmity nor irrational advocacy has hindered the continuous spread, in all parts of the scientific world, of the new system of investigation of intellectual and moral man. All the signs of the progressive success of a happy philosophical revolution are present in this case.

The positive theory of the affective and intellectual functions is therefore settled, irreversibly, to be this :—it consists in the experimental and rational study of the phenomena of interior sensibility proper to the cerebral ganglions, apart from all immediate external apparatus. These phenomena are the most complex and the most special of all belonging to physiology; and therefore they have naturally been the last to attain to a postive analysis; to say nothing of their relation to social considerations, which must be an impediment in the way of their study. . . .

We need not stop to draw out any parallel or contrast between phrenology and psychology. Gall has fully and clearly exposed the powerlessness of metaphysical methods for the study of intellectual and moral phenomena : and in the present state of the human mind, all discussion on this subject is superfluous. The great philosophical cause is tried and judged; and the metaphysicians have passed from a state of domination to one of protestation,—in the learned world at least, where their opposition would obtain no attention but for the inconvenience of their still impeding the progress of popular reason. The triumph of the positive method is so decided that it is needless to devote time and effort to any demonstration, except in the way of instruction : but, in order to characterize, by a striking contrast, the true general spirit of phrenological physiology, it may be useful here to analyse very briefly the radical vices of the pretended psychological method, considered merely in regard to what it has in common in the principal existing schools;—in those called the French, the German, and (the least consistent and also the least absurd of the three) the Scotch school :—that is, as far as we can talk of schools in a philosophy which, by its nature, must engender as many incompatible opinions as it has adepts gifted with any degree of imagination. We may, moreover, refer confidently to these sects for the mutual refutation of their most essential points of difference.

As for their fundamental principle of *interior observation,* it would certainly be superfluous to add anything to what I have already said about the absurdity of the supposition of a man seeing himself think. It was well remarked by M. Broussais, on this point, that such a method, if possible, would extremely restrict the study of the understanding, by necessarily limiting it to the case of adult and healthy Man, without any hope of illustrating this difficult doctrine by any comparison of different ages, or consideration of pathological states, which yet are unanimously recognized as indispensable auxiliaries in the simplest researches about Man. But, further, we must be also struck by the absolute interdict which is laid upon all intellectual and moral study of animals, from whom the psychologists can hardly be expecting any *interior observation.* It seems rather strange that the philosophers who have so attenuated this immense subject should be those who are for ever reproaching their adversaries with a want of comprehensiveness and elevation. The case of animals is the rock on which all psychological theories have split, since the naturalists have compelled the metaphysicians to part with the singular expedient imagined by Descartes, and to admit that animals, in the higher parts of the scale at least, manifest most of our affective, and even intellectual faculties, with mere differences of degree; a fact which no one at this day ventures to deny, and which is enough of itself to demonstrate the absurdity of these idle conceptions.

Recurring to the first ideas of philosophical common sense, it is at once evident that no function can be studied but with relation to the organ that fulfils it, or to the phenomena of its fulfilment : and, in the second place, that the affective functions, and yet more the intellectual, exhibit in the latter respect this particular characteristic,—that they cannot be observed during their operation, but only in their results,—more or less immediate, and more or less durable. There are then only two ways of studying such an order of functions; either determining, with all attainable precision, the various organic conditions on which they depend,—which is the chief object of phrenological physiology; or in directly observing the series of intellectual and moral acts,—which belongs rather to natural history, properly so called : these two inseparable aspects of one subject being always so conceived as to throw light on each other. Thus regarded, this great study is seen to be indissolubly connected on the one hand with the whole of the foregoing parts of natural philosophy, and especially with the fundamental doctrines of biology; and, on the other hand, with the whole of history,—of animals as well as of man and of humanity. But when, by the pretended psychological method, the consideration of both the agent and the act is discarded altogether, what material can remain but an unintelligible conflict of words, in which merely nominal entities are substituted for real phenomena? The most difficult study of all is thus set up in a state of isolation, without any one point of support in the most simple and perfect sciences, over which it is yet proposed to give it a majestic sovereignty : and in this all psychologists agree, however extreme may be their differences on other points.

About the method of psychology or ideology, enough has been said. As to the doctrine, the first glance shows a radical fault in it, common to all sects,—a false estimate of the general relations between the affective and the intellectual faculties. However various may be the theories about the preponderance of the latter, all metaphysicians assert that preponderance by making these faculties their starting-point. The intellect is almost exclusively the subject of their speculations, and the affections have been almost entirely neglected; and, moreover, always subordinated to the understanding. Now, such a conception represents precisely the reverse of the reality, not only for animals, but also for Man : for daily experience shows that the affections, the propensities, the passions, are the great springs of human life; and that, so far from resulting from intelligence, their spontaneous and independent impulse is indispensable to the first awakening and continuous development of the various intellectual faculties, by assigning to them a permanent end, without which—to say nothing of the vagueness of their general direction—they would remain dormant in the majority of men. It is even but too certain that the least noble and most animal propensities are habitually the most energetic, and therefore the most influential. The whole of human nature is thus very unfaithfully represented by these futile systems, which, if noticing the affective faculties at all, have vaguely connected them with one single principle, sympathy, and, above all, self-consciousness, always supposed to be directed by the intellect. Thus it is that, contrary to evidence, man has been represented as essentially a reasoning being, continually carrying on, unconsciously, a multitude of imperceptible calculations, with scarcely any spontaneity of action, from infancy upwards. This false conception has doubtless been supported by a consideration worthy of all respect,—that it is by the intellect that Man is modified and improved; but science requires, before all things, the reality of any views, independently of their desirableness; and it is always this reality which is the basis of genuine utility. Without denying the secondary influence of such a view, we can show that two purely philosophical causes, quite unconnected with any idea of application, and inherent in the nature of the method, have led the metaphysicians of all sects to this hypothesis of the supremacy of the intellect. The first is the radical separation which it was thought necessary to make between brutes and man, and which would have been effaced at once by the admission of the preponderance of the affective over the intellectual faculties; and the second was the necessity that the metaphysicians found themselves under, of preserving the unity of what they called the *I*, that it might correspond with the unity of the *soul*, in obedience to the requisitions of the theological philosophy, of which metaphysics is, as we must ever bear in mind, the final transformation. But the positive philosophers, who approach the question with the simple aim of ascertaining the true state of things, and reproducing it with all possible accuracy in their theories, have perceived that, according to universal experience, human nature is so far from being single that it is eminently multiple; that is, usually induced in various directions by distinct and independent powers, among which equilibrium is established with extreme difficulty when, as usually happens in civilized life, no one of them is, in itself, sufficiently marked to acquire spontaneously any considerable preponderance over the rest. Thus, the famous theory of the *I* is essentially without a scientific object, since it is destined to represent a purely fictitious state. There is, in this direction, as I have already pointed out, no other real subject of positive investigation than the study of the equilibrium of the various animal functions,—both of irritability and of sensibility,—which marks the normal state, in which each of them, duly moderated, is regularly and permanently associated with the whole of the others, according to the laws of sympathy, and yet more of synergy. The very abstract and indirect notion of the *I* proceeds from the continuous sense of such a harmony; that is, from the universal accordance of the entire organism. Psychologists have attempted in vain to make out of this idea, or rather sense, an attribute of humanity exclusively. It is evidently a necessary result of all animal life; and therefore it must belong to all animals, whether they are able to discourse upon it or not. No doubt a cat, or any other vertebrated animal, without knowing how to say "I," is not in the habit of taking itself for another. Moreover, it is probable that among the superior animals the sense of personality is still more marked than in Man, on account of their more isolated life; though if we descended too far in the zoological scale we should reach organisms in which the continuous degradation of the nervous system attentuates this compound sense, together with the various simple feelings on which it depends.

It must not be overlooked that though the psychologists have agreed in neglecting the intellectual and moral faculties of brutes, which have been happily left to the naturalists, they have occasioned great mischief by their obscure and indefinite distinction between intelligence and instinct, thus setting up a division between human and animal nature which has had too much effect even upon zoologists to this day. The only meaning that can be attributed to the word *instinct,* is any spontaneous impulse in a determinate direction, independently of any foreign influence. In this primitive sense, the term evidently applies to the proper and direct àctivity of any faculty whatever, intellectual as well as affective; and it therefore does not conflict with the term *intelligence* in any way, as we so often see when we speak of those who, without any education, manifest a marked talent for music, painting, mathematics, etc. In this way there is instinct, or rather, there are instincts in Man, as much or more than in brutes. If, on the other hand, we describe *intelligence* as the aptitude to modify conduct in conformity to the circumstances of each case,—which, in fact, is the main practical attribute of *reason,* in its proper sense,—it is more evident than before that there is no other essential difference between humanity and animality than that of the degree of development admitted by a faculty which is, by its nature, common to all animal life, and without which it could not even be conceived to exist. Thus the famous scholastic definition of Man as a *reasonable animal* offers a real no-meaning, since no animal, especially in the higher parts of the zoo-logical scale, could live without being to a certain extent reasonable, in proportion to the complexity of its organism. Though the moral nature of animals has been but little and very imperfectly explored, we can yet perceive, without possibility of mistake, among those that live with us and that are familiar with us,—judging of them by the same means of observation that we should employ about men whose language and ways were previously unknown to us,—that they not only apply their intelligence to the satisfaction of their organic wants, much as men do, aiding themselves also with some sort of language; but that they are, in like manner, susceptible of a kind of wants more disinter-ested, inasmuch as they consist in a need to exercise their faculties for the mere pleasure of the exercise. It is the same thing that leads children or savages to invent new sports, and that renders them, at the same time, liable to *ennui*. That state, erroneously set up as a special privilege of human nature, is sometimes sufficiently marked, in the case of certain animals, to urge them to suicide, when captivity has become intolerable. An attentive examination of the facts therefore discredits the perversion of the word *instinct* when it is used to signify the fatality under which animals are impelled to the mechanical performance of *acts* uniformly determinate, without any possible modification from corresponding circumstances, and neither requiring nor allowing any education, properly so called. This gratuitous supposition is evidently a remnant of the automatic hypothesis of Descartes. . . .

V

WHEWELL

WILLIAM WHEWELL (1794-1870) was born in Lancashire. An undergraduate at Trinity College, Cambridge, he was elected to a fellowship there in 1817, later becoming Master of the college. As his numerous publications show, Whewell was a man of vast learning and of very wide interests: his writings include contributions to the fields of mathematics, mechanics, theology, ethics, and political economy, and he was opposed to the rigid division between study of the arts and study of the natural sciences which was an established feature of the English educational system. A Fellow of the Royal Society, he was in close touch with some of the leading scientists of his time, including Faraday, Lyell, and Herschel, and was himself a pioneer in the development of crystallography. It was therefore as no mere armchair theorist, but as one possessed of considerable scientific knowledge and experience, that he embarked upon the two works for which he is now chiefly remembered: his *History of the Inductive Sciences* (1837) and his *Philosophy of the Inductive Sciences* (1840). These books were used as an important source by J. S. Mill when writing his own *A System of Logic;* yet, while acknowledging the debt, Mill at the same time found much to criticize in Whewell's conception of inductive procedure, thereby initiating a famous controversy between the two men which continued over a period of several years. Mill regarded Whewell as a somewhat reactionary rationalist, who not only upheld an outdated doctrine of necessary truth, but who also fatally misunderstood and misrepresented the problem of scientific proof. Whewell, on his side, accused Mill of overlooking the crucial part played by original ideas and interpretative conceptions in scientific discovery and of maintaining an unrealistic view of how inductive hypotheses are arrived at and established in practice: his principal objections

158

are to be found in the chapter on Mill's logic in the third edition of his *Philosophy of the Inductive Sciences* (1858-60).

From one point of view Whewell may be considered as having developed, in an interesting and novel way, the Kantian insight that the role of the human mind in knowledge is active rather than passive; we construct and impose upon nature our interpretations of experience as opposed to mechanically reading them off from the presented data. For Whewell, induction took the form of "a leap which is out of the reach of method," and he insisted upon invention and imagination, involving fresh modes of looking at and connecting empirical facts, as being integral to all genuine scientific discovery. Thus new conceptions are introduced which are never mere summaries of, or abstractions from, painstakingly accumulated observations; instead they should be seen for what they are—products of insight and genius. This did not mean that Whewell wished to advocate a kind of scientific apriorism, whereby truths concerning the nature of the world could be acquired independently of appeals to experience; on the contrary, he continually stressed the need to test and justify hypotheses by reference to their observable consequences. It did mean, however, that he presented the structure of scientific thought and inference in a perspicuous manner that contrasted favorably with conventional textbook interpretations of inductive reasoning. A general law or theory is *established* by showing that statements descriptive of the observed facts are deducible from it; it is wrong, on the other hand, to suppose that such a law or theory is typically *reached* or *discovered* as a consequence directly derivable from those facts. His "Inductive Tables"—in which propositions are arranged hierarchically, the most general statements of scientific law appearing at one end and particular observation-statements appearing at the other—were intended to illustrate this: to move up the table is to proceed by deductive steps in the direction of confirmation; to move down it is to follow the inductive pattern of discovery. In effect, he was describing what is now known as the "hypothetico-deductive" conception of scientific procedure, a conception which (it is sometimes maintained) obviates the classical "problem of induction"—the alleged difficulty of justifying extrapolation from observed to unobserved cases. Whewell himself spoke on occasions as if this were so, but the legitimacy of the claim was disputed by Mill and it is still disputed today.

The Colligation of Facts*

5. Let us now suppose that, besides common everyday perception of facts, we turn our attention to some other occurrences and appearances, with a design of obtaining from them speculative knowledge. This process is more peculiarly called *Observation,* or, when we ourselves occasion the facts, *Experiment.* But the same remark which we have already made, still holds good here. These facts can be of no value, except they are resolved into those exact Conceptions which contain the essential circumstances of the case. They must be determined, not indeed necessarily, as has sometimes been said, "according to Number, Weight, and Measure;" for, as we have endeavoured to show in the preceding Books, there are many other Conceptions to which phenomena may be subordinated, quite different from these, and yet not at all less definite and precise. But in order that the facts obtained by observation and experiment may be capable of being used in furtherance of our exact and solid knowledge, they must be apprehended and analyzed according to some Conceptions which, applied for this purpose, give distinct and definite results, such as can be steadily taken hold of and reasoned from; that is, the facts must be referred to Clear and Appropriate Ideas, according to the manner in which we have already explained this condition of the derivation of our knowledge. The phenomena of light, when they are such as to indicate sides in the ray, must be referred to the Conception of *polarization;* the phenomena of mixture, when there is an alteration of qualities as well as quantities, must be combined by a Conception of *elementary composition.* And thus, when mere position, and number, and resemblance, will no longer answer the purpose of enabling us to connect the facts, we call in other Ideas, in such cases more efficacious, though less obvious.

6. But how are we, in these cases, to discover such Ideas, and to

*From *The Philosophy of the Inductive Sciences,* rev. ed., Vol. II (London, 1847), Book XI, Chap. 4, pp. 39-46.

160

judge which will be efficacious, in leading to a scientific combination
of our experimental data? To this question, we must in the first place
answer, that the first and great instrument by which facts, so observed
with a view to the formation of exact knowledge, are combined into
important and permanent truths, is that peculiar Sagacity which belongs to the genius of a Discoverer; and which, while it supplies those
distinct and appropriate Conceptions which lead to its success, cannot
be limited by rules, or expressed in definitions. It would be difficult or
impossible to describe in words the habits of thought which led Archi-
medes to refer the conditions of equilibrium on the lever to the Conception of *pressure,* while Aristotle could not see in them anything more
than the results of the strangeness of the properties of the circle;—or
which impelled Pascal to explain by means of the Conception of the
weight of air, the facts which his predecessors had connected by the
notion of nature's horrour of a vacuum;—or which caused Vitello and
Roger Bacon to refer the magnifying power of a convex lens to the
bending of the rays of light towards the perpendicular by *refraction,*
while others conceived the effect to result from the matter of medium,
with no consideration of its form. These are what are commonly
spoken of as felicitous and inexplicable strokes of inventive talent; and
such, no doubt, they are. No rules can ensure to us similar success in new
cases; or can enable men who do not possess similar endowments, to
make like advances in knowledge.

7. Yet still, we may do something in tracing the process by which
such discoveries are made; and this it is here our business to do. We
may observe that these, and the like discoveries, are not improperly
described as happy *Guesses;* and that Guesses, in these as in other
instances, imply various suppositions made, of which some one turns out
to be the right one. We may, in such cases, conceive the discoverer as
inventing and trying many conjectures, till he finds one which answers
the purpose of combining the scattered facts into a single rule. The
discovery of general truths from special facts is performed, commonly
at least, and more commonly than at first appears, by the use of a series
of Suppositions, or *Hypotheses,* which are looked at in quick succession, and of which the one which really leads to truth is rapidly detected, and when caught sight of, firmly held, verified, and followed to its
consequences. In the minds of most discoverers, this process of invention, trial, and acceptance or rejection of the hypothesis, goes on so
rapidly that we cannot trace it in its successive steps. But in some
instances, we can do so; and we can also see that the other examples of
discovery do not differ essentially from these. The same intellectual
operations take place in other cases, although this often happens so

instantaneously that we lose the trace of the progression. In the discoveries made by Kepler, we have a curious and memorable exhibition of this process in its details. Thanks to his communicative disposition, we know that he made nineteen hypotheses with regard to the motion of Mars, and calculated the results of each, before he established the true doctrine, that the planet's path is an ellipse. We know, in like manner, that Galileo made wrong suppositions respecting the law of falling bodies, and Mariotte, concerning the motion of water in a siphon, before they hit upon the correct view of these cases.

8. But it has very often happened in the history of science, that the erroneous hypotheses which preceded the discovery of the truth have been made, not by the discoverer himself, but by his precursors; to whom he thus owed the service, often an important one in such cases, of exhausting the most tempting forms of errour. Thus the various fruitless suppositions by which Kepler endeavoured to discover the law of refraction, led the way to its real detection by Snell; Kepler's numerous imaginations concerning the forces by which the celestial motions are produced,—his "physical reasonings" as he termed them,— were a natural prelude to the truer physical reasonings of Newton. The various hypotheses by which the suspension of vapour in air had been explained, and their failure, left the field open for Dalton with his doctrine of the mechanical mixture of gases. In most cases, if we could truly analyze the operation of the thoughts of those who make, or who endeavour to make discoveries in science, we should find that many more suppositions pass through their minds than those which are expressed in words; many a possible combination of conceptions is formed and soon rejected. There is a constant invention and activity, a perpetual creating and selecting power at work, of which the last results only are exhibited to us. Trains of hypotheses are called up and pass rapidly in review; and the judgment makes its choice from the varied group.

9. It would, however, be a great mistake to suppose that the hypotheses, among which our choice thus lies, are constructed by an enumeration of obvious cases, or by a wanton alteration of relations which occur in some first hypothesis. It may, indeed, sometimes happen that the proposition which is finally established is such as may be formed, by some slight alteration, from those which are justly rejected. Thus Kepler's elliptical theory of Mars's motions, involved relations of lines and angles much of the same nature as his previous false suppositions : and the true law of refraction so much resembles those erroneous ones which Kepler tried, that we cannot help wondering how he chanced to miss it. But it more frequently happens that new truths

are brought into view by the application of new Ideas, not by new modifications of old ones. The cause of the properties of the Lever was learnt, not by introducing any new *geometrical* combination of lines and circles, but by referring the properties to genuine *mechanical* Conceptions. When the Motions of the Planets were to be explained, this was done, not by merely improving the previous notions, of cycles of time, but by introducing the new conception of *epicycles* in space. The doctrine of the Four Simple Elements was expelled, not by forming any new scheme of elements which should impart, according to new rules, their sensible qualities to their compounds, but by considering the elements of bodies as *neutralizing* each other. The Fringes of Shadows could not be explained by ascribing new properties to the single rays of light, but were reduced to law by referring them to the *interference* of several rays.

Since the true supposition is thus very frequently something altogether diverse from all the obvious conjectures and combinations, we see here how far we are from being able to reduce discovery to rule, or to give any precepts by which the want of real invention and sagacity shall be supplied. We may warn and encourage these faculties when they exist, but we cannot create them, or make great discoveries when they are absent.

10. The Conceptions which a true theory requires are very often clothed in a *Hypothesis* which connects with them several superfluous and irrelevant circumstances. Thus the Conception of the Polarization of Light was originally represented under the image of *particles* of light having their poles all turned in the same direction. The Laws of Heat may be made out perhaps most conveniently by conceiving Heat to be a *Fluid*. The Attraction of Gravitation might have been successfully applied to the explanation of facts, if Newton had throughout treated Attraction as the result of an *Ether* diffused through space; a supposition which he has noticed as a possibility. The doctrine of Definite and Multiple Proportions may be conveniently expressed by the hypothesis of *Atoms*. In such cases, the Hypothesis may serve at first to facilitate the introduction of a new Conception. Thus a pervading Ether might for a time remove a difficulty, which some persons find considerable, of imagining a body to exert force at a distance. A Particle with Poles is more easily conceived than Polarization in the abstract. And if hypotheses thus employed will really explain the facts by means of a few simple assumptions, the laws so obtained may afterwards be reduced to a simpler form than that in which they were first suggested. The general laws of Heat, of Attraction, of Polarization, of Multiple

Proportions, are now certain, whatever image we may form to ourselves of their ultimate causes.

11. In order, then, to discover scientific truths, suppositions consisting either of new Conceptions, or of new Combinations of old ones, are to be made, till we find one which succeeds in binding together the Facts. But how are we to find this? How is the trial to be made? What is meant by "success" in these cases? To this we reply, that our inquiry must be, whether the Facts have the same relation in the Hypothesis which they have in reality;—whether the results of our suppositions agree with the phenomena which nature presents to us. For this purpose, we must both carefully observe the phenomena, and steadily trace the consequences of our assumptions, till we can bring the two into comparison. The Conceptions which our hypotheses involve, being derived from certain Fundamental Ideas, afford a basis of rigorous reasoning, as we have shown in the Books respecting those Ideas. And the results to which this reasoning leads, will be susceptible of being verified or contradicted by observation of the facts. Thus the Epicyclical Theory of the Moon, once assumed, determined what the moon's place among the stars ought to be at any given time, and could therefore be tested by actually observing the moon's places. The doctrine that musical strings of the same length, stretched with weights of 1, 4, 9, 16, would give the musical intervals of an octave, a fifth, a fourth, in succession, could be put to the trial by any one whose ear was capable of appreciating those intervals : and the inference which follows from this doctrine by numerical reasoning,—that there must be certain imperfections in the concords of every musical scale,—could in like manner be confirmed by trying various modes of *Temperament*. In like manner all received theories in science, up to the present time, have been established by taking up some supposition, and comparing it, directly or by means of its remoter consequences, with the facts it was intended to embrace. Its agreement, under certain cautions and conditions, of which we may hereafter speak, it held to be the evidence of its truth. It answers its genuine purpose, the Colligation of Facts. . . .

Characteristics of Scientific Induction*

2. Induction is familiarly spoken of as the process by which we collect a *General Proposition* from a number of *Particular Cases;* and it appears to be frequently imagined that the general proposition results from a mere juxta-position of the cases, or at most, from merely conjoining and extending them. But if we consider the process more closely, as exhibited in the cases lately spoken of, we shall perceive that this is an inadequate account of the matter. The particular facts are not merely brought together, but there is a New Element added to the combination by the very act of thought by which they are combined. There is a Conception of the mind introduced in the general proposition, which did not exist in any of the observed facts. When the Greeks, after long observing the motions of the planets, saw that these motions might be rightly considered as produced by the motion of one wheel revolving in the inside of another wheel, these Wheels were Creations of their minds, added to the Facts which they perceived by sense. And even if the wheels were no longer supposed to be material, but were reduced to mere geometrical spheres or circles, they were not the less products of the mind alone,—something additional to the facts observed. The same is the case in all other discoveries. The facts are known, but they are insulated and unconnected, till the discoverer supplies from his own stores a Principle of Connexion. The pearls are there, but they will not hang together till some one provides the String. The distances and periods of the planets were all so many separate facts; by Kepler's Third Law they are connected into a single truth : but the Conceptions which this law involves were supplied by Kepler's mind, and without these, the facts were of no avail. The planets described ellipses round the sun, in the contemplation of others as well as of Newton; but Newton conceived the deflection from the tangent in these elliptical motions in a new light,—as the effect of a Central

*From Chap. 5, pp. 48-74.

Force following a certain law; and then it was, that such a force was discovered truly to exist.

Thus in each inference made by Induction, there is introduced some General Conception, which is given not by the phenomena, but by the mind. The conclusion is not contained in the premises, but includes them by the introduction of a New Generality. In order to obtain our inference, we travel beyond the cases which we have before us; we consider them as mere exemplifications of some Ideal Case in which the relations are complete and intelligible. We take a Standard, and measure the facts by it; and this Standard is constructed by us, not offered by Nature. We assert, for example, that a body left to itself will move on with unaltered velocity; not because our senses ever disclosed to us a body doing this, but because (taking this as our Ideal Case) we find that all actual cases are intelligible and explicable by means of the Conception of *Forces,* causing change and motion, and exerted by surrounding bodies. In like manner, we see bodies striking each other, and thus moving and stopping, accelerating and retarding each other: but in all this, we do not perceive by our senses that abstract quantity, *Momentum,* which is always lost by one body as it is gained by another. This Momentum is a creation of the mind, brought in among the facts, in order to convert their apparent confusion into order, their seeming chance into certainty, their perplexing variety into simplicity. This the Conception of *Momentum gained and lost* does: and in like manner, in any other case in which a truth is established by Induction, some Conception is introduced, some Idea is applied, as the means of binding together the facts, and thus producing the truth.

3. Hence in every inference by Induction, there is some Conception *superinduced* upon the Facts: and we may henceforth conceive this to be the peculiar import of the term *Induction.* I am not to be understood as asserting that the term was originally or anciently employed with this notion of its meaning; for the peculiar feature just pointed out in Induction has generally been overlooked. This appears by the accounts generally given of Induction. "Induction," says Aristotle, "is when by means of one extreme term we infer the other extreme term to be true of the middle term." Thus, (to take such exemplifications as belong to our subject), from knowing that Mercury, Venus, Mars, describe ellipses about the Sun, we infer that all Planets describe ellipses about the Sun. In making this inference syllogistically, we assume that the evident proposition, "Mercury, Venus, Mars, do what all Planets do," may be taken *conversely,* "All Planets do what Mercury, Venus, Mars, do." But we may remark that, in this passage,

Aristotle (as was natural in his line of discussion) turns his attention entirely to the *evidence* of the inference; and overlooks a step which is of far more importance to our knowledge, namely, the *invention* of the second extreme term. In the above instance, the particular luminaries, Mercury, Venus, Mars, are one logical *Extreme;* the general designation Planets is the *Middle Term;* but having these before us, how do we come to think of *description of ellipses,* which is the other Extreme of the syllogism? When we have once invented this "second Extreme Term," we may, or may not, be satisfied with the evidence of the syllogism; we may, or may not, be convinced that, so far as this property goes, the extremes are co-extensive with the middle term; but the *statement* of the syllogism is the important step in science. We know how long Kepler laboured, how hard he fought, how many devices he tried, before he hit upon this *Term,* the Elliptical Motion. He rejected, as we know, many other "second Extreme Terms," for example, various combinations of epicyclical constructions, because they did not represent with sufficient accuracy the special facts of observation. When he had established his premise, that "Mars does describe an Ellipse about the Sun," he does not hesitate to *guess* at least that, in this respect, he might *convert* the other premise, and assert that "All the Planets do what Mars does." But the main business was, the inventing and verifying the proposition respecting the Ellipse. The Invention of the Conception was the great step in the *discovery;* the Verification of the Proposition was the great step in the *proof* of the discovery. If Logic consists in pointing out the conditions of proof, the Logic of Induction must consist in showing what are the conditions of proof, in such inferences as this : but this subject must be pursued in the next chapter; I now speak principally of the act of *Invention,* which is requisite in every inductive inference.

4. Although in every inductive inference, an act of invention is requisite, the act soon slips out of notice. Although we bind together facts by superinducing upon them a new Conception, this Conception, once introduced and applied, is looked upon as inseparably connected with the facts, and necessarily implied in them. Having once had the phenomena bound together in their minds in virtue of the Conception, men can no longer easily restore them back to the detached and incoherent condition in which they were before they were thus combined. The pearls once strung, they seem to form a chain by their nature. Induction has given them a unity which it is so far from costing us an effort to preserve, that it requires an effort to imagine it dissolved. For instance, we usually represent to ourselves the Earth as *round,* the Earth and the Planets as *revolving* about the Sun, and as *drawn*

to the Sun by a Central Force; we can hardly understand how it could cost the Greeks, and Copernicus, and Newton, so much pains and trouble to arrive at a view which is to us so familiar. These are no longer to us Conceptions caught hold of and kept hold of by a severe struggle; they are the simplest modes of conceiving the facts : they are really Facts. We are willing to *own* our obligation to those discoverers, but we hardly *feel* it : for in what other manner (we ask in our thoughts,) could we represent the facts to ourselves?

Thus we see why it is that this step of which we now speak, the Invention of a new Conception in every inductive inference, is so generally overlooked that it has hardly been noticed by preceding philosophers. When once performed by the discoverer, it takes a fixed and permanent place in the understanding of every one. It is a thought which, once breathed forth, permeates all men's minds. All fancy they nearly or quite knew it before. It oft was thought, or almost thought, though never till now expressed. Men accept it and retain it, and know it cannot be taken from them, and look upon it as their own. They will not and cannot part with it, even though they may deem it trivial and obvious. It is a secret, which once uttered, cannot be recalled, even though it be despised by those to whom it is imparted. As soon as the leading term of a new theory has been pronounced and understood, all the phenomena change their aspect. There is a standard to which we cannot help referring them. We cannot fall back into the helpless and bewildered state in which we gazed at them when we possessed no principle which gave them unity. Eclipses arrive in mysterious confusion : the notion of a *Cycle* dispels the mystery. The Planets perform a tangled and mazy dance; but *Epicycles* reduce the maze to order. The Epicycles themselves run into confusion; the conception of an *Ellipse* makes all clear and simple. And thus from stage to stage, new elements of intelligible order are introduced. But this intelligible order is so completely adopted by the human understanding, as to seem part of its texture. Men ask Whether Eclipses follow a Cycle; Whether the Planets describe Ellipses; and they imagine that so long as they do not *answer* such questions rashly, they take nothing for granted. They do not recollect how much they assume in *asking* the question :—how far the conceptions of Cycles and of Ellipses are beyond the visible surface of the celestial phenomena :—how many ages elapsed, how much thought, how much observation, were needed, before men's thoughts were fashioned into the words which they now so familiarly use. And thus they treat the subject, as we have seen Aristotle treating it; as if it were a question, not of invention, but of proof; not of substance, but of form : as if the main thing were not what we assert, but *how* we assert it. But for our purpose, it is requisite to bear in mind the feature which we have thus attempted to mark; and to recollect that, in every inference by induction, there is a Conception supplied by the mind and superinduced upon the Facts.

5. In collecting scientific truths by Induction, we often find (as has already been observed), a Definition and a Proposition established at the same time,—introduced together, and mutually dependent on each other. The combination of the two constitutes the Inductive act; and we may consider the Definition as representing the superinduced Conception, and the proposition as exhibiting the Colligation of Facts.

. . .

6. To discover a Conception of the mind which will justly represent a train of observed facts is, in some measure, a process of conjecture, as I have stated already; and as I then observed, the business of conjecture is commonly conducted by calling up before our minds several suppositions, and selecting that one which most agrees with what we know of the observed facts. Hence he who has to discover the laws of nature may have to invent many suppositions before he hits upon the right one; and among the endowments which lead to his success, we must reckon that fertility of invention which ministers to him such imaginary schemes, till at last he finds the one which conforms to the true order of nature. A facility in devising hypotheses, therefore, is so far from being a fault in the intellectual character of a discoverer, that it is, in truth, a faculty indispensable to his task. It is, for his purposes, much better that he should be too ready in contriving, too eager in pursuing systems which promise to introduce law and order among a mass of unarranged facts, than that he should be barren of such inventions and hopeless of such success. Accordingly, as we have already noticed, great discoverers have often invented hypotheses which would not answer to all the facts, as well as those which would; and have fancied themselves to have discovered laws, which a more careful examination of the facts overturned.

The tendencies of our speculative nature, carrying us onwards in pursuit of symmetry and rule, and thus producing all true theories, perpetually show their vigour by overshooting the mark. They obtain something, by aiming at much more. They detect the order and connexion which exist, by conceiving imaginary relations of order and connexion which has no existence. Real discoveries are thus mixed with baseless assumptions; profound sagacity is combined with fanciful conjecture; not rarely, or in peculiar instances, but commonly, and in most cases; probably in all, if we could read the thoughts of discoverers as we read the books of Kepler. To try wrong guesses is, with most persons, the only way to hit upon right ones. The character of the true philosopher is, not that he never conjectures hazardously, but that his conjectures are clearly conceived, and brought into rigid contact with facts. He sees and compares distinctly the Ideas and Things;—the relations of the notions to each other and to phenomena. Under these conditions, it is not only excusable, but necessary for him, to snatch at every semblance of general rule,—to try all promising forms of simplicity and symmetry.

Hence advances in knowledge are not commonly made without the previous exercise of some boldness and license in guessing. The discovery of new truths requires, undoubtedly, minds careful and scrupulous in examining what is suggested; but it requires, no less, such as are quick and fertile in suggesting. What is Invention, except the talent of rapidly calling before us the many possibilities, and selecting the appropriate one? It is true, that when we have rejected all the inadmissible suppositions, they are often quickly forgotten; and few think it necessary to dwell on these discarded hypotheses, and on the process by which they were condemned. But all who discover truths, must have reasoned upon many errours to obtain each truth; every accepted doctrine must have been one chosen out of many candidates. If many of the guesses of philosophers of bygone times now appear fanciful and absurd, because time and observation have refuted them, others, which were at the time equally gratuitous, have been confirmed in a manner which makes them appear marvellously sagacious. To form hypotheses, and then to employ much labour and skill in refuting, if they do not succeed in establishing them, is a part of the usual process of inventive minds. Such a proceeding belongs to the *rule* of the genius of discovery, rather than (as has often been taught in modern times) to the *exception*.

7. But if it be an advantage for the discoverer of truth that he be ingenious and fertile in inventing hypotheses which may connect the phenomena of nature, it is indispensably requisite that he be diligent and careful in comparing his hypotheses with the facts, and ready to abandon his invention as soon as it appears that it does not agree with the course of actual occurrences. This constant comparison of his own conceptions and supposition with observed facts under all aspects, forms the leading employment of the discoverer : this candid and simple love of truth, which makes him willing to suppress the most favourite production of his own ingenuity as soon as it appears to be at variance with realities, constitutes the first characteristic of his temper. He must have neither the blindness which cannot, nor the obstinacy which will not, perceive the discrepancy of his fancies and his facts. He must allow

no indolence, or partial views, or self-complacency, or delight in seeming demonstration, to make him tenacious of the schemes which he devises, any further than they are confirmed by their accordance with nature. The framing of hypotheses is, for the inquirer after truth, not the end, but the beginning of his work. Each of his systems is invented, not that he may admire it and follow it into all its consistent consequences, but that he may make it the occasion of a course of active experiment and observation. And if the results of this process contradict his fundamental assumptions, however ingenious, however symmetrical, however elegant his system may be, he rejects it without hesitation. He allows no natural yearning for the offspring of his own mind to draw him aside from the higher duty of loyalty to his sovereign, Truth : to her he not only gives his affections and his wishes, but strenuous labour and scrupulous minuteness of attention. . . .

8. It has often happened that those who have undertaken to instruct mankind have not possessed this pure love of truth and comparative indifference to the maintenance of their own inventions. Men have frequently adhered with great tenacity and vehemence to the hypotheses which they have once framed; and in their affection for these, have been prone to overlook, to distort, and to misinterpret facts. In this manner, *Hypotheses* have so often been prejudicial to the genuine pursuit of truth, that they have fallen into a kind of obloquy; and have been considered as dangerous temptations and fallacious guides. Many warnings have been uttered against the fabrication of hypotheses by those who profess to teach philosophy; many disclaimers of such a course by those who cultivate science.

Thus we find Bacon frequently discommending this habit, under the name of "anticipation of the mind," and Newton thinks it necessary to say emphatically "hypotheses non fingo." It has been constantly urged that the inductions by which sciences are formed must be *cautious* and *rigorous;* and the various imaginations which passed through Kepler's brain, and to which he has given utterance, have been blamed or pitied as lamentable instances of an unphilosophical frame of mind. Yet it has appeared in the preceding remarks that hypotheses rightly used are among the helps, far more than the dangers, of science;— that scientific induction is not a "cautious" or a "rigorous" process in the sense of *abstaining from* such suppositions, but in *not adhering to* them till they are confirmed by fact, and in carefully seeking from facts confirmation or refutation. Kepler's character was, not that he was peculiarly given to the construction of hypotheses, but that he narrated with extraordinary copiousness and candour the course of his thoughts, his labours, and his feelings. In the minds of most persons, as we have

said, the inadmissible suppositions, when rejected, are soon forgotten :
and thus the trace of them vanishes from the thoughts, and the successful hypothesis alone holds its place in our memory. But in reality, many
other transient suppositions must have been made by all discoverers;—
hypotheses which are not afterwards asserted as true systems, but entertained for an instant;—"tentative hypotheses," as they have been called.
Each of these hypotheses is followed by its corresponding train of observations, from which it derives its power of leading to truth. The
hypothesis is like the captain, and the observations like the soldiers of
an army : while he appears to command them, and in this way to work
his own will, he does in fact derive all his power of conquest from their
obedience, and becomes helpless and useless if they mutiny. . . .

10. The hypotheses which we accept ought to explain phenomena
which we have observed. But they ought to do more than this : our
hypotheses ought to *foretell* phenomena which have not yet been
observed;—at least all of the same kind as those which the hypothesis
was invented to explain. For our assent to the hypothesis implies that
it is held to be true of all particular instances. That these cases belong
to past or to future times, that they have or have not already occurred,
makes no difference in the applicability of the rule to them. Because
the rule prevails, it includes all cases; and will determine them all, if
we can only calculate its real consequences. Hence it will predict the
results of new combinations, as well as explain the appearances which
have occurred in old ones. And that it does this with certainty and
correctness, is one mode in which the hypothesis is to be verified as right
and useful.

The scientific doctrines which have at various periods been established have been verified in this manner. For example, the *Epicyclical
Theory* of the heavens was confirmed by its *predicting* truly eclipses of
the sun and moon, configurations of the planets, and other celestial
phenomena; and by its leading to the construction of Tables by which
the places of the heavenly bodies were given at every moment of time.
The truth and accuracy of these predictions were a proof that the
hypothesis was valuable and, at least to a great extent, true; although,
as was afterwards found, it involved a false representation of the structure of the heavens. In like manner, the discovery of the *Laws of
Refraction* enabled mathematicians to *predict*, by calculation, what
would be the effect of any new form or combination of transparent
lenses. Newton's hypothesis of *Fits of Easy Transmission and Easy
Reflection* in the particles of light, although not confirmed by other
kinds of facts, involved a true statement of the law of the phenomena
which it was framed to include, and served to *predict* the forms and

colours of thin plates for a wide range of given cases. The hypothesis that Light operates by *Undulations* and *Interferences,* afforded the means of *predicting* results under a still larger extent of conditions. In like manner in the progress of chemical knowledge, the doctrine of *Phlogiston* supplied the means of *foreseeing* the consequence of many combinations of elements, even before they were tried; but the *Oxygen Theory,* besides affording predictions, at least equally exact, with regard to the general results of chemical operations, included all the facts concerning the relations of weight of the elements and their compounds, and enabled chemists to *foresee* such facts in untried cases. And the Theory of *Electromagnetic Forces,* as soon as it was rightly understood, enabled those who had mastered it to *predict* motions such as had not been before observed, which were accordingly found to take place.

Men cannot help believing that the laws laid down by discoverers must be in a great measure identical with the real laws of nature, when the discoverers thus determine effects beforehand in the same manner in which nature herself determines them when the occasion occurs. Those who can do this, must, to a considerable extent, have detected nature's secret;—must have fixed upon the conditions to which she attends, and must have seized the rules by which she applies them. Such a coincidence of untried facts with speculative assertions cannot be the work of chance, but implies some large portion of truth in the principles on which the reasoning is founded. To trace order and law in that which had been observed, may be considered as interpreting what nature has written down for us, and will commonly prove that we understand her alphabet. But to predict what has not been observed, is to attempt ourselves to use the legislative phrases of nature; and when she responds plainly and precisely to that which we thus utter, we cannot but suppose that we have in a great measure made ourselves masters of the meaning and structure of her language. The prediction of results, even of the same kind as those which have been observed, in new cases, is a proof of real success in our inductive processes.

11. We have here spoken of the prediction of facts *of the same kind* as those from which our rule was collected. But the evidence in favour of our induction is of a much higher and more forcible character when it enables us to explain and determine cases of a *kind different* from those which were contemplated in the formation of our hypothesis. The instances in which this has occurred, indeed, impress us with a conviction that the truth of our hypothesis is certain. No accident could give rise to such an extraordinary coincidence. No false supposition could, after being adjusted to one class of phenomena, exactly represent a

different class, when the agreement was unforeseen and uncontemplated. That rules springing from remote and unconnected quarters should thus leap to the same point, can only arise from *that* being the point where truth resides.

Accordingly the cases in which inductions from classes of facts altogether different have thus *jumped together,* belong only to the best established theories which the history of science contains. And as I shall have occasion to refer to this peculiar feature in their evidence, I will take the liberty of describing it by a particular phrase; and will term it the *Consilience of Inductions.*

It is exemplified principally in some of the greatest discoveries. Thus it was found by Newton that the doctrine of the Attraction of the Sun varying according to the Inverse Square of this distance, which explained Kepler's *Third Law* of the proportionality of the cubes of the distances to the squares of the periodic times of the planets, explained also his *First* and *Second Laws* of the elliptical motion of each planet; although no connexion of these laws had been visible before. Again, it appeared that the force of Universal Gravitation, which had been inferred from the *Perturbations* of the moon and planets by the sun and by each other, also accounted for the fact, apparently altogether dissimilar and remote, of the *Precession of the equinoxes.* Here was a most striking and surprising coincidence, which gave to the theory a stamp of truth beyond the power of ingenuity to counterfeit. . . .

12. In the preceding Article I have spoken of the hypothesis with which we compare our facts as being framed *all at once,* each of its parts being included in the original scheme. In reality, however, it often happens that the various suppositions which our system contains are *added* upon occasion of different researches. Thus in the Ptolemaic doctrine of the heavens, new epicycles and eccentrics were added as new inequalities of the motions of the heavenly bodies were discovered; and in the Newtonian doctrine of material rays of light, the supposition that these rays had "fits," was added to explain the colours of thin plates; and the supposition that they had "sides" was introduced on occasion of the phenomena of polarization. In like manner other theories have been built up of parts devised at different times.

This being the mode in which theories are often framed, we have to notice a distinction which is found to prevail in the progress of true and of false theories. In the former class all the additional suppositions *tend to simplicity* and harmony; the new suppositions resolve themselves into the old ones, or at least require only some easy modification of the hypothesis first assumed : the system becomes more coherent as it is further extended. The elements which we require for explaining a new class of facts are already contained in our system. Different members of the theory run together, and we have thus a constant convergence to unity. In false theories, the contrary is the case. The new suppositions are something altogether additional;—not suggested by the original scheme; perhaps difficult to reconcile with it. Every such addition adds to the complexity of the hypothetical system, which at last becomes unmanageable, and is compelled to surrender its place to some simpler explanation.

Such a false theory, for example, was the ancient doctrine of eccentrics and epicycles. It explained the general succession of the Places of the Sun, Moon, and Planets; it would not have explained the proportion of their Magnitudes at different times, if these could have been accurately observed; but this the ancient astronomers were unable to do. When, however, Tycho and other astronomers came to be able to observe the planets accurately in all positions, it was found that *no* combination of *equable* circular motions would exactly represent all the observations. We may see, in Kepler's works, the many new modifications of the epicyclical hypothesis which offered themselves to him; some of which would have agreed with the phenomena with a certain degree of accuracy, but not so great a degree as Kepler, fortunately for the progress of science, insisted upon obtaining. After these epicycles had been thus accumulated, they all disappeared and gave way to the simpler conception of an *elliptical* motion. In like manner, the discovery of new inequalities in the Moon's motions encumbered her system more and more with new machinery, which was at last rejected all at once in favour of the *elliptical* theory. Astronomers could not but suppose themselves in a wrong path, when the prospect grew darker and more entangled at every step. . . .

13. The two last sections of this chapter direct our attention to two circumstances, which tend to prove, in a manner which we may term irresistible, the truth of the theories which they characterize :—the *Consilience of Inductions* from different and separate classes of facts; —and the progressive *Simplification of the Theory* as it is extended to new cases. These two Characters are, in fact, hardly different; they are exemplified by the same cases. For if these Inductions, collected from one class of facts, supply an unexpected explanation of a new class, which is the case first spoken of, there will be no need for new machinery in the hypothesis to apply it to the newly-contemplated facts; and thus, we have a case in which the system does not become more complex when its application is extended to a wider field, which was the character of true theory in its second aspect. The Consiliences of

our Inductions give rise to a constant Convergence of our Theory towards Simplicity and Unity.

But, moreover, both these cases of the extension of the theory,
without difficulty or new suppositions, to a wider range and to new
classes of phenomena, may be conveniently considered in yet another
point of view; namely, as successive steps by which we gradually ascend
in our speculative views to a higher and higher point of generality.
For when the theory, either by the concurrence of two indications, or by
an extension without complications, has included a new range of phenomena, we have, in fact, a new induction of a more general kind, to
which the inductions formerly obtained are subordinate, as particular
cases to a general proposition. We have in such examples, in short, an
instance of *successive generalization*. This is a subject of great importance, and deserving of being well illustrated; it will come under our
notice in the next chapter.

The Logic of Induction*

1. The subject to which the present chapter refers is described by phrases which are at the present day familiarly used in speaking of the progress of knowledge. We hear very frequent mention of *ascending from particular to general* propositions, and from these to propositions still more general;—of truths *included* in other truths of a higher degree of generality;—of different *stages of generalization;*—and of the *highest step* of the process of discovery, to which all others are subordinate and preparatory. As these expressions, so familiar to our ears, especially since the time of Francis Bacon, denote, very significantly, processes and relations which are of great importance in the formation of science, it is necessary for us to give a clear account of them, illustrated with general exemplifications; and this we shall endeavour to do.

We have, indeed, already explained that science consists of propositions which include the facts from which they were collected; and other wider propositions, collected in like manner from the former, and including them. Thus, that the stars, the moon, the sun, rise, culminate, and set, are facts *included* in the proposition that the heavens, carrying with them all the celestial bodies, have a diurnal revolution about the axis of the earth. Again, the observed monthly motions of the moon, and the annual motions of the sun, are *included* in certain propositions concerning the movements of those luminaries with respect to the stars. But all these propositions are really *included* in the doctrine that the earth, revolving on its axis, moves round the sun, and the moon round the earth. These movements, again, considered as facts, are explained and *included* in the statement of the forces which the earth exerts upon the moon, and the sun upon the earth. Again, this doctrine of the forces of these two bodies is *included* in the assertion, that all the bodies of the solar system, and all parts of matter, exert forces, each upon each. And we might easily show that all the leading facts in astronomy are comprehended in the same generalization. In like

*From Chap. 6, pp. 74-95.

manner with regard to any other science, so far as its truths have been well established and fully developed, we might show that it consists of a gradation of propositions, proceeding from the most special facts to the most general theoretical assertions. We shall exhibit this gradation in some of the principal branches of science.

2. This gradation of truths, successively included in other truths, may be conveniently represented by *Tables* resembling the genealogical tables by which the derivation of descendants from a common ancestor is exhibited; except that it is proper in this case to invert the form of the Table, and to make it converge to unity downwards instead of upwards, since it has for its purpose to express, not the derivation of many from one, but the collection of one truth from many things. Two or more co-ordinate facts or propositions may be ranged side by side, and joined by some mark of connexion, (a bracket, as ⌣ or ⌣ ,) beneath which may be placed the more general proposition which is collected by induction from the former. Again, propositions co-ordinate with this more general one may be placed on a level with it; and the combination of these, and the result of the combination, may be indicated by brackets in the same manner; and so on, through any number of gradations. By this means the streams of knowledge from the various classes of facts will constantly run together into a smaller and smaller number of channels; like the confluent rivulets of a great river, coming together from many sources, uniting their ramifications so as to form larger branches, these again uniting in a single trunk. The *genealogical tree* of each great portion of science, thus formed, will contain all the leading truths of the science arranged in their due co-ordination and subordination. . . .

7. The Tables, as we have presented them, exhibit the course by which we pass from particular to general through various gradations, and so to the most general. They display the order of *discovery*. But by reading them in an inverted manner, beginning at the single comprehensive truths with which the Tables end, and tracing these back into the more partial truths, and these again into special facts, they answer another purpose;—they exhibit the process of *verification* of discoveries once made. For each of our general propositions is true in virtue of the truth of the narrower propositions which it involves; and we cannot satisfy ourselves of its truth in any other way than by ascertaining that these its constituent elements are true. To assure ourselves that the sun attracts the planets with forces varying inversely as the square of the distance, we must analyze by geometry the motion in an ellipse about the focus, so as to see that it does imply such a force. We must also verify those calculations by which the observed places of

each planet are stated to be included in an ellipse. These calculations involve assumptions respecting the path which the earth describes about the sun, which assumptions must again be verified by reference to observation. And thus, proceeding from step to step, we resolve the most general truths into their constituent parts; and these again into their parts; and by testing, at each step, both the reality of the asserted ingredients and the propriety of the conjunction, we establish the whole system of truths, however wide and various it may be. . . .

10. The analysis of doctrines inductively obtained, into their constituent facts, and the arrangement of them in such a form that the conclusiveness of the induction may be distinctly seen, may be termed *the Logic of Induction*. By *Logic* has generally been meant a system which teaches us so to arrange our reasonings that their truth or falsehood shall be evident in their form. In *deductive* reasonings, in which the general principles are assumed, and the question is concerning their application and combination in particular cases, the device which thus enables us to judge whether our reasonings are conclusive, is the *Syllogism;* and this *form,* along with the rules which belong to it, does in fact supply us with a criterion of deductive or demonstrative reasoning. The *Inductive Table,* such as it is presented in the present chapter, in like manner supplies the means of ascertaining the truth of our *inductive* inferences, so far as the *form* in which our reasoning may be stated can afford such a criterion. Of course some care is requisite in order to reduce a train of demonstration into the form of a series of syllogisms; and certainly not less thought and attention are required for resolving all the main doctrines of any great department of science into a graduated table of co-ordinate and subordinate inductions. But in each case, when this task is once executed, the evidence or want of evidence of our conclusions appears immediately in a most luminous manner. In each step of induction, our Table enumerates the particular facts, and states the general theoretical truth which includes these and which these constitute. The special act of attention by which we satisfy ourselves that the facts *are* so included,— that the general truth *is* so constituted,—then affords little room for errour, with moderate attention and clearness of thought. . . .

12. But when we say that the more general proposition *includes* the several more particular ones, we must recollect what has before been said, that these particulars form the general truth, not by being merely enumerated and added together, but by being seen *in a new light*. No mere verbal recitation of the particulars can decide whether the general proposition is true; a special act of thought is requisite in order to determine how truly each is included in the supposed induc-

tion. In this respect the Inductive Table is not like a mere schedule of accounts, where the rightness of each part of the reckoning is tested by mere addition of the particulars. On the contrary, the Inductive truth is never the mere *sum* of the facts. It is made into something more by the introduction of a new mental element; and the mind, in order to be able to supply this element, must have peculiar endowments and discipline. Thus looking back at the instances noticed in the last article, how are we to see that a convex surface of the earth is necessarily implied by the convergence of meridians towards the north, or by the visible descent of the north pole of the heavens as we travel south? Manifestly the student, in order to see this, must have clear conceptions of the relations of space, either naturally inherent in his mind, or established there by geometrical cultivation,—by studying the properties of circles and spheres. When he is so prepared, he will feel the force of the expressions we have used, that the facts just mentioned are *seen to be consistent* with a globular form of the earth; but without such aptitude he will not see this consistency : and if this be so, the mere assertion of it in words will not avail him in satisfying himself of the truth of the proposition. . . .

14. In the Common or Syllogistic Logic, a certain *Formula* of language is used in stating the reasoning, and is useful in enabling us more readily to apply the Criterion of Form to alleged demonstrations. This formula is the usual Syllogism; with its members, Major Premise, Minor Premise, and Conclusion. It may naturally be asked whether in Inductive Logic there is any such Formula? whether there is any standard form of words in which we may most properly express the inference of a general truth from particular facts?

At first it might be supposed that the formula of Inductive Logic need only be of this kind : "These particulars, and all known particulars of the same kind, are exactly included in the following general proposition." But a moment's reflection on what has just been said will show us that this is not sufficient : for the particulars are not merely *included* in the general proposition. It is not enough that they appertain to it by enumeration. It is, for instance, no adequate example of Induction to say, "Mercury describes an elliptical path, so does Venus, so do the Earth, Mars, Jupiter, Saturn, Uranus; therefore all the Planets describe elliptical paths." This is, as we have seen, the mode of stating the *evidence* when the proposition is once suggested; but the Inductive step consists in the *suggestion* of a conception not before apparent. When Kepler, after trying to connect the observed places of the planet Mars in many other ways, found at last that the conception of an ellipse would include them all, he obtained a truth by induction : for this conclusion was not obviously included in the phenomena, and had not been applied to these facts previously. Thus in our Formula, besides stating that the particulars are included in the general proposition, we must also imply that the generality is constituted by a new Conception, —new at least in its application.

Hence our Inductive Formula might be something like the following : "These particulars, and all known particulars of the same kind, are exactly expressed by adopting the Conceptions and Statement of the following Proposition." It is of course requisite that the Conceptions should be perfectly clear, and should precisely embrace the facts, according to the explanation we have already given of those conditions. . . .

17. I have said that the mind must be properly disciplined in order that it may see the necessary connexion between the facts and the general proposition in which they are included. And the perception of this connexion, though treated as *one step* in our inductive inference, may imply *many steps* of demonstrative proof. The connexion is this, that the particular case is included in the general one, that is, may be *deduced* from it : but this deduction may often require many links of reasoning. Thus in the case of the inference of the law of the force from the elliptical form of the orbit by Newton, the proof that in the ellipse the deflection from the tangent is inversely as the square of the distance from the focus of the ellipse, is a ratiocination consisting of several steps, and involving several properties of Conic Sections; these properties being supposed to be previously established by a geometrical system of demonstration on the special subject of the Conic Sections. In this and similar cases the Induction involves many steps of Deduction. And in such cases, although the Inductive Step, the Invention of the Conception, is really the most important, yet since, when once made, it occupies a familiar place in men's minds; and since the Deductive Demonstration is of considerable length and requires intellectual effort to follow it at every step; men often admire the deductive part of the proposition, the geometrical or algebraical demonstration, far more than that part in which the philosophical merit really resides.

18. Deductive reasoning is virtually a collection of syllogisms, as has already been stated; and in such reasoning, the general principles, the Definitions and Axioms, necessarily stand at the *beginning* of the demonstration. In an inductive inference, the Definitions and Principles are the *final result* of the reasoning, the ultimate effect of the proof. Hence when an Inductive Proposition is to be established by a proof involving several steps of demonstrative reasoning, the enunciation of the Proposition will contain, explicitly or implicitly, principles which

the demonstration proceeds upon as axioms, but which are really inductive inferences. Thus in order to prove that the force which retains a planet in an ellipse varies inversely as the square of the distance, it is taken for granted that the Laws of Motion are true, and that they apply to the planets. Yet the doctrine that this is so, as well as the law of the force, were established only by this and the like demonstrations. The doctrine which is the *hypothesis* of the deductive reasoning, is the *inference* of the inductive process. The special facts which are the basis of the inductive inference, are the conclusion of the train of deduction. And in this manner the deduction establishes the induction. The principle which we gather from the facts is true, because the facts can be derived from it by rigorous demonstration. Induction moves upwards, and deduction downwards, on the same stair.

But still there is a great difference in the character of their movements. Deduction descends steadily and methodically, step by step : Induction mounts by a leap which is out of the reach of method. She bounds to the top of the stair at once; and then it is the business of Deduction, by trying each step in order, to establish the solidity of her companion's footing. Yet these must be processes of the same mind. The Inductive Intellect makes an assertion which is subsequently justified by demonstration; and it shows its sagacity, its peculiar character, by enunciating the proposition when as yet the demonstration does not exist : but then it shows that it *is* sagacity, by also producing the demonstration.

It has been said that inductive and deductive reasoning are contrary in their scheme; that in Deduction we infer particular from general truths; while in Induction we infer general from particular : that Deduction consists of many steps, in each of which we apply known general propositions in particular cases; while in Induction we have a single step, in which we pass from many particular truths to one general proposition. And this is truly said; but though contrary in their motions, the two are the operation of the same mind travelling over the same ground. Deduction is a necessary part of Induction. Deduction justifies by calculation what Induction had happily guessed. Induction recognizes the ore of truth by its weight; Deduction confirms the recognition by chemical analysis. Every step of Induction must be confirmed by rigorous deductive reasoning, followed into such detail as the nature and complexity of the relations (whether of quantity or any other) render requisite. If not so justified by the supposed discoverer, it is *not* Induction.

19. Such Tabular arrangements of propositions as we have constructed may be considered as the *Criterion of Truth* for the doc-

trines which they include. They are the Criterion of Inductive Truth, in the same sense in which Syllogistic Demonstration is the Criterion of Necessary Truth,—of the certainty of conclusions, depending upon evident First Principles. And that such Tables are really a Criterion of the truth of the propositions which they contain, will be plain by examining their structure. For if the connexion which the inductive process assumes be ascertained to be in each case real and true, the assertion of the general proposition merely collects together ascertained truths; and in like manner each of those more particular propositions is true, because it merely expresses collectively more special facts : so that the most general theory is only the assertion of a great body of facts, duly classified and subordinated. When we assert the truth of the Copernican theory of the motions of the solar system, or of the Newtonian theory of the forces by which they are caused, we merely assert the groups of propositions which, in the Table of Astronomical Induction, are included in these doctrines; and ultimately, we may consider ourselves as merely asserting at once so many Facts, and therefore, of course, expressing an indisputable truth.

20. At any one of these steps of Induction in the Table, the inductive proposition is a *Theory* with regard to the Facts which it includes, while it is to be looked upon as a *Fact* with respect to the higher generalizations in which it is included. In any other sense, as was formerly shown, the opposition of Fact and Theory is untenable, and leads to endless perplexity and debate. Is it a Fact or a Theory that the planet Mars revolves in an Ellipse about the Sun? To Kepler, employed in endeavouring to combine the separate observations by the Conception of an Ellipse, it is a Theory; to Newton, engaged in inferring the law of force from a knowledge of the elliptical motion, it is a Fact. There are, as we have already seen, no special attributes of Theory and Fact which distinguish them from one another. Facts are phenomena apprehended by the aid of conceptions and mental acts, as Theories also are. We commonly call our observations *Facts*, when we apply, without effort or consciousness, conceptions perfectly familiar to us : while we speak of Theories, when we have previously contemplated the Facts and the connecting Conception separately, and have made the connexion by a conscious mental act. The real difference is a difference of relation; as the same proposition in a demonstration is the *premise* of one syllogism and the *conclusion* in another;—as the same person is a father and a son. Propositions are Facts and Theories, according as they stand above or below the Inductive Brackets of our Tables. . . .

Laws and Causes*

1. In the first attempts at acquiring an exact and connected knowledge of the appearances and operations which nature presents, men went no further than to learn *what* takes place, not *why* it occurs. They discovered an Order which the phenomena follow, Rules which they obey; but they did not come in sight of the Powers by which these rules are determined, the Causes of which this order is the effect. Thus, for example, they found that many of the celestial motions took place as if the sun and stars were carried round by the revolutions of certain celestial spheres; but what causes kept these spheres in constant motion, they were never able to explain. In like manner in modern times, Kepler discovered that the planets describe ellipses, before Newton explained why they select this particular curve, and describe it in a particular manner. The laws of reflection, refraction, dispersion, and other properties of light have long been known; the causes of these laws are at present under discussion. And the same might be said of many other sciences. The discovery of *the Laws of Phenomena* is, in all cases, the first step in exact knowledge; these Laws may often for a long period constitute the whole of our science; and it is always a matter requiring great talents and great efforts, to advance to a knowledge of the *Causes* of the phenomena.

Hence the larger part of our knowledge of nature, at least of the certain portion of it, consists of the knowledge of the Laws of Phenomena. In Astronomy indeed, besides knowing the rules which guide the appearances, and resolving them into the real motions from which they arise, we can refer these motions to the forces which produce them. In Optics, we have become acquainted with a vast number of laws by which varied and beautiful phenomena are governed; and perhaps we may assume, since the evidence of the undulatory theory has been so fully developed, that we know also the Causes of the Phenomena. But in a large class of sciences, while we have learnt many Laws of Phenomena, the causes by which these are produced are still unknown or

*From Chap. 7, pp. 95-106.

disputed. Are we to ascribe to the operation of a fluid or fluids, and if so, in what manner, the facts of heat, magnetism, electricity, galvanism? What are the forces by which the elements of chemical compounds are held together? What are the forces, of a higher order, as we cannot help believing, by which the course of vital action in organized bodies is kept up? In these and other cases, we have extensive departments of science; but we are as yet unable to trace the effects to their causes; and our science, so far as it is positive and certain, consists entirely of the laws of phenomena. . . .

10. Since it is thus difficult to know when we have seized the true cause of the phenomena in any department of science, it may appear to some persons that physical inquirers are imprudent and unphilosophical in undertaking this research of causes; and that it would be safer and wiser to confine ourselves to the investigation of the laws of phenomena, in which field the knowledge which we obtain is definite and certain. Hence there have not been wanting those who have laid it down as a maxism that "science must study only the laws of phenomena, and never the mode of production."* But it is easy to see that such a maxim would confine the breadth and depth of scientific inquiries to a most scanty and miserable limit. Indeed, such a rule would defeat its own object; for the laws of phenomena, in many cases, cannot be even expressed or understood without some hypothesis respecting their mode of production. How could the phenomena of polarization have been conceived or reasoned upon, except by imagining a polar arrangement of particles, or transverse vibrations, or some equivalent hypothesis? The doctrines of fits of easy transmission, the doctrine of moveable polarization, and the like, even when erroneous as representing the whole of the phenomena, were still useful in combining some of them into laws; and without some such hypotheses the facts could not have been followed out. The doctrine of a fluid caloric may be false; but without imagining such a fluid, how could the movement of heat from one part of a body to another be conceived? It may be replied that Fourier, Laplace, Poisson, who have principally cultivated the Theory of Heat, have not conceived it as a fluid, but have referred conduction to the radiation of the molecules of bodies, which they suppose to be separate points. But this molecular constitution of bodies is itself an assumption of the mode in which the phenomena are produced; and the radiation of heat suggests inquiries concerning a fluid emanation, no less than its conduction does. In like manner, the attempts to connect the laws of phenomena of heat and of gases, have led to hypotheses respecting the constitution of gases, and the combi-

*Comte, *Cours de philosophie positive.*

nation of their particles with those of caloric, which hypotheses may be false, but are probably the best means of discovering the truth.

To debar science from inquiries like these, on the ground that it is her business to inquire into facts, and not to speculate about causes, is a curious example of that barren caution which hopes for truth without daring to venture upon the quest of it. This temper would have stopped with Kepler's discoveries, and would have refused to go on with Newton to inquire into the mode in which the phenomena are produced. It would have stopped with Newton's optical facts, and would have refused to go on with him and his successors to inquire into the mode in which these phenomena are produced. And, as we have abundantly shown, it would, on that very account, have failed in seeing what the phenomena really are.

In many subjects the attempt to study the laws of phenomena, independently of any speculations respecting the causes which have produced them, is neither possible for human intelligence nor for human temper. Men cannot contemplate the phenomena without clothing them in terms of some hypothesis, and will not be schooled to suppress the questionings which at every moment rise up within them concerning the causes of the phenomena. Who can attend to the appearances which come under the notice of the geologist;—strata regularly bedded, full of the remains of animals such as now live in the depths of the ocean, raised to the tops of mountains, broken, contorted, mixed with rocks such as still flow from the mouths of volcanos; —who can see phenomena like these, and imagine that he best promotes the progress of our knowledge of the earth's history, by noting down the facts, and abstaining from all inquiry whether these are really proofs of past states of the earth and of subterraneous forces, or merely an accidental limitation of the effects of such causes? In this and similar cases, to proscribe the inquiry into causes would be to annihilate the science.

Finally, this caution does not even gain its own single end, the escape from hypotheses. For, as we have said, those who will not seek for new and appropriate causes of newly-studied phenomena, are almost inevitably led to ascribe the facts to modifications of causes already familiar. They may declare that they will not hear of such causes as vital powers, elective affinities, electric, or calorific, or luminiferous ethers or fluids; but they will not the less on that account assume hypotheses equally unauthorized; for instance—universal mechanical forces; a molecular constitution of bodies; solid, hard, inert matter;—and will apply these hypotheses in a manner which is arbitrary in itself as well as quite insufficient for its purpose.

11. It appears, then, to be required, both by the analogy of the most successful efforts of science in past times and by the irrepressible speculative powers of the human mind, that we should attempt to discover both the *laws of phenomena*, and their *causes*. In every department of science, when prosecuted far enough, these two great steps of investigation must succeed each other. The laws of phenomena must be known before we can speculate concerning causes; the causes must be inquired into when the phenomena have been reduced to rule. In both these speculations the suppositions and conceptions which occur must be constantly tested by reference to observation and experiment. In both we must, as far as possible, devise hypotheses which, when we thus test them, display those characters of truth of which we have already spoken;—an agreement with facts such as will stand the most patient and rigid inquiry; a provision for predicting truly the results of untried cases; a consilience of inductions from various classes of facts; and a progressive tendency of the scheme to simplicity and unity.

VI

MILL

JOHN STUART MILL (1806-73) was the eldest son of the philosopher and economist James Mill. He was from the start subjected by his father to an exceptionally rigorous education. When only three he began to learn Greek, and this was followed by intensive instruction, first in Latin, mathematics, and history and then, from twelve onward, in logic and political economy. At fourteen he was sent to France, where he attended courses in chemistry, zoology, and higher mathematics; on his return he was introduced to the study of Roman law. While undergoing this comprehensive training he was at the same time imbued with the doctrines of the Benthamite philosophy to which his father subscribed; he was familiar at an early age with the leading representatives of the Utilitarian school, and at eighteen took on the task of editing Bentham's *Rationale of Evidence*. In 1823 Mill entered the Examiner's Office of the East India Company, remaining there for thirty-five years; the work involved did not, however, prevent him from engaging in a range of other activities. Thus he was a frequent contributor to the *Westminster Review*, was a vigorous propagandist—at the London Debating Society and elsewhere —on behalf of radical causes, and from 1834 to 1840 edited the *London Review;* during this period he also published some of his principal writings, including the *System of Logic* (1843) and the *Principles of Political Economy* (1848). In 1858 he retired from his administrative post (he had been appointed Chief of the Examiner's Office two years before) and spent much of the rest of his life in the south of France, at Avignon. Nevertheless, he was a Member of Parliament at Westminster from 1865 to 1868, where he spoke in favor of the 1867 Reform Bill and where he was also active as an advocate of Irish land reform and of women's suffrage. Nor were these years unproductive from a literary point of view. His essay *On Liberty* appeared in 1859, *Considerations on Representative*

188

Government in 1861, *Utilitarianism* in 1863, and *An Examination of Sir William Hamilton's Philosophy* and *Auguste Comte and Positivism* in 1865.

Mill's attitude to the philosophical creed upheld by Bentham and his father was of a somewhat ambivalent character. Partly as a result of a psychological crisis which he suffered in 1826 and of his subsequent reading of Romantic thinkers and poets, he came to feel that the Benthamite outlook was unduly narrow and arid, and much of his own work—particularly in the fields of morals and politics—is expressive of the dissatisfaction he experienced at that time. Yet the moral he typically drew was that the principles of Benthamism required modification and supplementation, not that they should be rejected; moreover, he was at one with his predecessors in his opposition to all "intuitionist" or a priori modes of thinking, regarding these as dangerous in their practical implications as well as being indefensible theoretically. He was, however, acutely conscious that the crudities of traditional forms of empiricism exposed it to obvious objections, and believed that these could only be met by formulating its presuppositions and tenets in a more careful and sophisticated manner.

Mill's *System of Logic*, from which our selections of his work are mostly taken, can thus be seen as being largely an attempt to set the "philosophy of experience" upon a secure foundation, both by examining the nature and credentials of inductive inference and by systematizing the procedures involved in a way that demonstrated their epistemological priority and general applicability. He begins his discussion by criticizing what he thinks are incorrect notions of induction; in particular, he attacks the views of Whewell, which he regards as (among other things) obscuring the central problem of scientific validation or proof. In later chapters Mill develops at considerable length his own theory of the canons by which scientific conclusions may be experimentally assessed and finally justified; though it remains questionable whether he succeeded in the task he set himself. For the methods he describes themselves presuppose the truth of certain very general principles, such as the so-called "law of causation"; and although it is suggested that knowledge of the latter is safely grounded upon past experience, it is hard to see how the argument Mill propounds escapes circularity.

Mill's background and his deep interest in social reform would lead one to expect him to be particularly concerned with the possibility of extending scientific procedures to the investigation of human behavior, especially under its social aspects; and the last section of his book is in fact devoted to this problem. The objection, often made, that such a program would presuppose a denial of human "free-will" is dismissed as resting upon confusions: on the other hand, he was aware that the complexity of the subject matter and the difficulty of applying experimental techniques in this sphere raised special obstacles. Under the influence of Comte, Mill proposed the employment of a method according to which generalizations, arrived at in the first instance by observation and historical enquiry, would be confirmed by connecting them with what he conceived to be the fundamental principles of human nature. As the selection from the chapter on "laws of mind" shows, Mill adopted without demur the "associationist" psychology of Bentham and his father, parts of what he wrote here being among the texts used by F. H. Bradley in his later polemics against empiricist conceptions of the mind and its workings.

The concluding selection is from a different work. Sir William Hamilton (1788-1856) had subscribed to the view that in perception we have a direct or intuitive knowledge of the existence of a world external to ourselves. Mill provided, in his *Examination* of Hamilton's philosophy, an alternative account, giving an explanation in terms of associationist principles of how our belief in such a world arises and subsequently going on to claim that matter may be defined as a "permanent possibility of sensation." This phrase has been cited with approval by a number of contemporary phenomenalists, who have interpreted Mill's views as anticipating their own. Mill's ideas on this subject may also be compared with those of Mach, for their differences as well as for their resemblances.*

*See below, pp. 369-384.

Inductions Improperly So Called*

1. Induction, then, is that operation of the mind by which we infer that what we know to be true in a particular case or cases, will be true in all cases which resemble the former in certain assignable respects. In other words, Induction is the process by which we conclude that what is true of certain individuals of a class is true of the whole class, or that what is true at certain times will be true in similar circumstances at all times.

This definition excludes from the meaning of the term Induction, various logical operations, to which it is not unusual to apply that name.

Induction, as above defined, is a process of inference; it proceeds from the known to the unknown; and any operation involving no inference, any process in which what seems the conclusion is no wider than the premises from which it is drawn, does not fall within the meaning of the term. Yet in the common books of Logic we find this laid down as the most perfect, indeed the only quite perfect, form of induction. In those books, every process which sets out from a less general and terminates in a more general expression,—which admits of being stated in the form, "This and that A are B, therefore every A is B,"—is called an induction, whether anything be really concluded or not : and the induction is asserted not to be perfect, unless every single individual of the class is included in the antecedent, or premise : that is, unless what we affirm of the class has already been ascertained to be true of every individual in it, so that the nominal conclusion is not really a conclusion, but a mere reassertion of the premises. If we were to say, All the planets shine by the sun's light, from observation of each separate planet, or all the Apostles were Jews, because this is true of Peter, Paul, John, and every other apostle,—these, and such as these, would, in the phraseology in question, be called perfect, and the only perfect, Inductions. This, however, is a totally different kind

*From *A System of Logic* (London, 1895), Book III, Chap. 2, pp. 188-200.

of induction from ours; it is not an inference from facts known to facts unknown, but a mere shorthand registration of facts known. The two simulated arguments which we have quoted are not generalisations; the propositions purporting to be conclusions from them are not really general propositions. A general proposition is one in which the predicate is affirmed or denied of an unlimited number of individuals, namely, all, whether few or many, existing or capable of existing, which possess the properties connoted by the subject of the proposition. "All men are mortal" does not mean all now living, but all men past, present, and to come. When the signification of the term is limited so as to render it a name not for any and every individual falling under a certain general description, but only for each of a number of individuals designated as such, and as it were counted off individually, the proposition, though it may be general in its language, is no general proposition, but merely that number of singular propositions, written in an abridged character. The operation may be very useful, as most forms of abridged notation are; but it is no part of the investigation of truth, though often bearing the important part in the preparation of the materials for that investigation.

As we may sum up a definite number of singular propositions in one proposition, which will be apparently, but not really, general, so we may sum up a definite number of general propositions in one proposition, which will be apparently, but not really, more general. If by a separate induction applied to every distinct species of animals, it has been established that each possesses a nervous system, and we affirm thereupon that all animals have a nervous system; this looks like a generalisation though as the conclusion merely affirms of all what has already been affirmed of each, it seems to tell us nothing but what we knew before. A distinction however must be made. If in concluding that all animals have a nervous system, we mean the same thing and no more as if we had said "all known animals," the proposition is not general, and the process by which it is arrived at is not induction. But if our meaning is that the observations made of the various species of animals have discovered to us a law of animal nature, and that we are in a condition to say that a nervous system will be found even in animals yet undiscovered, this indeed is an induction; but in this case the general proposition contains more than the sum of the special propositions from which it is inferred. . . .

2. There are several processes used in mathematics which require to be distinguished from Induction, being not unfrequently called by that name, and being so far similar to Induction properly so called, that the propositions they lead to are really general propositions. For ex-

ample, when we have proved with respect to the circle that a straight line cannot meet it in more than two points, and when the same thing has been successively proved of the ellipse, the parabola, and the hyperbola, it may be laid down as an universal property of the sections of the cone. The distinction drawn in the two previous examples can have no place here, there being no difference between all *known* sections of the cone and *all* sections, since a cone demonstrably cannot be intersected by a plane except in one of these four lines. It would be difficult, therefore, to refuse to the proposition arrived at the name of a generalisation, since there is no room for any generalisation beyond it. But there is no induction, because there is no inference : the conclusion is a mere summing up of what was asserted in the various propositions from which it is drawn. . . .

3. There remains a third improper use of the term Induction, which it is of real importance to clear up, because the theory of Induction has been, in no ordinary degree, confused by it, and because the confusion is exemplified in the most recent and elaborate treatise on the inductive philosophy which exists in our language. The error in question is that of confounding a mere description, by general terms, of a set of observed phenomena, with an induction from them.

Suppose that a phenomenon consists of parts, and that these parts are only capable of being observed separately, and as it were piecemeal. When the observations have been made, there is a convenience (amounting for many purposes to a necessity) in obtaining a representation of the phenomenon as a whole, by combining, or, as we may say piecing those detached fragments together. A navigator sailing in the midst of the ocean discovers land : he cannot at first, or by any one observation, determine whether it is a continent or an island; but he coasts along it, and after a few days finds himself to have sailed completely round it : he then pronounces it an island. Now there was no particular time or place of observation at which he could perceive that this land was entirely surrounded by water; he ascertained the fact by a succession of partial observations, and then selected a general expression which summed up in two or three words the whole of what he so observed. But is there anything of the nature of an induction in this process? Did he infer anything that had not been observed, from something else which had? Certainly not. He had observed the whole of what the proposition asserts. That the land in question is an island, is not an inference from the partial facts which the navigator saw in the course of his circumnavigation; it is the facts themselves; it is a summary of those facts; the description of a complex fact, to which those simpler ones are as the parts of a whole.

Now there is, I conceive, no difference in kind between this simple operation, and that by which Kepler ascertained the nature of the planetary orbits; and Kepler's operation, all at least that was characteristic in it, was not more an inductive act than that of our supposed navigator.

The object of Kepler was to determine the real path described by each of the planets, or let us say by the planet Mars (since it was of that body that he first established the two of his three laws which did not require a comparison of planets). To do this there was no other mode than that of direct observation; and all which observation could do was to ascertain a great number of the successive places of the planet, or rather, of its apparent places. That the planets occupied successively all these positions, or at all events, positions which produced the same impressions on the eye, and that it passed from one of these to another insensibly, and without any apparent breach of continuity; thus much the senses, with the aid of the proper instruments, could ascertain. What Kepler did more than this, was to find what sort of a curve these different points would make, supposing them to be all joined together. He expressed the whole series of the observed places of Mars by what Dr. Whewell calls the general conception of an ellipse. This operation was far from being as easy as that of the navigator who expressed the series of his observations on successive points of the coast by the general conceptions of an island. But it is the very same sort of operation; and if the one is not an indication but a description, this must also be true of the other.

The only real induction concerned in the case consisted in inferring that because the observed places of Mars were correctly represented by points in an imaginary ellipse, therefore Mars would continue to revolve in that same ellipse; and in concluding (before the gap had been filled up by further observations) that the positions of the planet during the time which intervened between two observations, must have coincided with the intermediate points of the curve. For these were facts which had not been directly observed. They were inferences from the observations; facts inferred, as distinguished from facts seen. But these inferences were so far from being a part of Kepler's philosophical operation, that they had been drawn long before he was born. Astronomers had long known that the planets periodically returned to the same places. When this had been ascertained, there was no induction left for Kepler to make, nor did he make any further induction. He merely applied his new conception to the facts inferred, as he did to the facts observed. Knowing already that the planets continued to move in the same paths : when he found that an ellipse correctly represented the past path he knew that it would represent the future path. In finding a compendious expression for the one set of facts, he found one for the other : but he found the expression only, not the inference; nor did he (which is the true test of a general truth) add anything to the power of prediction already possessed.

4. The descriptive operation which enables a number of details to be summed up in a single proposition, Dr. Whewell, by an aptly chosen expression, has termed the Colligation of Facts. In most of his observations concerning that mental process I fully agree, and would gladly transfer all that portion of his book into my own pages. I only think him mistaken in setting up this kind of operation, which, according to the old and received meaning of the term, is not induction at all, as the type of induction generally; and laying down, throughout his work, as principles of induction, the principles of mere colligation.

Dr. Whewell maintains that the general proposition which binds together the particular facts, and makes them, as it were, one fact, is not the mere sum of those facts, but something more, since there is introduced a conception of the mind, which did not exist in the facts themselves. "The particular facts," says he, "are not merely brought together, but there is a new element added to the combination by the very act of thought by which they are combined. . . . When the Greeks, after long observing the motions of the planets, saw that these motions might be rightly considered as produced by the motion of one wheel revolving in the inside of another wheel, these wheels were creations of their minds, added to the facts which they perceived by sense. And even if the wheels were no longer supposed to be material, but were reduced to more geometrical, spheres or circles, they were not the less products of the mind alone,—something additional to the facts observed. The same is the case in all other discoveries. The facts are known, but they are insulated and unconnected, till the discoverer supplies from his own store a principle of connection. The pearls are there, but they will not hang together till some one provides the string."

Let me first remark that Dr. Whewell, in this passage, blends together, indiscriminately, examples of both the processes which I am endeavouring to distinguish from one another. When the Greeks abandoned the supposition that the planetary motions were produced by the revolutions of material wheels, and fell back upon the idea of "mere geometrical spheres or circles," there was more in this change of opinion than the mere substitution of an ideal curve for a physical one. There was the abandonment of a theory, and the replacement of it by a mere description. No one would think of calling the doctrine of material wheels a mere description. That doctrine was an attempt to point out the force by which the planets were acted upon, and compelled to move in their orbits. But when, by a great step in philosophy, the materiality of the wheels was discarded, and the geometrical forms alone retained, the attempt to account for the motions was given up, and what was left of the theory was a mere description of the orbits. The assertion that the planets were carried round by wheels revolving in the inside of other wheels, gave place to the proposition that they moved in the same lines which would be traced by bodies so carried : which was a mere mode of representing the sum of the observed facts; as Kepler's was another and a better mode of representing the same observations.

It is true that for these simply descriptive operations, as well as for the erroneous inductive one, a conception of the mind was required. The conception of an ellipse must have presented itself to Kepler's mind before he could identify the planetary orbits with it. According to Dr. Whewell, the conception was something added to the facts. He expresses himself as if Kepler had put something into the facts by his mode of conceiving them. But Kepler did no such thing. The ellipse was in the facts before Kepler recognised it; just as the island was an island before it had been sailed round. Kepler did not *put* what he had conceived into the facts, but *saw* it in them. A conception implies, and corresponds to, something conceived : and though the conception itself is not in the facts, but in our mind, yet if it is to convey any knowledge relating to them it must be a conception *of* something which really is in the facts, some property which they actually possess, and which they could manifest to our senses if our senses were able to take cognisance of it. If, for instance, the planet left behind it in space a visible track, and if the observer were in a fixed position at such a distance from the plane of the orbit as would enable him to see the whole of it at once, he would see it to be an ellipse; and if gifted with appropriate instruments and powers of locomotion, he would prove it to be such by measuring its different dimensions. Nay, further : if the track were visible, and he were so placed that he could see all parts of it in succession, but not all of them at once, he might be able, by piercing together his successive observations, to discover both that it was an ellipse and that the planet moved in it. The case would then exactly resemble that of the navigator who discovers the land to be an island by sailing round it. If the path was visible, no one I think would dispute that to identify it with an ellipse is to describe it : and I cannot see why any difference should be made by its not being directly an object of sense, when every point in it is as exactly ascertained as if it were so. . . .

5. Dr. Whewell has replied at some length to the preceding obser-

vations, re-stating his opinions, but without (as far as I can perceive) adding anything material to his former arguments. Since, however, mine have not had the good fortune to make any impression upon him, I will subjoin a few remarks, tending to show more clearly in what our difference of opinion consists, as well as, in some measure, to account for it.

Nearly all the definitions of induction, by writers of authority, make it consist in drawing inferences from known cases to unknown; affirming of a class a predicate which has been found true of some cases belonging to the class; concluding, because some things have a certain property, that other things which resemble them have the same property—or because a thing has manifested a property at a certain time, that it has and will have that property at other times.

It can scarcely be contended that Kepler's operation was an Induction in this sense of the term. The statement that Mars moves in an elliptical orbit was no generalisation from individual cases to a class of cases. Neither was it an extension to all time of what had been found true at some particular time. The whole amount of generalisation which the case admitted of was already completed, or might have been so. Long before the elliptic theory was thought of, it had been ascertained that the planets returned periodically to the same apparent places; the series of these places was, or might have been, completely determined, and the apparent course of each planet marked out on the celestial globe in an uninterrupted line. Kepler did not extend an observed truth to other cases than those in which it had been observed : he did not widen the *subject* of the proposition which expressed the observed facts. The alteration he made was in the predicate. Instead of saying, the successive places of Mars are so and so, he summed them up in the statement, that the successive places of Mars are points in an ellipse. It is true this statement, as Dr. Whewell says, was not the sum of the observations *merely;* it was the sum of the observations *seen under a new point of view.* But it was not the sum of *more* than the observations, as a real induction is. It took in no cases but those which had been actually observed, or which could have been inferred from the observations before the new point of view presented itself. There was not that transition from known cases to unknown which constitutes Induction in the original and acknowledged meaning of the term.

Old definitions, it is true, cannot prevail against new knowledge : and if the Keplerian operation, as a logical process, be really identical with what takes place in acknowledged induction, the definition of induction ought to be so widened as to take it in; since scientific language ought to adapt itself to the true relations which subsist be-

tween the things it is employed to designate. Here then it is that I
am at issue with Dr. Whewell. He does think the operations identical.
He allows of no logical process in any case of induction other than what
there was in Kepler's case, namely, guessing until a guess is found
which tallies with the facts; and accordingly, as we shall see hereafter,
he rejects all canons of induction, because it is not by means of them
that we guess. Dr. Whewell's theory of the logic of science would be
very perfect if it did not pass over altogether the question of Proof.
But in my apprehension there is such a thing as proof, and inductions
differ altogether from descriptions in their relation to that element.
Induction is proof; it is inferring something unobserved from something
observed : it requires, therefore, an appropriate test of proof; and to
provide that test is the special purpose of inductive logic. When, on
the contrary, we merely collate known observations, and, in Dr. Whewell's phraseology, connect them by means of a new conception; if the
conception does serve to connect the observations, we have all we want.
As the proposition in which it is embodied pretends to no other truth
than what it may share with many other modes of representing the
same facts, to be consistent with the facts is all it requires : it neither
needs nor admits of proof; though it may serve to prove other things,
inasmuch as, by placing the facts in mental connection with other facts
not previously seen to resemble them, it assimilates the case to another
class of phenomena, concerning which real Inductions have already
been made. Thus Kepler's so-called law brought the orbit of Mars
into the class ellipse, and by doing so, proved all the properties of an
ellipse to be true of the orbit : but in this proof Kepler's law supplied
the minor premise, and not (as is the case with real Inductions) the
major.

    Dr. Whewell calls nothing Induction where there is not a new
mental conception introduced, and everything induction where there
is. But this is to confound two very different things, Invention and
Proof. The introduction of a new conception belongs to Invention :
and invention may be required in any operation, but is the essence of
none. A new conception may be introduced for descriptive purposes,
and so it may for inductive purposes. But it is so far from constituting
induction, that induction does not necessarily stand in need of it.
Most inductions require no conception but what was present in every
one of the particular instances on which the induction is grounded.
That all men are mortal is surely an inductive conclusion; yet no new
conception is introduced by it. Whoever knows that any man has died,
has all the conceptions involved in the inductive generalisation. But
Dr. Whewell considers the process of invention, which consists in fram-

ing a new conception consistent with the facts, to be not merely a necessary part of all induction, but the whole of it.

The mental operation which extracts from a number of detached observations certain general characters in which the observed phenomena resemble one another, or resemble other known facts, is what Bacon, Locke, and most subsequent metaphysicians, have understood by the word Abstraction. A general expression obtained by abstraction, connecting known facts by means of common characters, but without concluding from them to unknown, may, I think, with strict logical correctness, be termed a Description; nor do I know in what other way things can ever be described. My position, however, does not depend on the employment of that particular word : I am quite content to use Dr. Whewell's term Colligation, or the more general phrases, "mode of representing, or of expressing, phenomena;" provided it be clearly seen that the process is not Induction, but something radically different. . . .

The Ground of Induction*

1. Induction, properly so called, as distinguished from those mental operations, sometimes though improperly designated by the name, which I have attempted in the preceding chapter to characterise, may, then, be summarily defined as Generalisation from Experience. It consists in inferring from some individual instances in which a phenomenon is observed to occur, that it occurs in all instances of a certain class; namely, in all which *resemble* the former, in what are regarded as the material circumstances.

In what way the material circumstances are to be distinguished from those which are immaterial, or why some of the circumstances are material and others not so, we are not yet ready to point out. We must first observe that there is a principle implied in the very statement of what Induction is an assumption with regard to the course of nature and the order of the universe; namely, that there are such things in nature as parallel cases; that what happens once will, under a sufficient degree of similarity of circumstances, happen again, and not only again, but as often as the same circumstances recur. This, I say, is an assumption involved in every case of induction. And if we consult the actual course of nature, we find that the assumption is warranted. The universe, so far as known to us, is so constituted, that whatever is true in any one case, is true in all cases of a certain description; the only difficulty is, to find what description.

This universal fact, which is our warrant for all inferences from experience, has been described by different philosophers in different forms of language; that the course of nature is uniform; that the universe is governed by general laws; and the like. One of the most usual of those modes of expression, but also one of the most inadequate, is that which has been brought into familiar use by the metaphysicians of the school of Reid and Stewart. The disposition of the human mind to generalise from experience,—a propensity considered

*Ibid., Chap. 3, pp. 200-206.

by these philosophers as an instinct of our nature,—they usually describe under some such name as "our intuitive conviction that the future will resemble the past." Now it has been well pointed out by Mr. Bailey, that (whether the tendency be or not an original and ulti- mate element of our nature) Time, in its modifications of past, present, and future, has no concern either with the belief itself, or with the grounds of it. We believe that fire will burn to-morrow, because it burned to-day and yesterday; but we believe, on precisely the same grounds, that it burned before we were born, and that it burns this very day in Cochin-China. It is not from the past to the future, as past and future, that we infer, but from the known to the unknown; from facts observed to facts unobserved; from what we have perceived, or been directly conscious of, to what has not come within our experience. In this last predicament is the whole region of the future; but also the vastly greater portion of the present and of the past.

Whatever be the most proper mode of expressing it, the proposi- tion that the course of nature is uniform is the fundamental principle, or general axiom, of Induction. It would yet be a great error to offer this large generalisation as any explanation of the inductive process. On the contrary, I hold it to be itself an instance of induction, and induction by no means of the most obvious kind. Far from being the first induction we make, it is one of the last, or at all events one of those which are latest in attaining strict philosophical accuracy. As a general maxim, indeed, it has secretly entered into the minds of any but phi- losophers; nor even by them, as we shall have many opportunities of remarking, have its extent and limits been always very justly conceived. The truth is, that this great generalisation is itself founded on prior generalisations. The obscurer laws of nature were discovered by means of it, but the more obvious ones must have been understood and as- sented to as general truths before it was ever heard of. We should never have thought of affirming that all phenomena take place according to general laws, if we had not first arrived, in the case of a great multitude of phenomena, at some knowledge of the laws themselves; which could be done no otherwise than by induction. In what sense, then, can a principle, which is so far from being our earliest induction, be regarded as our warrant for all the others? In the only sense in which (as we have already seen) the general propositions which we place at the head of our reasonings when we throw them into syllogisms ever really contrib- ute to their validity. As Archbishop Whately remarks, every induction is a syllogism with the major premise suppressed; or (as I prefer expres- sing it) every induction may be thrown into the form of a syllogism by supplying a major premise. If this be actually done, the principle which we are now considering, that of the uniformity of the course of nature, will appear as the ultimate major premise of all inductions, and will, therefore, stand to all inductions in the relation in which, as has been shown at so much length, the major proposition of a syllogism always stands to the conclusion; not contributing at all to prove it, but being a necessary condition of its being proved; since no conclusion is proved for which there cannot be found a true major premise.

The statement that the uniformity of the course of nature is the ultimate major premise in all cases of induction may be thought to require some explanation. The immediate major premise in every inductive argument it certainly is not. Of that Archbishop Whately's must be held to be the correct account. The induction, "John, Peter, &c., are mortal, therefore all mankind are mortal," may, as he justly says, be thrown into a syllogism prefixing as a major premise, (what is at any rate a necessary condition of the validity of the argument,) namely, that what is true of John, Peter, &c., is true of all mankind. But how came we by this major premise? It is not self-evident; nay, in all cases of unwarranted generalisation it is not true. How, then, is it arrived at? Necessarily either by induction or ratiocination; and if by induction, the process, like all other inductive arguments, may be thrown into the form of a syllogism. This previous syllogism it is, therefore, necessary to construct. There is, in the long-run, only one possible construction. The real proof that what is true of John Peter, &c., is true of all mankind, can only be, that a different supposition would be inconsistent with the uniformity which we know to exist in the course of nature. Whether there would be this inconsistency or not, may be a matter of long and delicate inquiry; but unless there would, we have no sufficient ground for the major of the inductive syllogism. It hence appears, that if we throw the whole course of any inductive argument into a series of syllogisms, we shall arrive by more or fewer steps at an ultimate syllogism, which will have for its major premise the principle or axiom of the uniformity of the course of nature.

It was not to be expected that in the case of this axiom, any more than of other axioms, there should be unanimity among thinkers with respect to the ground on which it is to be received as true. I have already stated that I regard it as itself a generalisation from experience. Others hold it to be a principle which, antecedently to any verification by experience, we are compelled by the constitution of our thinking faculty to assume as true. Having so recently, and at so much length, combated a similar doctrine as applied to the axioms of mathematics by arguments which are in a great measure applicable to the present case, I shall defer the more particular discussion of this controverted point in regard to the fundamental axiom of induction until a more advanced period of our inquiry. At present, it is of more importance to understand thoroughly the import of the axiom itself. For the proposition, that the course of nature is uniform, possesses rather the brevity suitable to popular, than the precision requisite in philosophical language : its terms require to be explained, and a stricter than their ordinary signification given to them, before the truth of the assertion can be admitted.

2. Every person's consciousness assures him that he does not always expect uniformity in the course of events; he does not always believe that the unknown will be similar to the known, that the future will resemble the past. Nobody believes that the succession of rain and fine weather will be the same in every future year as in the present. Nobody expects to have the same dreams repeated every night. On the contrary, everybody mentions it as something extraordinary if the course of nature is constant, and resembles itself in these particulars. To look for constancy where constancy is not to be expected, as, for instance, that a day which has once brought good fortune will always be a fortunate day, is justly accounted superstition.

The course of nature, in truth, is not only uniform, it is also infinitely various. Some phenomena are always seen to recur in the very same combinations in which we met with them at first; others seem altogether capricious; while some, which we had been accustomed to regard as bound down exclusively to a particular set of combinations, we unexpectedly find detached from some of the elements with which we had hitherto found them conjoined, and united to others of quite a contrary description. To an inhabitant of Central Africa fifty years ago no fact probably appeared to rest on more uniform experience than this, that all human beings are black. To Europeans not many years ago, the proposition, All swans are white, appeared an equally unequivocal instance of uniformity in the course of nature. Further experience has proved to both that they were mistaken; but they had to wait fifty centuries for this experience. During that long time, mankind believed in an uniformity of the course of nature where no such uniformity really existed.

According to the notion which the ancients entertained of induction, the foregoing were cases of as legitimate inference as any inductions whatever. In these two instances, in which, the conclusion being false, the ground of inference must have been insufficient, there was, nevertheless, as much ground for it as this conception of induction admitted of. The induction of the ancients has been well described by Bacon, under the name of "Inductio per enumerationem simplicem, ubi non reperitur instantia contradictoria." It consists in ascribing the character of general truths to all propositions which are true in every instance that we happen to know of. This is the kind of induction which is natural to the mind when unaccustomed to scientific methods. The tendency, which some call an instinct, and which others account for by association, to infer the future from the past, the known from the unknown, is simply a habit of expecting that what has been found true once or several times, and never yet found false, will be found true again. Whether the instances are few or many, conclusive or inconclusive, does not much affect the matter : these are considerations which occur only on reflection : the unprompted tendency of the mind is to generalise its experience, provided this points all in one direction; provided no other experience of a conflicting character comes unsought. The notion of seeking it, of experimenting for it, of *interrogating* nature (to use Bacon's expression) is of much later growth. The observation of nature by uncultivated intellects is purely passive : they accept the facts which present themselves, without taking the trouble of searching for more : it is a superior mind only which asks itself what facts are needed to enable it to come to a safe conclusion, and then looks out for these.

But though we have always a propensity to generalise from unvarying experience, we are not always warranted in doing so. Before we can be at liberty to conclude that something is universally true because we have never known an instance to the contrary, we must have reason to believe that if there were in nature any instances to the contrary, we should have known of them. This assurance, in the great majority of cases, we cannot have, or can have only in a very moderate degree. The possibility of having it is the foundation on which we shall see hereafter that induction by simple enumeration may in some remarkable cases amount practically to proof. No such assurance, however, can be had on any of the ordinary subjects of scientific inquiry. Popular notions are usually founded on induction by simple enumeration; in science it carries us but a little way. We are forced to begin with it; we must often rely on it provisionally, in the absence of means of more searching investigation. But, for the accurate study of nature, we require a surer and a more potent instrument.

It was, above all, by pointing out the insufficiency of this rude and loose conception of Induction that Bacon merited the title so generally awarded to him of Founder of the Inductive Philosophy. The value of his own contributions to a more philosophical theory of the subject has certainly been exaggerated. Although (along with some fundamental errors) his writings contain, more or less fully developed, several of the most important principles of the Inductive Method, physical investigation has now far outgrown the Baconian conception of Induction. Moral and political inquiry, indeed, are as yet far behind that conception. The current and improved modes of reasoning on these subjects are still of the same vicious description against which Bacon protested; the method almost exclusively employed by those professing to treat such matters inductively, is the very *inductio per enumerationem simplicem* which he condemns; and the experience which we hear so confidently appealed to by all sects, parties, and interests is still, in his own emphatic words, *mera palpatio.*

3. In order to[have]a better understanding of the problem which the logician must solve if he would establish a scientific theory of Induction, let us compare a few cases of incorrect inductions with others which are acknowledged to be legitimate. Some, we know, which were believed for centuries to be correct, were nevertheless incorrect. That all swans are white, cannot have been a good induction, since the conclusion has turned out erroneous. The experience, however, on which the conclusion rested was genuine. From the earliest records, the testimony of the inhabitants of the known world was unanimous on the point. The uniform experience, therefore, of the inhabitants of the known world, agreeing in a common result, without one known instance of deviation from that result, is not always sufficient to establish a general conclusion.

But let us now turn to an instance apparently not very dissimilar to this. Mankind were wrong, it seems, in concluding that all swans were white; are we also wrong when we conclude that all men's heads grow above their shoulders, and never below, in spite of the conflicting testimony of the naturalist Pliny? As there were black swans, though civilised people had existed for three thousand years on the earth without meeting with them, may there not also be "men whose heads do grow beneath their shoulders," notwithstanding a rather less perfect unanimity of negative testimony from observers? Most persons would answer No; it was more credible that a bird should vary in its colour than that man should vary in the relative position of their principal organs. And there is no doubt that in so saying they would be right; but to say why they are right would be impossible, without entering more deeply than is usually done into the true theory of Induction.

Again, there are cases in which we reckon with the most unfailing confidence upon uniformity, and other cases in which we do not count upon it at all. In some we feel complete assurance that the future will resemble the past, the unknown be precisely similar to the known. In others, however invariable may be the result obtained from the instances which have been observed, we draw from them no more than a very feeble presumption that the like result will hold in all other cases. That a straight line is the shortest distance between two points, we do not doubt to be true even in the region of the fixed stars. When a chemist announces the existence and properties of a newly discovered substance, if we confide in his accuracy, we feel assured that the conclusions he has arrived at will hold universally, though the induction be founded but on a single instance. We do not withhold our assent, waiting for a repetition or the experiment; or if we do, it is from a doubt whether the one experiment was properly made, not whether, if properly made, it would be conclusive. Here, then, is a general law of nature, inferred without hesitation from a single instance; an universal proposition from a singular one. Now mark another case, and contrast it with this. Not all the instances which have been observed since the beginning of the world in support of the general proposition that all crows are black would be deemed a sufficient presumption of the truth of the proposition, to outweigh the testimony of one unexceptionable witness who should affirm that in some region of the earth not fully explored he had caught and examined a crow, and had found it to be grey.

Why is a single instance, in some cases, sufficient for a complete induction, while in others myriads of concurring instances, without a single exception known or presumed, go such a very little way towards establishing an universal proposition? Whoever can answer this question knows more of the philosophy of logic than the wisest of the ancients, and has solved the problem of Induction.

Liberty and Necessity*

1. The question whether the law of causality applies in the same strict sense to human actions as to other phenomena, is the celebrated controversy concerning the freedom of the will, which, from at least as far back as the time of Pelagius, has divided both the philosophical and the religious world. The affirmative opinion is commonly called the doctrine of Necessity, as asserting human volitions and actions to be necessary and inevitable. The negative maintains that the will is not determined, like other phenomena, by antecedents, but determines itself; that our volitions are not, properly speaking, the effects of causes, or at least have no causes which they uniformly and implicitly obey.

I have already made it sufficiently apparent that the former of these opinions is that which I consider the true one; but the misleading terms in which it is often expressed, and the indistinct manner in which it is usually apprehended, have both obstructed its reception and perverted its influence when received. The metaphysical theory of free-will, as held by philosophers, (for the practical feeling of it, common in the greater or less degree to all mankind, is in no way inconsistent with the contrary theory,) was invented because the supposed alternative of admitting human actions to be *necessary* was deemed inconsistent with every one's instinctive consciousness, as well as humiliating to the pride, and even degrading to the moral nature, of man. Nor do I deny that the doctrine, as sometimes held, is open to these imputations; for the misapprehension in which I shall be able to show that they originate unfortunately is not confined to the opponents of the doctrine, but is participated in by many, perhaps we might say by most, of its supporters.

2. Correctly conceived, the doctrine called Philosophical Necessity is simply this : that given the motives which are present to an individual's mind, and given likewise the character and disposition of the individual, the manner in which he will act might be unerringly inferred; that if we

*From Book VI, Chap. 2, pp. 547-552.

knew the person thoroughly, and knew all the inducements which are acting upon him, we could foretell his conduct with as much certainty as we can predict any physical event. This proposition I take to be a mere interpretation of universal experience, a statement in words of what every one is internally convinced of. No one who believed that he knew thoroughly the circumstances of any case, and the characters of the different persons concerned, would hesitate to foretell how all of them would act. Whatever degree of doubt he may in fact feel arises from the uncertainty whether he really knows the circumstances, or the character of some one or other of the persons, with the degree of accuracy required; but by no means from thinking that if he did know these things, there could be any uncertainty what the conduct would be. Nor does this full assurance conflict in the smallest degree with what is called our feeling of freedom. We do not feel ourselves the less free because those to whom we are intimately known are well assured how we shall will to act in a particular case. We often, on the contrary, regard the doubt what our conduct will be as a mark of ignorance of our character, and sometimes even resent it as an imputation. The religious metaphysicians who have asserted the freedom of the will have always maintained it to be consistent with divine foreknowledge of our actions; and if with divine, then with any other foreknowledge. We may be free, and yet another may have reason to be perfectly certain what use we shall make of our freedom. It is not, therefore, the doctrine that our volitions and actions are invariable consequents of our antecedent states of mind, that is either contradicted by our consciousness or felt to be degrading.

But the doctrine of causation, when considered as obtaining between our volitions and their antecedents, is almost universally conceived as involving more than this. Many do not believe, and very few practically feel, that there is nothing in causation but invariable, certain, and unconditional sequence. There are few to whom mere constancy of succession appears a sufficiently stringent bond of union for so peculiar a relation as that of cause and effect. Even if the reason repudiates, the imagination retains the feeling of some more intimate connection, of some peculiar tie or mysterious constraint exercised by the antecedent over the consequent. Now this it is which, considered as applying to the human will, conflicts with our consciousness and revolts our feelings. We are certain that, in the case of our volitions, there is not this mysterious constraint. We know that we are not compelled, as by a magical spell, to obey any particular motive. We feel that if we wished to prove that we have the power of resisting the motive, we could do so, (that wish being, it needs scarcely be observed, a *new ante-*

cedent;) and it would be humiliating to our pride, and (what is of more importance) paralysing to our desire of excellence, if we thought otherwise. But neither is any such mysterious compulsion now supposed, by the best philosophical authorities, to be exercised by any other cause over its effect. Those who think that causes draw their effects after them by a mystical tie are right in believing that the relation between volitions and their antecedents is of another nature. But they should go farther, and admit that this is also true of all other effects and their antecedents. If such a tie is considered to be involved in the word necessity, the doctrine is not true of human actions; but neither is it then true of inanimate objects. It would be more correct to say that matter is not bound by necessity, than that mind is so.

That the free-will metaphysicians, being mostly of the school which rejects Hume's and Brown's analysis of Cause and Effect, should miss their way for want of the light which that analysis affords, cannot surprise us. The wonder is, that the Necessitarians, who usually admit that philosophical theory, should in practice equally lose sight of it. The very same misconception of the doctrine called Philosophical Necessity which prevents the opposite party from recognising its truth, I believe to exist more or less obscurely in the minds of most Necessitarians, however they may in words disavow it. I am much mistaken if they habitually feel that the necessity which they recognize in actions is but uniformity of order, and capability of being predicted. They have a feeling as if there were at bottom a stronger tie between the volitions and their causes : as if, when they asserted that the will is governed by the balance of motives, they meant something more cogent than if they had only said, that whoever knew the motives, and our habitual susceptibilities to them, could predict how we should will to act. They commit, in opposition to their own scientific system, the very same mistake which their adversaries commit in obedience to theirs; and in consequence do really in some instances suffer those depressing consequences which their opponents erroneously impute to the doctrine itself.

3. I am inclined to think that this error is almost wholly an effect of the associations with a word, and that it would be prevented by forbearing to employ, for the expression of the simple fact of causation, so extremely inappropriate a term as Necessity. That word, in its other acceptations, involves much more than mere uniformity of sequence : it implies irresistibleness. Applied to the will, it only means that the given cause will be followed by the effect, subject to all possibilities of counteraction by other causes; but in common use it stands for the operation of those causes exclusively, which are supposed too powerful

to be counteracted at all. When we say that all human actions take place of necessity, we only mean that they will certainly happen if nothing prevents :—when we say that dying of want, to those who cannot get food, is a necessity, we mean that it will certainly happen, whatever may be done to prevent it. The application of the same term to the agencies on which human actions depend as is used to express those agencies of nature which are really uncontrollable, cannot fail, when habitual, to create a feeling of uncontrollableness in the former also. This, however, is a mere illusion. There are physical sequences which we call necessary, as death for want of food or air; there are others which, though as much cases of causation as the former, are not said to be necessary, as death from poison, which an antidote, or the use of the stomach-pump, will sometimes avert. It is apt to be forgotten by people's feelings, even if remembered by their understandings, that human actions are in this last predicament : they are never (except in some cases of mania) ruled by any one motive with such absolute sway that there is no room for the influence of any other. The causes, therefore, on which action depends are never uncontrollable, and any given effect is only necessary provided that the causes tending to produce it are not controlled. That whatever happens could not have happened otherwise unless something had taken place which was capable of preventing it, no one surely needs hesitate to admit. But to call this by the name necessity is to use the term in a sense so different from its primitive and familiar meaning, from that which it bears in the common occasions of life, as to amount almost to a play upon words. The associations derived from the ordinary sense of the term will adhere to it in spite of all we can do; and though the doctrine of Necessity, as stated by most who hold it, is very remote from fatalism, it is probable that most Necessitarians are Fatalists, more or less, in their feelings.

A Fatalist believes, or half believes, (for nobody is a consistent Fatalist,) not only that whatever is about to happen will be the infallible result of the causes which produce it, (which is the true Necessitarian doctrine,) but, moreover, that there is no use in struggling against it; that it will happen however we may strive to prevent it. Now, a Necessitarian, believing that our actions follow from our characters, and that our characters follow from our organisation, our education, and our circumstances, is apt to be, with more or less of consciousness on his part, a Fatalist as to his own actions, and to believe that his nature is such, or that his education and circumstances have so moulded his character, that nothing can now prevent him from feeling and acting in a particular way, or at least that no effort of his own can hinder

it. In the words of the sect which in our own day has most perseveringly
inculcated and most perversely misunderstood this great doctrine, his
character is formed *for* him. and not *by* him; therefore his wishing that
it had been formed differently is of no use; he has no power to alter it.
But this is a grand error. He has, to a certain extent a power to alter
his character. Its being, in the ultimate resort, formed for him, is not
inconsistent with its being, in part, formed *by* him as one of the intermediate agents. His character is formed by his circumstances, (including among these his particular organisation,) but his own desire to
mould it in a particular way is one of those circumstances, and by the
means one of the least influential. We cannot, indeed, directly will to
be different from what we are; but neither did those who are supposed
to have formed our characters directly will that we should be what we
are. Their will had no direct power except over their own actions.
They made us what they did make us by willing, not the end, but the
requisite means; and we, when our habits are not too inveterate, can,
by similarly willing the requisite means, make ourselves different. If
they could place us under the influence of certain circumstances, we in
like manner can place ourselves under the influence of other circumstances. We are exactly as capable of making our own character, *if
we will*, as others are of making it for us.

Yes, (answers the Owenite,) but these words, "if we will," surrender
the whole point, since the will to alter our own character is given us,
not by any efforts of ours, but by circumstances which we cannot
help; it comes to us either from external causes or not at all. Most
true : if the Owenite stops here, he is in a position from which nothing
can expel him. Our character is formed by us as well as for us, but the
wish which induces us to attempt to form it is formed for us; and how?
Not, in general, by our organisation, nor wholly by our education, but
by our experience—experience of the painful consequences of the
character we previously had, or by some strong feeling of admiration
or aspiration accidentally aroused. But to think that we have no power
of altering our character, and to think that we shall not use our power
unless we desire to us it, are very different things and have a very
different effect on the mind. A person who does not wish to alter his
character cannot be the person who is supposed to feel discouraged
or paralysed by thinking himself unable to do it. The depressing effect
of the Fatalist doctrine can only be felt where there *is* a wish to do
what that doctrine represents as impossible. It is of no consequence
what we think forms our character, when we have no desire of our own
about forming it, but it is of great consequence that we should not be
prevented from forming such a desire by thinking the attainment im-

practicable, and that if we have the desire we should know that the work is not so irrevocably done as to be incapable of being altered.

And, indeed if we examine closely, we shall find that this feeling, of our being able to modify our own character *if we wish* is itself the feeling of moral freedom which we are conscious of. A person feels morally free who feels that his habits or his temptations are not his masters, but he theirs : who even in yielding to them knows that he could resist : that were he desirous of altogether throwing them off, there would not be required for that purpose a stronger desire than he knows himself to be capable of feeling. It is of course necessary, to render our consciousness of freedom complete, that we should have succeeded in making our character all we have hitherto attempted to make it; for if we have wished and not attained, we have, to that extent, not power over our own character—we are not free. Or at least, we must feel that our wish, if not strong enough to alter our character, is strong enough to conquer our character when the two are brought into conflict in any particular case of conduct. And hence it is said with truth, that none but a person of confirmed virtue is completely free.

The application of so improper a term as Necessity to the doctrine of cause and effect in the matter of human character seems to me one of the most signal instances in philosophy of the abuse of terms, and its practical consequences one of the most striking examples of the power of language over our associations. The subject will never be generally understood until that objectionable term is dropped. The free-will doctrine, by keeping in view precisely that portion of the truth which the word Necessity puts out of sight, namely, the power of the mind to co-operate in the formation of its own character, has given to its adherents a practical feeling much nearer to the truth than has generally (I believe) existed in the minds of Necessitarians. The latter may have had a stronger sense of the importance of what human beings can do to shape the characters of one another; but the free-will doctrine has, I believe, fostered in its supporters a much stronger spirit of self-culture.

4. There is still one fact which requires to be noticed (in addition to the existence of a power of self-formation) before the doctrine of the causation of human actions can be freed from the confusion and misapprehensions which surround it in many minds. When the will is said to be determined by motives, a motive does not mean always, or solely, the anticipation of a pleasure or of a pain. I shall not here inquire whether it be true that, in the commencement, all our voluntary actions are mere means consciously employed to obtain some pleasure or avoid some pain. It is at least certain that we gradually,

through the influence of association, come to desire the means without thinking of the end : the action itself becomes an object of desire, and is performed without reference to any motive beyond itself. Thus far, it may still be objected, that the action having through association become pleasurable, we are, as much as before, moved to act by the anticipation of a pleasure, namely, the pleasure of the action itself. But granting this, the matter does not end here. As we proceed in the formation of habits, and become accustomed to will a particular act or a particular course of conduct because it is pleasurable, we at last continue to will it without any reference to its being pleasurable. Although, from some change in us or in our circumstances, we have ceased to find any pleasure in the action, or perhaps to anticipate any pleasure as the consequence of it, we still continue to desire the action, and consequently to do it. In this manner it is that habits of hurtful excess continue to be practised although they have ceased to be pleasurable; and in this manner also it is that the habit of willing to persevere in the course which he has chosen does not desert the moral hero, even when the reward, however real, which he doubtless receives from the consciousness of well-doing, is anything but an equivalent for the sufferings he undergoes or the wishes which he may have to renounce.

A habit of willing is commonly called a purpose; and among the causes of our volitions, and of the actions which flow from them, must be reckoned not only likings and aversions, but also purposes. It is only when our purposes have become independent of the feelings of pain or pleasure from which they originally took their rise that we are said to have a confirmed character. "A character," says Novalis, "is a completely fashioned will," and the will, once so fashioned, may be steady and constant, when the passive susceptibilities of pleasure and pain are greatly weakened or materially changed.

With the corrections and explanations now given, the doctrine of the causation of our volitions by motives, and of motives by the desirable objects offered to us, combined with our particular susceptibilities of desire, may be considered, I hope, as sufficiently established for the purposes of this treatise.

Human Nature as a Subject of Science*

1. It is a common notion or at least it is implied in many common modes of speech, that the thoughts, feelings, and actions of sentient beings are not a subject of science, in the same strict sense in which this is true of the objects of outward nature. This notion seems to involve some confusion of ideas, which it is necessary to begin by clearing up.

Any facts are fitted, in themselves, to be a subject of science, which follow one another according to constant laws; although those laws may not have been discovered, nor even be discoverable by our existing resources. Take, for instance, the most familiar class of meteorological phenomena, those of rain and sunshine. Scientific inquiry has not yet succeeded in ascertaining the order of antecedence and consequence among these phenomena, so as to be able, at least in our regions of the earth, to predict them with certainty or even with any high degree of probability. Yet no one doubts that the phenomena depend on laws, and that these must be derivative laws resulting from known ultimate laws, those of heat, electricity, vaporisation, and elastic fluids. Nor can it be doubted that if we were acquainted with all the antecedent circumstances, we could, even from those more general laws, predict (saving difficulties of calculation) the state of the weather at any future time. Meteorology, therefore, not only has in itself every natural requisite for being, but actually is, a science; though, from the difficulty of observing the facts on which the phenomena depend, (a difficulty inherent in the peculiar nature of those phenomena,) the science is extremely imperfect; and were it perfect, might probably be of little avail in practice, since the data requisite for applying its principles to particular instances would rarely be procurable.

A case may be conceived of an intermediate character between the perfection of science and this its extreme imperfection. It may happen that the greater causes, those on which the principal part of the phe-

Ibid., Chap. 3, pp. 552-555.

nomena depends, are within the reach of observation and measurement; so that if no other causes intervened, a complete explanation could be given not only of the phenomenon in general, but of all the variations and modifications which it admits of. But inasmuch as other, perhaps many other causes, separately insignificant in their effects, co-operate or conflict in many or in all cases with those greater causes, the effect, accordingly, presents more or less of aberration from what would be produced by the greater causes alone. Now if these minor causes are not so constantly accessible, or not accessible at all to accurate observation, the principal mass of the effect may still, as before, be accounted for, and even predicted; but there will be variations and modifications which we shall not be competent to explain thoroughly, and our predictions will not be fulfilled accurately, but only approximately.

It is thus, for example, with the theory of the tides. No one doubts that Tidology (as Dr. Whewell proposes to call it) is really a science. As much of the phenomena as depends on the attraction of the sun and moon is completely understood, and may in any, even unknown, part of the earth's surface be foretold with certainty; and the far greater part of the phenomena depends on those causes. But circumstances of a local or casual nature, such as the configuration of the bottom of the ocean, the degree of confinement from shores, the direction of the wind, &c., influence in many or in all places the height and time of the tide; and a portion of these circumstances being either not accurately knowable, nor precisely measurable, or not capable of being certainly foreseen, the tide in known places commonly varies from the calculated result of general principles by some difference that we cannot explain, and in unknown ones may vary from it by a difference that we are not able to foresee or conjecture. Nevertheless, not only is it certain that these variations depend on causes, and follow their causes by laws of unerring uniformity; not only, therefore, is tidology a science, like meteorology, but it is what, hitherto at least, meteorology is not, a science largely available in practice. General laws may be laid down respecting the tides; predictions may be founded on those laws but the result will in the main, though often not with complete accuracy, correspond to the predictions.

And this is what is or ought to be meant by those who speak of sciences which are not *exact* sciences. Astronomy was once a science, without being an exact science. It could not become exact until not only the general course of the planetary motions, but the perturbations also, were accounted for, and referred to their causes. It has become an exact science, because its phenomena have been brought under laws comprehending the whole of the causes by which the phenomena are influenced, whether in a great or only in a trifling degree, whether in all or only in some cases, and assigning to each of those causes the share of effect which really belongs to it. But in the theory of the tides, the only laws as yet accurately ascertained are those of the causes which affect the phenomenon in all cases, and in a considerable degree; while others which affect it in some cases only, or, if in all, only in a slight degree, have not been sufficiently ascertained and studied to enable us to lay down their laws, still less to deduce the completed law of the phenomenon, by compounding the effects of the greater with those of the minor causes. Tidology, therefore, is not yet an exact science; not from any inherent incapacity of being so, but from the difficulty of ascertaining with complete precision the real derivative uniformities. By combining, however, the exact laws of the greater causes, and of such of the minor ones as are sufficiently known, with such empirical laws or such approximate generalisations respecting the miscellaneous variations as can be obtained by specific observation, we can lay down general propositions which will be true in the main, and on which, with allowance for the degree of their probable inaccuracy, we may safely ground our expectations and our conduct.

2. The science of human nature is of this description. It falls far short of the standard of exactness now realised in Astronomy; but there is no reason that it should not be as much a science as Tidology is, or as Astronomy was when its calculations had only mastered the main phenomena, but not the perturbations.

The phenomena with which this science is conversant being the thoughts, feelings, and actions of human beings, it would have attained the ideal perfection of a science if it enabled us to foretell how an individual would think, feel, or act throughout life, with the same certainty with which astronomy enables us to predict the places and the occultations of the heavenly bodies. It needs scarcely be stated that nothing approaching to this can be done. The actions of individuals could not be predicted with scientific accuracy, were it only because we cannot foresee the whole of the circumstances in which those individuals will be placed. But further, even in any given combination of (present) circumstances, no assertion, which is both precise and universally true, can be made respecting the manner in which human beings will think, feel, or act. This is not, however, because every person's modes of thinking, feeling, and acting do not depend on causes; nor can we doubt that if, in the case of any individual, our data could be complete, we even now know enough of the ultimate laws by which mental phenomena are determined to enable us in many cases to predict, with tolerable certainty, what, in the greater number of supposable combinations of circumstances, his conduct or sentiments would be. But the impressions and actions of human beings are not solely the result of their present circumstances, but the joint result of those circumstances and of the characters of the individuals; and the agencies which determine human character are so numerous and diversified, (nothing which has happened to the person throughout life being without its portion of influence,) that in the aggregate they are never in any two cases exactly similar. Hence, even if our science of human nature were theoretically perfect, that is, if we could calculate any character as we can calculate the orbit of any planet *from given data;* still, as the data are never all given, nor ever precisely alike in different cases, we could neither make positive predictions, nor lay down universal propositions.

Inasmuch, however, as many of those effects which it is of most importance to render amenable to human foresight and control are determined, like the tides, in an incomparably greater degree by general causes, than by all partial causes taken together; depending in the main on those circumstances and qualities which are common to all mankind, or at least to large bodies of them, and only on a small degree on the idiosyncrasies of organisation or the peculiar history of individuals; it is evidently possible, with regard to all such effects, to make predictions which will *almost* always be verified, and general propositions which are almost always true. And whenever it is sufficient to know how the great majority of the human race, or of some nation or class of persons, will think, feel, and act, these propositions are equivalent to universal ones. For the purposes of political and social science this *is* sufficient. As we formerly remarked, an approximate generalisation is, in social inquiries, for most practical purposes equivalent to an exact one; that which is only probable when asserted of individual human beings indiscriminately selected, being certain when affirmed of the character and collective conduct of masses.

It is no disparagement, therefore, to the science of Human Nature that those of its general propositions which descend sufficiently into detail to serve as a foundation for predicting phenomena in the concrete are for the most part only approximately true. But in order to give a genuinely scientific character to the study, it is indispensible that these approximate generalisations, which in themselves would amount only to the lowest kind of empirical laws, should be connected deductively with the laws of nature from which they result—should be resolved into the properties of the causes on which the phenomena depend. In other words, the science of Human Nature may be said to exist in proportion as the approximate truths which compose a practical knowledge of mankind can be exhibited as corollaries from the universal laws of human nature on which they rest, whereby the proper limits of these approximate truths would be shown, and we should be enabled to deduce others for any new state of circumstances, in anticipation of specific experience.

The Laws of Mind*

1. What the Mind is, as well as what Matter is, or any other question respecting Things in themselves, as distinguished from their sensible manifestations, it would be foreign to the purposes of this treatise to consider. Here, as throughout our inquiry, we shall keep clear of all speculations respecting the mind's own nature, and shall understand by the laws of mind those of mental phenomena—of the various feelings or states of consciousness of sentient beings. These, according to the classification we have uniformly followed, consist of Thoughts, Emotions, Volitions, and Sensations; the last being as truly states of Mind as the three former. It is usual, indeed, to speak of sensations as states of body, not of mind. But this is the common confusion of giving one and the same name to a phenomenon and to the proximate cause or conditions of the phenomenon. The immediate antecedent of a sensation is a state of body, but the sensation itself is a state of mind. If the word mind means anything, it means that which feels. Whatever opinion we hold respecting the fundamental identity or diversity of matter and mind, in any case the distinction between mental and physical facts, between the internal and the external world, will always remain as a matter of classification; and in that classification, sensations, like all other feelings, must be ranked as mental phenomena. The mechanism of their production, both in the body-itself and in what is called outward nature, is all that can with any propriety be classed as physical.

The phenomena of mind, then, are the various feelings of our nature, both those improperly called physical and those peculiarly designated as mental; and by the laws of mind I mean the laws according to which those feelings generate one another.

2. All states of mind are immediately caused either by other states of mind or by states of body. When a state of mind is produced by a state of mind, I call the law concerned in the case a law of Mind.

*Ibid., pp. 555-559.

When a state of mind is produced directly by a state of body, the law is a law of Body, and belongs to physical science.

With regard to those states of mind which are called sensations, all are agreed that these have for their immediate antecedents states of body. Every sensation has for its proximate cause some affection of the portion of our frame called the nervous system, whether this affection originate in the action of some external object, or in some pathological condition of the nervous organisation itself. The laws of this portion of our nature—the varieties of our sensations and the physical conditions on which they proximately depend—manifestly belong to the province of Physiology.

Whether the remainder of our mental states are similarly dependent on physical conditions, is one of the *vexatæ questiones* in the science of human nature. It is still disputed whether our thoughts, emotions, and volitions are generated through the intervention of material mechanism; whether we have organs of thought and of emotion in the same sense in which we have organs of sensation. Many eminent physiologists hold the affirmative. These contend that a thought (for example) is as much the result of nervous agency as a sensation; that some particular state of our nervous system, in particular of that central portion of it called the brain, invariably precedes, and is presupposed by, every state of our consciousness. According to this theory, one state of mind is never really produced by another; all are produced by states of body. When one thought seems to call up another by association, it is not really a thought which recalls a thought; the association did not exist between the two thoughts, but between the two states of the brain or nerves which preceded the thoughts : one of those states recalls the other, each being attended, in its passage, by the particular state of consciousness which is consequent on it. On this theory the uniformities of succession among states of mind would be mere derivative uniformities, resulting from the laws of succession of the bodily states which cause them. There would be no original mental laws, no Laws of Mind in the sense in which I use the term, at all; and mental science would be a mere branch, though the highest and most recondite branch, of the science of Physiology. M. Comte, accordingly, claims the scientific cognisance of moral and intellectual phenomena exclusively for physiologists; and not only denies to Psychology, or Mental Philosophy properly so called, the character of a science, but places it, in the chimerical nature of its objects and pretensions, almost on a par with astrology.

But, after all has been said which can be said, it remains incontestable that there exist uniformities of succession among states of mind, and that these can be ascertained by observation and experiment. Further, that every mental state has a nervous state for its immediate antecedent and proximate cause, though extremely probable, cannot hitherto be said to be proved, in the conclusive manner in which this can be proved of sensations; and even were it certain, yet every one must admit that we are wholly ignorant of the characteristics of these nervous states; we know not, and at present have no means of knowing, in what respect one of them differs from another; and our only mode of studying their successions or co-existences must be by observing the successions and co-existences of the mental states of which they are supposed to be the generators or causes. The successions, therefore, which obtain among mental phenomena do not admit of being deduced from the physiological laws of our nervous organisation; and all real knowledge of them must continue, for a long time at least, if not always, to be sought in the direct study, by observation and experiment, of the mental successions themselves. Since, therefore, the order of our mental phenomena must be studied in those phenomena, and not inferred from the laws of any phenomena more general, there is a distinct and separate Science of Mind.

The relations, indeed, of that science to the science of physiology must never be overlooked or undervalued. It must by no means be forgotten that the laws of mind may be derivative laws resulting from laws of animal life, and that their truth therefore may ultimately depend on physical conditions; and the influence of physiological states or physiological changes in altering or counteracting the mental successions is one of the most important departments of psychological study. But, on the other hand, to reject the resource of psychological analysis, and construct the theory of the mind solely on such data as physiology at present affords, seems to me as great an error in principle, and an even more serious one in practice. Imperfect as is the science of mind, I do not scruple to affirm that it is in a considerably more advanced state than the portion of physiology which corresponds to it; and to discard the former for the latter appears to me an infringement of the true canons of inductive philosophy, which must produce, and which does produce, erroneous conclusions in some very important departments of the science of human nature.

3. The subject, then, of Psychology is the uniformities of succession, the laws, whether ultimate or derivative, according to which one mental state succeeds another—is caused by, or at least is caused to follow, another. Of these laws, some are general, others more special. The following are examples of the most general laws.

First, Whenever any state of consciousness has once been excited in us, no matter by what cause, an inferior degree of the same state of consciousness, a state of consciousness resembling the former, but inferior in intensity, is capable of being reproduced in us, without the presence of any such cause as excited it at first. Thus, if we have once seen or touched an object, we can afterwards think of the object though it be absent from our sight or from our touch. If we have been joyful or grieved at some event, we can think of or remember our past joy or grief, though no new event of a happy or painful nature has taken place. When a poet has put together a mental picture of an imaginary object, a Castle of Indolence, a Una, or a Hamlet, he can afterwards think of the ideal object he has created without any fresh act of intellectual combination. This law is expressed by saying, in the language of Hume, that every mental *impression* has its *idea*.

Secondly, These ideas, or secondary mental states, are excited by our impressions, or by other ideas, according to certain laws which are called Laws of Association. Of these laws the first is, that similar ideas tend to excite one another. The second is, that when two impressions have been frequently experienced (or even thought of), either simultaneously or in immediate succession, then whenever one of these impressions, or the idea of it, recurs, it tends to excite the idea of the other. The third law is, that greater intensity in either or both of the impressions is equivalent, in rendering them excitable by one another, to a greater frequency of conjunction. These are the laws of ideas, on which I shall not enlarge in this place, but refer the reader to works professedly psychological, in particular to Mr. James Mill's *Analysis of the Phenomena of the Human Mind,* where the principal laws of association, along with many of their applications, are copiously exemplified, and with a masterly hand.

These simple or elementary Laws of Mind have been ascertained by the ordinary methods of experimental inquiry; nor could they have been ascertained in any other manner. But a certain number of elementary laws having thus been obtained, it is a fair subject of scientific inquiry how far those laws can be made to go in explaining the actual phenomena. It is obvious that complex laws of thought and feeling not only may, but must be generated from these simple laws. And it is to be remarked that the case is not always one of Composition of Causes : the effect of concurring causes is not always precisely the sum of the effects of those causes when separate, nor even always an effect of the same kind with them. Reverting to the distinction which occupies so prominent a place in the theory of induction, the laws of the phenomena of mind are sometimes analogous to mechanical, but sometimes also to chemical laws. When many impressions or ideas are operating in the mind together, there sometimes takes place a process of a similar kind to chemical combination. When impressions have been so often experienced in conjunction that each of them calls up readily and instantaneously the ideas of the whole group, those ideas sometimes melt and coalesce into one another, and appear not several ideas, but one, in the same manner as, when the seven prismatic colours are presented to the eye in rapid succession the sensation produced is that of white. But as in this last case it is correct to say that the seven colours when they rapidly follow one another *generate* white, but not that they actually *are* white; so it appears to me that the Complex Idea, formed by the blending together of several simpler ones, should, when it really appears simple, (that is, when the separate elements are not consciously distinguishable in it), be said to *result from,* or *be generated by,* the simple ideas, not to *consist* of them. Our idea of an orange really *consists* of the simple ideas of a certain colour, a certain form, a certain taste and smell, &c., because we can, by interrogating our consciousness, perceive all these elements in the idea. But we cannot perceive, in so apparently simple a feeling as our perception of the shape of an object by the eye, all that multitude of ideas derived from other senses, without which it is well ascertained that no such visual perception would ever have had existence; nor, in our idea of Extension, can we discover those elementary ideas of resistance derived from our muscular frame in which it has been conclusively shown that the idea originates. These, therefore, are cases of mental chemistry, in which it is proper to say that the simple ideas generate, rather than that they compose, the complex ones.

With respect to all the other constituents of the mind, its beliefs, its abstruser conceptions, its sentiments, emotions, and volitions, there are some (among whom are Hartley and the author of the *Analaysis*) who think that the whole of these are generated from simple ideas of sensation by a chemistry similar to that which we have just exemplified. These philosophers have made out a great part of their case, but I am not satisfied that they have established the whole of it. They have shown that there is such a thing as mental chemistry; that the heterogeneous nature of a feeling A, considered in relation to B and C, is no conclusive argument against its being generated from B and C. Having proved this, they proceed to show that where A is found B and C were or may have been present; and why, therefore, they ask, should not A have been generated from B and C? But even if this evidence were carried to the highest degree of completeness which it admits of; if it were shown (which hitherto it has not, in all cases, been) that certain groups of associated ideas not only might have been, but actually were present whenever the more recondite mental feeling was experienced, this would amount only to the Method of Agreement, and could not prove causation until confirmed by the more conclusive evidence of the Method of Difference. If the question be whether Belief is a mere case of close association of ideas, it would be necessary to examine experimentally if it be true that any ideas whatever, provided they are associated with the required degree of closeness, give rise to belief. If the inquiry be into the origin of moral feelings, the feeling, for example, of moral reprobation, it is necessary to compare all the varieties of actions or states of mind which are ever morally disapproved, and see whether in all these cases it can be shown, or reasonably surmised, that the action or state of mind had become connected by association, in the disapproving mind, with some particular class of hateful or disgusting ideas; and the method employed is, thus far, that of Agreement. But this is not enough. Supposing this proved, we must try further by the Method of Difference whether this particular kind of hateful or disgusting ideas, when it becomes associated with an action previously indifferent, will render that action a subject of moral disapproval. If this question can be answered in the affirmative, it is shown to be a law of the human mind that an association of that particular description is the generating cause of moral reprobation. That all this is the case has been rendered extremely probable, but the experiments have not been tried with the degree of precision necessary for a complete and absolutely conclusive induction.

It is further to be remembered, that even if all which this theory of mental phenomena contends for could be proved, we should not be the more enabled to resolve the laws of the more complex feelings into those of the simpler ones. The generation of one class of mental phenomena from another, whenever it can be made out, is a highly interesting fact in psychological chemistry; but it no more supersedes the necessity of an experimental study of the generated phenomenon, than a knowledge of the properties of oxygen and sulphur enables us to deduce those of sulphuric acid without specific observation and experiment. Whatever, therefore, may be the final issue of the attempt to account for the origin of our judgments, our desires, or our volitions, from simpler mental phenomena, it is not the less imperative to ascertain the sequences of the complex phenomena themselves by special study in conformity to the canons of Induction. Thus, in respect to Belief, psychologists will always have to inquire what beliefs we have by direct consciousness, and according to what laws one belief produces another; what are the laws in virtue of which one thing is recognised by the mind, either rightly or erroneously, as evidence of another thing. In regard to Desire, they will have to examine what objects we desire naturally, and by what causes we are made to desire things originally indifferent, or even disagreeable to us; and so forth. It may be remarked, that the general laws of association prevail among these more intricate states of mind, in the same manner as among the simpler ones. A desire, an emotion, an idea of the higher order of abstraction, even our judgments and volitions when they have become habitual, are called up by association, according to precisely the same laws as our simple ideas.

The Psychological Theory of the Belief in an External World*

We have seen Sir W. Hamilton at work on the question of the reality of Matter, by the introspective method, and, as it seems, with little result. Let us now approach the same subject by the psychological. I proceed, therefore, to state the case of those who hold that the belief in an external world is not intuitive, but an acquired product.

This theory postulates the following psychological truths, all of which are proved by experience, and are not contested, though their force is seldom adequately felt, by Sir W. Hamilton and the other thinkers of the introspective school.

It postulates, first, that the human mind is capable of Expectation. In other words, that after having had actual sensations, we are capable of forming the conception of Possible sensations; sensations which we are not feeling at the present moment, but which we might feel, and should feel if certain conditions were present, the nature of which conditions we have, in many cases, learnt by experience.

It postulates, secondly, the laws of the Association of Ideas. So far as we are here concerned, these laws are the following : 1st. Similar phenomena tend to be thought of together. 2nd. Phenomena which have either been experienced or conceived in close contiguity to one another, tend to be thought of together. The contiguity is of two kinds; simultaneity, and immediate succession. Facts which have been experienced or thought of simultaneously, recall the thought of one another. Of facts which have been experienced or thought of in immediate succession, the antecedent, or the thought of it, recalls the thought of the consequent, but not conversely. 3rd. Associations produced by contiguity become more certain and rapid by repetition. When two phenomena have been very often experienced in conjunction, and have

*From *An Examination of Sir William Hamilton's Philosophy* (London, 1889), pp. 225-239.

not, in any single instance, occurred separately either in experience or in thought, there is produced between them what has been called Inseparable, or less correctly, Indissoluble Association : by which is not meant that the association must inevitably last to the end of life—that no subsequent experience or process of thought can possibly avail to dissolve it; but only that as long as no such experience or process of thought has taken place, the association is irresistible; it is impossible for us to think the one thing disjoined from the other. 4th. When an association has acquired this character of inseparability—when the bond between the two ideas has been thus firmly riveted, not only does the idea called up by association become, in our consciousness, inseparable from the idea which suggested it, but the facts or phenomena answering to those ideas come at last to seem inseparable in existence : things which we are unable to conceive apart, appear incapable of existing apart; and the belief we have in their coexistence, though really a product of experience, seems intuitive. Innumerable examples might be given of this law. One of the most familiar, as well as the most striking, is that of our acquired perceptions of sight. Even those who, with Mr. Bailey, consider the perception of distance by the eye as not acquired, but intuitive, admit that there are many perceptions of sight which, though instantaneous and unhesitating, are not intuitive. What we see is a very minute fragment of what we think we see. We see artificially that one thing is hard, another soft. We see artificially that one thing is hot, another cold. We see artificially that what we see is a book, or a stone, each of these being not merely an inference, but a heap of inferences, from the signs which we see, to things not visible. We see, and cannot help seeing, what we have learnt to infer, even when we know that the inference is erroneous, and that the apparent perception is deceptive. We cannot help seeing the moon larger when near the horizon, though we know that she is of precisely her usual size. We cannot help seeing a mountain as nearer to us and of less height, when we see it through a more than ordinarily transparent atmosphere.

Setting out from these premises, the Psychological Theory maintains, that there are associations naturally and even necessarily generated by the order of our sensations and of our reminiscences of sensation, which supposing no intuition of an external world to have existed in consciousness, would inevitably generate the belief, and would cause it to be regarded as an intuition.

What is it we mean, or what is it which leads us to say, that the objects we perceive are external to us, and not a part of our own thoughts? We mean, that there is concerned in our perceptions something which exists when we are not thinking of it; which existed before we had ever thought of it, and would exist if we were annihilated; and further, that there exist things which we never saw, touched, or otherwise perceived, and things which never have been perceived by man. This idea of something which is distinguished from our fleeting impressions by what, in Kantian language, is called Perdurability; something which is fixed and the same, while our impressions vary; something which exists whether we are aware of it or not, and which is always square (or of some other given figure) whether it appears to us square or round—constitutes altogether our idea of external substance. Whoever can assign an origin to this complex conception, has accounted for what we mean by the belief in matter. Now all this, according to the Psychological Theory, is but the form impressed by the known laws of association, upon the conception or notion, obtained by experience, of Contingent Sensations; by which are meant, sensations that are not in our present consciousness, and individually never were in our consciousness at all, but which in virtue of the laws to which we have learnt by experience that our sensations are subject, we know that we should have felt under given supposable circumstances, and under these same circumstances, might still feel.

I see a piece of white paper on a table. I go into another room. If the phenomenon always followed me, or if, when it did not follow me, I believed it to disappear è rerum naturâ, I should not believe it to be an external object. I should consider it as a phantom—a mere affection of my senses : I should not believe that there had been any Body there. But, though I have ceased to see it, I am persuaded that the paper is still there. I no longer have the sensations which it gave me; but I believe that when I again place myself in the circumstances in which I had those sensations, that is, when I go again into the room, I shall again have them; and further, that there has been no intervening moment at which this would not have been the case. Owing to this property of my mind, my conception of the world at any given instant consists, in only a small proportion, of present sensations. Of these I may at the time have none at all, and they are in any case a most insignificant portion of the whole which I apprehend. The conception I form of the world existing at any moment, comprises, along with the sensations I am feeling, a countless variety of possibilities of sensation : namely, the whole of those which past observation tells me that I could, under any supposable circumstances, experience at this moment, together with an indefinite and illimitable multitude of others which though I do not know that I could, yet it is possible that I might, experience in circumstances not known to me. These various possibilities are the important thing to me in the world. My present sensations are generally of little importance, and are moreover fugitive : the possibilities, on the contrary, are permanent, which is the character that mainly distinguishes our idea of Substance or Matter from our notion of sensation. These possibilities, which are conditional certainties, need a special name to distinguish them from mere vague possibilities, which experience gives no warrant for reckoning upon. Now as soon as a distinguishing name is given, though it be only to the same thing regarded in a different aspect, one of the most familiar experiences of our mental nature teaches us, that the different name comes to be considered as the name of a different thing.

There is another important important peculiarity of these certified or guaranteed possibilities of sensation; namely, that they have reference, not to single sensations, but to sensations joined together in groups. When we think of anything as a material substance, or body, we either have had, or we think that on some given supposition we should have, not some *one* sensation, but a great and even indefinite number and variety of sensations, generally belonging to different senses, but so linked together, that the presence of one announces the possible presence at the very same instant of any or all of the rest. In our mind, therefore, not only is this particular Possibility of sensation invested with the quality of permanence when we are not actually feeling any of the sensations at all; but when we are feeling some of them, the remaining sensations of the group are conceived by us in the form of Present Possibilities, which might be realised at the very moment. And as this happens in turn to all of them, the group as a whole presents itself to the mind as permanent, in contrast not solely with the temporariness of my bodily presence, but also with the temporary character of each of the sensations composing the group; in other words, as a kind of permanent substratum, under a set pf passing experiences or manifestations : which is another leading character of our idea of substance or matter, as distinguished from sensation.

Let us now take into consideration another of the general characters of our experience, namely, that in addition to fixed groups, we also recognise a fixed Order in our sensations; an Order of succession, which, when ascertained by observation, gives rise to the ideas of Cause and Effect, according to what I hold to be the true theory of that relation, and is on any theory the source of all our knowledge what causes produce what effects. Now, of what nature is this fixed order among our sensations? It is a constancy of antecedence and sequence. But the constant antecedence and sequence do not generally exist between one actual sensation and another. Very few such sequences are presented to us by experience. In almost all the constant sequences which occur in Nature, the antecedence and consequence do not obtain between sensations, but between the groups we have been speaking about, of which a very small portion is actual sensation, the greater part being permanent possibilities of sensation, evidenced to us by a small and variable number of sensations actually present. Hence, our ideas of causation, power, activity, do not become connected in thought with our sensations as *actual* at all, save in the few physiological cases where these figure by themselves as the antecedents in some uniform sequence. Those ideas become connected, not with sensations, but with groups of possibilities of sensation. The sensations conceived do not, to our habitual thoughts, present themselves as sensations actually experienced, inasmuch as not only any one or any number of them may be supposed absent, but none of them need be present. We find that the modifications which are taking place more or less regularly in our possibilities of sensation, are mostly quite independent of our consciousness, and of our presence or absence. Whether we are asleep or awake the fire goes out, and puts an end to one particular possibility of warmth and light. Whether we are present or absent the corn ripens, and brings a new possibility of food. Hence we speedily learn to think of Nature as made up solely of these groups of possibilities, and the active force in Nature as manifested in the modification of some of these by others. The sensations, though the original foundation of the whole, come to be looked upon as a sort of accident depending on us, and the possibilities as much more real than the actual sensations, nay, as the very realities of which these are only the representations, appearances, or effects. When this state of mind has been arrived at, then, and from that time forward, we are never conscious of a present sensation without instantaneously referring it to some one of the groups of possibilities into which a sensation of that particular description enters; and if we do not yet know to what group to refer it, we at least feel an irresistible conviction that it must belong to some group or other; *i.e.* that its presence proves the existence, here and now, of a great number and variety of possibilities of sensation, without which it would not have been. The whole set of sensations as possible, form a permanent background to any one or more of them that are, at a given moment, actual; and the possibilities are conceived as standing to the actual sensations in the relation of a cause to its effects, or of canvas to the figures painted on it, or of a root to the trunk, leaves, and flowers, or of a substratum to that which is spread over it, or, in transcendental language, of Matter to Form.

When this point has been reached, the Permanent Possibilities in question have assumed such unlikeness of aspect, and such difference of apparent relation to us, from any sensations, that it would be contrary to all we know of the constitution of human nature that they should not be conceived as, and believed to be, at least as different from sensations as sensations are from one another. Their groundwork in sensation is forgotten, and they are supposed to be something intrinsically distinct from it. We can withdraw ourselves from any of our (external) sensations, or we can be withdrawn from them by some other agency. But though the sensations cease, the possibilities remain in existence; they are independent of our will, our presence, and everything which belongs to us. We find, too, that they belong as much to other human or sentient beings as to ourselves. We find other people grounding their expectations and conduct upon the same permanent possibilities on which we ground ours. But we do not find them experiencing the same actual sensations. Other people do not have our sensations exactly when and as we have them : but they have our possibilities of sensations; whatever indicates a present possibility of sensations to ourselves, indicates a present possibility of similar sensations to them, except so far as their organs of sensation may vary from the type of ours. This puts the final seal to our conception of the groups of possibilities as the fundamental reality in Nature. The permanent possibilities are common to us and to our fellow-creatures; the actual sensations are not. That which other people become aware of when, and on the same grounds, as I do, seems more real to me than that which they do not know of unless I tell them. The world of Possible Sensations succeeding one another according to laws, is as much in other beings as it is in me; it has therefore an existence outside me; it is an External World.

If this explanation of the origin and growth of the idea of Matter, or External Nature, contains nothing at variance with natural laws, it is at least an admissible supposition, that the element of Non-ego which Sir W. Hamilton regards as an original datum of consciousness, and which we certainly do find in what we now call our consciousness, may not be one of its primitive elements—may not have existed at all in its first manifestations. But if this supposition be admissible, it ought, on Sir W. Hamilton's principles, to be received as true. The first of the laws laid down by him for the interpretation of Consciousness, the law (as he terms it) of Parsimony, forbids to suppose an original principle of our nature in order to account for phenomena which admit of possible explanation from known causes. If the supposed ingredient of consciousness be one which might grow up (though we cannot prove that it did grow up) through later experience; and if, when it had so grown up, it would, by known laws of our nature, appear as completely intuitive as our sensations themselves; we are bound, according to Sir W. Hamilton's and all sound philosophy, to assign to it that origin. Where there is a known cause adequate to account for a phenomenon, there is no justification for ascribing it to an unknown one. And what evidence does Consciousness furnish of the intuitiveness of an impression, except instantaneousness, apparent simplicity, and unconsciousness on our part of how the impression came into our minds? These features can only prove the impression to be intuitive, on the hypothesis that there are no means of accounting for them otherwise. If they not only might, but naturally would, exist, even on the supposition that it is not intuitive, we must accept the conclusion to which we are led by the Psychological Method, and which the Introspective Method furnishes absolutely nothing to contradict.

Matter, then, may be defined, a Permanent Possibility of Sensation. If I am asked, whether I believe in matter, I ask whether the questioner accepts this definition of it. If he does, I believe in matter : and so do all Berkeleians. In any other sense than this, I do not. But I affirm with confidence, that this conception of Matter includes the whole meaning attached to it by the common world, apart from philosophical, and sometimes from theological, theories. The reliance of mankind on the real existence of visible and tangible objects, means reliance on the reality and permanence of Possibilities of visual and tactual sensations, when no such sensations are actually experienced. We are warranted in believing that this is the meaning of Matter in the minds of many of its most esteemed metaphysical champions, though they themselves would not admit as much : for example, of Reid, Stewart, and Brown. For these three philosophers alleged that all mankind, including Berkeley and Hume, really believed in Matter, inasmuch as unless they did, they would not have turned aside to save themselves from running against a post. Now all which this manoeuvre really proved is, that they believed in Permanent Possibilities of Sensation. We have therefore the unintentional sanction of these three eminent defenders of the existence of matter, for affirming, that to believe in Permanent Possibilities of Sensation is believing in Matter. It is hardly necessary, after such authorities, to mention Dr. Johnson, or any one else who resorts to the *argumentum baculinum* of knocking a stick against the ground. Sir W. Hamilton, a far subtler thinker than any of these, never reasons in this manner. He never supposes that a disbeliever in what he means by Matter, ought in consistency to act in any different mode from those who believe in it. He knew that the belief on which all the practical consequences depend, is the belief in Permanent Possibilities of Sensation, and that if nobody believed in a material universe in any other sense, life would go on exactly as it now does. He, however, did believe in more than this, but, I think, only because it had never occurred to him that mere Possibilities of Sensation could, to our artificialised consciousness, present the character of objectivity which, as we have now shown, they not only can, but unless the known laws of the human mind were suspended, must necessarily, present.

Perhaps it may be objected, that the very possibility of framing such a notion of Matter as Sir W. Hamilton's—the capacity in the human mind of imagining an external world which is anything more than what the Psychological Theory makes it—amounts to a disproof of the theory. If (it may be said) we had no revelation in consciousness, of a world which is not in some way or other identified with sensation, we should be unable to have the notion of such a world. If the only ideas we had of external objects were ideas of our sensations, supplemented by an acquired notion of permanent possibilities of sensation, we must (it is thought) be incapable of conceiving, and therefore still more incapable of fancying that we perceive, things which are not sensations at all. It being evident however that some philosophers believe this, and it being maintainable that the mass of mankind do so, the existence of a perdurable basis of sensations, distinct from sensations themselves, is proved, it might be said, by the possibility of believing it.

Let me first restate what I apprehend the belief to be. We believe that we perceive a something closely related to all our sensations, but different from those which we are feeling at any particular minute; and distinguished from sensations altogether, by being permanent and always the same, while these are fugitive, variable, and alternately displace one another. But these attributes of the object of perception are properties belonging to all the possibilities of sensation which experience guarantees. The belief in such permanent possibilities seems to me to include all that is essential or characteristic in the belief in substance. I believe that Calcutta exists, though I do not perceive it, and that it would still exist if every percipient inhabitant were suddenly to leave the place, or be struck dead. But when I analyse the belief, all I find in it is, that were these events to take place, the Permanent Possibility of Sensation which I call Calcutta would still remain; that if I were suddenly transported to the banks of the Hoogly, I should still have the sensations which, if now present, would lead me to affirm that Calcutta exists here and now. We may infer, therefore, that both philosophers and the world at large, when they think of matter, conceive it really as a Permanent Possibility of Sensation. But the majority of philosophers fancy that it is something more; and the world at large, though they have really, as I conceive, nothing in their minds but a

Permanent Possibility of Sensation, would, if asked the question, undoubtedly agree with the philosophers : and though this is sufficiently explained by the tendency of the human mind to infer difference of things from difference of names, I acknowledge the obligation of showing how it can be possible to believe in an existence transcending all possibilities of sensation, unless on the hypothesis that such an existence actually is, and that we actually perceive it.

The explanation, however, is not difficult. It is an admitted fact, that we are capable of all conceptions which can be formed by generalising from the observed laws of our sensations. Whatever relation we find to exist between any one of our sensations and something different from *it,* that same relation we have no difficulty in conceiving to exist between the sum of all our sensations and something different from *them.* The differences which our consciousness recognises between one sensation and another, give us the general notion of difference, and inseparably associate with every sensation we have, the feeling of its being different from other things : and when once this association has been formed, we can no longer conceive anything, without being able, and even being compelled, to form also the conception of something different from it. This familiarity with the idea of something different from *each* thing we know, makes it natural and easy to form the notion of something different from *all* things that we know, collectively as well as individually. It is true we can form no conception of what such a thing can be; our notion of it is merely negative; but the idea of a substance, apart from its relation to the impressions which we conceive it as making on our senses, *is* a merely negative one. There is thus no psychological obstacle to our forming the notion of a something which is neither a sensation nor a possibility of sensation, even if our consciousness does not testify to it; and nothing is more likely than that the Permanent Possibilities of sensation, to which our consciousness does testify, should be confounded in our minds with this imaginary conception. All experience attests the strength of the tendency to mistake mental abstractions, even negative ones, for substantive realities; and the Permanent Possibilities of sensation which experience guarantees, are so extremely unlike in many of their properties to actual sensations, that since we are capable of imagining something which transcends sensation, there is a great natural probability that we should suppose these to be it.

But this natural probability is converted into certainty, when we take into consideration that universal law of our experience which is termed the law of Causation, and which makes us mentally connect with the beginning of everything, some antecedent condition, or Cause.

The case of Causation is one of the most marked of all the cases in which we extend to the sum total of our consciousness, a notion derived from its parts. It is a striking example of our power to conceive, and our tendency to believe, that a relation which subsists between every individual item of our experience and some other item, subsists also between our experience as a whole, and something not within the sphere of experience. By this extension to the sum of all our experiences, of the internal relations obtaining between its several parts, we are led to consider sensation itself—the aggregate whole of our sensations—as deriving its origin from antecedent existences transcending sensation. That we should do this, is a consequence of the particular character of the uniform sequences, which experience discloses to us among our sensations. As already remarked, the constant antecedent of a sensation is seldom another sensation, or set of sensations, actually felt. It is much oftener the existence of a group of possibilities, not necessarily including any actual sensations, except such as are required to show that the possibilities are really present. Nor are actual sensations indispensable even for this purpose; for the presence of the object (which is nothing more than the immediate presence of the possibilities) may be made known to us by the very sensation which we refer to it as its effect. Thus, the real antecedent of an effect—the only antecedent which, being invariable and unconditional, we consider to be the cause—may be, not any sensation really felt, but solely the presence, at that or the immediately preceding moment, of a group of possibilities of sensation. Hence it is not with sensations as actually experienced, but with their Permanent Possibilities, that the idea of Cause comes to be identified : and we, by one and the same process, acquire the habit of regarding Sensation in general, like all our individual sensations, as an Effect, and also that of conceiving as the causes of most of our individual sensations, not other sensations, but general possibilities of sensation. If all these considerations put together do not completely explain and account for our conceiving these Possibilities as a class of independent and substantive entities, I know not what psychological analysis can be conclusive.

It may perhaps be said, that the preceding theory gives, indeed, some account of the idea of Permanent Existence which forms part of our conception of matter, but gives no explanation of our believing these permanent objects to be external, or out of ourselves. I apprehend, on the contrary, that the very idea of anything out of ourselves is derived solely from the knowledge experience gives us of the Permanent Possibilities. Our sensations we carry with us wherever we go, and they never exist where we are not; but when we change our place we

do not carry away with us the Permanent Possibilities of Sensation :
they remain until we return, or arise and cease under conditions with
which our presence has in general nothing to do. And more than all—
they are, and will be after we have ceased to feel, Permanent Possibilities of sensation to other beings than ourselves. Thus our actual sensations and the permanent possibilities of sensation, stand out in obtrusive
constrast to one another : and when the idea of Cause has been
acquired, and extended by generalisation from the parts of our experience to its aggregate whole, nothing can be more natural than that
the Permanent Possibilities should be classed by us as existences generi-
cally distinct from our sensations, but of which our sensations are the
effect.

The same theory which accounts for our ascribing to an aggregate
of possibilities of sensation, a permanent existence which our sensations themselves do not possess, and consequently a greater reality than
belongs to our sensations, also explains our attributing greater objectivity to the Primary Qualities of bodies than to the Secondary. For the
sensations which correspond to what are called the Primary Qualities
(as soon at least as we come to apprehend them by two senses, the eye
as well as the touch) are always present when any part of the group
is so. But colours, tastes, smells, and the like, being, in comparison,
fugacious, are not, in the same degree, conceived as being always
there, even when nobody is present to perceive them. The sensations
answering to the Secondary Qualities are only occasional, those to the
Primary, constant. The Secondary, moreover, vary with different
persons, and with the temporary sensibility of our organs; the Primary,
when perceived at all, are, as far as we know, the same to all persons
and at all times.

VII

FEUERBACH

Ludwig Feuerbach (1804-72) began his university career at Heidelberg, where he studied theology. Subsequently he moved to Berlin and, despite parental opposition, turned his attention to philosophy. He worked under Hegel for two years, submitting his dissertation in 1828 and at the same time becoming a *Privatdozent* at the University of Erlangen. He did not, however, continue his pursuit of an academic career. Instead he retired into private life, devoting himself first to producing studies in the history of philosophy and later to undertaking a radical reassessment of the Hegelian position. Feuerbach's most famous work in this connection was *The Essence of Christianity* (1841), from which the selections below are taken. It was followed by a number of other books, including *Preliminary Theses on the Reform of Philosophy* (1842), *Fundamental Tenets of the Philosophy of the Future* (1843), and *The Essence of Religion* (1845).

Feuerbach tends today to be remembered more as a seminal influence in the development of Marxism than as an important thinker in his own right. Yet, despite the rather turgid and repetitive quality of much of his writing, there is considerable penetration in his conception of Hegelian metaphysics as an "esoteric psychology" which contains the truth about the role of religion in human life and history in a hidden or misleading form. According to him, the Hegelian system was the "rational expression" of Christianity; the notion that spirit goes outside itself in nature and then returns to consciousness of itself in man represented the inner meaning of theological doctrine, however much it might seem to conflict with certain tenets of orthodoxy, such as those that treat God as an external personal being. Hegel had treated God and man as intrinsically connected; his error, on the other hand, was to regard God (or absolute spirit) as the true subject, man being relegated to the status of

237

a mere manifestation of this. In fact, man was fundamental, God being only a reified idea representing his own alienated human essence; it was thus a case of man coming to a consciousness of himself through his image of God rather than of God (or the Absolute) achieving self-consciousness through man. In this sense, Feuerbach could fairly claim to have "turned speculative philosophy upside down."

The Essence of Religion Considered Generally*

Religion, at least the Christian, is the relation of man to himself, or more correctly to his own nature (*i.e.,* his subjective nature); but a relation to it, viewed as a nature apart from his own. The divine thing is nothing else than the human being, or, rather, the human nature purified, freed from the limits of the individual man, made objective—*i.e.,* contemplated and revered as another, a distinct being. All the attributes of the divine nature are, therefore, attributes of the human nature.

In relation to the attributes, the predicates, of the Divine Being, this is admitted without hesitation, but by no means in relation to the subject of these predicates. The negation of the subject is held to be irreligion, nay, atheism; though not so the negation of the predicates. But that which has no predicates or qualities, has no effect upon me; that which has no effect upon me has no existence for me. To deny all the qualities of a being is equivalent to denying the being himself. A being without qualities is one which cannot become an object to the mind, and such a being is virtually non-existent. Where man deprives God of all qualities, God is no longer anything more to him than a negative being. To the truly religious man, God is not a being without qualities, because to him he is a positive, real being. The theory that God cannot be defined, and consequently cannot be known by man, is therefore the offspring of recent times, a product of modern unbelief.

As reason is and can be pronounced finite only where man regards sensual enjoyment, or religious emotion, or aesthetic contemplation, or moral sentiment, as the absolute, the true; so the proposition that God is unknowable or undefinable, can only be enunciated and become fixed as a dogma, where this object has no longer any interest for the intellect; where the real, the positive, alone has any hold on man, where the real

*From *The Essence of Christianity* (trans. Marian Evans [George Eliot]; London 1881), pp. 14-32.

alone has for him the significance of the essential, of the absolute, divine object, but where at the same time, in contradiction with this purely worldly tendency, there yet exist some old remains of religiousness. On the ground that God is unknowable, man excuses himself to what is yet remaining of his religious conscience for his forgetfulness of God, his absorption in the world : he denies God practically by his conduct,—the world has possession of all his thoughts and inclinations, —but he does not deny him theoretically, he does not attack his existence; he lets that rest. But this existence does not affect or incommode him; it is a merely negative existence, an existence without existence, a self-contradictory existence,—a state of being which, as to its effects, is not distinguishable from non-being. The denial of determinate, positive predicates concerning the divine nature is nothing else than a denial of religion, with, however, an appearance of religion in its favour, so that it is not recognised as a denial; it is simply a subtle disguised atheism. The alleged religious horror of limiting God by positive predicates is only the irreligious wish to know nothing more of God, to banish God from the mind. Dread of limitation is dread of existence. All real existence, *i.e.*, all existence which is truly such, is qualitative, determinative existence. He who earnestly believes in the Divine existence is not shocked at the attributing even of gross sensuous qualities to God. He who dreads an existence that may give offence, who shrinks from the grossness of a positive predicate, may as well renounce existence altogether. A God who is injured by determinate qualities has not the courage and the strength to exist. Qualities are the fire, the vital breath, the oxygen, the salt of existence. An existence in general, an existence without qualities, is an insipidity, an absurdity. But there can be no more in God than is supplied by religion. Only where man loses his taste for religion, and thus religion itself becomes insipid, does the existence of God become an insipid existence—an existence without qualities.

There is, however, a still milder way of denying the divine predicates than the direct one just described. It is admitted that the predicates of the divine nature are finite, and, more particularly, human qualities, but their rejection is rejected; they are even taken under protection, because it is necessary to man to have a definite conception of God, and since he is man he can form no other than a human conception of him. In relation to God, it is said, these predicates are certainly without any objective validity; but to me, if he is to exist for me, he cannot appear otherwise than as he does appear to me, namely, as a being with attributes analogous to the human. But this distinction between what God is in himself, and what he is for me destroys the peace of religion, and is besides in itself an unfounded and untenable distinction. I cannot know whether God is something else in himself or for himself than he is for me; what he is to me is to me all that he is. For me, there lies in these predicates under which he exists for me, what he is in himself, his very nature; he is for me what he can alone ever be for me. The religious man finds perfect satisfaction in that which God is in relation to himself; of any other relation he knows nothing, for God is to him what he can alone be to man. In the distinction above stated, man takes a point of view above himself, *i.e.*, above his nature, the absolute measure of his being; but this transcendentalism is only an illusion; for I can make the distinction between the object as it is in itself, and the object as it is for me, only where an object can really appear otherwise to me, not where it appears to me such as the absolute measure of my nature determines it to appear—such as it must appear to me. It is true that I may have a merely subjective conception, *i.e.*, one which does not arise out of the general constitution of my species; but if my conception is determined by the constitution of my species, the distinction between what an object is in itself, and what it is for me ceases; for this conception is itself an absolute one. The measure of the species is the absolute measure, law, and criterion of man. And, indeed, religion has the conviction that its conceptions, its predicates of God, are such as every man ought to have, and must have, if he would have the true ones —that they are the conceptions necessary to human nature; nay, further, that they are objectively true, representing God as he is. To every religion the gods of *other* religions are only notions concerning God, but its own conception of God is to it God himself, the true God—God such as he is in himself. Religion is satisfied only with a complete Deity, a God without reservation; it will not have a mere phantasm of God; it demands God himself. Religion gives up its own existence when it gives up the nature of God; it is no longer a truth when it renounces the possession of the true God. Scepticism is the arch-enemy of religion; but the distinction between object and conception—between God as he is in himself, and God as he is for me—is a sceptical distinction, and therefore an irreligious one.

That which is to man the self-existent, the highest being, to which he can conceive nothing higher—that is to him the Divine Being. How then should he inquire concerning this being, what he is in himself? If God were an object to the bird, he would be a winged being : the bird knows nothing higher, nothing more blissful, than the winged condition. How ludicrous would it be if this bird pronounced : To me God appears as a bird, but what he is in himself I know not. To the bird the highest nature is the bird-nature; take from him the conception of this, and you take from him the conception of the highest being. How, then, could he ask whether God in himself were winged? To ask whether God is in himself what he is for me, is to ask whether God is God, is to lift oneself above one's God, to rise up against him. . . .

Thou believest in love as a divine attribute because thou thyself lovest; thou believest that God is a wise, benevolent being because thou knowest nothing better in thyself than benevolence and wisdom; and thou believest that God exists, that therefore he is a subject—whatever exists is a subject, whether it be defined as substance, person, essence, or otherwise—because thou thyself existest, art thyself a subject. Thou knowest no higher human good than to love, than to be good and wise; and even so thou knowest no higher happiness than to exist, to be a subject; for the consciousness of all reality, of all bliss, is for thee bound up in the consciousness of being a subject, of existing. God is an existence, a subject to thee, for the same reason that he is to thee a wise, a blessed, a personal being. The distinction between the divine predicates and the divine subject is only this, that to thee the subject, the existence, does not appear an anthropomorphism, because the conception of it is necessarily involved in thy own existence as a subject, whereas the predicates do appear anthropomorphisms, because their necessity—the necessity that God should be conscious, wise, good, &c., —is not an immediate necessity, identical with the being of man, but is evolved by his self-consciousness, by the activity of his thought. I am a subject, I exist, whether I be wise or unwise, good or bad. To exist is to man the first datum; it constitutes the very idea of the subject; it is presupposed by the predicates. Hence man relinquishes the predicates, but the existence of God is to him a settled, irrefragable, absolutely certain, objective truth. But, nevertheless, this distinction is merely an apparent one. The necessity of the subject lies only in the necessity of the predicate. Thou art a subject only in so far as thou art a human subject; the certainty and reality of thy existence lie only in the certainty and reality of thy human attributes. What the subject is lies only in the predicate; the predicate is the *truth* of the subject—the subject only the personified, existing predicate, the predicate conceived as existing. Subject and predicate are distinguished only as existence and essence. The negation of the predicates is therefore the negation of the subject. What remains of the human subject when abstracted from the human attributes? Even in the language of common life the divine predicates—Providence, Omniscience, Omnipotence—are put for the divine subject. . . .

Now, when it is shown that what the subject is lies entirely in the attributes of the subject; that is, that the predicate is the true subject;

it is also proved that if the divine predicates are attributes of the human nature, the subject of those predicates is also of the human nature. But the divine predicates are partly general, partly personal. The general predicates are the metaphysical, but these serve only as external points of support to religion; they are not the characteristic definitions of religion. It is the personal predicates alone which constitute the essence of religion—in which the Divine Being is the object of religion. Such are, for example, that God is a Person, that he is the moral Lawgiver, the Father of mankind, the Holy One, the Just, the Good, the Merciful. It is, however, at once clear, or it will at least be clear in the sequel, with regard to these and other definitions, that, especially as applied to a personality, they are purely human definitions, and that consequently man in religion—in his relation to God—is in relation to his own nature; for to the religious sentiment these predicates are not mere conceptions, mere images, which man forms of God, to be distinguished from that which God is in himself, but truths, facts, realities. Religion knows nothing of anthropomorphisms; to it they are not anthropomorphisms. It is the very essence of religion, that to it these definitions express the nature of God. They are pronounced to be images only by the understanding, which reflects on religion, and which while defending them yet before its own tribunal denies them. But to the religious sentiment God is a real Father, real Love and Mercy; for to it he is a real, living, personal being, and therefore his attributes are also living and personal. Nay, the definitions which are the most sufficing to the religious sentiment are precisely those which give the most offence to the understanding, and which in the process of reflection on religion it denies. Religion is essentially emotion; hence, objectively also, emotion is to it necessarily of a divine nature. Even anger appears to it an emotion not unworthy of God, provided only there be a religious motive at the foundation of this anger.

But here it is also essential to observe, and this phenomenon is an extremely remarkable one, characterising the very core of religion, that in proportion as the divine subject is in reality human, the greater is the apparent difference between God and man; that is, the more, by reflection on religion, by theology, is the identity of the divine and human denied, and the human, considered as such, is depreciated. The reason of this is, that as what is positive in the conception of the divine being can only be human, the conception of man, as an object of consciousness, can only be negative. To enrich God, man must become poor; that God may be all, man must be nothing. But he desires to be nothing in himself, because what he takes from himself is not lost to him, since it is preserved in God. Man has his being in God; why then should he have it in himself? Where is the necessity of positing the same thing twice, of having it twice? What man withdraws from himself, what he renounces in himself, he only enjoys in an incomparably higher and fuller measure in God. . . .

Man—this is the mystery of religion—projects his being into objectivity, and then again makes himself an object to this projected image of himself thus converted into a subject; he thinks of himself, is an object to himself, but as the object of an object, of another being than himself. Thus here. Man is an object to God. That man is good or evil is not indifferent to God; no! He has a lively, profound interest in man's being good; he wills that man should be good, happy—for without goodness there is no happiness. Thus the religious man virtually retracts the nothingness of human activity, by making his dispositions and actions an object to God, by making man the end of God—for that which is an object to the mind is an end in action; by making the divine activity a means of human salvation. God acts, that man may be good and happy. Thus man, while he is apparently humiliated to the lowest degree, is in truth exalted to the highest. Thus, in and through God, man has in view himself alone. It is true that man places the aim of his action in God, but God has no other aim of action than the moral and eternal salvation of man : thus man has in fact no other aim than himself. The divine activity is not distinct from the human.

How could the divine activity work on me as its object, nay, work in me, if it were essentially different from me; how could it have a human aim, the aim of ameliorating and blessing man, if it were not itself human? Does not the purpose determine the nature of the act? When man makes his moral improvement an aim to himself, he has divine resolutions, divine projects; but also, when God seeks the salvation of man, he has human ends and a human mode of activity corresponding to these ends. Thus in God man has only his own activity as an object. But for the very reason that he regards his own activity as objective, goodness only as an object, he necessarily receives the impulse, the motive not from himself, but from this object. He contemplates his nature as external to himself, and this nature as goodness; thus it is self-evident, it is mere tautology to say that the impulse to good comes only from thence where he places the good.

God is the highest subjectivity of man abstracted from himself; hence man can do nothing of himself, all goodness comes from God. The more subjective God is, the more completely does man divest himself of his subjectivity, because God is, *per se,* his relinquished self, the possession of which he however again vindicates to himself. As the action of the arteries drives the blood into the extremities, and the action of the veins brings it back again, as life in general consists in a perpetual systole and diastole; so is it in religion. In the religious systole man propels his own nature from himself, he throws himself outward; in the religious diastole he receives the rejected nature into his heart again. God alone is the being who acts of himself,—this is the force of repulsion in religion; God is the being who acts in me, with me, through me, upon me, for me, is the principle of my salvation, of my good dispositions and actions, consequently my own good principle and nature,—this is the force of attraction in religion.

The course of religious development which has been generally indicated consists specifically in this, that man abstracts more and more from God, and attributes more and more to himself. This is especially apparent in the belief in revelation. That which to a later age or a cultured people is given by nature or reason, is to an earlier age, or to a yet uncultured people, given by God. Every tendency of man, however natural—even the impulse to cleanliness, was conceived by the Israelities as a positive divine ordinance. From this example we again see that God is lowered, is conceived more entirely on the type of ordinary humanity, in proportion as man detracts from himself. How can the self-humiliation of man go further than when he disclaims the capability of fulfilling spontaneously the requirements of common decency? The Christian religion, on the other hand, distinguished the impulses and passions of man according to their quality, their character; it represented only good emotions, good dispositions, good thoughts, as revelations, operations—that is, as dispositions, feelings, thoughts,—of God; for what God reveals is a quality of God himself : that of which the heart is full overflows the lips; as is the effect such is the cause; as the revelation, such the being who reveals himself. A God who reveals himself in good dispositions is a God whose essential attribute is only moral perfection. The Christian religion distinguishes inward moral purity from external physical purity; the Israelites identified the two. In relation to the Israelitish religion, the Christian religion is one of criticism and freedom. The Israelite trusted himself to do nothing except what was commanded by God; he was without will even in external things; the authority of religion extended itself even to his food. The Christian religion, on the other hand, in all these external things made man dependent on himself, *i.e.*, placed in man what the Israelite placed out of himself in God. Israel is the most complete presentation of Positivism in religion. In relation to the Israelite, the Christian is an *esprit fort,* a free-thinker. Thus do things change. What yesterday was still religion is no longer such to-day; and what to-day is atheism, to-morrow will be religion.

The Contradiction in the Speculative Doctrine of God*

The personality of God is thus the means by which man converts the qualities of his own nature into the qualities of another being,— of a being external to himself. The personality of God is nothing else than the projected personality of man.

On this process of projecting self outwards rests also the Hegelian speculative doctrine, according to which *man's* consciousness of God is the *self*-consciousness of God. God is thought, cognised by us. According to speculation, God, in being thought by us, thinks himself or is conscious of himself; speculation identifies the two sides which religion separates. In this it is far deeper than religion, for the fact of God being thought is not like the fact of an external object being thought. God is an inward, spiritual being; thinking, consciousness, is an inward, spiritual act; to think God is therefore to affirm what God is, to establish the being of God as an act. That God is thought, cognised, is essential; that this tree is thought, is to the tree accidental, unessential. God is an indispensable thought, a necessity of thought. But how is it possible that this necessity should simply express the subjective, and not the objective also?—how is it possible that God—if he is to exist for us, to be an object to us—must necessarily be thought, if he is in himself like a block, indifferent whether he be thought, cognised or not? No! it is not possible. We are necessitated to regard the fact of God being thought by us, as his thinking himself, or his self-consciousness.

Religious objectivism has two passives, two modes in which God is thought. On the one hand, God is thought by us, on the other, he is thought by himself. God thinks himself, independently of his being thought by us : he has a self-consciousness distinct from, independent of, our consciousness. This is certainly consistent when once God is conceived as a real personality; for the real human person thinks

Ibid., pp. 226-231.

himself, and is thought by another; my thinking of him is to him an indifferent, external fact. This is the last degree of anthropopathism. In order to make God free and independent of all that is human, he is regarded as a formal, real person, his thinking is confined within himself, and the fact of his being thought is excluded from him, and is represented as occurring in another being. This indifference or independence with respect to us, to our thought, is the attestation of a self-subsistent, *i.e.*, external, personal existence. It is true that religion also makes the fact of God being thought into the self-thinking of God; but because this process goes forward *behind* its consciousness, since God is immediately presupposed as a self-existent personal being, the religious consciousness only embraces the indifference of the two facts.

Even religion, however, does not abide by this indifference of the two sides. God creates in order to reveal himself : creation is the revelation of God. But for stones, plants, and animals there is no God, but only for man; so that Nature exists for the sake of man, and man purely for the sake of God. God glorifies himself in man : man is the pride of God. God indeed knows himself even without man; but so long as there is no other *me,* so long is he only a possible, conceptional person. First when a difference from God, a non-divine is posited, is God conscious of himself; first when he knows what is not God, does he know what it is to be God, does he know the bliss of his Godhead. First in the positing of what is other than himself, of the world, does God posit himself as God. Is God almighty without creation? No! Omnipotence first realises, proves itself in creation. What is a power, a property, which does not exhibit, attest itself? What is a force which affects nothing? a light that does not illuminate? a wisdom which knows nothing, *i.e.*, nothing real? And what is omnipotence, what all other divine attributes, if man does not exist? Man is nothing without God; but also, God is nothing without man; for only in man is God an object as God; only in man is he God. The various qualities of man first give difference, which is the ground of reality in God. The physical qualities of man make God a physical being—God the Father, who is the creator of Nature, *i.e.*, the personified, anthropomorphised essence of Nature; the intellectual qualities of man make God an intellectual being, the moral, a moral being. Human misery is the triumph of divine compassion; sorrow for sin is the delight of the divine holiness. Life, fire, emotion comes into God only through man. With the stubborn sinner God is angry; over the repentant sinner he rejoices. Man is the revealed God : in man the divine essence first realises and unfolds itself. In the creation of Nature God goes out of himself, he has relation to what is other than himself, but in man he returns into himself :—man knows God, because in him God finds and knows himself, feels himself as God. Where there is no pressure, no want, there is no feeling;—and feeling is alone real knowledge. Who can know compassion without having felt the want of it? justice without the experience of injustice? happiness without the experience of distress? Thou must feel what a thing is; otherwise thou wilt never learn to know it. It is in man that the divine properties first become feelings, *i.e.*, man is the self-feeling of God;— and the feeling of God is the real God; for the qualities of God are indeed only real qualities, realities, as felt by man,—as feelings. If the experience of human misery were outside of God, in a being personally separate from him, compassion also would not be in God, and we should hence have again the Being destitute of qualities, or more correctly the *nothing,* which God was before man or without man. For example : —Whether I be a good or sympathetic being—for that alone is good which gives, imparts itself, *bonum est communicativum sui,*—is un- known to me before the opportunity presents itself of showing goodness to another being. Only in the act of imparting do I experience the happiness of beneficence, the joy of generosity, of liberality. But is this joy apart from the joy of the recipient? No; I rejoice because he rejoices. I feel the wretchedness of another, I suffer with him; in alleviating his wretchedness I alleviate my own;—sympathy with suffering is itself suffering. The joyful feeling of the giver is only the reflex, the self- consciousness of the joy in the receiver. Their joy is a common feeling, which accordingly makes itself visible in the union of hands, of lips. So it is here. Just as the feeling of human misery is human, so the feeling of divine compassion is human. It is only a sense of the poverty of finiteness that gives a sense of the bliss of infiniteness. Where the one is not, the other is not. The two are inseparable,—inseparable the feeling of God as God, and the feeling of man as man, inseparable the knowledge of man and the self-knowledge of God. God is a Self only in the human self,—only in the human power of discrimination, in the principle of difference that lies in the human being. Thus compassion is only felt as a *me,* a self, a force, *i.e.*, as something special, through its opposite. The opposite of God gives qualities to God, realises him, makes him a Self. God is God, only through that which is not God. Herein we have also the mystery of Jacob Böhme's doctrine. It must only be borne in mind that Jacob Böhme, as a mystic and theologian, places outside of man the feelings in which the divine being first realises himself, passes from nothing to something, to a qualitative being apart from the feelings of man (at least in imagination),—and that he makes them objective in the form of natural qualities, but in such a way that these qualities still only represent the impressions made on his feelings. It will then be obvious that what the empirical religious consciousness first posits with the real creation of Nature and of man, the mystical consciousness places before the creation in the premundane God, in doing which, however, it does away with the reality of the creation. For if God has what is not-God, already in himself, he has no need first to create what is not-God in order to be God. The creation of the world is here a pure superfluity, or rather an impossibility; this God for very reality does not come to reality; he is already in himself the full and restless world. This is especially true of Schelling's doctrine of God, who though made up of innumerable "potences" is yet thoroughly impotent. Far more reasonable, therefore, is the empirical religious consciousness, which makes God reveal, *i.e.*, realise himself in real man, real nature, and according to which man is created purely for the praise and glory of God. That is to say, man is the mouth of God, which articulates and accentuates the divine qualities as human feelings. God wills that he be honoured, praised. Why? because the passion of man for God is the self-consciousness of God. Nevertheless, the religious consciousness separates these two properly inseparable sides, since by means of the idea of personality it makes God and man independent existences. Now the Hegelian speculation identifies the two sides, but so as to leave the old contradiction still at the foundation;— it is therefore only the consistent carrying out, the completion of a religious truth. The learned mob was so blind in its hatred towards Hegel as not to perceive that his doctrine, at least in this relation, does not in fact contradict religion;—that it contradicts it only in the same way as, in general, a developed, consequent process of thought contradicts an undeveloped, inconsequent, but nevertheless radically identical conception.

But if it is only in human feelings and wants that the divine "nothing" becomes something, obtains qualities, then the being of man is alone the real being of God,—man is the real God. And if in the consciousness which man has of God first arises the self-consciousness of God, then the human consciousness is, *per se,* the divine consciousness. Why then dost thou alienate man's consciousness from him, and make it the self-consciousness of a being distinct from man, of that which is an object to him? Why dost thou vindicate existence to God, to man only the consciousness of that existence? God has his consciousness in man, and man his being in God? Man's knowledge of God is God's knowledge of himself? What a divorcing and contradiction! The true statement is this : man's knowledge of God is man's knowledge of himself, of his own nature. Only the unity of being and consciousness is

truth. Where the consciousness of God is, there is the being of God,—
in man, therefore; in the being of God it is only thy own being which
is an object to thee, and what presents itself *before* thy consciousness is
simply what lies *behind* it. If the divine qualities are human, the human
qualities are divine.

Only when we abandon a philosophy of religion, or a theology,
which is distinct from psychology and anthropology, and recognise
anthropology as itself theology, do we attain to a true, self-satisfying
identity of the divine and human being, the identity of the human
being with itself. In every theory of the identity of the divine and
human which is not true identity, unity of the human nature with
itself, there still lies at the foundation a division, a separation into two,
since the identity is immediately abolished, or rather is supposed to
be abolished. Every theory of this kind is in contradiction with itself
and with the understanding—is a half measure—a thing of the imagination—a perversion, a distortion; which, however, the more perverted
and false it is, all the more *appears* to be profound.

VIII

STIRNER

Max Stirner (1806-56)—his real name was Johann Kaspar Schmidt— studied philosophy at Berlin under Schleiermacher and Hegel, later becoming a member of the *Doktorklub*, a graduates' society of radically minded students to which Marx also at one time belonged. Together with writers like Bauer, Ruge, and Hess, he took a leading part in the philosophical and political controversies which engaged German intellectuals in the eighteen thirties and forties, his best known work appearing in 1845 under the title of *Der Einzige und sein Eigentum* (rendered, somewhat inexactly, as *The Ego and His Own* by its English translator). Both book and author were extravagantly pilloried by Marx, who in his *German Ideology* treated Stirner as ideologically representative of the egoism of a decaying bourgeois society and at the same time attacked him for making ideas, rather than the "real historical relations" that give rise to them, the driving force of history. Toward the end of the century the affinities between some of Stirner's conceptions and those of Nietzsche led to revived interest in his work, while in more recent times it has attracted attention as anticipating certain typical existentialist themes.

Like other left-wing Hegelians, Stirner tended to see alienation everywhere. In contrast to them, however, he propounded a romantically individualistic philosophy, as sharply critical of contemporary humanitarian and communistic theories as it was of the religious orthodoxies of earlier times. In the past men had conjured up "ghosts" and "specters," in the shape of personified ideals and reified systems of thought, by which they allowed themselves to be dominated and enslaved: what was at root the same tendency displayed itself in the modern period when theorists spoke of abstractions like "humanity" or "society" or "the State." Feuerbach had described religious man as projecting his own true essence upon an external mythical being;

Stirner, on the other hand, challenged the whole conception of a pre-existent human essence, which it was the task or destiny of men to realize, as itself embodying a myth. In opposition to it, he set up the notion of the free independent individual, the unique "I" or ego, who was the ultimate creator and master of his own nature and thoughts, and who clearly recognized himself to be such. Value was not an objective property inherent in things, nor was it something ordained by an external authority; it was the individual alone who had to decide what he wanted, what he stood for, what he believed. For, in the last resort, each man was entitled to rely upon nothing except himself and his own powers of appropriation.

The Mythology of Essence*

With the strength of *despair* Feuerbach clutches at the total substance of Christianity, not to throw it away, no, to drag it to himself,
to draw it, the long-yearned-for, ever-distant, out of its heaven with
a last effort, and keep it by him forever. Is not that a clutch of the
uttermost despair, a clutch for life or death, and is it not at the same
time the Christian yearning and hungering for the other world? The
hero wants not to go into the other world, but to draw the other
world to him, and compel it to become this world! And since then
has not all the world, with more or less consciousness, been crying that
"this world" is the vital point, and heaven must come down on earth
and be experienced even here?

Let us, in brief, set Feuerbach's theological view and our contradiction over against each other! "The essence of man is man's supreme
being; now by religion, to be sure, the *supreme being* is called *God*
and regarded as an *objective* essence, but in truth it is only man's own
essence; and therefore the turning point of the world's history is that
henceforth no longer *God*, but man, is to appear to man as God."

To this we reply : The supreme being is indeed the essence of man,
but, just because it is his *essence* and not he himself, it remains quite
immaterial whether we see it outside him and view it as "God," or
find it in him and call it "Essence of Man" or "Man." *I* am neither God
nor *Man*, neither the supreme essence nor my essence, and therefore it
is all one in the main whether I think of the essence as in me or outside
me. Nay, we really do always think of the supreme being as in both
kinds of otherworldliness, the inward and outward, at once; for the
"Spirit of God" is, according to the Christian view, also "our spirit,"
and "dwells in us." It dwells in heaven and dwells in us; we poor
things are just its "dwelling," and, if Feuerbach goes on to destroy its

*From *The Ego and His Own* (trans. Steven T. Byington; London & New York,
1913), pp. 40-62.

253

heavenly dwelling and force it to move to us bag and baggage, then we, its earthly apartments, will be badly overcrowded. . . .

Atheists keep up their scoffing at the higher being, which was also honored under the name of the "highest" or *être suprême,* and trample in the dust one "proof of his existence" after another, without noticing that they themselves, out of need for a higher being, only annihilate the old to make room for a new. Is "Man" perchance not a higher essence than an individual man, and must not the truths, rights, and ideas which result from the concept of him be honored and—counted sacred, as revelations of this very concept? For, even though we should abrogate again many a truth that seemed to be made manifest by this concept, yet this would only evince a misunderstanding on our part, without in the least degree harming the sacred concept itself or taking their sacredness from those truths that must "rightly" be looked upon as its revelations. *Man* reaches beyond every individual man, and yet— though he be "his essence"—is not in fact *his* essence (which rather would be as single as he the individual himself), but a general and "higher," yes, for atheists "the highest essence." And, as the divine revelations were not written down by God with his own hand, but made public through "the Lord's instruments," so also the new highest essence does not write out its revelations itself, but lets them come to our knowledge through "true men." Only the new essence betrays, in fact, a more spiritual style of conception than the old God, because the latter was still represented in a sort of embodiedness or form, while the un-dimmed spirituality of the new is retained, and no special material body is fancied for it. And withal it does not lack corporeity, which even takes on a yet more seductive appearance because it looks more natural and mundane and consists in nothing less than in every bodily man,—yes, or outright in "humanity" or "all men." Thereby the spectralness of the spirit in a seeming-body has once again become really solid and popular.

Sacred, then, is the highest essence and everything in which this highest essence reveals or will reveal itself; but hallowed are they who recognize this highest essence together with its own, *i.e.* together with its revelations. The sacred hallows in turn its reverer, who by his worship becomes himself a saint, as likewise what he does is saintly, a saintly walk, saintly thoughts and actions, imaginations and aspirations, etc.

It is easily understood that the conflict over what is revered as the highest essence can be significant only so long as even the most embittered opponents concede to each other the main point,—that there is a highest essence to which worship or service is due. If one should smile compassionately at the whole struggle over a highest essence, as a Christian might at the war of words between a Shiite and a Sunnite or between a Brahman and a Buddhist, then the hypothesis of a highest essence would be null in his eyes, and the conflict on this basis an idle play. Whether then the one God or the three in one, whether the Lutheran God or the *être suprême* or not God at all, but "Man," may represent the highest essence, that makes no difference at all for him who denies the highest essence itself, for in his eyes those servants of a highest essence are one and all—pious people, the most raging atheist not less than the most faith-filled Christian. . . .

Piety has for a century received so many blows, and had to hear its superhuman essence reviled as an "inhuman" one so often, that one cannot feel tempted to draw the sword against it again. And yet it has almost always been only moral opponents that have appeared in the arena, to assail the supreme essence in favor of—another supreme essence. So Proudhon, unabashed, says : "Man is destined to live without religion, but the moral law is eternal and absolute. Who would dare to-day to attack morality?" Moral people skimmed off the best fat from religion, ate it themselves, and are now having a tough job to get rid of the resulting scrofula. If, therefore, we point out that religion has not by any means been hurt in its inmost part so long as people reproach it only with its superhuman essence, and that it takes its final appeal to the "spirit" alone (for God is spirit), then we have sufficiently indicated its final accord with morality, and can leave its stubborn conflict with the latter lying behind us. It is a question of a supreme essence with both, and whether this is a superhuman or a human one can make (since it is in any case an essence over me, a super mine one, so to speak) but little difference to me. In the end the relation to the human essence, or to "Man," as soon as ever it has shed the snake-skin of the old religion, will yet wear a religious snake-skin again.

So Feuerbach instructs us that, "if one only *inverts* speculative philosophy, *i.e.* always makes the predicate the subject, and so makes the subject the object and principle, one has the undraped truth, pure and clean." Herewith, to be sure, we lose the narrow religious standpoint, lose the *God,* who from this standpoint is subject; but we take in exchange for it the other side of the religious standpoint, the *moral* standpoint. *E.g.,* we no longer say "God is love," but "love is divine." If we further put in place of the predicate "divine" the equivalent "sacred," then, as far as concerns the sense, all the old comes back again. According to this, love is to be the *good* in man, his divineness, that which does him honor, his true *humanity* (it "makes him Man for the first time," makes for the first time a man out of him). So then it would be more accurately worded thus : Love is what is *human* in man, and what is inhuman is the loveless egoist. But precisely all that which Christianity and with it speculative philosophy (*i.e.* theology) offers as the good, the absolute, is to self-ownership simply not the good (or, what means the same, it is *only the good*). Consequently, by the transformation of the predicate into the subject, the Christian *essence* (and it is the predicate that contains the essence, you know) would only be fixed yet more oppressively. God and the divine would entwine themselves all the more inextricably with me. To expel God from his heaven and to rob him of his *"transcendence"* cannot yet support a claim of complete victory, if therein he is only chased into the human breast and gifted with indelible *immanence.* Now they say, "The divine is the truly human !"

The same people who oppose Christianity as the basis of the State, *i.e.* oppose the so-called Christian State, do not tire of repeating that morality is "the fundamental pillar of social life and of the State." As if the dominion of morality were not a complete dominion of the sacred, a "hierarchy." . . .

Man as Owner*

Every one has a relation to objects, and more, every one is differently related to them. Let us choose as an example that book to which millions of men had a relation for two thousand years, the Bible. What is it, what was it, to each? Absolutely, only what he *made out of it!* For him who makes to himself nothing at all out of it, it is nothing at all; for him who uses it as an amulet, it has solely the value, the significance, of a means of sorcery; for him who, like children, plays with it, it is nothing but a plaything; etc.

Now, Christianity asks that it shall *be the same for all:* say, the sacred book or the "sacred Scriptures." This means as much as that the Christian's view shall also be that of other men, and that no one may be otherwise related to that object. And with this the ownness of the relation is destroyed, and one mind, one disposition, is fixed as the *"true,"* the "only true" one. In the limitation of the freedom to make of the Bible what I will, the freedom of making in general is limited; and the coercion of a view or a judgment is put in its place. He who should pass the judgment that the Bible was a long error of mankind would judge—*criminally.*

In fact, the child who tears it to pieces or plays with it, the Inca Atahualpa who lays his ear to it and throws it away contemptuously when it remains dumb, judges just as correctly about the Bible as the priest who praises in it the "Word of God," or the critic who calls it a job of men's hands. For how we toss things about is the affair of our *option,* our *free will:* we use them according to our *heart's pleasure,* or, more clearly, we use them just as we *can.* Why, what do the parsons scream about when they see how Hegel and the speculative theologians make speculative thoughts out of the contents of the Bible? Precisely this, that they deal with it according to their heart's pleasure, or "proceed arbitrarily with it." . . .

What a man is, he makes out of things; "as you look at the world, so

*Ibid., pp. 447-483.

it looks at you again." Then the wise advice makes itself heard again at once, You must only look at it "rightly, unbiasedly," etc. As if the child did not look at the Bible "rightly and unbiasedly" when it makes it a plaything. That shrewd precept is given us, *e.g.*, by Feuerbach. One does look at things rightly when one makes of them what one *will* (by things objects in general are here understood, such as God, our fellow-men, a sweetheart, a book, a beast, etc.). And therefore the things and the look-ing at them are not first, but I am, my will is. One *will* bring thoughts out of the things, *will* discover reason in the world, *will* have sacredness in it : therefore one shall find them. "Seek and ye shall find." *What* I will seek, *I* determine: I want, *e.g.*, to get edification from the Bible; it is to be found; I want to read and test the Bible thoroughly; my outcome will be a thorough instruction and criticism—to the extent of my powers. I elect for myself what I have a fancy for, and in electing I show myself— arbitrary.

Connected with this is the discernment that every judgment which I pass upon an object is the *creature* of my will; and that discernment again leads me to not losing myself in the *creature,* the judgment, but remaining the *creator,* the judger, who is ever creating anew. All pred-icates of objects are my statements, my judgments, my—creatures. If they want to tear themselves loose from me and be something for them-selves, or actually overawe me, then I have nothing more pressing to do than to take them back into their nothing, *i.e.* into me the creator. God, Christ, trinity, morality, the good, etc., are such creatures, of which I must not merely allow myself to say that they are truths, but also that they are deceptions. As I once willed and decreed their exist-ence, so I want to have license to will their non-existence too; I must not let them grow over my head, must not have the weakness to let them become something "absolute," whereby they would be eternal-ized and withdrawn from my power and decision. With that I should fall a prey to the *principle of stability,* the proper life-principle of religion, which concerns itself with creating "sanctuaries that must not be touched," "eternal truths,"—in short, that which shall be "sacred," —and depriving you of what is *yours.* . . . .

Only as the property of me do the spirits, the truths, get to rest; and they then for the first time really are, when they have been deprived of their sorry existence and made a property of mine, when it is no longer said "the truth develops itself, rules, asserts itself; history (also a concept) wins the victory," and the like. The truth never has won a victory, but was always my *means* to the victory, like the sword ("the sword of truth"). The truth is dead, a letter, a word, a material that I can use up. All truth by itself is dead, a corpse; it is alive only in the

same way as my lungs are alive,—to wit, in the measure of my own
vitality. Truths are material, like vegetables and weeds; as to whether
vegetable or weed, the decision lies in me.

Objects are to me only material that I use up. Wherever I put my
hand I grasp a truth, which I trim for myself. The truth is certain to
me, and I do not need to long after it. To do the truth a service is
in no case my intent; it is to me only a nourishment for my thinking
head, as potatoes are for my digesting stomach, or as a friend is for my
social heart. As long as I have the humor and force for thinking, every
truth serves me only for me to work it up according to my powers. As
reality or worldliness is "vain and a thing of naught" for Christians, so
is the truth for me. It exists, exactly as much as the things of this world
go on existing although the Christian has proves their nothingness;
but it is vain, because it has its *value* not *in itself* but *in me*. *Of itself* it is
valueless. The truth is a—*creature*. . . .

Whether what I think and do is Christian, what do I care?
Whether it is human, liberal, humane, whether unhuman, illiberal, in-
humane, what do I ask about that? If only it accomplishes what I want,
if only I satisfy myself in it, then overlay it with predicates as you will;
it is all alike to me.

Perhaps I too, in the very next moment, defend myself against my
former thoughts; I too am likely to change suddenly my mode of action;
but not on account of its not corresponding to Christianity, not on
account of its running counter to the eternal rights of man,
not on account of its affronting the idea of mankind, humanity,
and humanitarianism, but—because I am no longer all in it, because
it no longer furnishes me any full enjoyment, because I doubt the earlier
thought or no longer please myself in the mode of action just now
practised.

As the world as property has become a *material* with which I
undertake what I will, so the spirit too as property must sink down into
a *material* before which I no longer entertain any sacred dread. Then,
firstly, I shall shudder no more before a thought, let it appear as presumptuous and "devilish" as it will, because, if it threatens to become
too inconvenient and unsatisfactory for *me*, its end lies in my power;
but neither shall I recoil from any deed because there dwells in it a
spirit of godlessness, immorality, wrongfulness, as little as St. Boniface
pleased to desist, through religious scrupulousness, from cutting down
the sacred oak of the heathens. If the *things* of the world have once
become vain, the *thoughts* of the spirit must also become vain.

No thought is sacred, for let no thought rank as "devotions"; no
feeling is sacred (no sacred feeling of friendship, mother's feelings, etc.),

no belief is sacred. They are all *alienable,* my alienable property, and are annihilated, as they are created, by *me. . . .*

Self-enjoyment is embittered to me by my thinking I must serve another, by my fancying myself under obligation to him, by my holding myself called to "self-sacrifice," "resignation," "enthusiasm." All right : if I no longer serve any idea, any "higher essence," then it is clear of it-self that I no longer serve any man either, but—under all circumstances —*myself.* But thus I am not merely in fact or in being, but also for my consciousness, the—unique.

There pertains to *you* more than the divine, the human, etc.; *yours* pertains to you.

Look upon yourself as more powerful than they give you out for, and you have more power; look upon yourself as more, and you have more.

You are then not merely *called* to everything divine, *entitled* to everything human, but *owner* of what is yours, *i.e.* of all that you possess the force to make your own; *i.e.* you are *appropriate* and capacitated for everything that is yours.

People have always supposed that they must give me a destiny lying outside myself, so that at last they demanded that I should lay claim to the human because I am = man. This is the Christian magic circle. Fichte's ego too is the same essence outside me, for every one is ego; and, if only this ego has rights, then it is "the ego," it is not I. But I am not an ego along with other egos, but the sole ego : I am unique. Hence my wants too are unique, and my deeds; in short, everything about me is unique. And it is only as this unique I that I take everything for my own, as I set myself to work, and develop myself, only as this. I do not develop man, nor as man, but, as I, I develop—myself. . . .

MARX

KARL MARX (1818-83) was born in Trier, Germany, the son of a Jewish lawyer of mildly liberal views. In 1835 he attended the University of Bonn as a law student, subsequently transferring to Berlin. Here he abandoned law for philosophy, made a concentrated study of Hegel's thought, and became associated with the so-called "Young Hegelians"—a group of men who sought to interpret the Hegelian system in a more progressive manner than had previously been done. In 1842 Marx was in Cologne, where he edited the radical *Rheinische Zeitung* with a subversive venom which finally led to its suppression by the Prussian authorities in April of the following year. He decided to emigrate to Paris, where he remained until 1845. Marx's stay in the French capital was fruitful in a number of ways. It brought him into contact with leading socialists like Proudhon and Louis Blanc, as well as providing him with an opportunity to further his researches into the doctrines of such political economists as Adam Smith, Quesnay, Ricardo, and Say. Moreover, it was in Paris that he first met Friedrich Engels (1820-95) who, as the son of a wealthy cotton manufacturer, possessed a first-hand acquaintance with labor conditions in contemporary industrial society. This meeting marked the beginning of a lifetime of collaboration in revolutionary writing and activity, of which the most important immediate products were *The German Ideology* (completed, though not published, in 1846) and the *Communist Manifesto* (1848). In 1849, after the collapse of the revolutionary movements on the continent, Marx moved to London where he spent the rest of his life. The first volume of his *Capital* appeared in Hamburg in 1867, the succeeding two volumes being published posthumously in 1885 and 1894.

It is arguable that Marx's principal contributions to nineteenth-century thought belong to the field of social and economic analysis rather than to that of philosophy, and he himself certainly spoke as if the time had come for the latter, conceived as a purely contemplative or speculative pursuit, to give way to a theory of society with a practical, i.e., revolutionary, purpose. The fact remains, however, that it was Hegelian philosophy that provided Marx with a framework within which to develop his ideas, and his writings in the eighteen forties, when he was working out the main outlines of his theory of history and social change, draw heavily upon Hegel and upon the materialistic or "naturalized" Hegelianism of Feuerbach. It is, indeed, sometimes suggested that there are really two distinct stages in Marx's intellectual career: an initial "humanistic" period, to which the semiphilosophical writings of 1842-44 belong, and a later sociological one, in which the empirical analysis of class structures and conflicts tended to supplant the previous philosophizing about the nature of man as a "species being." In view of the evident continuities that exist between much of Marx's early work and the "scientific socialism" of his maturity, such a sharp division seems somewhat artificial; the differences, it might be claimed, are more often ones of emphasis and mode of formulation (Marx was capable of using a contorted jargon that rivalled Hegel's in opacity) than of essential content. But, however this may be, it is in the early writings that the influence of Hegelian and Feuerbachian notions of human alienation and self-development is most marked; it is here, too, that the precise nature of Marx's reaction against the philosophical doctrines current in the Germany of his time is most clearly exhibited.

Critique of Hegel's Dialectic and General Philosophy*

. . . Hegel's *Encyclopaedia* begins with logic, with *pure speculative thought*, and ends with *absolute knowledge*, the self-conscious and self-conceiving philosophical or absolute mind, i.e., the superhuman abstract mind. The whole of the *Encyclopaedia* is nothing but the extended being of the philosophical mind, its self-objectification; and the philosophical mind is nothing but the alienated world-mind thinking within the bounds of its self-alienation, i.e. conceiving itself in an abstract manner. *Logic* is the *money* of the mind, the speculative *thought-value* of man and of nature, their essence indifferent to any real determinate character and thus unreal; *thought* which is *alienated* and abstract and ignores real nature and man. *The external character of this abstract thought . . . nature* as it exists for this abstract thought. Nature is external to it, loss of itself, and is only conceived as something external, as abstract thought, but alienated abstract thought. Finally, spirit, this thought which returns to its own origin and which, as anthropological, phenomenological, psychological, customary, artistic-religious spirit, is not valid for itself until it discovers itself and relates itself to itself as absolute knowledge in the absolute (i.e. abstract) spirit, and so receives its conscious and fitting existence. For its real mode of existence is *abstraction*.

Hegel commits a double error. The first appears most clearly in the *Phenomenology*, the birthplace of his philosophy. When Hegel conceives wealth, the power of the state, etc. as entities alienated from the human being, he conceives them only in their thought form. They are entities of thought and thus simply an alienation of *pure* (i.e. abstract) philosophical thought. The whole movement, therefore, ends in absolute knowledge. It is precisely abstract thought from which these

*From *Economic and Philosophical Manuscripts* (1844), (trans. T. B. Bottomore in *Karl Marx: Early Writings*; London, 1963), pp. 199-214. Reprinted by permission of C. A. Watts & Co. Ltd.

objects are alienated, and which they confront with their presumptuous reality. The *philosopher,* himself an abstract form of alienated man, sets himself up as the *measure* of the alienated world. The whole *history of alienation,* and of the retraction of alienation, is, therefore, only the *history of the production* of abstract thought, i.e. of absolute, logical, speculative thought. *Estrangement,* which thus forms the real interest of this alienation and of the supersession of this alienation, is the opposition of *in itself* and *for itself,* of *consciousness* and *self-consciousness,* of *object* and *subject, i.e.* the opposition in thought itself between abstract thought and sensible reality or real sensuous existence. All other contradictions and movements are merely the *appearance,* the *cloak,* the *exoteric* form of these two opposites which are alone important and which constitute the *significance* of the other, profane contradictions. It is not the fact that the human being *objectifies* himself *inhumanly,* in opposition to himself, but that he *objectifies* himself by *distinction* from and in *opposition* to abstract thought, which constitutes alienation as it exists and as it has to be transcended.

The appropriation of man's objectified and alienated faculties is thus, in the first place, only an *appropriation* which occurs in *consciousness,* in *pure thought,* i.e. in abstraction. It is the appropriation of these objects as *thoughts* and as *movements of thoughts.* For this reason, despite its thoroughly negative and critical appearance, and despite the genuine criticism which it contains and which often anticipates later developments, there is already implicit in the *Phenomenology,* as a germ, as a potentiality and a secret, the uncritical positivism and uncritical idealism of Hegel's later works—the philosophical dissolution and restoration of the existing empirical world. *Secondly,* the vindication of the objective world for man (for example, the recognition that *sense* perception is not *abstract* sense perception but *human* sense perception, that religion, wealth, etc. are only the alienated reality of *human* objectification, of *human* faculties put to work, and are, therefore, a *way* to genuine *human* reality), this appropriation, or the insight into this process, appears in Hegel as the recognition of *sensuousness, religion,* state power, etc. as *mental* phenomena, for *mind* alone is the *true* essence of man, and the true form of mind is thinking mind, the logical, speculative mind. The *human character* of nature, of historically produced nature, of man's products, is shown by their being *products* of abstract mind, and thus phases of *mind, entities of thought.* The *Phenomenology* is a concealed, unclear and mystifying criticism, but in so far as it grasps the *alienation* of man (even though man appears only as mind) *all* the elements of criticism are contained in it, and are often *presented* and *worked out* in a manner which goes far beyond Hegel's

own point of view. The sections devoted to the "unhappy consciousness," the "honest consciousness," the struggle between the "noble"
and the "base" consciousness, etc., etc. contains the *critical* elements
(though still in an alienated form) of whole areas such as religion, the
state, civil life, etc. Just as the *entity,* the *object,* appears as an entity of
thought, so also the *subject* is always *consciousness* or *self-consciousness;*
or rather, the object appears only as *abstract* consciousness and man
as *self-consciousness.* Thus the distinctive forms of alienation which are
manifested are only different forms of consciousness and self-consciousness. Since abstract consciousness (the form in which the object is conceived) is in *itself* merely a distinctive moment of self-consciousness,
the outcome of the movement is the identity of self-consciousness and
consciousness—absolute knowledge—the movement of abstract thought
not directed outwards but proceeding within itself; i.e. the dialectic of
pure thought is the result.

The outstanding achievement of Hegel's *Phenomenology*—the
dialectic of negativity as the moving and creating principle—is, first,
that Hegel grasps the self-creation of man as a process, objectification
as loss of the object, as alienation and transcendence of this alienation,
and that he, therefore, grasps the nature of *labour,* and conceives
objective man (true, because real man) as the result of his *own labour.*
The *real,* active orientation of man to himself as a species-being, or the
affirmation of himself as a real species-being (i.e. as a human being)
is only possible so far as he really brings forth all his *species-powers*
(which is only possible through the co-operative endeavours of mankind and as an outcome of history) and treats these powers as objects,
which can only be done at first in the form of alienation.

We shall next show in detail Hegel's one-sidedness and limitations,
as revealed in the final chapter of the *Phenomenology,* on absolute
knowledge. . . .

The main point is that the *object of consciousness* is nothing else
but *self-consciousness,* that the object is only *objectified* self-consciousness, self-consciousness as an object. (Positing man = self-consciousness.)

It is necessary, therefore, to surmount the *object of consciousness.*
Objectivity as such is regarded as an alienated human relationship
which does not correspond with the *essence of man,* self-consciousness.
The reappropriation of the objective essence of man, which was produced as something alien and determined by alienation, signifies the
supersession not only of *alienation* but also of *objectivity;* that is, man
is regarded as a *non-objective, spiritual* being.

The process of *overcoming the object of consciousness* is described
by Hegel as follows : The *object* does not reveal itself only as *returning*

into the Self (according to Hegel that is a *one-sided* conception of the movement, considering only one aspect). Man is equated with self. The Self, however, is only man conceived *abstractly* and produced by abstraction. Man is self-referring. His eye, his ear, etc. are *self-refer-ring;* every one of his faculties has this quality of *self*-reference. But it is entirely false to say on that account, *"Self-consciousness* has eyes, ears, faculties." Self-consciousness is rather a quality of human nature, of the human eye, etc.; human nature is not a quality of *self-conscious-ness.*

The Self, abstracted and determined for itself, is man as an *abstract egoist,* purely abstract *egoism* raised to the level of thought. (We shall return to this point later.)

For Hegel, *human life, man,* is equivalent to *self-consciousness.* All alienation of human life is, therefore, *nothing* but *alienation of self-consciousness.* The alienation of self-consciousness is not regarded as the *expression,* reflected in knowledge and thought, of the *real* aliena-tion of human life. Instead, *actual* alienation, that which appears real, is in its *innermost* hidden nature (which philosophy first discloses) only the *phenomenal being* of the alienation of real human life, of *self-consciousness.* The science which comprehends this is therefore called *Phenomenology.* All reappropriation of alienated objective life appears, therefore, as an incorporation in self-consciousness. The person who takes possession of his being is only the self-consciousness which takes possession of objective being; the return of the object into the Self is, therefore, the reappropriation of the object.

Expressed in a *more comprehensive way* the *supersession of the object of consciousness* means: (1) that the object as such presents itself to consciousness as something disappearing; (2) that it is the alienation of self-consciousness which establishes "thinghood"; (3) that this aliena-tion has *positive* as well as *negative* significance; (4) that it has this significance not only *for us* or in itself, but also *for self-consciousness itself;* (5) that for *self-consciousness* the negative of the object, its self-supersession, has *positive* significance, or self-consciousness *knows* there-by the nullity of the object in that self-consciousness alienates itself, for in this alienation it establishes *itself* as object or, for the sake of the indivisible unity of *being-for-itself,* establishes the object as itself; (6) that, on the other hand, this other "moment" is equally present, that self-consciousness has superseded and reabsorbed this alienation and objectivity, and is thus *at home* in its other being as such; (7) that this is the movement of consciousness, and consciousness is, therefore, the totality of its "moments"; (8) that similarly, consciousness must have related itself to the object in all its determinations, and have conceived it in terms of each of them. This totality of determinations makes the object *intrinsically* a *spiritual being,* and it becomes truly so for consciousness by the apprehension of every one of these determinations as the Self, or by what was called earlier the *spiritual* attitude towards them.

ad (1) That the object as such presents itself to consciousness as something disappearing is the above-mentioned *return of the object into the Self.*

ad (2) *The alienation of self-consciousness* establishes "thinghood." Because man equals self-consciousness, his alienated objective being or *"thinghood"* is equivalent to *alienated self-consciousness,* and "thinghood" is established by this alienation. ("Thinghood" is that which is *an object for him,* and an object for him is really only that which is an essential object, consequently his *objective* essence. And since it is not the *real man,* nor *nature*—man being *human nature*—who becomes as such a subject, but only an abstraction of man, self-consciousness, "thinghood" can only be *alienated self-consciousness.*) It is quite understandable that a living, natural being endowed with objective (i.e. material) faculties should have *real natural objects* of its being, and equally that its self-alienation should be the establishment of a *real, objective world,* but in the form of *externality,* as a world which does not belong to, and dominates, its being. There is nothing incomprehensible or mysterious about this. The converse, rather, would be mysterious. But it is equally clear that a self-consciousness, i.e. its alienation, can only establish *"thinghood,"* i.e. only an abstract thing, a thing created by abstraction and not a real thing. It is clear, moreover, that "thinghood" is totally lacking in *independence,* in *being,* vis-à-vis self-consciousness; it is a mere *construct* established by self-consciousness. And what is established is not self-confirming; it is the confirmation of the act of establishing, which for an instant, but only for an instant, fixes its energy as a product and *apparently* confers upon it the role of an independent, real being.

When real, corporeal *man,* with his feet firmly planted on the solid ground, inhaling and exhaling all the powers of nature, *posits* his real objective faculties, as a result of his alienation, as alien objects, the *positing* is not the subject of this act but the subjectivity of *objective* faculties whose action must also, therefore, be *objective.* An objective being acts objectively, and it would not act objectively if objectivity were not part of its essential being. It creates and establishes *only objects, because* it is established by objects, and because it is fundamentally *natural.* In the act of establishing it does not descend from its "pure activity" to the *creation of objects;* its *objective* product simply confirms its *objective* activity, its activity as an objective, natural being.

We see here how consistent naturalism or humanism is distinguished from both idealism and materialism, and at the same time constitutes their unifying truth. We see also that only naturalism is able to comprehend the process of world history.

Man is directly *a natural being*. As a natural being, and as a living natural being he is, on the one hand, endowed with *natural powers* and *faculties*, which exist in him as tendencies and abilities, as *drives*. On the other hand, as a natural, embodied, sentient, objective being he is a *suffering*, conditioned and limited being, like animals and plants. The *objects* of his drives exist outside himself as *objects* independent of him, yet they are *objects* of his *needs*, essential *objects* which are indispensable to the exercise and confirmation of his faculties. The fact that man is an *embodied*, living, real, sentient, objective being with natural powers, means that he has *real, sensuous objects* as the objects of his being, or that he can only express his being in real, sensuous objects. *To be* objective, natural, sentient and at the same time to have object, nature and sense outside oneself, or to be oneself object, nature and sense for a third person, is the same thing. *Hunger* is a natural *need;* it requires, therefore, a *nature* outside itself, an *object* outside itself, in order to be satisfied and stilled. Hunger is the objective need of a body for an *object* which exists outside itself and which is essential for its integration and the expression of its nature. The sun is an *object*, a necessary and life-assuring object, for the plant, just as the plant is an object for the sun, an *expression* of the sun's life-giving power and *objective* essential powers.

A being which does not have its nature outside itself is not a *natural* being and does not share in the being of nature. A being which has no object outside itself is not an objective being. A being which is not itself an object for a third being has no being for its *object*, i.e. it is not objectively related and its being is not objective.

A non-objective being is a *non-being*. Suppose a being which neither is an object itself nor has an object. In the first place, such a being would be the *only* being; no other being would exist outside itself and it would be solitary and alone. For as soon as there exist objects outside myself, as soon as I am not *alone*, I am *another, another reality* from the object outside me. For this third object I am thus an *other reality* than itself, i.e. *its object*. To suppose a being which is not the object of another being would be to suppose that *no* objective being exists. As soon as I have an object, this being has for me its object. But a *non-objective* being is an unreal, non-sensuous, merely conceived being; i.e. a merely imagined being, an abstraction. To be *sensuous*, i.e. real, is to be an object of sense or *sensuous* object, and thus to have sensuous objects outside oneself, objects of one's sensations. To be sentient is to *suffer* (to experience). . . .

We have already seen that the appropriation of alienated objective being, or the supersession of objectivity in the form of *alienation* (which has to develop from indifferent otherness to real antagonistic alienation), signifies for Hegel also, or primarily, the supersession of *objectivity,* since it is not the determinate character of the object but its *objective* character which is the scandal of alienation for self-consciousness. The object is therefore negative, self-annulling, a *nullity.* This nullity of the object has a positive significance because it *knows* this nullity, objective being, as its *self-alienation,* and knows that this nullity exists only through its self-alienation. . . .

The way in which consciousness is, and in which something is for it, is *knowing.* Knowing is its only act. Thus something comes to exist for consciousness so far as it *knows* this *something.* Knowing is its only objective relation. It knows, then, the nullity of the object (i.e. knows the nonexistence of the distinction between itself and the object, the nonexistence of the object for it) because it knows the object as its *self-alienation.* That is to say, it knows itself (knows knowing as an object), because the object is only the *semblance* of an object, a deception, which is intrinsically nothing but knowing itself which has confronted itself with itself, has established in face of itself a *nullity,* a "something" which has *no* objective existence outside the knowing itself. Knowing knows that in relating itself to an object it is only *outside* itself, alienates itself, and that *it* only *appears* to itself as an object; or in other words, that which appears to it as an object is only itself.

On the other hand, Hegel says, this other "moment" is present at the same time; namely, the consciousness has equally superseded and reabsorbed this alienation and objectivity, and consequently is *at home in its other being as such.*

In this discussion all the illusions of speculation are assembled.

First, consciousness—self-consciousness—is *at home in its other being as such.* It is, therefore—if we abstract from Hegel's abstraction and substitute the self-consciousness of man for self-consciousness—*at home in its other being as such.* This implies, first, that consciousness (knowing as knowing, thinking as thinking) claims to be directly the *other* of itself, the sensuous world, reality, life; it is thought over-reaching itself in thought (Feuerbach). This aspect is contained in it, in so far as consciousness as mere consciousness is offended not by the alienated objectivity but by *objectivity as such.*

Secondly, it implies that self-conscious man, in so far as he has recognized and superseded the spiritual world (or the universal spiritual mode of existence of his world) then confirms it again in this alienated form and presents it as his true existence; he re-establishes it and claims to *be at home in his other being*. Thus, for example, after superseding religion, when he has recognized religion as a product of self-alienation, he then finds a confirmation of himself in *religion as religion*. *This is* the root of Hegel's *false* positivism, or of his merely *apparent* criticism : what Feuerbach calls the positing, negation and re-establishment of religion or theology, but which has to be conceived in a more general way. Thus reason is at home in unreason as such. Man, who has recognized that he leads an alienated life in law, politics, etc. leads his true human life in this alienated life as such. Self-affirmation, in contradiction with itself, with the knowledge and the nature of the object, is thus the true *knowledge* and *life*.

There can no longer be any question about Hegel's compromise with religion, the state, etc., for this falsehood is the falsehood of his whole argument.

If I *know* religion as *alienated* human self-consciousness what I know in it as religion is not my self-consciousness but my alienated self-consciousness confirmed in it. Thus my own self, and the self-consciousness which is its essence, is not confirmed in *religion* but in the *abolition* and *supersession* of religion.

In Hegel, therefore, the negation of the negation is not the confirmation of true being by the negation of illusory being. It is the confirmation of illusory being, or of self-alienating being in its denial; or the denial of this illusory being as an objective being existing outside man and independently of him, and its transformation into a subject.

The act of *supersession* plays a strange part in which *denial* and preservation, denial and affirmation, are linked together. Thus, for example, in Hegel's *Philosophy of Right, private right* superseded equals *morality,* morality superseded equals *the family,* the family superseded equals *civil society,* civil society superseded equals the *state,* and the state superseded equals *world history*. But in *actuality* private right, morality, the family, civil society, the state, etc. remain; only they have become "moments," modes of existence of man, which have no validity in isolation but which mutually dissolve and engender one another. *They are "moments" of the movement. . . .*

We have now to consider the *positive* moments of Hegel's dialectic, within the condition of alienation.

(a) Supersession as an objective movement which *reabsorbs* alienation into itself. This is the insight, expressed within alienation, into the *appropriation* of the objective being through the supersession of its

alienation. It is the alienated insight into the real objectification of man, into the real appropriation of his objective being by the destruction of the *alienated* character of the objective world, by the annulment of its alienated mode of existence. In the same way, atheism as the annulment of God is the emergence of theoretical humanism, and communism as the annulment of private property is the vindication of real human life as man's property. The latter is also the emergence of practical humanism, for atheism is humanism mediated to itself by the annulment of religion, while communism is humanism mediated to itself by the annulment of private property. It is only by the supersession of this mediation (which is, however, a necessary pre-condition) that the self-originating *positive* humanism can appear.

But atheism and communism are not flight or abstraction from, nor loss of, the objective world which men have created by the objectification of their faculties. They are not an impoverished return to unnatural, primitive simplicity. They are rather the first real emergence, the genuine actualization, of man's nature as something real.

Thus Hegel, in so far as he sees the *positive* significance of the self-referring negation (though in an alienated mode) conceives man's self-estrangement, alienation of being, loss of objectivity and reality, as self-discovery, change of nature, objectification and realization. In short, Hegel conceives labour as man's *act of self-creation* (though in abstract terms); he grasps man's relation to himself as an alien being and the emergence of *species-consciousness* and *species-life* as the demonstration of his alien being.

(b) But in Hegel, apart from, or rather as a consequence of, the inversion we have already described, this act of genesis appears, in the first place, as one which is merely *formal,* because it is abstract, and because human nature itself is treated as merely *abstract, thinking nature,* as self-consciousness.

Secondly, because the conception is *formal* and *abstract* the annulment of alienation becomes a confirmation of alienation. For Hegel, this movement of *self-creation* and *self-objectification* in the form of *self-estrangement* is the *absolute* and hence final *expression of human life,* which has its end in itself, is at peace with itself and at one with its own nature.

This movement, in its abstract form as dialectic, is regarded therefore as *truly human life,* and since it is nevertheless an abstraction, an alienation of human life, it is regarded as a *divine process* and thus as the divine process of mankind; it is a process which man's abstract, pure, absolute being, as distinguished from himself, traverses.

Thirdly, this process must have a bearer, a subject; but the subject first emerges as a result. This result, the subject knowing itself as absolute self-consciousness, is therefore *God, absolute spirit, the self-knowing and self-manifesting idea.* Real man and real nature become mere predicates, symbols of this concealed unreal man and unreal nature. Subject and predicate have, therefore, an inverted relation to each other; a *mystical subject-object,* or a *subjectivity reaching beyond the object,* the *absolute subject* as a process of self-alienation and of return from alienation into itself, and at the same time of reabsorption of this alienation, the *subject* as this process; pure, *unceasing* revolving within itself. . . .

Alienated Labor*

... We shall begin from a *contemporary* economic fact. The worker becomes poorer the more wealth he produces and the more his production increases in power and extent. The worker becomes an ever cheaper commodity the more goods he creates. The *devaluation* of the human world increases in direct relation with the *increase in value* of the world of things. Labour does not only create goods; it also produces itself and the worker as a *commodity,* and indeed in the same proportion as it produces goods.

This fact simply implies that the object produced by labour, its product, now stands opposed to it as an *alien being,* as a *power independent* of the producer. The product of labour is labour which has been embodied in an object and turned into a physical thing; this product is an *objectification* of labour. The performance of work is at the sametime its objectification. The performance of work appears in the sphere of political economy as a *vitiation* of the worker, objectification as a *loss* and as *servitude to the object,* and appropriation as *alienation.*

So much does the performance of work appear as vitiation that the worker is vitiated to the point of starvation. So much does objectification appear as loss of the object that the worker is deprived of the most essential things not only of life but also of work. Labour itself becomes an object which he can acquire only by the greatest effort and with unpredictable interruptions. So much does the appropriation of the object appear as alienation that the more objects the worker produces the fewer he can possess and the more he falls under the domination of his product, of capital.

All these consequences follow from the fact that the worker is related to the *product of his labour* as to an *alien* object. For it is clear on this presupposition that the more the worker expends himself in work the more powerful becomes the world of objects which he creates in face of himself, the poorer he becomes in his inner life, and the less

*Ibid., pp. 121-131.

he belongs to himself. It is just the same as in religion. The more of himself man attributes to God the less he has left in himself. The worker puts his life into the object, and his life then belongs no longer to himself but to the object. The greater his activity, therefore, the less he possesses. What is embodied in the product of his labour is no longer his own. The greater this product is, therefore, the more he is diminished. The *alienation* of the worker in his product means not only that his labour becomes an object, assumes an *external* existence, but that it exists independently, *outside himself*, and alien to him, and that it stands opposed to him as an autonomous power. The life which he has given to the object sets itself against him as an alien and hostile force.

Let us now examine more closely the phenomenon of *objectfication*; the worker's production and the *alienation* and *loss* of the object it produces, which is involved in it. The worker can create nothing without *nature*, without the *sensuous external world*. The latter is the material in which his labour is realized, in which it is active, out of which and through which it produces things.

But just as nature affords the *means of existence* of labour, in the sense that labour cannot *live* without objects upon which it can be exercised, so also it provides the *means of existence* in a narrower sense; namely the means of physical existence for the *worker* himself. Thus, the more the worker *appropriates* the external world of sensuous nature by his labour the more he deprives himself of *means of existence*, in two respects : first, that the sensuous external world becomes progressively less an object belonging to his labour or a means of existence of his labour, and secondly, that it becomes progressively less a means of existence in the direct sense, a means for the physical subsistence of the worker.

In both respects, therefore, the worker becomes a slave of the object; first, in that he receives an *object of work*, i.e. receives *work*, and secondly, in that he receives *means of subsistence*. Thus the object enables him to exist, first as a *worker* and secondly, as a *physical subject*. The culmination of this enslavement is that he can only maintain himself as a *physical subject* so far as he is a *worker,* and that it is as a *physical subject* that he is a worker.

(The alienation of the worker in his object is expressed as follows in the laws of political economy : the more the worker produces the less he has to consume; the more value he creates the more worthless he becomes; the more refined his product the more crude and misshapen the worker; the more civilized the product the more barbarous the worker; the more powerful the work the more feeble the worker; the more the work manifests intelligence the more the worker declines in intelligence and becomes a slave of nature.)

Political economy conceals the alienation in the nature of labour in so far is it does not examine the direct relationship between the worker (work) and production. Labour certainly produces marvels for the rich but it produces privation for the worker. It produces palaces, but hovels for the worker. It produces beauty, but deformity for the worker. It replaces labour by machinery, but it cases some of the workers back into a barbarous kind of work and turns the others into machines. It produces intelligence, but also supidity and cretinism for the workers.

The direct relationship of labour to its products is the relationship of the worker to the objects of his production. The relationship of property owners to the objects of production and to production itself is merely a *consequence* of this first relationship and confirms it. We shall consider this second aspect later.

Thus, when we ask what is the important relationship of labour, we are concerned with the relationship of the *worker* to production.

So far we have considered the alienation of the worker only from one aspect; namely, *his relationship with the products of his labour.* However, alienation appears not merely in the result but also in the *process of production,* within *productive activity* itself. How could the worker stand in an alien relationship to the product of his activity if he did not alienate himself in the act of production itself? The product is indeed only the *résumé* of activity, of production. Consequently, if the product of labour is alienation, production itself must be active alienation—the alienation of activity and the activity of alienation. The alienation of the object of labour merely summarizes the alienation in the work activity itself.

What constitutes the alienation of labour? First, that the work is *external* to the worker, that it is not part of his nature; and that, consequently, he does not fulfil himself in his work but denies himself, has a feeling of misery rather than well-being, does not develop freely his mental and physical energies but is physically exhausted and mentally debased. The worker, therefore, feels himself at home only during his leisure time, whereas at work he feels homeless. His work is not voluntary but imposed, *forced labour.* It is not the satisfaction of a need, but only a *means* for satisfying other needs. Its alien character is clearly shown by the fact that as soon as there is no physical or other compulsion it is avoided like the plague. External labour, labour in which man alienates himself, is a labour of self-sacrifice, of mortification. Finally, the external character of work for the worker is shown by the fact that it is not his own work but work for someone else, that in work he does not belong to himself but to another person.

Just as in religion the spontaneous activity of human fantasy, of the human brain and heart, reacts independently as an alien activity of gods or devils upon the individual, so the activity of the worker is not his own spontaneous activity. It is another's activity and a loss of his own spontaneity.

We arrive at the result that man (the worker) feels himself to be freely active only in his animal functions—eating, drinking and pro-creating, or at most also in his dwelling and in personal adorn-ment—while in his human functions he is reduced to an animal. The animal becomes human and the human becomes animal.

Eating, drinking and procreating are of course also genuine human functions. But abstractly considered, apart from the environment of human activities, and turned into final and sole ends, they are animal functions.

We have now considered the act of alienation of practical human activity, labour, from two aspects: (1) the relationship of the worker to the *product of labour* as an alien object which dominates him. This relationship is at the same time the relationship to the sensuous external world, to natural objects, as an alien and hostile world; (2) the relationship of labour to the *act of production* within *labour*. This is the relationship of the worker to his own activity as something alien and not belonging to him, activity as suffering (passivity), strength as powerlessness, creation as emasculation, the *personal* physical and mental energy of the worker, his personal life (for what is life but activity?), as an activity which is directed against himself, independent of him and not belonging to him. This is *self-alienation* as against the above-mentioned alienation of the *thing*.

We have now to infer a third characteristic of *alienated labour* from the two we have considered.

Man is a species-being not only in the sense that he makes the community (his own as well as those of other things) his object both practically and theoretically, but also (and this is simply another ex-pression for the same thing) in the sense that he treats himself as the present, living species, as a *universal* and consequently free being.

Species-life, for man as for animals, has its physical basis in the fact that man (like animals) lives from inorganic nature, and since man is more universal than an animal so the range of inorganic nature from which he lives is more universal. Plants, animals, minerals, air, light, etc. constitute, from the theoretical aspect, a part of human consciousness as objects of natural science and art; they are man's spiritual inorganic nature, his intellectual means of life, which he must first prepare for enjoyment and perpetuation. So also, from the practical aspect, they form a part of human life and activity. In practice man lives only from these natural products, whether in the form of food, heating, clothing, housing, etc. The universality of man appears in practice in the universality which makes the whole of nature into his inorganic body: (1) as a direct means of life; and equally (2) as the material object and instrument of his life activity. Nature is the inorganic body of man; that is to say nature, excluding the human body itself. To say that man *lives* from nature means that nature is his *body* with which he must remain in a continuous interchange in order not to die. The statement that the physical and mental life of man, and nature, are interdependent means simply that nature is interdependent with itself, for man is a part of nature.

Since alienated labour: (1) alienates nature from man; and (2) alienates man from himself, from his own active function, his life activity; so it alienates him from the species. It makes *species-life* into a means of individual life. In the first place it alienates species-life and individual life, and secondly, it turns the latter, as an abstraction, into the purpose of the former, also in its abstract and alienated form.

For labour, *life activity, productive life,* now appear to man only as *means* for the satisfaction of a need, the need to maintain his physical existence. Productive life is, however, species-life. It is life creating life. In the type of life activity resides the whole character of a species, its species-character; and free, conscious activity is the species-character of human beings. Life itself appears only as a *means of life.*

The animal is one with its life activity. It does not distinguish the activity from itself. It is *its activity.* But man makes his life activity itself an object of his will and consciousness. He has a conscious life activity. It is not a determination with which he is completely identified. Conscious life activity distinguishes man from the life activity of animals. Only for this reason is he is a species-being. Or rather, he is only a self-conscious being, i.e. his own life is an object for him, because he is a species-being. Only for this reason is his activity free activity. Alienated labour reverses the relationship, in that man because he is a self-conscious being makes his life activity, his *being,* only a means for his *existence.*

The practical construction of an *objective world,* the *manipulation* of inorganic nature, is the confirmation of man as a conscious species-being, i.e. a being who treats the species as his own being or himself as a species-being. Of course, animals also produce. They construct nests, dwellings, as in the case of bees, beavers, ants, etc. But they only produce what is strictly necessary for themselves or their young. They produce only in a single direction, while man produces universally. They produce only under the compulsion of direct physical needs, while man produces when he is free from physical need and only truly produces in freedom from such need. Animals produce only themselves, while man reproduces the whole of nature. The products of animal production belong directly to their physical bodies, while man is free in face of his product. Animals construct only in accordance with the standards and needs of the species to which they belong, while man knows how to produce in accordance with the standards of every species and knows how to apply the appropriate standard to the object. Thus man constructs also in accordance with the laws of beauty.

It is just in his work upon the objective world that man really proves himself as a *species-being*. This production is his active species-life. By means of it nature appears as *his* work and his reality. The object of labour is, therefore, the *objectification of man's species-life;* for he no longer reproduces himself merely intellectually, as in consciousness, but actively and in a real sense, and he sees his own reflection in a world which he has constructed. While, therefore, alienated labour takes away the object of production from man, it also takes away his *species*-life, his real objectivity as a species-being, and changes his advantage over animals into a disadvantage in so far as his inorganic body, nature, is taken from him.

Just as alienated labour transforms free and self-directed activity into a means, so it transforms the species-life of man into a means of physical existence.

Consciousness, which man has from his species, is transformed through alienation so that species-life becomes only a means for him. (3) Thus alienated labour turns the *species-life of man*, and also nature as his mental species-property, into an *alien* being and into a *means* for his *individual existence*. It alienates from man his own body, external nature, his mental life and his *human* life. (4) A direct consequence of the alienation of man from the product of his labour, from his life activity and from his species-life, is that *man* is *alienated* from other *men*. When man confronts himself he also confronts *other* men. What is true of man's relationship to his work, to the product of his work and to himself, is also true of his relationship to other men, to their labour and to the objects of their labour.

In general, the statement that man is alienated from his species-life means that each man is alienated from others, and that each of the others is likewise alienated from human life.

Human alienation, and above all the relation of man to himself, is first realized and expressed in the relationship between each man and other men. Thus in the relationship of alienated labour every man regards other men according to the standards and relationships in which he finds himself placed as a worker.

We began with an economic fact, the alienation of the worker and his production. We have expressed this fact in conceptual terms as *alienated labour*, and in analysing the concept we have merely analysed an economic fact.

Let us now examine further how this concept of alienated labour must express and reveal itself in reality. If the product of labour is alien to me and confronts me as an alient power, to whom does it belong? If my own activity does not belong to me but is an alien, forced activity, to whom does it belong? To a being *other* than myself. And who is this being? The *gods*? It is apparent in the earliest stages of advanced production, e.g. temple building, etc. in Egypt, India, Mexico, and in the service rendered to gods, that the product belonged to the gods. But the gods alone were never the lords of labour. And no more was *nature*. What a contradiction it would be if the more man subjugates nature by his labour, and the more the marvels of the gods are rendered superfluous by the marvels of industry, the more he should abstain from his joy in producing and his enjoyment of the product for love of these powers.

The *alien* being to whom labour and the product of labour belong, to whose service labour is devoted, and to whose enjoyment the product of labour goes, can only be *man* himself. If the product of labour does not belong to the worker, but confronts him as an alien power, this can only be because it belongs to *a man other than the worker*. If his activity is a torment to him it must be a source of *enjoyment* and pleasure to another. Not the gods, nor nature, but only man himself can be this alien power over men.

Consider the earlier statement that the relation of man to himself is first *realized, objectified*, through his relation to other men. If he is related to the product of his labour, his objectified labour, as to an *alien*, hostile, powerful and independent object, he is related in such a way that another alien, hostile, powerful and independent man is the lord of this object. If he is related to his own activity as to unfree activity, then he is related to it as activity in the service, and under the domination, coercion and yoke, of another man.

Every self-alienation of man, from himself and from nature, appears in the relation which he postulates between other men and himself and nature. Thus religious self-alienation is necessarily exemplified in the relation between laity and priest, or, since it is here a question of the spiritual world, between the laity and a mediator. In the real world of practice this self-alienation can only be expressed in the real, practical relation of man to his fellow men. The medium through which alienation occurs is itself a *practical* one. Through alienated labour, therefore, man not only produces his relation to the object and to the process of production as to alien and hostile men; he also produces the relation of other men to his production and his product, and the relation between himself and other men. Just as he creates his own production as a vitiation, a punishment, and his own product as a loss, as a product which does not belong to him, so he creates the domination of the non-producer over production and its product. As he alienates his own activity, so he bestows upon the stranger an activity which is not his own.

We have so far considered this relation only from the side of the worker, and later on we shall consider it also from the side of the non-worker.

Thus, through alienated labour the worker creates the relation of another man, who does not work and is outside the work process, to this labour. The relation of the worker to work also produces the relation of the capitalist (or whatever one likes to call the lord of labour) to work. *Private property* is, therefore, the product, the necessary result, of *alienated labour*, of the external relation of the worker to nature and to himself.

Private property is thus derived from the analysis of the concept of *alienated labour*; that is, alienated man, alienated labour, alienated life, and estranged man.

Theses on Feuerbach*

I

The chief defect of all previous materialism (including that of Feuerbach) is that things (*Gegenstand*), reality, the sensible world, are conceived only in the form of *objects* (*Objekt*) *of observation*, but not as *human sense activity*, not as *practical activity*, not subjectively. Hence, in opposition to materialism, the *active* side was developed abstractly by idealism, which of course does not know real sense activity as such. Feuerbach wants sensible objects really distinguished from the objects of thought, but he does not understand human activity itself as *objective* (*gegenständlich*) activity. Consequently, in *The Essence of Christianity*, he regards the theoretical attitude as the only genuine human attitude, while practical activity is apprehended only in its dirty Jewish manifestation. He therefore does not grasp the significance of "revolutionary," "practical-critical" activity.

II

The question whether human thinking can pretend to objective (*gegenständlich*) truth is not a theoretical but a *practical* question. Man must prove the truth, i.e. the reality and power, the "this-sidedness" of his thinking in practice. The dispute over the reality or non-reality of thinking that is isolated from practice is a purely *scholastic* question.

III

The materialist doctrine concerning the changing of circumstances and education forgets that circumstances are changed by men and that the educator must himself be educated. This doctrine has therefore to divide society into two parts, one of which is superior to society.

*From *Theses on Feuerbach* (1845), (trans. T. B. Bottomore in *Karl Marx: Selected Writings in Sociology and Social Philosophy*, ed. T. B. Bottomore and M. Rubel; London, 1956), pp. 67-69. Reprinted by permission of C. A. Watts & Co. Ltd.

The coincidence of the changing of circumstances and of human activity or self-changing can only be grasped and rationally understood as revolutionary *practice*.

IV

Feuerbach sets out from the fact of religious self-alienation, the duplication of the world into a religious and a secular one. His work consists in resolving the religious world into its secular basis. But the fact that the secular basis deserts its own sphere and establishes an independent realm in the clouds, can only be explained by the cleavage and self-contradictions within this secular basis. The latter therefore, must itself be both understood in its contradictions and revolutionized in practice. Thus, for instance, once the earthly family is discovered to be the secret of the heavenly family the former must itself be destroyed in theory and in practice.

V

Feuerbach, not satisfied with *abstract thought*, wants *empirical observation*, but he does not conceive the sensible world as *practical*, human sense activity.

VI

Feuerbach resolves the essence of religion into the essence of *man*. But the essence of man is not an abstraction inherent in each particular individual. The real nature of man is the totality of social relations.

Feuerbach, who does not enter upon a criticism of this real nature, is therefore obliged:

1. to abstract from the historical process, to hypostatize the religious sentiment, and to postulate an abstract—*isolated*—human individual;
2. to conceive the nature of man only in terms of a "genus," as an inner and mute universal quality which unites the many individuals in a purely natural (biological) way.

VII

Feuerbach therefore does not see that the "religious sentiment" is itself a social product, and that the abstract individual whom he analyses belongs to a particular form of society.

VIII

All social life is essentially *practical*. All the mysteries which lead theory towards mysticism find their rational solution in human practice and in the comprehension of this practice.

IX

The highest point attained by that materialism which only observes the world, i.e. which does not conceive sensuous existence as practical activity, is the observation of particular individuals and of civil society.

X

The standpoint of the old type of materialism is civil society; the standpoint of the new materialism is human society or social humanity.

XI

The philosophers have only *interpreted* the world in different ways; the point is to *change* it.

Ideology in General, German Ideology in Particular*

German criticism has, right up to its latest efforts, never quitted the realm of philosophy. Far from examining its general philosophic premises, the whole body of its inquiries has actually sprung from the soil of a definite philosophical system, that of Hegel. Not only in their answers but in their very questions there was a mystification. This dependence on Hegel is the reason why not one of these modern critics has even attempted a comprehensive criticism of the Hegelian system, however much each professes to have advanced beyond Hegel. Their polemics against Hegel and against one another are confined to this—each extracts one side of the Hegelian system and turns this against the whole system as well as against the sides extracted by the others. To begin with they extracted pure unfalsified Hegelian categories such as "substance" and "self-consciousness," later they desecrated these categories with more secular names such as "species," "the Unique," "Man," etc. . . .

The Old Hegelian had *comprehended* everything as soon as it was reduced to an Hegelian logical category. The Young Hegelians *criticized* everything by attributing to it religious conceptions or by pronouncing it a theological matter. The Young Hegelians are in agreement with the Old Hegelians in their belief in the rule of religion, of concepts, of an abstract general principle in the existing world. Only, the one party attacks this dominion as usurpation, while the other extols it as legitimate.

Since the Young Hegelians consider conceptions, thoughts, ideas, in fact all the products of consciousness, to which they attribute an independent existence, as the real chains of men (just as the Old Hegelians declared them the true bonds of human society) it is evident

*From *The German Ideology* (ed. R. Pascal; New York, 1967), pp. 4-16. Reprinted by permission of International Publishers, Inc. Copyright © 1947. Permission also granted by Lawrence & Wishart Ltd.

that the Young Hegelians have to fight only against these illusions of the consciousness. Since, according to their fantasy, the relationships of men, all their doings, their chains and their limitations are products of their consciousness, the Young Hegelians logically put to men the moral postulate of exchanging their present consciousness for human, critical or egoistic consciousness, and thus of removing their limitations. This demand to change consciousness amounts to a demand to interpret reality in another way, i.e. to accept it by means of another interpretation. The Young-Hegelian ideologists, in spite of their allegedly "world-shattering" statements, are the staunchest conservatives. The most recent of them have found the correct expression for their activity when they declare they are only fighting against "phrases." They forget, however, that to these phrases they themselves are only opposing other phrases, and that they are in no way combating the real existing world when they are merely combating the phrases of this world. The only results which this philosophic criticism could achieve were a few (and at that thoroughly one-sided) elucidations of Christianity from the point of view of religious history; all the rest of their assertions are only further embellishments of their claim to have furnished, in these unimportant elucidations, discoveries of universal importance.

It has not occurred to any one of these philosophers to inquire into the connection of German philosophy with German reality, the relation of their criticism to their own material surroundings. . . .

The premises from which we begin are not arbitrary ones, not dogmas, but real premises from which abstraction can only be made in the imagination. They are the real individuals, their activity and the material conditions under which they live, both those which they find already existing and those produced by their activity. These premises can thus be verified in a purely empirical way.

The first premise of all human history is, of course, the existence of living human individuals. Thus the first fact to be established is the physical organization of these individuals and their consequent relation to the rest of nature. Of course, we cannot here go either into the actual physical nature of man, or into the natural conditions in which man finds himself—geological, orohydrographical, climatic and so on. The writing of history must always set out from these natural bases and their modification in the course of history through the action of man.

Men can be distinguished from animals by consciousness, by religion or anything else you like. They themselves begin to distinguish themselves from animals as soon as they begin to *produce* their means

of subsistence, a step which is conditioned by their physical organization. By producing their means of subsistence men are indirectly producing their actual material life.

The way in which men produce their means of subsistence depends first of all on the nature of the actual means they find in existence and have to reproduce. This mode of production must not be
considered simply as being the reproduction of the physical existence of
the individuals. Rather it is a definite form of activity of these individuals, a definite form of expressing their life, a definite *mode of life*
on their part. As individuals express their life, so they are. What they
are, therefore, coincides with their production, both with *what* they
produce and with *how* they produce. The nature of individuals thus
depends on the material conditions determining their production.

This production only makes its appearance with the increase of
population. In its turn this presupposes the intercourse of individuals
with one another. The form of this intercourse is again determined by
production.

The relations of different nations among themselves depend upon
the extent to which each has developed its productive forces, the division of labour and internal intercourse. This statement is generally
recognized. But not only the relation of one nation to others, but
also the whole internal structure of the nation itself depends on the
stage of development reached by its production and its internal and
external intercourse. How far the productive forces of a nation are
developed is shown most manifestly by the degree to which the division
of labour has been carried. Each new productive force, in so far as it
is not merely a quantitative extension of productive forces already
known, (for instance the bringing into cultivation of fresh land), brings
about a further development of the division of labour.

The division of labour inside a nation leads at first to the separation of industrial and commercial from agricultural labour, and hence
to the separation of town and country and a clash of interests between
them. Its further development leads to the separation of commercial
from industrial labour. At the same time through the division of labour
there develop further, inside these various branches, various divisions
among the individuals co-operating in definite kinds of labour. The
relative position of these individual groups is determined by the
methods employed in agriculture, industry and commerce (patri-
archalism, slavery, estates, classes). These same conditions are to be
seen (given a more developed intercourse) in the relations of different
nations to one another. . . .

The fact is, therefore, that definite individuals who are productively active in a definite way enter into these definite social and political relations. Empirical observation must in each separate instance bring out empirically, and without any mystification and speculation, the connection of the social and political structure with production. The social structure and the State are continually evolving out of the life-process of definite individuals, but of individuals, not as they may appear in their own or other people's imagination, but as they really are; i.e. as they are effective, produce materially, and are active under definite material limits, presuppositions and conditions independent of their will.

The production of ideas, of conceptions, of consciousness, is at first directly interwoven with the material activity and the material intercourse of men, the language of real life. Conceiving, thinking, the mental intercourse of men, appear at this stage as the direct efflux of their material behaviour. The same applies to mental production as expressed in the language of the politics, laws, morality, religion, metaphysics of a people. Men are the producers of their conceptions, ideas, etc.—real, active men, as they are conditioned by a definite development of their productive forces and of the intercourse corresponding to these, up to its furthest forms. Consciousness can never be anything else than conscious existence, and the existence of men is their actual life-process. If in all ideology men and their circumstances appear upside down as in a *camera obscura*, this phenomenon arises just as much from their historical life-process as the inversion of objects on the retina does from their physical life-process.

In direct contrast to German philosophy which descends from heaven to earth, here we ascend from earth to heaven. That is to say, we do not set out from what men say, imagine, conceive, nor from men as narrated, thought of, imagined, conceived, in order to arrive at men in the flesh. We set out from real, active men, and on the basis of their real life-process we demonstrate the development of the ideological reflexes and echoes of this life-process. The phantoms formed in the human brain are also, necessarily, sublimates of their material life-process, which is empirically verifiable and bound to material premises. Morality, religion, metaphysics, all the rest of ideology and their corresponding forms of consciousness, thus no longer retain the semblance of independence. They have no history, no development; but men, developing their material production and their material intercourse, alter, along with this their real existence, their thinking and the products of their thinking. Life is not determined by consciousness, but consciousness by life. In the first method of approach the starting-point is consciousness taken as the living individual; in the second it is the real living individuals themselves, as they are in actual life, and consciousness is considered solely as *their* consciousness.

This method of approach is not devoid of premises. It starts out from the real premises and does not abandon them for a moment. Its premises are men, not in any fantastic isolation or abstract definition, but in their actual, empirically perceptible process of development under definite conditions. As soon as this active life-process is described, history ceases to be a collection of dead facts as it is with the empiricists (themselves still abstract), or an imagined activity of imagined subjects, as with the idealists.

Where speculation ends—in real life—there real, positive science begins: the representation of the practical activity, of the practical process of development of men. Empty talk about consciousness ceases, and real knowledge has to take its place. When reality is depicted, philosophy as an independent branch of activity loses its medium of existence. At the best its place can only be taken by a summing-up of the most general results, abstractions which arise from the observation of the historical development of men. Viewed apart from real history, these abstractions have in themselves no value whatsoever. They can only serve to facilitate the arrangement of historical material, to indicate the sequence of its separate strata. But they by no means afford a recipe or schema, as does philosophy, for neatly trimming the epochs of history. On the contrary, our difficulties begin only when we set about the observation and the arrangement—the real depiction of our historical material, whether of a past epoch or of the present. The removal of these difficulties is governed by premises which it is quite impossible to state here, but which only the study of the actual life-process and the activity of the individuals of each epoch will make evident.

X

KIERKEGAARD

SØREN AABYE KIERKEGAARD (1813-55) was born in Copenhagen, a city in which he spent almost the whole of his life. From 1830 he attended Copenhagen University as a theology student, but his interests at this time were primarily philosophical and literary, and a decade was to elapse before he finally took his examinations. In the same year (1840) he became engaged, but later broke off the relationship; this episode was to haunt him afterwards and references to it recur in his writings. In 1843 he published *Either Or,* a book in which two forms of life—an "aesthetic" and an "ethical"—are contrasted, and it was followed by a succession of works with philosophical, religious, and psychological themes; they include *Fear and Trembling* (1843), *The Concept of Dread* (1844), *Philosophical Fragments* (1844), *Concluding Unscientific Postscript* (1846), and *The Sickness Unto Death* (1849). He also kept a journal in which he recorded in considerable detail his personal and spiritual development. During the two years that preceded his death Kierkegaard was involved in a bitter controversy with the Danish state church, which he accused of perverting and emasculating the faith it claimed to represent.

As the first of the selections given below indicates, Kierkegaard, though himself a dedicated Christian, had no use for attempts to justify religious belief in rational terms; and for similar reasons he was deeply hostile to the Hegelian claim to have preserved the essential content of Christianity within the framework of an all-embracing metaphysical theory. As against the "System," with its vaunted reconciliation of opposites, its unification of thought and existence, its subordination of the individual to universal categories and historical forces, he stressed separation and division, insisting upon the priority of concrete human reality to abstract thinking and underlining the significance of personal choice and commitment; despite his differences

289

from them on other counts, his polemics against Hegel often recall the criticisms being made at the same time by Feuerbach, Stirner, and Marx. For Kierkegaard faith had the character of a venture or "leap," involving beliefs the individual was prepared to maintain in the face of all intellectual doubt and uncertainty, and this led him into undertaking a penetrating investigation of its psychological nature and conditions; especially noteworthy here are his analyses of "melancholy" and of "dread" (*Angst*), and his discussions of the ways in which men may, by evasion and self-deception, seek to absolve themselves from the responsibility of taking ultimate decisions concerning themselves and their lives. Kierkegaard's accounts are presented in a religious context, with prominence given to notions like sin and guilt; even so, one can discern in his writings the emergence of ideas which have since become familiar—though in a greatly altered form—through the secular works of twentieth-century philosophers like Sartre and Heidegger.

The Absolute Paradox*

In spite of the fact that Socrates studied with all diligence to acquire a knowledge of human nature and to understand himself, and in spite of the fame accorded him through the centuries as one who beyond all other men had an insight into the human heart, he has himself admitted that the reason for his shrinking from reflection upon the nature of such beings as Pegasus and the Gorgons was that he, the life-long student of human nature, had not yet been able to make up his mind whether he was a stranger monster than Typhon, or a creature of a gentler and simpler sort, partaking of something divine (*Phaedrus*, 229 E). This seems to be a paradox. However, one should not think slightingly of the paradoxical; for the paradox is the source of the thinker's passion, and the thinker without a paradox is like a lover without feeling: a paltry mediocrity. But the highest pitch of every passion is always to will its own downfall; and so it is also the supreme passion of the Reason to seek a collision, though this collision must in one way or another prove its undoing. The supreme paradox of all thought is the attempt to discover something that thought cannot think. This passion is at bottom present in all thinking, even in the thinking of the individual, in so far as in thinking he participates in something transcending himself. But habit dulls our sensibilities, and prevents us from perceiving it....

But what is this unknown something with which the Reason collides when inspired by its paradoxical passion, with the result of unsettling even man's knowledge of himself? It is the Unknown. It is not a human being, in so far as we know what man is; nor is it any other known thing. So let us call this unknown something: *the God*. It is nothing more than a name we assign to it. The idea of demonstrating that this unknown something (the God) exists, could scarcely suggest

*From *Philosophical Fragments* (trans. D. F. Swenson; revised by H. V. Hong; Princeton, 1962), pp. 46-57. Reprinted by permission of Princeton Univ. Press. Copyright ©, 1936, 1962 by Princeton University Press.

itself to the Reason. For if the God does not exist it would of course be impossible to prove it; and if he does exist it would be folly to attempt it. For at the very outset, in beginning my proof, I would have presupposed it, not as doubtful but as certain (a presuppositon is never doubtful, for the very reason that it is a presupposition), since otherwise I would not begin, readily understanding that the whole would be impossible if he did not exist. But if when I speak of proving the God's existence I mean that I propose to prove that the Unknown, which exists, is the God, then I express myself unfortunately. For in that case I do not prove anything, least of all an existence, but merely develop the content of a conception. Generally speaking, it is a difficult matter to prove that anything exists; and what is still worse for the intrepid souls who undertake the venture, the difficulty is such that fame scarcely awaits those who concern themselves with it. The entire demonstration always turns into something very different and becomes an additional development of the consequences that flow from my having assumed that the object in question exists. Thus I always reason from existence, not toward existence, whether I move in the sphere of palpable sensible fact or in the realm of thought. I do not for example prove that a stone exists, but that some existing thing is a stone. The procedure in a court of justice does not prove that a criminal exists, but that the accused, whose existence is given, is a criminal. Whether we call existence an *accessorium* or the eternal *prius,* it is never subject to demonstration. Let us take ample time for consideration. We have no such reason for haste as have those who from concern for themselves or for the God or for some other thing, must make haste to get existence demonstrated. Under such circumstances there may indeed be need for haste, especially if the prover sincerely seeks to appreciate the danger that he himself, or the thing in question, may be non-existent unless the proof is finished and does not surreptitiously entertain the thought that it exists whether he succeeds in proving it or not.

If it were proposed to prove Napoleon's existence from Napoleon's deeds, would it not be a most curious proceeding? His existence does indeed explain his deeds, but the deeds do not prove *his* existence, unless I have already understood the word "his" so as thereby to have assumed his existence. But Napoleon is only an individual, and in so far there exists no absolute relationship between him and his deeds; some other person might have performed the same deeds. Perhaps this is the reason why I cannot pass from the deeds to existence. If I call these deeds the deeds of Napoleon the proof becomes superfluous, since I have already named him; if I ignore this, I can never prove from the deeds that they are Napoleon's, but only in a purely ideal manner that such deeds are the deeds of a great general, and so forth. But between the God and his works there is an absolute relationship; God is not a name but a concept. Is this perhaps the reason that his *essentia involvit existentiam?*[1] The works of God are such that only the God can perform them. Just so, but where then are the works of the God? The works from which I would deduce his existence are not directly and immediately given. The wisdom in nature, the goodness, the wisdom in the governance of the world—are all these manifest, perhaps, upon the very face of things? are we not here confronted with the most terrible temptations to doubt, and is it not impossible finally to dispose of all these doubts? But from such an order of things I will surely not attempt to prove God's existence; and even if I began I would never

1. So Spinoza, who probes the depths of the God-idea in order to bring being out of it by way of thought, but not, it should be noted, as if being were an accidental characteristic, but rather as if it constituted an essential determination of content. Here lies Spinoza's profundity, but let us examine his reasoning. In *principia philosophiae Cartesianae, pars I, propositio VII, lemma I,* he says: *"quo res sua natura perfectior est, eo majorem existentiam et magis necessariam involvit; et contra, quo magis necessariam existentiam res sua natura involvit, eo perfectior."* The more perfect therefore a thing is, the more being it has; the more being it has, the more perfect it is. This is however a tautology, which becomes still more evident in a note, *nota II: "quod hic non loquimur de pulchritudine et aliis perfectionibus, quas homines ex superstitione et igonorantia perfectiones vocare voluerunt. Sed per perfectionem intelligo tantum realitatem sive esse."* He explains *perfectio* by *realitas, esse;* so that the more perfect a thing is, the more it is; but its perfection consists in having more *esse* in itself; that is to say, the more a thing is, the more it is. So much for the tautology, but now further. What is lacking here is a distinction between factual being and ideal being. The terminology which permits us to speak of more or less of being, and consequently of degrees of reality or being, is in itself lacking in clearness, and becomes still more confusing when the above distinction is neglected—in other words, when Spinoza does indeed speak profoundly but fails first to consider the difficulty. In the case of factual being it is meaningless to speak of more or less of being. A fly, when it is, has as much being as the God; with respect to factual being the stupid remark I here set down has as much being as Spinoza's profundity, for factual being is subject to the dialectic of Hamlet: to be or not to be. Factual being is wholly indifferent to any and all variations in essence, and everything that exists participates without petty jealousy in being, and participates in the same degree. Ideally, to be sure, the case is quite different. *But the moment I speak of being in the ideal sense I no longer speak of being, but of essence.* Highest ideality has this necessity and therefore it is. But this its being is identical with its essence; such being does not involve it dialectically in the determinations of factual being, since it is; nor can it be said to have more or less being in relation to other things. In the old days this used to be expressed, if somewhat imperfectly, by saying that if God is possible, he is *eo ipso* necessary (Leibniz). Spinoza's principle is thus quite correct and his tautology in order; but it is also certain that he altogether evades the difficulty. For the difficulty is to lay hold of God's factual being and to introduce God's ideal essence dialectically into the sphere of factual being.

finish, and would in addition have to live constantly in suspense, lest something so terrible should suddenly happen that my bit of proof would be demolished. From what works then do I propose to derive the proof? From the works as apprehended through an ideal interpretation, i.e., such as they do not immediately reveal themselves. But in that case it is not from the works that I make the proof; I merely develop the ideality I have presupposed, and because of my confidence in *this* I make so bold as to defy all objections, even those that have not yet been made. In beginning my proof I presuppose the ideal interpretation, and also that I will be successful in carrying it through; but what else is this but to presuppose that the God exists, so that I really begin by virtue of confidence in him?

And how does the God's existence emerge from the proof? Does it follow straightway, without any breach of continuity? Or have we not here an analogy to the behaviour of the little Cartesian dolls? As soon as I let go of the doll it stands on its head. As soon as I let it go—I must therefore let it go. So also with the proof. As long as I keep my hold on the proof, i.e., continue to demonstrate, the existence does not come out, if for no other reason than that I am engaged in proving it; but when I let the proof go, the existence is there. But this act of letting go is surely also something; it is indeed a contribution of mine. Must not this also be taken into the account, this little moment, brief as it may be—it need not be long, for it is a *leap*. However brief this moment, if only an instantaneous now, this "now" must be included in the reckoning. If anyone wishes to have it ignored, I will use it to tell a little anecdote, in order to show that it nevertheless does exist. Chrysippus was experimenting with a sorites to see if he could not bring about a break in its quality, either progressively or retrogressively. But Carneades could not get it in his head when the new quality actually emerged. Then Chrysippus told him to try making a little pause in the reckoning, and so—so it would be easier to understand. Carneades replied: With the greatest pleasure, please do not hesitate on my acount; you may not only pause, but even lie down to sleep, and it will help you just as little; for when you awake we will begin again where you left off. Just so; it boots as little to try to get rid of something by sleeping as to try to come into the possession of something in the same manner.

Whoever therefore attempts to demonstrate the existence of God (except in the sense of clarifying the concept, and without the *reservatio finalis* noted above, that the existence emerges from the demonstration by a leap) proves in lieu thereof something else, something which at times perhaps does not need a proof, and in any case needs none better; for the fool says in his heart that there is no God, but whoever says in his heart or to men: Wait just a little and I will prove it—what a rare man of wisdom is he![2] If in the moment of beginning his proof it is not absolutely undetermined whether the God exists or not, he does not prove it; and if it is thus undetermined in the beginning he will never come to begin, partly from fear of failure, since the God perhaps does not exist, and partly because he has nothing with which to begin.—A project of this kind would scarcely have been undertaken by the ancients. Socrates at least, who is credited with having put forth the physico-teleological proof for God's existence, did not go about it in any such manner. He always presupposes the God's existence, and under this presupposition seeks to interpenetrate nature with the idea of purpose. Had he been asked why he pursued this method, he would doubtless have explained that he lacked the courage to venture out upon so perilous a voyage of discovery without having made sure of the God's existence behind him. At the word of the God he casts his net as if to catch the idea of purpose; for nature herself finds many means of frightening the inquirer, and distracts him by many a digression.

The paradoxical passion of the Reason thus comes repeatedly into collision with this Unknown, which does indeed exist, but is unknown, and in so far does not exist. The Reason cannot advance beyond this point, and yet it cannot refrain in its paradoxicalness from arriving at this limit and occupying itself therewith. It will not serve to dismiss its relation to it simply by asserting that the Unknown does not exist, since this itself involves a relationship. But what then is the Unknown, since the designation of it as the God merely signifies for us that it is unknown? To say that it is the Unknown because it cannot be known, and even if it were capable of being known, it could not be expressed, does not satisfy the demands of passion, though it correctly interprets the Unknown as a limit; but a limit is precisely a torment for passion, though it also serves as an incitement. And yet the Reason can come no further, whether it risks an issue *via negationis* or *via eminentia*.

What then is the Unknown? It is the limit to which the Reason repeatedly comes, and in so far, substituting a static form of conception for the dynamic, it is the different, the absolutely different. But because it is absolutely different, there is no mark by which it could be distinguished. When qualified as absolutely different it seems on the verge of disclosure, but this is not the case; for the Reason cannot even con-

---

2. What an excellent subject for a comedy of the higher lunacy!

ceive an absolute unlikeness. The Reason cannot negate itself absolutely, but uses itself for the purpose, and thus conceives only such an
unlikeness within itself as it can conceive by means of itself; it cannot
absolutely transcend itself, and hence conceives only such a superiority
over itself as it can conceive by means of itself. Unless the Unknown
(the God) remains a mere limiting conception, the single idea of
difference will be thrown into a state of confusion, and become many
ideas of many differences. The Unknown is then in a condition of dispersion (διασπορά), and the Reason may choose at pleasure from
what is at hand and the imagination may suggest (the monstrous, the
ludicrous, etc.).

But it is impossible to hold fast to a difference of this nature.
Every time this is done it is essentially an arbitrary act, and deepest
down in the heart of piety lurks the mad caprice which knows that it
has itself produced the God. If no specific determination of difference
can be held fast, because there is no distinguishing mark, like and unlike
finally become identified with one another, thus sharing the fate of all
such dialectical opposites. The unlikeness clings to the Reason and
confounds it, so that the Reason no longer knows itself and quite consistently confuses itself with the unlikeness. On this point paganism
has been sufficiently prolific in fantastic inventions. As for the last
named supposition, the self-irony of the Reason, I shall attempt to
delineate it merely by a stroke or two, without raising any question of its
being historical. There exists an individual whose appearance is precisely like that of other men; he grows up to manhood like others, he
marries, he has an occupation by which he earns his livelihood, and
he makes provision for the future as befits a man. For though it may be
beautiful to live like the birds of the air, it is not lawful, and may lead
to the sorriest of consequences: either starvation if one has enough persistence, or dependence on the bounty of others. This man is also
the God. How do I know? I cannot know it, for in order to know it I
would have to know the God, and the nature of the difference between
the God and man; and this I cannot know, because the Reason has
reduced it to likeness with that from which it was unlike. Thus the
God becomes the most terrible of deceivers, because the Reason has
deceived itself. The Reason has brought the God as near as possible,
and yet he is as far away as ever. . . .

An Existential System Is Impossible*

An existential system cannot be formulated. Does this mean that no such system exists? By no means; nor is this implied in our assertion. Reality itself is a system—for God; but it cannot be a system for any existing spirit. System and finality correspond to one another, but existence is precisely the opposite of finality. It may be seen, from a purely abstract point of view, that system and existence are incapable of being thought together; because in order to think existence at all systematic thought must think it as abrogated, and hence as not existing. Existence separates, and holds the various moments of existence discretely apart; the systematic thought consists of the finality which brings them together. . . .

Respecting the impossibility of an existential system, let us then ask quite simply, as a Greek youth might have asked his teacher (and if the superlative wisdom can explain everything, but cannot answer a simple question, it is clear that the world is out of joint) : "Who is to write or complete such a system?" Surely a human being, unless we propose again to begin using the strange mode of speech which assumes that a human being becomes speculative philosophy in the abstract, or becomes the identity of subject and object. So then, a human being —and surely a living human being, i.e. an existing individual. Or if the speculative thought which brings the systems to light is the joint effort of different thinkers: in what last concluding thought does this fellowship finally realize itself, how does it reach the light of day? Surely through some human being? And how are the individual participants related to the joint effort, what are the categories which mediate between the individual and world-process, and who is it again who strings them all together on the systematic thread? Is he a human being, or is he speculative philosophy in the abstract? But if he is a human

*From *Concluding Unscientific Postscript* (trans. D. F. Swenson and Walter Lowrie; Princeton, 1941), pp. 107-113. Reprinted by permission of Princeton Univ. Press. Copyright © 1941.

being, then he is also an existing individual. Two ways, in general, are open for an existing individual: *Either* he can do his utmost to forget that he is an existing individual, by which he becomes a comic figure, since existence has the remarkable trait of compelling an existing individual to exist whether he wills it or not. (The comical contradiction in willing to be what one is not, as when a man wills to be a bird, is not more comical than the contradiction of not willing to be what one is, as *in casu* an existing individual; just as the language finds it comical that a man forgets his name, which does not so much mean forgetting a designation, as it means forgetting the distinctive essence of one's being.) *Or* he can concentrate his entire energy upon the fact that he is an existing individual. It is from this side, in the first instance, that objection must be made to modern philosophy; not that it has a mistaken presupposition, but that it has a comical presupposition, occasioned by its having forgotten, in a sort of world-historical absent-mindedness, what it means to be a human being. Not indeed, what it means to be a human being in general; for this is the sort of thing that one might even induce a speculative philosopher to agree to; but what it means that you and I and he are human beings, each one for himself. . . .

So-called pantheistic systems have often been characterized and challenged in the assertion that they abrogate the distinction between good and evil, and destroy freedom. Perhaps one would express oneself quite as definitely, if one said that every such system fantastically dissipates the concept *existence*. But we ought to say this not merely of pantheistic systems; it would be more to the point to show that every system must be pantheistic precisely on account of its finality. Existence must be revoked in the eternal before the system can round itself out; there must be no existing remainder, not even such a little minikin as the existing Herr Professor who writes the system. But this is not the way in which the problem is usually dealt with. No, pantheistic systems are attacked, partly in tumultuous aphorisms which again and again promise a new system; and partly by way of scraping together something supposed to be a system, and inserting in it a special paragraph in which it is laid down that the concept *existence*, or actuality, is intended to be especially emphasized. That such a paragraph is a mockery of the entire system, that instead of being a paragraph in a system it is an absolute protest against the system, makes no difference to busy systematists. If the concept of existence is really to be stressed, this cannot be given a direct expression as a paragraph in a system; all direct swearing and oath-supported assurances serve only to make the topsy-turvy profession of the paragraph more and more ridiculous. An actual emphasis on existence must be expressed in an essential form; in view of the elusiveness of existence, such a form will have to be an indirect form, namely, the absence of a system. But this again must not degenerate into an asseverating formula, for the indirect character of the expression will constantly demand renewal and rejuvenation in the form. In the case of committee reports, it may be quite in order to incorporate in the report a dissenting opinion; but an existential system which includes the dissenting opinion as a paragraph in its own logical structure, is a curious monstrosity. What wonder that the System continues to sustain its life as a going concern. In general, objections are haughtily ignored; if a particular objection seems to attract a little attention, the systematic entrepreneurs engage a copyist to copy off the objection, which thereupon is incorporated in the System; and when the book is bound the System is complete.

The systematic Idea is the identity of subject and object, the unity of thought and being. Existence, on the other hand, is their separation. It does not by any means follow that existence is thoughtless; but it has brought about, and brings about, a separation between subject and object, thought and being. In the objective sense, thought is understood as being pure thought; this corresponds in an equally abstract-objective sense to its object, which object is therefore the thought itself, and the truth becomes the correspondence of thought with itself. This objective thought has no relation to the existing subject; and while we are always confronted with the difficult question of how the existing subject slips into this objectivity, where subjectivity is merely pure abstract subjectivity (which again is an objective determination, not signifying any existing human being), it is certain that the existing subjectivity tends more and more to evaporate. And finally, if it is possible for a human being to become anything of the sort, and it is merely something of which at most he becomes aware through the imagination, he becomes the pure abstract conscious participation in and knowledge of this pure relationship between thought and being, this pure identity; aye, this tautology, because this being which is ascribed to the thinker does not signify that he is, but only that he is engaged in thinking.

The existing subject, on the other hand, is engaged in existing, which is indeed the case with every human being. Let us therefore not deal unjustly with the objective tendency, by calling it an ungodly and pantheistic self-deification; but let us rather view it as an essay in the comical. For the notion that from now on until the end of the world nothing could be said except what proposed a further improvement in an almost completed system, is merely a systematic consequence for systematists.

By beginning at once to use ethical categories in criticism of the objective tendency, one does it an injustice, and fails to make contact with it, because one has nothing in common with what is under attack. But by remaining in the metaphysical sphere, one is enabled to use the comical, which also lies in the metaphysical, so as to bring such a transfigured professor to book. If a dancer could leap very high, we would admire him. But if he tried to give the impression that he could fly, let laughter single him out for suitable punishment; even though it might be true that he could leap as high as any dancer ever had done. Leaping is the accomplishment of a being essentially earthly, one who respects the earth's gravitational force, since the leaping is only momentary. But flying carries a suggestion of being emancipated from telluric conditions, a privilege reserved for winged creatures, and perhaps also shared by the inhabitants of the moon—and there perhaps the System will first find its true readers.

Being an individual man is a thing that has been abolished, and every speculative philosopher confuses himself with humanity at large; whereby he becomes something infinitely great, and at the same time nothing at all. He confounds himself with humanity in sheer distraction of mind, just as the opposition press uses the royal "we," and sailors say: "devil take me!" But when a man has indulged in oaths for a long time, he returns at last to the simple utterance, because all swearing is self-nugatory; and when one discovers that every street urchin can say "we," one perceives that it means a little more, after all, to be a particular individual. And when one finds that every cellar-dweller can play the game of being humanity, one learns at last, that being purely and simply a human being is a more significant thing than playing the society game in this fashion. And one thing more. When a cellar-dweller plays this game everyone thinks it ridiculous; and yet it is equally ridiculous for the greatest man in the world to do it. And one may very well permit oneself to laugh at him for this, while still entertaining a just and proper respect for his talents and his learning, and so forth.

Faith and the Absurd*

... If an existing individual were really able to transcend himself,
the truth would be for him something final and complete; but where is
the point at which he is outside himself? The I-am-I is a mathematical
point which does not exist, and in so far there is nothing to prevent
everyone from occupying this standpoint; the one will not be in the
way of the other. It is only momentarily that the particular individual
is able to realize existentially a unity of the infinite and the finite which
transcends existence. This unity is realized in the moment of passion.
Modern philosophy has tried anything and everything in the effort
to help the individual to transcend himself objectively, which is a
wholly impossible feat; existence exercises its restraining influence,
and if philosophers nowadays had not become mere scribblers in the
service of a fantastic thinking and its preoccupation, they would long
ago have perceived that suicide was the only tolerable practical interpretation of its striving. But the scribbling modern philosophy holds
passion in contempt, and yet passion is the culmination of existence
for an existing individual—and we are all of us existing individuals. In
passion the existing subject is rendered infinite in the eternity of the
imaginative representation, and yet he is at the same time most definitely himself. The fantastic I-am-I is not an identity of the infinite
and the finite, since neither the one nor the other is real; it is a fantastic
rendezvous in the clouds, an unfruitful embrace, and the relationship
of the individual self to this mirage is never indicated.

All essential knowledge relates to existence, or only such knowledge as has an essential relationship to existence is essential knowledge.
All knowledge which does not inwardly relate itself to existence, in the
reflection of inwardness, is, essentially viewed, accidental knowledge;
its degree and scope is essentially indifferent. That essential knowledge
is essentially related to existence does not mean the above-mentioned
identity which abstract thought postulates between thought and being;

*Ibid., pp. 176-190.

nor does it signify, objectively, that knowledge corresponds to something existent as its object. But it means that knowledge has a relationship to the knower, who is essentially[1] an existing individual, and that for this reason all essential knowledge is essentially related to existence. Only ethical and ethico-religious knowledge has an essential relationship to the existence of the knower. . . .

In an attempt to make clear the difference of way that exists between an objective and a subjective reflection, I shall now proceed to show how a subjective reflection makes its way inwardly in inwardness. Inwardness in an existing subject culminates in passion; corresponding to passion in the subject the truth becomes a paradox; and the fact that the truth becomes a paradox is rooted precisely in its having a relationship to an existing subject. Thus the one corresponds to the other. By forgetting that one is an existing subject, passion goes by the board and the truth is no longer a paradox; the knowing subject becomes a fantastic entity rather than a human being, and the truth becomes a fantastic object for the knowledge of this fantastic entity.

When the question of truth is raised in an objective manner, reflection is directed objectively to the truth, as an object to which the knower is related. Reflection is not focussed upon the relationship, however, but upon the question of whether it is the truth to which the knower is related. If only the object to which he is related is the truth, the subject is accounted to be in the truth. When the question of the truth is raised subjectively, reflection is directed subjectively to the nature of the individual's relationship; if only the mode of this relationship is in the truth, the individual is in the truth even if he should happen to be thus related to what is not true.[1] Let us take as an example the knowledge of God. Objectively, reflection is directed to the problem of whether this object is the true God; subjectively, reflection is directed to the question whether the individual is related to a something *in such a manner* that his relationship is in truth a God-relationship. On which side is the truth now to be found? Ah, may we not here resort to a mediation, and say: It is on neither side, but in the mediation of both? Excellently well said, provided we might have it explained how an existing individual manages to be in a state of mediation. For to be in a state of mediation is to be finished, while to exist is to become. Nor can an existing individual be in two places at the same time—he cannot be an identity of subject and object. When he is nearest to being in two places at the same time he is in passion;

1. The reader will observe that the question here is about essential truth, or about the truth which is essentially related to existence, and that it is precisely for the sake of clarifying it as inwardness or as subjectivity that this contrast is drawn.

but passion is momentary, and passion is also the highest expression of subjectivity.

The existing individual who chooses to pursue the objective way enters upon the entire approximation-process by which it is proposed to bring God to light objectively. But this is in all eternity impossible, because God is a subject, and therefore exists only for subjectivity in inwardness. The existing individual who chooses the subjective way apprehends instantly the entire dialectical difficulty involved in having to use some time, perhaps a long time, in finding God objectively; and he feels this dialectical difficulty in all its painfulness, because every moment is wasted in which he does not have God.[2] That very instant he has God, not by virtue of any objective deliberation, but by virtue of the infinite passion of inwardness. The objective inquirer, on the other hand, is not embarrassed by such dialectical difficulties as are involved in devoting an entire period of investigation to finding God— since it is possible that the inquirer may die tomorrow; and if he lives he can scarcely regard God as something to be taken along if convenient, since God is precisely that which one takes *a tout prix*, which in the understanding of passion constitutes the true inward relationship to God.

It is at this point, so difficult dialectically, that the way swings off for everyone who knows what it means to think, and to think existentially; which is something very different from sitting at a desk and writing about what one has never done, something very different from writing *de omnibus dubitandum* and at the same time being as credulous existentially as the most sensuous of men. Here is where the way swings off, and the change is marked by the fact that while objective knowledge rambles comfortably on by way of the long road of approximation without being impelled by the urge of passion, subjective knowledge counts every delay a deadly peril, and the decision so infinitely important and so instantly pressing that it is as if the opportunity had already passed.

Now when the problem is to reckon up on which side there is most truth, whether on the side of one who seeks the true God objectively, and pursues the approximate truth of the God-idea; or on the side of

2. In this manner God certainly becomes a postulate, but not in the otiose manner in which this word is commonly understood. It becomes clear rather that the only way in which an existing individual comes into relation with God, is when the dialectical contradiction brings his passion to the point of despair, and helps him to embrace God with the "category of despair" (faith). Then the postulate is so far from being arbitrary that it is precisely a life-necessity. It is then not so much that God is a postulate, as that the existing individual's postulation of God is a necessity.

one who, driven by the infinite passion of his need of God, feels an
infinite concern for his own relationship to God in truth (and to be
at one and the same time on both sides equally, is as we have noted
not possible for an existing individual, but is merely the happy delusion
of an imaginary I-am-I): the answer cannot be in doubt for anyone
who has not been demoralized with the aid of science. If one who
lives in the midst of Christendom goes up to the house of God, the
house of the true God, with the true conception of God in his knowledge, and prays, but prays in a false spirit; and one who lives in an
idolatrous community prays with the entire passion of the infinite,
although his eyes rest upon the image of an idol: where is there most
truth? The one prays in truth to God though he worships an idol;
the other prays falsely to the true God, and hence worships in fact an
idol. . . .

*The objective accent falls on WHAT is said, the subjective accent
on HOW it is said.* This distinction holds even in the aesthetic realm,
and receives definite expression in the principle that what is in itself
true may in the mouth of such and such a person become untrue. In
these times this distinction is particularly worthy of notice, for if we
wish to express in a single sentence the difference between ancient
times and our own, we should doubtless have to say: "In ancient times
only an individual here and there knew the truth; now all know it,
except that the inwardness of its appropriation stands in an inverse
relationship to the extent of its dissemination.[3] Aesthetically the contradiction that truth becomes untruth in this or that person's mouth,
is best construed comically: In the ethico-religious sphere, accent is
again on the "how." But this is not to be understood as referring to
demeanor, expression, or the like; rather it refers to the relationship
sustained by the existing individual, in his own existence, to the con-

3. *Stages on Life's Way*, Note on p. 426. Though ordinarily not wishing an expression
of opinion on the part of reviewers, I might at this point almost desire it, provided
such opinions, so far from flattering me, amounted to an assertion of the daring truth
that what I say is something that everybody knows, even every child, and that the
cultured know infinitely much better. If it only stands fast that everyone knows it,
my standpoint is in order, and I shall doubtless make shift to manage with the unity
of the comic and the tragic. If there were anyone who did not know it I might perhaps be in danger of being dislodged from my position of equilibrium by the thought
that I might be in a position to communicate to someone the needful preliminary
knowledge. It is just this which engages my interest so much, this that the cultured
are accustomed to say: that everyone knows what the highest is. This was not the
case in paganism, nor in Judaism, nor in the seventeen centuries of Christianity.
Hail to the nineteenth century! Everyone knows it. What progress has been made
since the time when only a few knew it. To make up for this, perhaps, we must
assume that no one nowadays does it.

tent of his utterance. Objectively the interest is focussed merely on the
thought-content, subjectively on the inwardness. At its maximum this
inward "how" is the passion of the infinite, and the passion of the
infinite is the truth. But the passion of the infinite is precisely subjectivity, and thus subjectivity becomes the truth. Objectively there is
no infinite decisiveness, and hence it is objectively in order to annul
the difference between good and evil, together with the principle of
contradiction, and therewith also the infinite difference between the
true and the false. Only in subjectivity is there decisiveness, to seek
objectivity is to be in error. It is the passion of the infinite that is the
decisive factor and not its content, for its content is precisely itself. In
his manner subjectivity and the subjective "how" constitute the truth.

But the "how" which is thus subjectively accentuated precisely because the subject is an existing individual, is also subject to a dialectic
with respect to time. In the passionate moment of decision, where the
road swings away from objective knowledge, it seems as if the infinite
decision were thereby realized. But in the same moment the existing
individual finds himself in the temporal order, and the subjective
"how" is transformed into a striving, a striving which receives indeed
its impulse and a repeated renewal from the decisive passion of the
infinite, but is nevertheless a striving.

When subjectivity is the truth, the conceptual determination of the
truth must include an expression for the antithesis to objectivity, a
memento of the fork in the road where the way swings off; this expression will at the same time serve as an indication of the tension of
the subjective inwardness. Here is such a definition of truth: *An objective uncertainty held fast in an appropriation-process of the most passionate inwardness is the truth,* the highest truth attainable for an
existing individual. At the point where the way swings off (and where
this is cannot be specified objectively, since it is a matter of subjectivity), there objective knowledge is placed in abeyance. Thus the subject
merely has, objectively, the uncertainty; but it is this which precisely
increases the tension of that infinite passion which constitutes his inwardness. The truth is precisely the venture which chooses an objective
uncertainty with the passion of the infinite. I contemplate the order of
nature in the hope of finding God, and I see omnipotence and wisdom;
but I also see much else that disturbs my mind and excites anxiety. The
sum of all this is an objective uncertainty. But it is for this very reason
that the inwardness becomes as intense as it is, for it embraces this
objective uncertainty with the entire passion of the infinite. In the case
of a mathematical proposition the objectivity is given, but for this
reason the truth of such a proposition is also an indifferent truth.

But the above definition of truth is an equivalent expression for faith. Without risk there is no faith. Faith is precisely the contradiction between the infinite passion of the individual's inwardness and the objective uncertainty. If I am capable of grasping God objectively, I do not believe, but precisely because I cannot do this I must believe. If I wish to preserve myself in faith I must constantly be intent upon holding fast the objective uncertainty, so as to remain out upon the deep, over seventy thousand fathoms of water, still preserving my faith. . . .

When Socrates believed that there was a God, he held fast to the objective uncertainty with the whole passion of his inwardness, and it is precisely in this contradiction and in this risk, that faith is rooted. Now it is otherwise. Instead of the objective uncertainty, there is here a certainty, namely, that objectively it is absurd; and this absurdity, held fast in the passion of inwardness, is faith. The Socratic ignorance is as a witty jest in comparison with the earnestness of facing the absurd; and the Socratic existential inwardness is as Greek light-mindedness in comparison with the grave strenuosity of faith.

What now is the absurd? The absurd is—that the eternal truth has come into being in time, that God has come into being, has been born, has grown up, and so forth, precisely like any other individual human being, quite indistinguishable from other individuals. For every assumption of immediate recognizability is pre-Socratic paganism, and from the Jewish point of view, idolatry; and every determination of what really makes an advance beyond the Socratic must essentially bear the stamp of having a relationship to God's having come into being; for faith *sensu strictissimo*, as was developed in the *Fragments*, refers to becoming. When Socrates believed that there was a God, he saw very well that where the way swings off there is also an objective way of approximation, for example by the contemplation of nature and human history, and so forth. His merit was precisely to shun this way, where the quantitative siren song enchants the mind and deceives the existing individual.

In relation to the absurd, the objective approximation-process is like the comedy, *Misunderstanding upon Misunderstanding,* which is generally played by *Privatdocents* and speculative philosophers. The absurd is precisely by its objective repulsion the measure of the intensity of faith in inwardness. Suppose a man who wishes to acquire faith; let the comedy begin. He wishes to have faith, but he wishes also to safeguard himself by means of an objective inquiry and its approximation-process. What happens? With the help of the approximation-process the absurd becomes something different; it becomes probable, *impossionated,*

it becomes increasingly probable, it becomes extremely and emphatically probable. Now he is ready to believe it, and he ventures to claim for himself that he does not believe as shoemakers and tailors and simple folk believe, but only after long deliberation. Now he is ready to believe it; and lo, now it has become precisely impossible to believe it. Anything that is almost probable, or probable, or extremely and emphatically probable, is something he can almost know, or as good as know, or extremely and emphatically almost *know*—but it is impossible to *believe*. For the absurd is the object of faith, and the only object that can be believed.

Or suppose a man who says that he has faith, but desires to make his faith clear to himself, so as to understand himself in his faith. Now the comedy again begins. The object of faith becomes almost probable, as good as probable, extremely and emphatically probable. He has completed his investigations, and he ventures to claim for himself that he does not believe as shoemakers and tailors and other simple folk believe, but that he has also understood himself in his believing. Strange understanding! On the contrary, he has in fact learned something else about faith than when he believed; and he has learned that he no longer believes, since he almost knows, or as good as knows, or extremely and emphatically almost knows.

In so far as the absurd comprehends within itself the factor of becoming, one way of approximation will be that which confuses the absurd fact of such a becoming (which is the object of faith) with a simple historical fact, and hence seeks historical certainty for that which is absurd, because it involves the contradiction that something which can become historical only in direct opposition to all human reason, has become historical. It is this contradiction which constitutes the absurd, and which can only be believed. If historical certainty with respect to it is assumed, the certainty attained is merely that the something which is thus assumed as certain is not the thing in question. A witness can testify that he has believed it, and hence that so far from being an historical certainty it is directly contrary to his own reason; but such a witness thrusts the individual away in precisely the same sense that the absurd itself does. And a witness who does not so repel is *eo ipso* a deceiver, or a man who talks about something quite different, and can help only to obtain certainty about something quite different. A hundred thousand individual witnesses, who are individual witnesses precisely on account of the peculiar character of their testimony (that they have believed the absurd), cannot *en masse* become anything else, so as to make the absurd less absurd—and why less absurd? Because a hundred thousand human beings have separately, each one for himself, believed that it was absurd? On the contrary, these hundred thousand witnesses again exercise a repellent influence in nearly the same way that the absurd itself exercises it.

But this I need not here expound in greater detail. In the *Fragments* (especially where the distinction between the disciple at first-hand and at second-hand is shown to be illusory), and in the first part of this book, I have already carefully enough expounded the thesis that all approximation is useless, since on the contrary it behooves us to get rid of introductory guarantees of security, proofs from consequences, and the whole mob of public pawnbrokers and guarantors, so as to permit the absurd to stand out in all its clarity—in order that the individual may believe if he wills it; I merely say that it must be strenuous in the highest degree so to believe.

If speculative philosophy wishes to take cognizance of this, and say as always, that there is no paradox when the matter is viewed eternally, divinely, theocentrically—then I admit that I am not in a position to determine whether the speculative philosopher is right, for I am only a poor existing human being, not competent to contemplate the eternal either eternally or divinely or theocentrically, but compelled to content myself with existing. So much is certain, however, that speculative philosophy carries everything back, back past the Socratic position, which at least comprehended that for an existing individual existence is essential; to say nothing of the failure of speculative philosophy to take time to grasp what it means to be so critically situated in existence as the existing individual in the experiment. . . .

Melancholy*

... What, then, is melancholy? It is hysteria of the spirit. There comes a moment in a man's life when his immediacy is, as it were, ripened and the spirit demands a higher form in which it will apprehend itself as spirit. Man, so long as he is immediate spirit, coheres with the whole earthly life, and now the spirit would collect itself, as it were, out of this dispersion and become in itself transformed, the personality would be conscious of itself in its eternal validity. If this does not come to pass, if the movement is checked, if it is forced back, melancholy ensues. One may do much by way of inducing forgetfulness, one may work, one may employ other expedients ... but melancholy remains. There is something inexplicable in melancholy. The man who has sorrow and anxiety knows why he is sorrowful or anxious. If a melancholy man is asked what ground he has for it, what it is that weighs upon him, he will reply, "I know not, I cannot explain it." Herein lies the infinity of melancholy. This reply is perfectly correct, for as soon as a man knows the cause, the melancholy is done away with, whereas, on the contrary, in the case of the sorrowful the sorrow is not done away when a man knows why he sorrows. But melancholy is sin, really it is a sin *instar omnium,* for not to will deeply and sincerely is sin, and this is the mother of all sins. This sickness, or rather this sin, is very common in our age, and so it is under this all young Germany and France now sighs. I do not wish to provoke you, I would threaten you as leniently as possible. I am willing to admit that in a way melancholy is not a bad sign, for as a rule only the most gifted natures are subject to it. Neither shall I vex you by assuming that everyone who suffers from indigestion has for this cause a right to call himself melancholy—a thing often enough to be seen in our time when to be melancholy is the dignity to which everybody

*From *Either/Or,* Vol. 2 (trans. Walter Lowrie; New York, 1959), pp. 193-194. Reprinted by permission of Princeton Univ. Press. Copyright, 1944 by Princeton University Press. Copyright © 1959 by Doubleday & Company, Inc.

aspires. But he who would claim to be more eminently gifted must put up with it when I charge him with the accountability of being also more guilty than other men. If he will see this situation rightly, he will not see in it a disparagement of his personality, though it will teach him to bow with genuine humility before the eternal Power. As soon as that movement comes about, melancholy is essentially done away with, although to the same individual it may well happen that his life has in store many sorrows and anxieties, and à propos of this you know that I am the last man to teach the wretched commonplace that sorrow is of no avail, that one must drive sorrow away. I should be ashamed of myself if with these words I were to approach a person in sorrow. But even the man in whose life this movement comes about quietly, peaceably and seasonably, will, nevertheless, always retain a little melancholy; but this is connected with something far deeper, with original sin, and it is due to the fact that no man can become perfectly transparent to himself. On the other hand, the men whose souls are acquainted with no melancholy are those whose souls have no presentiment of a metamorphosis. With them I have nothing to do here, for I am writing only to and about you, and to you I believe this explanation will be satisfactory, for you hardly assume like many physicians that melancholy is an ailment of the body—and for all that, strangely enough, the physicians cannot relieve it. Only spirit can relieve it, for it is a spiritual ailment. And when the spirit finds itself, all the small troubles vanish, all the causes which according to some people produced melancholy, for example, that one cannot find oneself in the world, that one comes to the world both too late and too early, that one cannot find one's place in life; for he who owns his own self eternally can come neither too early nor too late, and he who possesses himself in his eternal validity surely finds his significance in this life. . . .

The Concept of Dread*

Innocence is ignorance. In his innocence man is not determined as spirit but is soulishly determined in immediate unity with his natural condition. Spirit is dreaming in man. This view is in perfect accord with that of the Bible, and by refusing to ascribe to man in the state of innocence a knowledge of the difference between good and evil it condemns all the notions of merit Catholicism has imagined.

In this state there is peace and repose; but at the same time there is something different, which is not dissension and strife, for there is nothing to strive with. What is it then? Nothing. But what effect does nothing produce? It begets dread. This is the profound secret of innocence, that at the same time it is dread. Dreamingly the spirit projects its own reality, but this reality is nothing, but this nothing constantly sees innocence outside of it.

Dread is a qualification of the dreaming spirit, and as such it has its place in psychology. When awake, the difference between myself and my other is posited; sleeping, it is suspended; dreaming, it is a nothing vaguely hinted at. The reality of the spirit constantly shows itself in a form which entices its possibility, but it is away as soon as one grasps after it, and it is a nothing which is able only to alarm. More it cannot do so long as it only shows itself. One almost never sees the concept dread dealt with in psychology, and I must therefore call attention to the fact that it is different from fear and similar concepts which refer to something definite, whereas dread is freedom's reality as possibility for possibility. One does not therefore find dread in the beast, precisely for the reason that by nature the beast is not qualified by spirit.

When we consider the dialectical determinants in dread, it ap-

*From The Concept of Dread (trans. Walter Lowrie; Princeton, 1957), pp. 37-41. Reprinted by permission of Princeton Univ. Press. Copyright © 1957 by Princeton University Press.

pears that they have precisely the characteristic ambiguity of psychology. Dread is a *sympathetic antipathy and an antipathetic sympathy*. One easily sees, I think, that this is much more truly a psychological subject than is the concupiscence of which we have spoken. Language confirms this completely. One speaks of a sweet dread, a sweet feeling of apprehension, one speaks of a strange dread, a shrinking dread, etc.

The dread which is posited in innocence is, in the first place, not guilt; in the second place, it is not a heavy burden, not a suffering which cannot be brought into harmony with the felicity of innocence. If we observe children, we find this dread more definitely indicated as a seeking after adventure, a thirst for the prodigious, the mysterious. The fact that there are children in whom this is not found proves nothing, for neither in the beast does it exist, and the less spirit, the less dread. This dread belongs to the child so essentially that it cannot do without it; even though it alarms him, it captivates him nevertheless by its sweet feeling of apprehension. In all nations in which the childish character is preserved as the dreaming of the spirit this dread is found, and the deeper it is, the more profound is the nation. It is only a prosaic stupidity which thinks that this is a disorganization. Dread has here the same significance melancholy has at a far later point where freedom, after having passed through imperfect forms of its history, has to come to itself in a deeper sense.[1]

Just as the relation of dread to its object, to something which is nothing (language in this instance also is pregnant; it speaks of being in dread of nothing), is altogether ambiguous, so will the transition here from innocence to guilt be correspondingly so dialectical that the explanation is and must be psychological. The qualitative leap is outside of ambiguity, but he who through dread becomes guilty is innocent, for it was not he himself but dread, an alien power, which laid hold of him, a power he did not love but dreaded—and yet he is guilty, for he sank in the dread which he loved even while he feared it. There is nothing in the world more ambiguous, and therefore this is the only psychological explanation, although (to repeat what I have said) it never occurs to it to want to be the explanation which explains the qualitative leap. Every theory about the prohibition tempting Adam or the seducer deceiving him has only for a superficial observation sufficient ambiguity, while it perverts ethics, introduces a quanti-

1. With regard to this one may consult *Either/Or* (Copenhagen 1843), noting especially that Part I represents melancholy, in its anguished sympathy and egotism, which in Part II is explained.

tative determination, and would by the help of psychology pay man a compliment from which everyone who is ethically developed would beg to be excused, regarding it as a new and deeper seduction.

Everything turns upon dread coming into view. Man is a synthesis of the soulish and the bodily. But a synthesis is unthinkable if the two are not united in a third factor. This third factor is the spirit. In the state of innocence man is not merely an animal, for if at any time of his life he was merely an animal, he never would become a man. So then the spirit is present, but in a state of immediacy, a dreaming state. Forasmuch as it is present, it is in one way a hostile power, for it constantly disturbs the relation between soul and body, a relation which endures, and yet does not endure, inasmuch as it has endurance only by means of the spirit. On the other hand, it is a friendly power which has precisely the function of constituting the relationship. What then is man's relation to this ambiguous power? How is spirit related to itself and to its situation? It is related as dread. The spirit cannot do away with itself; nor can it grasp itself so long as it has itself outside of itself. Neither can man sink down into the vegetative life, for he is determined as spirit. He cannot flee from dread, for he loves it; really he does not love it, for he flees from it. Innocence has now reached its apex. It is ignorance, but not an animal brutality, but an ignorance which is qualified by spirit, but which precisely is dread, because its ignorance is about nothing. Here there is no knowledge of good and evil, etc., but the whole reality of knowledge is projected in dread as the immense nothing of ignorance.

Innocence still *is*, but one word suffices, and with that ignorance is concentrated. Innocence of course cannot understand this word; but dread has as it were obtained its first prey; instead of nothing, innocence gets an enigmatic word. So when it is related in Genesis that God said to Adam, "Only of the tree of the knowledge of good and evil thou shalt not eat," it is a matter of course that Adam did not really understand this word. For how could he have understood the difference between good and evil, seeing that this distinction was in fact consequent upon the enjoyment of the fruit?

When one assumes that the prohibition awakens the desire, one posits a knowledge instead of ignorance; for Adam would have had to have a knowledge of freedom, since his desire was to use it. The explanation therefore anticipates what was subsequent. The prohibition alarms Adam [induces a state of dread] because the prohibition awakens in him the possibility of freedom. That which passed innocence by as the nothing of dread has now entered into him, and here again it is a nothing, the alarming possibility of *being able*. What it is he is able to do, of that he has no conception; to suppose that he had some conception is to presuppose, as commonly is done, what came later, the distinction between good and evil. There is only the possibility of being able, as a higher form of ignorance, as a heightened expression of dread, because this in a more profound sense is and is not, because in a more profound sense he loves it and flees from it.

After the word of prohibition follows the word of judgment: "Thou shalt surely die." What it means to die, Adam of course cannot conceive; but if one assumes that these words were said to him, there is nothing to prevent his having a notion of the terrible. Indeed even the beast is able to understand the mimic expression and movement in the speaker's voice, without understanding the word. In case one lets the prohibition awaken desire, one may also let the word about punishment awaken a deterring conception. However, this confuses things. The terrible becomes in this instance merely dread; for Adam has not understood what was said, and here again we have only the ambiguity of dread. The infinite possibility of being able (awakened by the prohibition) draws closer for the fact that this possibility indicates a possibility as its consequence.

Thus innocence is brought to its last extremity. It is in dread in relation to the prohibition and the punishment. It is not guilty, and yet it is in dread, as though it were lost.

Further than this psychology cannot go, but so far it can reach, and moreover it can verify this point again and again in its observation of human life.

Subjective Dread*

The more reflective we venture to assume dread is, the easier it might seem to get it to pass over into guilt. But here it is important not to let ourselves be beguiled by gradual approximations, but to hold fast to the fact that it is not a "more" which gives rise to the leap, and that the "easier" does not in truth make the explanation easier. If we do not hold fast to this, we run the risk of stumbling suddenly upon a phenomenon where everything goes so easily that the transition becomes a simple transition, or else the risk of never daring to bring our thought to a conclusion, because the purely empirical observation can never be finished. Therefore even though the dread become more and more reflective, the guilt which breaks forth in dread by the qualitative leap retains nevertheless the same accountability as that of Adam, and dread retains the same ambiguity.

To wish to deny that every subsequent individual has or may be assumed to have had a state of innocence analogous to that of Adam, would not only offend every man but would abrogate all rational thought, because then there would be an individual who was not an individual but was related as a sample to the species in spite of the fact that at the same time he would be viewed under the category of the individual, that is, as a guilty man.

One may liken dread to dizziness. He whose eye chances to look down into the yawning abyss becomes dizzy. But the reason for it is just as much his eye as it is the precipice. For suppose he had not looked down.

Thus dread is the dizziness of freedom which occurs when the spirit would posit the synthesis, and freedom then gazes down into its own possibility, grasping at finiteness to sustain itself. In this dizziness freedom succumbs. Further than this psychology cannot go and will not. That very instant everything is changed, and when freedom rises again it sees that it is guilty. Between these two in-

*Ibid., pp. 54-56.

stants lies the leap, which no science has explained or can explain.
He who becomes guilty in dread becomes as ambiguously guilty as
it is possible to be. Dread is a womanish debility in which freedom
swoons. Psychologically speaking, the fall into sin always occurs in
impotence. But dread is at the same time the most egoistic thing,
and no concrete expression of freedom is so egoistic as is the possibility
of every concretion. This again is the overwhelming experience which
determines the individual's ambiguous relation, both sympathetic and
antipathetic. In dread there is the egoistic infinity of possibility, which
does not tempt like a definite choice, but alarms (ængster) and fascin-
ates with its sweet anxiety (Beængstelse).

In the later individual dread is more reflective. This may be
expressed by saying that the nothing which is the object of dread
becomes, as it were, more and more a something. We do not say
that it really becomes something or really signifies something, we do
not say that now instead of nothing there should be substituted sin
or something else, for here what was true of Adam's innocence is
true also of the later individual. All this applies only to freedom,
and only when the individual himself by the qualitative leap posits
sin. Here then the nothing of dread is a complex of presentiments
which reflect themselves in themselves, coming nearer and nearer to
the individual, notwithstanding that in dread they signify again essentially nothing, not, however, be it noted, a nothing with which the
individual has nothing to do, but a nothing in lively communication
with the ignorance of innocence. This reflectiveness is a predisposition
which, before the individual becomes guilty, signifies essentially nothing, whereas when by the qualitative leap he becomes guilty it is the
presupposition in which the individual goes beyond himself because
sin presupposes itself, not of course before it is posited (that would be
a predestination), but presupposes itself when it is posited. . . .

Dread as a Saving Experience*

In one of Grimm's Fairy Tales there is the story of a youth who went out in search of adventures for the sake of learning what it is to fear or be in dread. We will let that adventurer go his way without troubling ourselves to learn whether in the course of it he encountered the dreadful. On the other hand I would say that learning to know dread is an adventure which every man has to affront if he would not go to perdition either by not having known dread or by sinking under it. He therefore who has learned rightly to be in dread has learned the most important thing. . . .

Dread is the possibility of freedom. Only this dread is by the aid of faith absolutely educative, consuming as it does all finite aims and discovering all their deceptions. And no Grand Inquisitor has in readiness such terrible tortures as has dread, and no spy knows how to attack more artfully the man he suspects, choosing the instant when he is weakest, nor knows how to lay traps where he will be caught and ensnared, as dread knows how, and no sharp-witted judge knows how to interrogate, to examine the accused, as dread does, which never lets him escape, neither by diversion nor by noise, neither at work nor at play, neither by day nor by night.

He who is educated by dread is educated by possibility, and only the man who is educated by possibility is educated in accordance with its infinity. Possibility is therefore the heaviest of all categories. One often hears, it is true, the opposite affirmed, that possibility is so light but reality is heavy. But from whom does one hear such talk? From a lot of miserable men who never have known what possibility is, and who, since reality showed them that they were not fit for anything and never would be, mendaciously bedizened a possibility which was so beautiful, so enchanting; and the only foundation of this possibility was a little youthful tomfoolery of which they might rather have been ashamed. Therefore by this possibility which is said to be

*Ibid., pp. 139-142.

light one commonly understands the possibility of luck, good fortune, etc. But this is not possibility, it is a mendacious invention which human depravity falsely embellishes in order to have reason to complain of life, of providence, and as a pretext for being self-important. No, in possibility everything is possible, and he who truly was brought up by possibility has comprehended the dreadful as well as the smiling. When such a person, therefore, goes out from the school of possibility, and knows more thoroughly than a child knows the alphabet that he can demand of life absolutely nothing, and that terror, perdition, annihilation, dwell next door to every man, and has learned the profitable lesson that every dread which alarms [*ængste*] may the next instant become a fact, he will then interpret reality differently, he will extol reality, and even when it rests upon him heavily he will remember that after all it is far, far lighter than the possibility was. Only thus can possibility educate; for finiteness and the finite relationships in which the individual is assigned a place, whether it be small and commonplace or world-historical, educate only finitely, and one can always talk them around, always make something a little different out of them, always chaffer, always escape a little way from them, always keep a little apart, always prevent oneself from learning absolutely from them; and if one is to learn absolutely, the individual must in turn have the possibility in himself and himself fashion that from which he is to learn, even though the next instant it does not recognize that it was fashioned by him, but absolutely takes the power from him.

But in order that the individual may thus absolutely and infinitely be educated by possibility, he must be honest towards possibility and must have faith. By faith I mean what Hegel in his fashion calls very rightly "the inward certainty which anticipates infinity." When the discoveries of possibility are honestly administered, possibility will then disclose all finitudes but idealize them in the form of infinity, and by dread overwhelm the individual, until he in turn conquers them by the anticipation of faith.

What I say here appears perhaps to many an obscure and foolish saying, since they even boast of never having been in dread. To this I would reply that doubtless one should not be in dread of men, of finite things, but that only the man who has gone through the dread of possibility is educated to have no dread—not because he avoids the dreadful things of life, but because they always are weak in comparison with those of possibility. If on the other hand the speaker means that the great thing about him is that he has never been in dread, then I shall gladly initiate him into my explanation, that this comes from the fact that he is spirit-less.

If the individual cheats the possibility by which he is to be educated, he never reaches faith; his faith remains the shrewdness of finitude, as his school was that of finitude. But men cheat possibility in every way—if they did not, one has only to stick one's head out of the window, and one would see enough for possibility to begin its exercises forthwith. There is an engraving by Chodowiecki which represents the surrender of Calais as viewed by the four temperaments, and the theme of the artist was to let the various impressions appear mirrored in the faces which express the various temperaments. The most commonplace life has events enough, no doubt, but the question is about possibility in the individual who is honest with himself. It is recounted of an Indian hermit who for two years had lived upon dew, that he came once to the city, tasted wine, and then became addicted to drink. This story, like every other of the sort, can be understood in many ways, one can make it comic, one can make it tragic; but the man who is educated by possibility has more than enough to occupy him in such a story. Instantly he is absolutely identified with that unfortunate man, he knows no finite evasion by which he might escape. Now the dread of possibility holds him as its prey, until it can deliver him saved into the hands of faith. In no other place does he find repose, for every other point of rest is mere nonsense, even though in men's eyes it is shrewdness. This is the reason why possibility is so absolutely educative. No man has ever become so unfortunate in reality that there was not some little residue left to him, and, as common sense observes quite truly, if a man is canny, he will find a way. But he who went through the curriculum of misfortune offered by possibility lost everything, absolutely everything, in a way that no one has lost it in reality. If in this situation he did not behave falsely towards possibility, if he did not attempt to talk around the dread which would save him, then he received everything back again, as in reality no one ever did even if he received everything tenfold, for the pupil of possibility received infinity, whereas the soul of the other expired in the finite. No one ever sank so deep in reality that he could not sink deeper, or that there might not be one or another sunk deeper than he. But he who sank in the possibility has an eye too dizzy to see the measuring rod which Tom, Dick, and Harry hold out as a straw to the drowning man; his ear is closed so that he cannot hear what the market price for men is in his day, cannot hear that he is just as good as most of them. He sank absolutely, but then in turn he floated up from the depth of the abyss, lighter now than all that is

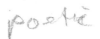

oppressive and dreadful in life. Only I do not deny that he who is educated by possibility is exposed—not to the danger of bad company and dissoluteness of various sorts, as are those who are educated by the finite, but—to one danger of downfall, and that is self-slaughter. If at the beginning of his education he misunderstands the anguish of dread, so that it does not lead him to faith but away from faith, then he is lost. On the other hand, he who is educated by possibility remains with dread, does not allow himself to be deceived by its countless counterfeits, he recalls the past precisely; then at last the attacks of dread, though they are fearful, are not such that he flees from them. For him dread becomes a serviceable spirit which against its will leads him whither he would go. Then when it announces itself, when it craftily insinuates that it has invented a new instrument of torture far more terrible than anything employed before, he does not recoil, still less does he attempt to hold it off with clamor and noise, but he bids it welcome, he hails it solemnly, as Socrates solemnly flourished the poisoned goblet, he shuts himself up with it, he says, as a patient says to the surgeon when a painful operation is about to begin, "Now I am ready." Then dread enters into his soul and searches it thoroughly, constraining out of him all the finite and the petty, and leading him hence whither he would go. . . .

NIETZSCHE

FRIEDRICH WILHELM NIETZSCHE (1844-1900) was born in Röcken, Germany, the son of a Lutheran pastor who died when Nietzsche was four. He studied classical philology, first at Bonn and later at Leipzig, where he greatly impressed one of the professors, Friedrich Ritschl; it was Ritschl's enthusiastic recommendation that was largely responsible for Nietzsche's being appointed to a chair at the University of Basle at the age of only twenty-five. Nietzsche's significant relationship with the Swiss historian Jacob Burckhardt and his more short-lived friendship with Richard Wagner both date from this time; the deep impression Wagner made upon him is apparent in his first book, *The Birth of Tragedy out of the Spirit of Music,* in which, among other things, he presented a fundamental revaluation of traditional notions of Greek culture. While at Basle he also published four essays under the title of *Untimely Meditations* and a book of aphorisms called *Human, All Too Human* (1878). In 1879 bad health and a dissatisfaction with his career as an academic led to his resigning his professorship; he now entered upon a lonely existence as a writer, spending much of his time in Italy and Switzerland and producing, often in conditions of extreme physical distress, the works upon which his reputation as a philosopher largely rests. In 1881 *Dawn* was published, and in the following year another book of aphorisms which he called *The Gay Science* (given the title of *Joyful Wisdom* by its English translator). Nietzsche's most popular book, *Thus Spoke Zarathustra,* which contains his curious doctrine of "eternal recurrence," came out in four installments between 1883 and 1885, and it was succeeded by three works that are more succinct and less eccentrically presented: *Beyond Good and Evil* (1886), *A Genealogy of Morals* (1887), and *The Twilight of the Idols* (1889). In 1889 Nietzsche became insane, probably as a result of a syphilitic infection which he contracted as a student, and never recovered. He was looked after in his last years by his sister, who also undertook, with a certain lack of scholarly accuracy and scruple, the editing and publication of his writings: *The Antichrist* and *Nietzsche contra Wagner* appeared in 1895, *The Will to Power* (embodying material for a projected but uncompleted treatise) in 1901, and *Ecce Homo* in 1908.

Though a prolific writer Nietzsche was far from being a systematic one; his books tend to comprise a patchwork of ideas rather than a continuous line of argument, and passages expressing original and shrewd insights are often interspersed with others of a grating shrillness and moral crudity. Partly as a consequence of such unevenness of temper and quality, Nietzsche's significant philosophical perceptions have tended to suffer neglect by comparison with his more dubious and unsavory apocalyptic utterances. In particular, his contributions to the understanding of mind and consciousness—e.g., his conception of thought as answering personal or social needs, his theory of language as determining fundamental attitudes to experience, his analysis in depth of systems of ethics as institutions developed by men for their own purposes and therefore always in principle open to revision or replacement—are only beginning to be fully or fairly appreciated. The selections given below have been chosen with a view to illustrating some of his central themes.

Life, Knowledge, and Self-consciousness*

108

New Struggles—After Buddha was dead people showed his shadow for centuries afterwards in a cave,—an immense frightful shadow. God is dead: but as the human race is constituted, there will perhaps be caves for millenniums yet, in which people will show his shadow.—And we—we have still to overcome his shadow!

109

Let us be on our Guard—Let us be on our guard against thinking that the world is a living being. Where could it extend itself? What could it nourish itself with? How could it grow and increase? We know tolerably well what the organic is; and we are to reinterpret the emphatically derivative, tardy, rare and accidental, which we only perceive on the crust of the earth, into the essential, universal and eternal, as those do who call the universe an organism? That disgusts me. Let us now be on our guard against believing that the universe is a machine; it is assuredly not constructed with a view to *one* end; we invest it with far too high an honour with the word "machine." Let us be on our guard against supposing that anything so methodical as the cyclic motions of our neighbouring stars obtains generally and throughout the universe; indeed a glance at the Milky Way induces doubt as to whether there are not many cruder and more contradictory motions there, and even stars with continuous, rectilinearly gravitating orbits, and the like. The astral arrangement in which we live is an exception; this arrangement, and the relatively long durability which is determined by it, has again made possible the exception of exceptions, the formation of organic life. The general character of the world, on the other hand, is to all eternity chaos; not by the absence of neces-

*From *The Joyful Wisdom* (trans. T. Common; Edinburgh & London, 1910), pp. 151-164 and 296-301.

sity, but in the sense of the absence of order, structure, form, beauty, wisdom, and whatever else our aesthetic humanities are called. Judged by our reason, the unlucky casts are far oftenest the rule, the exceptions are not the secret purpose; and the whole musical box repeats eternally its air, which can never be called a melody,—and finally the very expression, "unlucky cast" is already an anthropomorphising which involves blame. But how could we presume to blame or praise the universe! Let us be on our guard against ascribing to it heartlessness and unreason, or their opposites; it is neither perfect, nor beautiful, nor noble; nor does it seek to be anything of the kind, it does not at all attempt to imitate man! It is altogether unaffected by our aesthetic and moral judgments! Neither has it any self-preservative instinct, nor instinct at all; it also knows no law. Let us be on our guard against saying that there are laws in nature. There are only necessities : there is no one who commands, no one who obeys, no one who transgresses. When you know that there is no design, you know also that there is no chance: for it is only where there is a world of design that the word "chance" has a meaning. Let us be on our guard against saying that death is contrary to life. The living being is only a species of dead being, and a very rare species.—Let us be on our guard against thinking that the world eternally creates the new. There are no eternally enduring substances; matter is just another such error as the God of the Eleatics. But when shall we be at an end with our foresight and precaution! When will all these shadows of God cease to obscure us? When shall we have nature entirely undeified! When shall we be permitted to *naturalise* ourselves by means of the pure, newly discovered, newly redeemed nature?

110

Origin of Knowledge—Throughout immense stretches of time the intellect has produced nothing but errors; some of them proved to be useful and preservative of the species: he who fell in with them, or inherited them, waged the battle for himself and his offspring with better success. Those erroneous articles of faith which were successively transmitted by inheritance, and have finally become almost the property and stock of the human species, are, for example, the following:—that there are enduring things, that there are equal things, that there are things, substances, and bodies, that a thing is what it appears, that our will is free, that what is good for me is also good absolutely. It was only very late that the deniers and doubters of such propositions came forward,—it was only very late that truth made its appearance as the most impotent form of knowledge. It seemed as

if it were impossible to get along with truth, our organism was adapted
for the very opposite; all its higher functions, the perceptions of the
senses, and in general every kind of sensation co-operated with those
primevally embodied, fundamental errors. Moreover, those propositions became the very standards of knowledge according to which
the "true" and the "false" were determined—throughout the whole
domain of pure logic. The *strength* of conceptions does not, therefore,
depend on their degree of truth, but on their antiquity, their embodiment, their character as conditions of life. Where life and knowledge
seemed to conflict, there has never been serious contention; denial
and doubt have there been regarded as madness. The exceptional
thinkers like the Eleatics, who, in spite of this, advanced and maintained the antitheses of the natural errors, believed that it was possible
also *to live* these counterparts: it was they who devised the sage as the
man of immutability, impersonality and universality of intuition, as
one and all at the same time, with a special faculty for that reverse
kind of knowledge; they were of the belief that their knowledge was
at the same time the principle of *life*. To be able to affirm all this,
however, they had to *deceive* themselves concerning their own condition: they had to attribute to themselves impersonality and unchang-
ing permanence, they had to mistake the nature of the philosophic
individual, deny the force of the impulses in cognition, and conceive
of reason generally as an entirely free and self-originating activity;
they kept their eyes shut to the fact that they also had reached their
doctrines in contradiction to valid methods, or through their longing
for repose or for exclusive possession or for domination. The subtler
development of sincerity and of scepticism finally made these men
impossible; their life also and their judgments turned out to be dependent on the primeval impulses and fundamental errors of all sentient being.—The subtler sincerity and scepticism arose whenever two
antithetical maxims appeared to be *applicable* to life, because both
of them were compatible with the fundamental errors; where, therefore, there could be contention concerning a higher or lower degree of
utility for life; and likewise where new maxims proved to be, not
in fact useful, but at least not injurious, as expressions of an intellectual
impulse to play a game that was, like all games, innocent and happy.
The human brain was gradually filled with such judgments and convictions; and in this tangled skein there arose ferment, strife and lust
for power. Not only utility and delight, but every kind of impulse took
part in the struggle for "truths": the intellectual struggle became a
business, an attraction, a calling, a duty, an honour—: cognizing and
striving for the true finally arranged themselves as needs among other

needs. From that moment not only belief and conviction, but also examination, denial, distrust and contradiction became *forces*; all "evil" instincts were subordinated to knowledge, were placed in its service, and acquired the prestige of the permitted, the honoured, the useful, and finally the appearance and innocence of the *good*. Knowledge, thus became a portion of life itself, and as life it became a continually growing power: until finally the cognitions and those primeval, fundamental errors clashed with each other, both as life, both as power, both in the same man. The thinker is now the being in whom the impulse to truth and those life-preserving errors wage their first conflict, now that the impulse to truth has also *proved* itself to be a life-preserving power. In comparison with the importance of this conflict everything else is indifferent; the final question concerning the conditions of life is here raised, and the first attempt is here made to answer it by experiment. How far is truth susceptible of embodiment?—that is the question, that is the experiment.

111

Origin of the Logical—Where has logic originated in men's heads? Undoubtedly out of the illogical, the domain of which must originally have been immense. But numberless beings who reasoned otherwise than we do at present, perished; albeit that they may have come nearer to truth than we! Whoever, for example, could not discern the "like" often enough with regard to food, and with regard to animals dangerous to him, whoever, therefore, deduced too slowly, or was too circumspect in his deductions, had smaller probability of survival than he who in all similar things immediately divined the equality. The preponderating inclination, however, to deal with the similar as the equal—an illogical inclination, for there is nothing equal in itself—first created the whole basis of logic. It was just so (in order that the conception of substance might originate, this being indispensable to logic, although in the strictest sense nothing actual corresponds to it) that for a long period the changing process in things had to be overlooked, and remain unperceived; the beings not seeing correctly had an advantage over those who saw everything "in flux." In itself every high degree of circumspection in conclusions, every sceptical inclination, is a great danger to life. No living being would have been preserved unless the contrary inclination—to affirm rather than suspend judgment, to mistake and fabricate rather than wait, to assent rather than deny, to decide rather than be in the right— had been cultivated with extraordinary assiduity.—The course of logical thought and reasoning in our modern brain corresponds to a process and struggle of impulses, which singly and in themselves are all very illogical and unjust; we experience usually only the result of the struggle, so rapidly and secretly does this primitive mechanism now operate in us.

112

Cause and Effect—We say it is "explanation"; but it is only in "description" that we are in advance of the older stages of knowledge and science. We describe better,—we explain just as little as our predecessors. We have discovered a manifold succession where the naïve man and investigator of older cultures saw only two things, "cause" and "effect," as it was said; we have perfected the conception of becoming, but have not got a knowledge of what is above and behind the conception. The series of "causes" stands before us much more complete in every case; we conclude that this and that must first precede in order that that other may follow—but we have not *grasped* anything thereby. The peculiarity, for example, in every chemical process seems a "miracle," the same as before, just like all locomotion; nobody has "explained" impulse. How could we ever explain! We operate only with things which do not exist, with lines, surfaces, bodies, atoms, divisible times, divisible spaces—how can explanation ever be possible when we first make everything a *conception*, our conception! It is sufficient to regard science as the exactest humanising of things that is possible; we always learn to describe ourselves more accurately by describing things and their successions. Cause and effect: there is probably never any such duality; in fact there is a *continuum* before us, from which we isolate a few portions;—just as we always observe a motion as isolated points, and therefore do not properly see it, but infer it. The abruptness with which many effects take place leads us into error; it is however only an abruptness for us. There is an infinite multitude of processes in that abrupt moment which escape us. An intellect which could see cause and effect as a *continuum*, which could see the flux of events not according to our mode of perception, as things arbitrarily separated and broken—would throw aside the conception of cause and effect, and would deny all conditionality. . . .

121

Life no Argument—We have arranged for ourselves a world in which we can live—by the postulating of bodies, lines, surfaces, causes and effects, motion and rest, form and content: without these articles of faith no one could manage to live at present! But for all that they are still unproved. Life is no argument; error might be among the conditions of life. . . .

354

The "Genius of the Species"—The problem of consciousness (or more correctly: of becoming conscious of oneself) meets us only when we begin to perceive in what measure we could dispense with it: and it is at the beginning of this perception that we are now placed by physiology and zoology (which have thus required two centuries to overtake the hint thrown out in advance by Leibnitz). For we could in fact think, feel, will, and recollect, we could likewise "act" in every sense of the term, and nevertheless nothing of it all would require to "come into consciousness" (as one says metaphorically). The whole of life would be possible without its seeing itself as it were in a mirror: as in fact even at present the far greater part of our life still goes on without this mirroring,—and even our thinking, feeling, volitional life as well, however painful this statement may sound to an older philosopher. *What* then is the *purpose* of consciousness generally, when it is in the main *superfluous?*—Now it seems to me, if you will hear my answer and its perhaps extravagant supposition, that the subtlety and strength of consciousness are always in proportion to the *capacity for communication* of a man (or an animal), the capacity for communication in its turn being in proportion to the *necessity for communication*: the latter not to be understood as if precisely the individual himself who is master in the art of communication and making known his necessities would at the same time have to be most dependent upon others for his necessities. It seems to me, however, to be so in relation to whole races and successions of generations : where necessity and need have long compelled men to communicate with their fellows and understand one another rapidly and subtly, a surplus of the power and art of communication is at last acquired, as if it were a fortune which had gradually accumulated, and now waited for an heir to squander it prodigally (the so-called artists are these heirs, in like manner the orators, preachers. and authors: all of them men who come at the end of a long succession, "late-born" always, in the best sense of the word, and as has been said, *squanderers* by their very nature). Granted that this observation is correct, I may proceed further to the conjecture that *consciousness generally has only been developed under the pressure of the necessity for communication,*—that from the first it has been necessary and useful only between man and man (especially between those commanding and those obeying), and has only developed in proportion to its utility. Consciousness is properly only a connecting network between man and man,—it is only as such that it has had to develop; the recluse and wild-beast species of men would not have needed it. The very fact that our actions, thoughts, feelings and motions come within the range of our consciousness— at least a part of them—is the result of a terrible, prolonged "must" ruling man's destiny: as the most endangered animal he *needed* help and protection; he needed his fellows, he was obliged to express his distress, he had to know how to make himself understood—and for all this he needed "consciousness" first of all, consequently, to "know" himself what he lacked, to "know" how he felt and to "know" what he thought. For, to repeat it once more, man, like every living creature, thinks unceasingly, but does not know it; the thinking which is becoming *conscious of itself* is only the smallest part thereof, we may say, the most superficial part, the worst part:—for this conscious thinking alone *is done in words, that is to say, in the symbols for communication,* by means of which the origin for consciousness is revealed. In short, the development of speech and the development of consciousness (not of reason, but of reason becoming self-conscious) go hand in hand. Let it be further accepted that it is not only speech that serves as a bridge between man and man, but also the looks, the pressure and the gestures; our becoming conscious of our sense impressions, our power of being able to fix them, and as it were to locate them outside of ourselves, has increased in proportion as the necessity has increased for communicating them to *others* by means of signs. The sign-inventing man is at the same time the man who is always more acutely self-conscious; it is only as a social animal that man has learned to become conscious of himself,—he is doing so still, and doing so more and more.—As is obvious, my idea is that consciousness does not properly belong to the individual existence of man, but rather to the social and gregarious nature in him; that, as follows therefrom, it is only in relation to communal and gregarious utility that it is finely developed; and that consequently each of us, in spite of the best intention of *understanding* himself as individually as possible, and of "knowing himself," will always just call into consciousness the non-individual in him, namely, his "averageness";—that our thought itself is continuously as it were *outvoted* by the character of consciousness— by the imperious "genius of the species" therein—and is translated back into the perspective of the herd. Fundamentally our actions are in an incomparable manner altogether personal, unique and absolutely individual—there is no doubt about it; but as soon as we translate them into consciousness, they *do not appear so any longer.* . . . This is the proper phenomenalism and perspectivism as I understand

it : the nature of *animal consciousness* involves the notion that the
world of which we can become conscious is only a superficial and
symbolic world, a generalised and vulgarised world;—that everything which becomes conscious *becomes* just thereby shallow, meagre,
relatively stupid,—a generalisation, a symbol, a characteristic of the
herd; that with the evolving of consciousness there is always combined
a great, radical perversion, falsification, superficialisation, and generalisation. Finally, the growing consciousness is a danger, and whoever
lives among the most conscious Europeans knows even that it is a
disease. As may be conjectured, it is not the antithesis of subject and
object with which I am here concerned: I leave that distinction to the
epistemologists who have remained entangled in the toils of grammar
(popular metaphysics). It is still less the antithesis of "thing in itself"
and phenomenon, for we do not "know" enough to be entitled even
to make such a distinction. Indeed, we have not any organ at all for
knowing or for "truth": we "know" (or believe, or fancy) just as much
as may be *of use* in the interest of the human herd, the species; and
even what is here called "usefulness" is ultimately only a belief, a
fancy, and perhaps precisely the most fatal stupidity by which we shall
one day be ruined.

355

The Origin of our Conception of "Knowledge"—I take this explanation from the street. I heard one of the people saying that "he
knew me," so I asked myself: What do the people really understand
by knowledge? what do they want when they seek "knowledge"?
Nothing more than that what is strange is to be traced back to something *known*. And we philosophers—have we really understood *anything more* by knowledge? The known, that is to say, what we are
accustomed to, so that we no longer marvel at it, the commonplace,
any kind of rule to which we are habituated, all and everything in
which we know ourselves to be at home:—what? is our need of knowing not just this need of the known? the will to discover in everything
strange, unusual, or questionable, something which no longer disquiets
us? Is it not possible that it should be the *instinct of fear* which en-
joins upon us to know? Is it not possible that the rejoicing of the
discerner should be just his rejoicing in the regained feeling of
security? . . . One philosopher imagined the world "known" when he
had traced it back to the "idea": alas, was it not because the idea was
so known, so familiar to him? because he had so much less fear of the
"idea"—Oh, this moderation of the discerners! let us but look at their
principles, and at their solutions of the riddle of the world in this

connection! When they again find aught in things, among things, or behind things, that is unfortunately very well known to us, for example, our multiplication table, or our logic, or our willing and desiring, how happy they immediately are! For "what is known is understood": they are unanimous as to that. Even the most circumspect among them think that the known is at least *more easily understood* than the strange; that for example, it is methodically ordered to proceed outward from the "inner world," from "the facts of consciousness," because it is the world which is *better known to us!* Errors of errors! The known is the accustomed, and the accustomed is the most difficult of all to "understand," that is to say, to perceive as a problem, to perceive as strange, distant, "outside of us." ... The great certainty of the natural sciences in comparison with psychology and the criticism of the elements of consciousness—*unnatural* sciences as one might almost be entitled to call them—rests precisely on the fact that they take *what is strange* as their object: while it is almost like something contradictory and absurd *to wish* to take generally what is not strange as an object. ...

Prejudices of Philosophers*

1

The Will to Truth, which is to tempt us to many a hazardous enterprise, the famous Truthfulness of which all philosophers have hitherto spoken with respect, what questions has this Will to Truth not laid before us! What strange, perplexing, questionable questions! It is already a long story; yet it seems as if it were hardly commenced. Is it any wonder if we at last grow distrustful, lose patience, and turn impatiently away? That this Sphinx teaches us at last to ask questions ourselves? *Who* is it really that puts questions to us here? *What* really is this "Will to Truth" in us? In fact we made a long halt at the question as to the origin of this Will—until at last we came to an absolute standstill before a yet more fundamental question. We inquired about the *value* of this Will. Granted that we want the truth: *why not rather* untruth? And uncertainty? Even ignorance? The problem of the value of truth presented itself before us—or was it we who presented ourselves before the problem? Which of us is the Œdipus here? Which the Sphinx? It would seem to be a rendezvous of questions and notes of interrogation. And could it be believed that it at last seems to us as if the problem had never been propounded before, as if we were the first to discern it, get a sight of it, and *risk raising* it. For there is risk in raising it; perhaps there is no greater risk.

3

Having kept a sharp eye on philosophers, and having read between their lines long enough, I now say to myself that the greater part of conscious thinking must be counted amongst the instinctive functions, and it is so even in the case of philosophical thinking; one has here to learn anew, as one learned anew about heredity and

*From *Beyond Good and Evil* (trans. Helen Zimmern in *The Philosophy of Nietzsche*; New York, 1927), pp. 381-407. Reprinted by permission of George Allen & Unwin Ltd.

"innateness." As little as the act of birth comes into consideration
in the whole process and procedure of heredity, just as little is "being-
conscious" *opposed* to the instinctive in any decisive sense; the greater
part of the conscious thinking of a philosopher is secretly influenced by
his instincts, and forced into definite channels. And behind all logic
and its seeming sovereignty of movement, there are valuations, or to
speak more plainly, physiological demands, for the maintenance of a
definite mode of life. For example, that the certain is worth more than
the uncertain, that illusion is less valuable than "truth": such valuations, in spite of their regulative importance for *us*, might notwithstanding be only superficial valuations, special kinds of *niaiserie*, such
as may be necessary for the maintenance of beings such as ourselves.
Supposing, in effect, that man is not just the "measure of things." . . .

4

The falseness of an opinion is not for us any objection to it: it
is here, perhaps, that our new language sounds most strangely. The
question is, how far an opinion is life-furthering, life-preserving,
species-preserving, perhaps species-rearing; and we are fundamentally
inclined to maintain that the falsest opinions (to which the synthetic
judgments *a priori* belong), are the most indispensable to us; that without a recognition of logical fictions, without a comparison of reality
with the purely *imagined* world of the absolute and immutable, without a constant counterfeiting of the world by means of numbers, man
could not live—that the renunciation of false opinions would be a
renunciation of life, a negation of life. *To recognise untruth as a condition of life*; that is certainly to impugn the traditional ideas of
value in a dangerous manner, and a philosophy which ventures to do
so, has thereby alone placed itself beyond good and evil.

5

That which causes philosophers to be regarded half-distrustfully
and half-mockingly, is not the oft-repeated discovery how innocent
they are—how often and easily they make mistakes and lose their
way, in short, how childish and childlike they are,—but that there is
not enough honest dealing with them, whereas they all raise a loud
and virtuous outcry when the problem of truthfulness is even hinted
at in the remotest manner. They all pose as though their real opinions
had been discovered and attained through the self-evolving of a cold,
pure, divinely indifferent dialectic (in contrast to all sorts of mystics,
who, fairer and foolisher, talk of *"inspiration"*); whereas, in fact,
a prejudiced proposition, idea, or "suggestion," which is generally their

heart's desire abstracted and refined, is defended by them with arguments sought out after the event. They are all advocates who do not
wish to be regarded as such, generally astute defenders, also, of their
prejudices, which they dub "truths,"—and *very* far from having the
conscience which bravely admits this to itself; very far from having the
good taste of the courage which goes so far as to let this be understood,
perhaps to warn friend or foe, or in cheerful confidence amd self-
ridicule. The spectacle of the Tartuffery of old Kant, equally stiff and
decent, with which he entices us into the dialectic by-ways that lead
(more correctly mislead) to his "categorical imperative"—makes us
fastidious ones smile, we who find no small amusement in spying out
the subtle tricks of old moralists and ethical preachers. Or, still more
so, the hocus-pocus in mathematical form, by means of which Spinoza
has, as it were, clad his philosophy in mail and mask—in fact, the
"love of *his* wisdom," to translate the term fairly and squarely—in
order thereby to strike terror at once into the heart of the assailant who
should dare to cast a glance on that invincible maiden, that Pallas
Athene:—how much of personal timidity and vulnerability does this
masquerade of a sickly recluse betray! . . .

9

You desire to *live* "according to Nature"? Oh, you noble Stoics,
what fraud of words! Imagine to yourselves a being like Nature,
boundlessly extravagant, boundlessly indifferent, without purpose or
consideration, without pity or justice, at once fruitful and barren and
uncertain: imagine to yourselves *indifference* as a power—how *could*
you live in accordance with such indifference? To live—is not that
just endeavouring to be otherwise than this Nature? Is not living
valuing, preferring, being unjust, being limited, endeavouring to be
different? And granted that your imperative, "living according to
Nature," means actually the same as "living according to life"—how
could you do *differently?* Why should you make a principle out of
what you yourselves are, and must be? In reality, however, it is quite
otherwise with you: while you pretend to read with rapture the canon
of your law in Nature, you want something quite the contrary, you
extraordinary stage-players and self-deluders! In your pride you wish
to dictate your morals and ideals to Nature, to Nature herself, and
to incorporate them therein; you insist that it shall be Nature "according to the Stoa," and would like everything to be made after your own
image, as a vast, eternal glorification and generalism of Stoicism!
With all your love for truth, you have forced yourselves so long, so
persistently, and with such hypnotic rigidity to see Nature *falsely,*

that is to say, Stoically, that you are no longer able to see it otherwise
—and to crown all, some unfathomable superciliousness gives you the
Bedlamite hope that *because* you are able to tyrannise over yourselves
—Stoicism is self-tyranny—Nature will also allow herself to be
tyrannised over: is not the Stoic a *part* of Nature? . . . But this is an
old and everlasting story: what happened in old times with the Stoics
still happens today, as soon as ever a philosophy begins to believe in
itself. It always creates the world in its own image; it cannot do
otherwise; philosophy is this tyrannical impulse itself; the most
spiritual Will to Power, the will to "creation of the world," the will to
the *causa prima*. . . .

11

It seems to me that there is everywhere an attempt at present to
divert attention from the actual influence which Kant exercised on
German philosophy, and especially to ignore prudently the value
which he set upon himself. Kant was first and foremost proud of his
Table of Categories; with it in his hand he said: "This is the most
difficult thing that could ever be undertaken on behalf of metaphysics."
Let us only understand this "could be"! He was proud of having
discovered a new faculty in man, the faculty of synthetic judgment *a
priori*. Granting that he deceived himself in this matter; the development and rapid flourishing of German philosophy depended nevertheless on his pride, and on the eager rivalry of the younger generation to
discover if possible something—at all events "new faculties"—of which
to be still prouder!—But let us reflect for a moment—it is high time
to do so. "How are synthetic judgments *a priori possible*?" Kant asks
himself—and what is really his answer? *"By means of a means
(faculty)"*—but unfortunately not in five words, but so circumstantially,
imposingly, and with such display of German profundity and verbal
flourishes, that one altogether loses sight of the comical *niaiserie allemande* involved in such an answer. People were beside themselves
with delight over this new faculty, and the jubilation reached its
climax when Kant further discovered a moral faculty in man—for at
that time Germans were still moral, not yet dabbling in the "Politics
of hard fact." Then came the honeymoon of German philosophy.
All the young theologians of the Tübingen institution went immediately into the groves—all seeking for "faculties." And what did they
find—in that innocent, rich, and still youthful period of the
German spirit, to which Romanticism, the malicious fairy, piped and
sang, when one could not yet distinguish between "finding" and
"inventing"! Above all a faculty for the "transcendental"; Schelling

336 NIETZSCHE

christened it "intellectual intuition," and thereby gratified the most earnest longings of the naturally pious-inclined Germans. One can do no greater wrong to the whole of this exuberant and eccentric movement (which was really youthfulness, notwithstanding that it disguised itself so boldly in hoary and senile conceptions), than to take it seriously, or even treat it with moral indignation. Enough, however—the world grew older, and the dream vanished. A time came when people rubbed their foreheads, and they still rub them today. People had been dreaming, and first and foremost—old Kant. "By means of a means (faculty)"—he had said, or at least meant to say. But, is that—an answer? An explanation? Or is it not rather merely a repetition of the question, How does opium induce sleep? "By means of a means (faculty)," namely the *virtus dormitiva*, replies the doctor in Molière :

> *Quia est in eo virtus dormitiva,*
> *Cujus est natura sensus assoupire.*

But such replies belong to the realm of comedy, and it is high time to replace the Kantian question, "How are synthetic judgments *a priori* possible?" by another question. "Why is belief in such judgments *necessary?*"—in effect, it is high time that we should understand that such judgments must be *believed* to be true, for the sake of the preservation of creatures like ourselves; though they still might naturally be *false* judgments! Or, more plainly spoken, and roughly and readily—synthetic judgments *a priori* should not "be possible" at all; we have no right to them; in our mouths they are nothing but false judgments. Only, of course, the belief in their truth is necessary, as plausible belief and ocular evidence belonging to the perspective view of life. And finally, to call to mind the enormous influence which "German philosophy"—I hope you understand its right to inverted commas (goosefeet)?—has exercised throughout the whole of Europe, there is no doubt that a certain *virtus dormitiva* had a share in it; thanks to German philosophy, it was a delight to the noble idlers, the virtuous, the mystics, the artists, the three-fourths Christians, and the political obscurantists of all nations, to find an antidote to the still overwhelming sensualism which overflowed from the last century into this, in short—*"sensus assoupire."* . . .

13

Psychologists should bethink themselves before putting down the instinct of self-preservation as the cardinal instinct of an organic being. A living thing seeks above all to *discharge* its strength—life itself is

Will to Power; self-preservation is only one of the indirect and most frequent *results* thereof. In short, here, as everywhere else, let us beware of *superfluous* teleological principles!—one of which is the instinct of self-preservation (we owe it to Spinoza's inconsistency). It is thus, in effect, that method ordains, which must be essentially economy of principles. . . .

16

There are still harmless self-observers who believe that there are "immediate certainties"; for instance, "I think," or as the superstition of Schopenhauer puts it, "I will"; as though cognition here got hold of its object purely and simply as "the thing in itself," without any falsification taking place either on the part of the subject or the object. I would repeat it, however, a hundred times, that "immediate certainty," as well as "absolute knowledge" and the "thing in itself," involve a *contradictio in adjecto*; we really ought to free ourselves from the misleading significance of words! The people on their part may think that cognition is knowing all about things, but the philosopher must say to himself: "When I analyse the process that is expressed in the sentence, 'I think,' I find a whole series of daring assertions, the argumentative proof of which would be difficult, perhaps impossible: for instance, that it is *I* who think, that there must necessarily be something that thinks, that thinking is an activity and operation on the part of a being who is thought of as a cause, that there is an 'ego,' and finally, that it is already determined what is to be designated by thinking—that I *know* what thinking is. For if I had not already decided within myself what it is, by what standard could I determine whether that which is just happening is not perhaps 'willing' or 'feeling'? In short, the assertion 'I think,' assumes that I *compare* my state at the present moment with other states of myself which I know, in order to determine what it is; on account of this retrospective connection with further 'knowledge,' it has, at any rate, no immediate certainty for me."—In place of the "immediate certainty" in which the people may believe in the special case, the philosopher thus finds a series of metaphysical questions presented to him, veritable conscience questions of the intellect, to wit: "From whence did I get the notion of 'thinking'? Why do I believe in cause and effect? What gives me the right to speak of an 'ego,' and even of an 'ego' as cause, and finally of an 'ego' as cause of thought?" He who ventures to answer these metaphysical questions at once by an appeal to a sort of *intuitive* perception, like the person who says, "I think, and know that this, at least, is true, actual, and certain"—will encounter a smile and two notes of interrogation in a philosopher nowadays. "Sir," the philosopher will perhaps give him to understand, "it is improbable that you are not mistaken, but why should it be the truth?"

17

With regard to the superstitions of logicians, I shall never tire of emphasising a small, terse fact, which is unwillingly recognised by these credulous minds—namely, that a thought comes when "it" wishes, and not when "I" wish; so that it is a *perversion* of the facts of the case to say that the subject "I" is the condition of the predicate "think." *One* thinks; but that this "one" is precisely the famous old "ego," is, to put it mildly, only a supposition, an assertion, and assuredly not an "immediate certainty." After all, one has even gone too far with this "one thinks"—even the "one" contains an *interpretation* of the process, and does not belong to the process itself. One infers here according to the usual grammatical formula—"To think is an activity; every activity requires an agency that is active; consequently" ... It was pretty much on the same lines that the older atomism sought, besides the operating "power," the material particle wherein it resides and out of which it operates—the atom. More rigorous minds, however, learned at last to get along without this "earth-residuum," and perhaps some day we shall accustom ourselves, even from the logician's point of view, to get along without the little "one" (to which the worthy old "ego" has refined itself).

18

It is certainly not the least charm of a theory that it is refutable; it is precisely thereby that it attracts the more subtle minds. It seems that the hundred-times-refuted theory of the "free will" owes its persistence to this charm alone; some one is always appearing who feels himself strong enough to refute it.

19

Philosophers are accustomed to speak of the will as though it were the best-known thing in the world; indeed, Schopenhauer has given us to understand that the will alone is really known to us, absolutely and completely known, without deduction or addition. But it again and again seems to me that in this case Schopenhauer also only did what philosophers are in the habit of doing—he seems to have adopted a *popular prejudice* and exaggerated it. Willing—seems to me to be above all something *complicated*, something that is a unity only in name—and it is precisely in a name that popular prejudice lurks, which has got the mastery over the inadequate precautions of philosophers in all ages. So let us for once be more cautious, let us be "unphilosophical": let us say that in all willing there is firstly a plurality of sensations, namely, the sensation of the condition "*away from which* we go," the sensation of the condition "*towards which* we go," the sensation of this "*from*" and "*towards*" itself, and then besides, an accompanying muscular sensation, which, even without our putting in motion "arms and legs," commences its action by force of habit, directly we "will" anything. Therefore, just as sensations (and indeed many kinds of sensations) are to be recognised as ingredients of the will, so, in the second place, thinking is also to be recognised; in every act of the will there is a ruling thought;—and let us not imagine it possible to sever this thought from the "willing," as if the will would then remain over! In the third place, the will is not only a complex of sensation and thinking, but it is above all an *emotion*, and in fact the emotion of the command. That which is termed "freedom of the will" is essentially the emotion of supremacy in respect to him who must obey: "I am free, 'he' must obey"—this consciousness is inherent in every will; and equally so the straining of the attention, the straight look which fixes itself exclusively on one thing, the unconditional judgment that "this and nothing else is necessary now," the inward certainty that obedience will be rendered—and whatever else pertains to the position of the commander. A man who *wills* commands something within himself which renders obedience, or which he believes renders obedience. But now let us notice what is the strangest thing about the will,—this affair so extremely complex, for which the people have only one name. Inasmuch as in the given circumstances we are at the same time the commanding *and* the obeying parties, and as the obeying party we know the sensations of constraint, impulsion, pressure, resistance, and motion, which usually commence immediately after the act of will; inasmuch as, on the other hand, we are accustomed to disregard this duality, and to deceive ourselves about it by means of the synthetic term "I": a whole series of erroneous conclusions, and consequently of false judgments about the will itself, has become attached to the act of willing—to such a degree that he who wills believes firmly that willing *suffices* for action. Since in the majority of cases there has only been exercise of will when the effect of the command—consequently obedience, and therefore action —was to be *expected,* the *appearance* has translated itself into the sentiment, as if there were a *necessity of effect;* in a word, he who wills believes with a fair amount of certainty that will and action are somehow one; he ascribes the success, the carrying out of the willing, to the will itself, and thereby enjoys an increase of the sensation of power which accompanies all success. "Freedom of Will"—that is the expression for the complex state of delight of the person exercising volition, who commands and at the same time identifies himself with the executor of the order—who, as such, enjoys also the triumph over obstacles, but thinks within himself that it was really his own will that overcame them. In this way the person exercising volition adds the feelings of delight of his successful executive instruments, the useful "underwills" or under-souls—indeed, our body is but a social structure composed of many souls—to his feelings of delight as commander. *L'effet c'est moi*: what happens here is what happens in every well-constructed and happy commonwealth, namely, that the governing class identifies itself with the successes of the commonwealth. In all willing it is absolutely a question of commanding and obeying, on the basis, as already said, of a social structure composed of many "souls"; on which account a philosopher should claim the right to include willing-as-such within the sphere of morals—regarded as the doctrine of the relations of supremacy under which the phenomenon of "life" manifests itself.

20

That the separate philosophical ideas are not anything optional or autonomously evolving, but grow up in connection and relationship with each other; that, however suddenly and arbitrarily they seem to appear in the history of thought, they nevertheless belong just as much to a system as the collective members of the fauna of a continent —is betrayed in the end by the circumstance: how unfailingly the most diverse philosophers always fill in again a definite fundamental scheme of *possible* philosophies. Under an invisible spell, they always revolve once more in the same orbit; however independent of each other they may feel themselves with their critical or systematic wills, something within them leads them, something impels them in definite order the one after the other—to wit, the innate methodology and relationship of their ideas. Their thinking is, in fact, far less a discovery than a re-recognising, a remembering, a return and a home-coming to a far-off, ancient common-household of the soul, out of which those ideas formerly grew: philosophising in so far a kind of atavism of the highest order. The wonderful family resemblance of all Indian, Greek, and German philosophising is easily enough explained. In fact, where there is affinity of language, owing to the common philosophy of grammar—I mean owing to the unconscious domination and guidance of similar grammatical functions—it cannot but be that everything is prepared at the outset for a similar development and succession of philosophical systems; just as the way seems barred against certain other possibilities of world-interpretation. It is highly probable that philosophers within the domain of the Ural-Altaic languages (where the conception of the subject is least developed) look otherwise "into the world," and will be found on paths of thought different from those of the Indo-Germans and Mussulmans : the spell of certain grammatical functions is ultimately also the spell of *physiological* valuations and racial conditions.—So much by way of rejecting Locke's superficiality with regard to the origin of ideas.

21

The *causa sui* is the best self-contradiction that has yet been conceived, it is a sort of logical violation and unnaturalness; but the extravagant pride of man has managed to entangle itself profoundly and frightfully with this very folly. The desire for "freedom of will" in the superlative, metaphysical sense, such as still holds sway, unfortunately, in the minds of the half-educated, the desire to bear the entire and ultimate responsibility for one's actions oneself, and to absolve God, the world, ancestors, chance, and society therefrom, involves nothing less than to be precisely this *causa sui,* and with more than Munchausen daring, to pull oneself up into existence by the hair, out of the slough of nothingness. If any one should find out in this manner the crass stupidity of the celebrated conception of "free will" and put it out of his head altogether, I beg of him to carry his "enlightenment" a step further, and also put out of his head the contrary of this monstrous conception of "free will": I mean "non-free will," which is tantamount to a misuse of cause and effect. One should not wrongly *materialise* "cause" and "effect," as the natural philosophers do (and whoever like them naturalises in thinking at present), according to the prevailing mechanical doltishness which makes the cause press and push until it "effects" its end; one should use "cause" and "effect" only as pure *conceptions,* that is to say, as conventional fictions for the purpose of designation and mutual understanding,— *not* for explanation. In "being-in-itself" there is nothing of "causal-connection," of "necessity," or of "psychological non-freedom"; there the effect does *not* follow the cause, there "law" does not obtain. It is *we* alone who have devised cause, sequence, reciprocity, relativity, constraint, number, law, freedom, motive, and purpose; and when we interpret and intermix this symbol-world, as "being in itself," with things, we act once more as we have always acted—*mythologically.* The "non-free will" is mythology; in real life it is only a question of *strong* and *weak* wills.—It is almost always a symptom of what is lacking in himself, when a thinker, in every "causal-connection" and "psychological necessity," manifests something of compulsion, indigence, obsequiousness, oppression, and non-freedom; it is suspicious to have such feelings—the person betrays himself. And in general, if I have observed correctly, the "non-freedom of the will" is regarded as a problem from two entirely opposite standpoints, but always in a profoundly *personal* manner: some will not give up their "responsibility," their belief in *themselves,* the personal right to *their* merits, at any price (the vain races belong to this class); others on the contrary, do not wish to be answerable for anything, or blamed for anything, and owing to an inward self-contempt, seek *to get out of the business,* no matter how. The latter, when they write books, are in the habit at present of taking the side of criminals; a sort of socialistic sympathy is their favourite disguise. And as a matter of fact, the fatalism of the weak-willed embellishes itself surprisingly when it can pose as "*la religion de la souffrance humaine*"; that is *its* "good taste."

22

Let me be pardoned, as an old philologist who cannot desist from the mischief of putting his finger on bad modes of interpretation, but "Nature's conformity of law," of which you physicists talk so proudly, as though—why, it exists only owing to your interpretation and bad "philology." It is no matter of fact, no "text," but rather just a naïvely humanitarian adjustment and perversion of meaning, with which you make abundant concessions to the democratic instincts of the modern soul! "Everywhere equality before the law—Nature is not different in that respect, nor better than we:" a fine instance of secret motive, in which the vulgar antagonism to everything privileged and autocratic—likewise a second and more refined atheism—is once more disguised. "*Ni Dieu, ni maître*"—that, also, is what you want; and therefore "Cheers for natural law!"—is it not so? But, as has been said, that is interpretation, not text; and somebody might come along, who, with opposite intentions and modes of interpretation, could read out of the same "Nature," and with regard to the same phenomena, just the tyrannically inconsiderate and relentless enforcement of the claims of power—an interpreter who should so place the unexceptionalness and unconditionalness of all "Will to Power" before your eyes, that almost every word, and the word "tyranny" itself, would eventually seem unsuitable, or like a weakening and softening metaphor—as being too human; and who should, nevertheless, end by asserting the same about this world as you do, namely, that it has a "necessary" and "calculable" course, *not,* however, because laws obtain in it, but because they are absolutely *lacking*, and every power effects its ultimate consequences every moment. Granted that this also is only interpretation—and you will be eager enough to make this objection?—well, so much the better.

23

All psychology hitherto has run aground on moral prejudices and timidities, it has not dared to launch out into the depths. In so far as it is allowable to recognise in that which has hitherto been written, evidence of that which has hitherto been kept silent, it seems as if nobody had yet harboured the notion of psychology as the Morphology and *Development-doctrine of the Will to Power*, as I conceive of it. The power of moral prejudices has penetrated deeply into the most intellectual world, the world apparently most indifferent and unprejudiced, and has obviously operated in an injurious, obstructive, blinding, and distorting manner. A proper physio-psychology has to contend with unconscious antagonism in the heart of the investigator, it has "the heart" against it: even a doctrine of the reciprocal conditionalness of the "good" and the "bad" impulses, causes (as refined immorality) distress and aversion in a still strong and manly conscience —still more so, a doctrine of the derivation of all good impulses from bad ones. If, however, a person should regard even the emotions of hatred, envy, covetousness, and imperiousness as life-conditioning emotions, as factors which must be present, fundamentally and essentially, in the general economy of life (which must, therefore, be further developed if life is to be further developed), he will suffer from such a view of things as from sea-sickness. And yet this hypothesis is far from being the strangest and most painful in this immense and almost new domain of dangerous knowledge; and there are in fact a hundred good reasons why every one should keep away from it who *can* do so! On the other hand, if one has once drifted hither with one's bark, well! very good! now let us set our teeth firmly! let us open our eyes and keep our hand fast on the helm! We sail away right *over* morality, we crush out, we destroy perhaps the remains of our own morality by daring to make our voyage thither—but what do *we* matter! Never yet did a *profounder* world of insight reveal itself to daring travellers and adventurers, and the psychologist who thus "makes a sacrifice"— it is *not* the *sacrifizio dell' intelletto*, on the contrary!—will at least be entitled to demand in return that psychology shall once more be recognised as the queen of the sciences, for whose service and equipment the other sciences exist. For psychology is once more the path to the fundamental problems.

Master-Morality and Slave-Morality*

I

The English psychologists to whom we owe the only attempts
that have thus far been made to write a genealogy of morals are no
mean posers of riddles, but the riddles they pose are themselves, and
being incarnate have one advantage over their books—they are
interesting. What are these English psychologists really after? One
finds them always, whether intentionally or not, engaged in the same
task of pushing into the foreground the nasty part of the psyche,
looking for the effective motive forces of human development in the
very last place we would wish to have them found, e.g., in the inertia
of habit, in forgetfulness, in the blind and fortuitous association of
ideas: always in something that is purely passive, automatic, reflexive,
molecular, and, moreover, profoundly stupid. What drives these psychologists forever in the same direction? A secret, malicious desire to
belittle humanity, which they do not acknowledge even to themselves?
A pessimistic distrust, the suspiciousness of the soured idealist? Some
petty resentment of Christianity (and Plato) which does not rise above
the threshold of consciousness? Or could it be a prurient taste for whatever is embarrassing, painfully paradoxical, dubious and absurd in
existence? Or is it, perhaps, a kind of stew—a little meanness, a little
bitterness, a bit of anti-Christianity, a touch of prurience and desire
for condiments? . . . But, again, people tell me that these men are
simply dull old frogs who hop and creep in and around man as in their
own element—as though man were a bog. However, I am reluctant
to listen to this, in fact I refuse to believe it; and if I may express a wish
where I cannot express a conviction, I do wish wholeheartedly that
things may be otherwise with these men—that these microscopic ex-
aminers of the soul may be really courageous, magnanimous, and

*From "The Genealogy of Morals," *The Birth of Tragedy and The Genealogy of
Morals* by Friedrich Nietzsche (trans. Francis Golffing), First Essay, pp. 158-180.
Copyright © 1956 by Doubleday & Company, Inc. Reprinted by permission of the
publisher.

proud animals, who know how to contain their emotions and have trained themselves to subordinate all wishful thinking to the truth—any truth, even a homespun, severe, ugly, obnoxious, un-Christian, unmoral truth. For such truths do exist.

II

All honor to the beneficent spirits that may motivate these historians of ethics! One thing is certain, however, they have been quite deserted by the true spirit of history. They all, to a man, think unhistorically, as is the age-old custom among philosophers. The amateurishness of their procedure is made plain from the very beginning, when it is a question of explaining the provenance of the concept and judgment *good*. "Originally," they decree, "altruistic actions were praised and approved by their recipients, that is, by those to whom they were useful. Later on, the origin of that praise having been forgotten, such actions were felt to be good simply because it was the habit to commend them." We notice at once that this first derivation has all the earmarks of the English psychologists' work. Here are the key ideas of utility, forgetfulness, habit, and, finally, error, seen as lying at the root of that value system which civilized man had hitherto regarded with pride as the prerogative of all men. This pride must now be humbled, these values devalued. Have the debunkers succeeded?

Now it is obvious to me, first of all, that their theory looks for the genesis of the concept *good* in the wrong place: the judgment *good* does not originate with those to whom the good has been done. Rather it was the "good" themselves, that is to say the noble, mighty, highly placed, and high-minded who decreed themselves and their actions to be good, i.e., belonging to the highest rank, in contradistinction to all that was base, low-minded and plebeian. It was only this *pathos of distance* that authorized them to create values and name them—what was utility to them? The notion of utility seems singularly inept to account for such a quick jetting forth of supreme value judgments. Here we come face to face with the exact opposite of that lukewarmness which every scheming prudence, every utilitarian calculus presupposes —and not for a time only, for the rare, exceptional hour, but permanently. The origin of the opposites *good* and *bad* is to be found in the pathos of nobility and distance, representing the dominant temper of a higher, ruling class in relation to a lower, dependent one. (The lordly right of bestowing names is such that one would almost be justified in seeing the origin of language itself as an expression of the rulers' power. They say, "This *is* that or that"; they seal off each thing and action with a sound and thereby take symbolic possession of it.) Such an origin would suggest that there is no *a priori* necessity for associating the word *good* with altruistic deeds, as those moral psychologists are fond of claiming. In fact, it is only after aristocratic values have begun to decline that the egotism-altruism dichotomy takes possession of the human conscience; to use my own terms, it is the herd instinct that now asserts itself. Yet it takes quite a while for this instinct to assume such sway that it can reduce all moral valuations to that dichotomy—as is currently happening throughout Europe, where the prejudice equating the terms *moral, altruistic,* and *disinterested* has assumed the obsessive force of an *idée fixe.*

III

Quite apart from the fact that this hypothesis about the origin of the value judgment *good* is historically untenable, its psychology is instrinsically unsound. Altruistic deeds were originally commended for their usefulness, but this original reason has now been forgotten— so the claim goes. How is such a forgetting conceivable? Has there ever been a point in history at which such deeds lost their usefulness? Quite the contrary, this usefulness has been apparent to every age, a thing that has been emphasized over and over again. Therefore, instead of being forgotten, it must have impressed itself on the consciousness with ever increasing clearness. The opposite theory is far more sensible, though this does not necessarily make it any the truer— the theory held by Herbert Spencer, for example, who considers the concept *good* qualitatively the same as the concepts *useful* or *practical;* so that in the judgments *good* and *bad,* humanity is said to have summed up and sanctioned precisely its unforgotten and unforgettable experiences of the *useful practical* and the *harmful impractical.* According to this theory, the *good* is that which all along has proved itself and which therefore may lay the highest claim to be considered valuable. As I have said, the derivation of this theory is suspect, but at least the explanation is self-consistent and psychologically tenable within its limits.

IV

The clue to the correct explanation was furnished me by the question "What does the etymology of the terms for good in various languages tell us?" I discovered that all these terms lead us back to the same conceptual transformation. The basic concept is always *noble* in the hierarchical, class sense, and from this has developed, by historical necessity, the concept *good* embracing nobility of mind, spiritual distinction. This development is strictly parallel to that other which eventually converted the notions *common, plebeian, base* into the notion *bad*.[1] Here we have an important clue to the actual genealogy of morals; that it has not been hit upon earlier is due to the retarding influence which democratic prejudice has had upon all investigation of origins. Ths holds equally true with regard to the seemingly quite objective areas of natural science and physiology, though I cannot enlarge upon the question now. . . .

VI

Granting that political supremacy always gives rise to notions of spiritual supremacy, it at first creates no difficulties (though difficulties might arise later) if the ruling caste is also the priestly caste and elects to characterize itself by a term which reminds us of its priestly function. In this context we encounter for the first time concepts of *pure* and *impure* opposing each other as signs of class, and here, too, *good* and *bad* as terms no longer referring to class, develop before long. The reader should be cautioned, however, against taking pure and impure in too large or profound or symbolic a sense: all the ideas of ancient man were understood in a sense much more crude, narrow, superficial and non-symbolic than we are able to imagine today. The pure man was originally one who washed himself, who refused to eat certain foods entailing skin diseases, who did not sleep with the unwashed plebeian women, who held blood in abomination—hardly more than that. At the same time, given the peculiar nature of a priestly aristocracy, it becomes clear why the value opposites would early turn inward and become dangerously exacerbated; and in fact the tension between such opposites has opened abysses between man and man, over which not even an Achilles of free thought would leap without a shudder. There is from the very start something unwholesome about such priestly aristocracies, about their way of life, which is turned away from action and swings between brooding and emotional explosions: a way of life which may be seen as responsible for the morbidity and neurasthenia of priests of all periods. Yet are we not right in maintaining that the cures which they have developed for their morbidities have proved a hundred times more dangerous than the ills themselves? Humanity is still suffering from the after-effects of those priestly cures.

1. The most eloquent proof of this is the etymological relationship between the German words *schlecht* (bad) and *schlicht* (simple). For a long time the first term was used interchangeably with the second, without any contemptuous connotation as yet, merely to designate the commoner as opposed to the nobleman. About the time of the Thirty Years' War the meaning changed to the present one.

Think, for example, of certain forms of diet (abstinence from meat), fasting, sexual continence, escape "into the desert"; think further of the whole anti-sensual metaphysics of the priests, conducive to inertia and false refinement; of the self-hypnosis encouraged by the example of fakirs and Brahmans, where a glass knob and an *idée fixe* take the place of the god. And at last, supervening on all this, comes utter satiety, together with its radical remedy, nothingness—or God, for the desire for a mystical union with God is nothing other than the Buddhist's desire to sink himself in nirvana. Among the priests everything becomes more dangerous, not cures and specifics alone but also arrogance, vindictiveness, acumen, profligacy, love, the desire for power, disease. In all fairness it should be added, however, that only on this soil, the precarious soil of priestly existence, has man been able to develop into an interesting creature; that only here has the human mind grown both profound and evil; and it is in these two respects, after all, that man has proved his superiority over the rest of creation.

VII

By now the reader will have got some notion how readily the priestly system of valuations can branch off from the aristocratic and develop into its opposite. An occasion for such a division is furnished whenever the priest caste and the warrior caste jealously clash with one another and find themselves unable to come to terms. The chivalrous and aristocratic valuations presuppose a strong physique, blooming, even exuberant health, together with all the conditions that guarantee its preservation : combat, adventure, the chase, the dance, war games, etc. The value system of the priestly aristocracy is founded on different presuppositions. So much the worse for them when it becomes a question of war! As we all know, priests are the most evil enemies to have—why should this be so? Because they are the most impotent. It is their impotence which makes their hate so violent and sinister, so cerebral and poisonous. The greatest haters in history—but also the most intelligent haters—have been priests. Beside the brilliance of priestly vengeance all other brilliance fades. Human history would be a dull and stupid thing without the intelligence furnished by its impotents. Let us begin with the most striking example. Whatever else has been done to damage the powerful and great of this earth seems trivial compared with what the Jews have done, that priestly people who succeeded in avenging themselves on their enemies and oppressors by radically inverting all their values, that is, by an act of the most spiritual vengeance. This was a strategy entirely appropriate to a priestly people in whom vindictiveness had gone most deeply underground. It was the Jew who, with frightening consistency, dared to invert the aristocratic value equations good/noble/powerful/beautiful/happy/favored-of-the-gods and maintain, with the furious hatred of the underprivileged and impotent, that "only the poor, the powerless, are good; only the suffering, sick, and ugly, truly blessed. But you noble and mighty ones of the earth will be, to all eternity, the evil, the cruel, the avaricious, the godless, and thus the cursed and damned!"... We know who has fallen heir to this Jewish inversion of values.... In reference to the grand and unspeakably disastrous initiative which the Jews have launched by this most radical of all declarations of war, I wish to repeat a statement I made in a different context (*Beyond Good and Evil*), to wit, that it was the Jews who started the slave revolt in morals; a revolt with two millennia of history behind it, which we have lost sight of today simply because it has triumphed so completely....

X

The slave revolt in morals begins by rancor turning creative and giving birth to values—the rancor of beings who, deprived of the direct outlet of action, compensate by an imaginary vengeance. All truly noble morality grows out of triumphant self-affirmation. Slave ethics, on the other hand, begins by saying *no* to an "outside," an "other," a non-self, and that *no* is its creative act. This reversal of direction of the evaluating look, this invariable looking outward instead of inward, is a fundamental feature of rancor. Slave ethics requires for its inception a sphere different from and hostile to its own. Physiologically speaking, it requires an outside stimulus in order to act at all; all its action is reaction. The opposite is true of aristocratic valuations: such values grow and act spontaneously, seeking out their contraries only in order to affirm themselves even more gratefully and delightedly. Here the negative concepts, *humble, base, bad*, are late, pallid counterparts of the positive, intense and passionate credo, "We noble, good, beautiful, happy ones." Aristocratic valuations may go amiss and do violence to reality, but this happens only with regard to spheres which they do not know well, or from the knowledge of which they austerely guard themselves: the aristocrat will, on occasion, misjudge a sphere which he holds in contempt, the sphere of the common man, the people. On the other hand we should remember that the emotion of contempt, of looking down, provided that it falsifies at all, is as nothing compared with the falsification which suppressed hatred, impotent vindictiveness, effects upon its opponent, though only in effigy. There is in all contempt too much casualness and nonchalance, too much blinking of facts and impatience, and too much inborn gaiety for it ever to make of its object a downright caricature and monster. Hear the almost benevolent nuances the Greek aristocracy, for example, puts into all its terms for the commoner; how emotions of compassion, consideration, indulgence, sugar-coat these words until, in the end, almost all terms referring to the common man survive as expressions for "unhappy," "pitiable" (cf. *deilos, deilaios, poneros, mochtheros,* the last two of which properly characterize the common man as a drudge and beast of burden); how, on the other hand, the words *bad, base, unhappy* have continued to strike a similar note for the Greek ear, with the timbre "unhappy" preponderating. The "wellborn" really felt that they were also the "happy." They did not have to construct their happiness factitiously by looking at their enemies, as all rancorous men are wont to do, and being fully active, energetic people they were incapable of divorcing happiness from action. They accounted activity a necessary part of happiness (which explains the origin of the phrase *eu prattein*).

All this stands in utter contrast to what is called happiness among the impotent and oppressed, who are full of bottled-up aggressions. Their happiness is purely passive and takes the form of drugged tranquillity, stretching and yawning, peace, "sabbath," emotional slackness. Whereas the noble lives before his own conscience with confidence and frankness (*gennaïos* "nobly bred" emphasizes the nuance "truthful" and perhaps also "ingenuous"), the rancorous person is neither truthful nor ingenuous nor honest and forthright with himself. His soul squints; his mind loves hide-outs, secret paths, and back doors; everything that is hidden seems to him his own world, his security, his comfort; he is expert in silence, in long memory, in waiting, in provisional self-depreciation, and in self-humiliation. A race of such men will, in the end, inevitably be cleverer than a race of aristocrats, and it will honor sharp-wittedness to a much greater degree, i.e., as an absolutely vital condition for its existence. Among the noble, mental acuteness always tends slightly to suggest luxury and overrefinement. The fact is that with them it is much less important than is the perfect functioning of the ruling, unconscious instincts or even a certain temerity to follow sudden impulses, court danger, or indulge spurts of violent rage, love, worship, gratitude, or vengeance. When a noble man feels resentment, it is absorbed in his instantaneous reaction and therefore does not poison him. Moreover, in countless cases where we might expect it, it never arises, while with weak and impotent people it occurs without fail. It is a sign of strong, rich temperaments that they cannot for long take seriously their enemies, their misfortunes, their

misdeeds; for such characters have in them an excess of plastic cura-
tive power, and also a power of oblivion. (A good modern example of
the latter is Mirabeau, who lacked all memory for insults and mean-
nesses done him, and who was unable to forgive because he had forgotten). Such a man simply shakes off vermin which would get beneath another's skin—and only here, if anywhere on earth, is it possible to speak of "loving one's enemy." The noble person will respect
his enemy, and respect is already a bridge to love. . . . Indeed he requires his enemy for himself, as his mark of distinction, nor could he
tolerate any other enemy than one in whom he finds nothing to despise
and much to esteem. Imagine, on the other hand, the "enemy" as conceived by the rancorous man! For this is his true creative achievement:
he has conceived the "evil enemy," the Evil One, as a fundamental
idea, and then as a pendant he has conceived a Good One—himself.

XI

The exact opposite is true of the noble-minded, who spontaneously
creates the notion *good*, and later derives from it the conception of
the *bad*. How ill-matched these two concepts look, placed side by side:
the bad of noble origin, and the *evil* that has risen out of the cauldron
of unquenched hatred! The first is a by-product, a complementary
color, almost an afterthought; the second is the beginning, the original
creative act of slave ethics. . . .

XIII

But to return to business: our inquiry into the origins of that
other notion of goodness, as conceived by the resentful, demands to
be completed. There is nothing very odd about lambs disliking birds of
prey, but this is no reason for holding it against large birds of prey
that they carry off lambs. And when the lambs whisper among themselves, "These birds of prey are evil, and does not this give us a right
to say that whatever is the opposite of a bird of prey must be good?"
there is nothing intrinsically wrong with such an argument—though
the birds of prey will look somewhat quizzically and say, "*We* have
nothing against these good lambs; in fact, we love them; nothing
tastes better than a tender lamb."—To expect that strength will not
manifest itself as strength, as the desire to overcome, to appropriate,
to have enemies, obstacles, and triumphs, is every bit as absurd as to
expect that weakness will manifest itself as strength. A quantum of
strength is equivalent to a quantum of urge, will, activity, and it is only
the snare of language (of the arch-fallacies of reason petrified in
language), presenting all activity as conditioned by an agent—the

"subject"—that blinds us to this fact. For, just as popular superstition divorces the lightning from its brilliance, viewing the latter as an activity whose subject is the lightning, so does popular morality divorce strength from its manifestations, as though there were behind the strong a neutral agent, free to manifest its strength or contain it. But no such agent exists; there is no "being" behind the doing, acting, becoming; the "doer" has simply been added to the deed by the imagination—the doing is everything. The common man actually doubles the doing by making the lightning flash; he states the same event once as cause and then again as effect. The natural scientists are no better when they say that "energy *moves*," "energy *causes*." For all its detachment and freedom from emotion, our science is still the dupe of linguistic habits; it has never yet got rid of those changelings called "subjects." The atom is one such changeling, another is the Kantian "thing-in-itself." Small wonder, then, that the repressed and smoldering emotions of vengeance and hatred have taken advantage of this superstition and in fact espouse no belief more ardently than that it is within the discretion of the strong to be weak, of the bird of prey to be a lamb. Thus they assume the right of calling the bird of prey to account for being a bird of prey. We can hear the oppressed, down-trodden, violated whispering among themselves with the wily vengefulness of the impotent, "Let us be unlike those evil ones. Let us be good. And the good shall be he who does not do violence, does not attack or retaliate, who leaves vengeance to God, who, like us, lives hidden, who shuns all that is evil, and altogether asks very little of life —like us, the patient, the humble, the just ones." Read in cold blood, this means nothing more than "We weak ones are, in fact, weak. It is a good thing that we do nothing for which we are not strong enough." But this plain fact, this basic prudence, which even the insects have (who, in circumstances of great danger, sham death in order not to have to "do" too much) has tricked itself out in the garb of quiet, virtuous resignation, thanks to the duplicity of impotence—as though the weakness of the weak, which is after all his essence, his natural way of being, his sole and inevitable reality, were a spontaneous act, a meritorious deed. This sort of person requires the belief in a "free subject" able to choose indifferently, out of that instinct of self-preservation which notoriously justifies every kind of lie. It may well be that to this day the subject, or in popular language the soul, has been the most viable of all articles of faith simply because it makes it possible for the majority of mankind—i.e., the weak and oppressed of every sort—to practice the sublime sleight of hand which gives weakness the appearance of free choice and one's natural disposition the distinction of merit.

Bad Conscience*

XVI

I can no longer postpone giving tentative expression to my own hypothesis concerning the origin of "bad conscience." It is one that may fall rather strangely on our ears and that requires close meditation. I take bad conscience to be a deep-seated malady to which man succumbed under the pressure of the most profound transformation he ever underwent—the one that made him once and for all a sociable and pacific creature. Just as happened in the case of those sea creatures who were forced to become land animals in order to survive, these semi-animals, happily adapted to the wilderness, to war, free roaming, and adventure, were forced to change their nature. Of a sudden they found all their instincts devalued, unhinged. They must walk on legs and carry themselves, where before the water had carried them: a terrible heaviness weighed upon them. They felt inapt for the simplest manipulations, for in this new, unknown world they could no longer count on the guidance of their unconscious drives. They were forced to think, deduce, calculate, weigh cause and effect—unhappy people, reduced to their weakest, most fallible organ, their consciousness! I doubt that there has ever been on earth such a feeling of misery, such a leaden discomfort. It was not that those old instincts had abruptly ceased making their demands; but now their satisfaction was rare and difficult. For the most part they had to depend on new, covert satisfactions. All instincts that are not allowed free play turn inward. This is what I call man's interiorization; it alone provides the soil for the growth of what is later called man's *soul.* Man's interior world, originally meager and tenuous, was expanding in every dimension, in proportion as the outward discharge of his feelings was curtailed. The formidable bulwarks by means of which the polity protected itself against the ancient instincts of freedom (punishment was one of the

Ibid., Second Essay, pp. 217-227.

strongest of these bulwarks) caused those wild, extravagant instincts to turn in upon man. Hostility, cruelty, the delight in persecution, raids, excitement, destruction all turned against their begetter. Lacking external enemies and resistances, and confined within an oppressive narrowness and regularity, man began rending, persecuting, terrifying himself, like a wild beast hurling itself against the bars of its cage. This languisher, devoured by nostalgia for the desert, who had to turn *himself* into an adventure, a torture chamber, an insecure and dangerous wilderness—this fool, this pining and desperate prisoner, became the inventor of "bad conscience." Also the generator of the greatest and most disastrous of maladies, of which humanity has not to this day been cured: his sickness of himself, brought on by the violent severance from his animal past, by his sudden leap and fall into new layers and conditions of existence, by his declaration of war against the old instincts that had hitherto been the foundation of his power, his joy, and his awesomeness. Let me hasten to add that the phenomenon of an animal soul turning in upon itself, taking arms against itself, was so novel, profound, mysterious, contradictory, and pregnant with possibility, that the whole complexion of the universe was changed thereby. This spectacle (and the end of it is not yet in sight) required a divine audience to do it justice. It was a spectacle too sublime and paradoxical to pass unnoticed on some trivial planet. Henceforth man was to figure among the most unexpected and breathtaking throws in the game of dice played by Heracleitus' great "child," be he called Zeus or Chance. Man now aroused an interest, a suspense, a hope, almost a conviction—as though in him something were heralded, as though he were not a goal but a way, an interlude. a bridge, a great promise. . . .

XVII

My hypothesis concerning the origin of bad conscience presupposes that this change was neither gradual nor voluntary, that it was not an organic growing into new conditions but rather an abrupt break, a leap, a thing compelled, an ineluctable disaster, which could neither be struggled against nor even resented. It further presupposes that the fitting of a hitherto unrestrained and shapeless populace into a tight mold, as it had begun with an act of violence, had to be brought to conclusion by a series of violent acts; that the earliest commonwealth constituted a terrible despotism, a ruthless, oppressive machinery for not only kneading and suppling a brutish populace but actually shaping it. I have used the word "commonwealth," but it should be clearly understood what I mean: a pack of savages, a race of conquerors, themselves organized for war and able to organize others, fiercely dominating a population perhaps vastly superior in numbers yet amorphous and nomadic. Such was the beginning of the human polity; I take it we have got over that sentimentalism that would have it begin with a contract. What do men who can command, who are born rulers, who evince power in act and deportment, have to do with contracts? Such beings are unaccountable; they come like destiny, without rhyme or reason, ruthlessly, bare of pretext. Suddenly they are here, like a stroke of lightning, too terrible, convincing, and "different" for hatred even. Their work is an instinctive imposing of forms. They are the most spontaneous, most unconscious artists that exist. They appear, and presently something entirely new has arisen, a live dominion whose parts and functions are delimited and inter-related, in which there is room for nothing that has not previously received its meaning from the whole. Being natural organizers, these men know nothing of guilt, responsibility, consideration. They are actuated by the terrible egotism of the artist, which is justified by the work he must do, as the mother by the child she will bear. Bad conscience certainly did not originate with these men, yet, on the other hand, that unseemly growth could not have developed *without* them, without their hammer blows, their artist's violence, which drove a great quantity of freedom out of sight and made it latent. In its earliest phase bad conscience is nothing other than the instinct of freedom forced to become latent, driven underground, and forced to vent its energy upon itself.

XVIII

We should guard against taking too dim a view of this phenomenon simply because it is both ugly and painful. After all, the same will to power which in those violent artists and organizers created polities, in the "labyrinth of the heart"—more pettily, to be sure, and in inverse direction—created negative ideals and humanity's bad conscience. Except that now the material upon which this great natural force was employed was man himself, his old animal self—and not, as in that grander and more spectacular phenomenon—his fellow man. This secret violation of the self, this artist's cruelty, this urge to impose on recalcitrant matter a form, a will, a distinction, a feeling of contradiction and contempt, this sinister task of a soul divided against itself, which makes itself suffer for the pleasure of suffering, this most energetic "bad conscience"—has it not given birth to a wealth of strange beauty and affirmation? Has it not given birth to beauty itself? Would beauty exist if ugliness had not first taken cognizance of itself, not said to itself, "I am ugly"? This hint will serve, at any rate, to solve the riddle of why contradictory terms such as *selflessness, self-denial, self-sacrifice* may intimate an ideal, a beauty. Nor will the reader doubt henceforth that the *joy* felt by the self-denying, self-sacrificing, selfless person was from the very start a *cruel* joy.—So much for the origin of altruism as a moral value. Bad conscience, the desire for self-mortification, is the wellspring of all altruistic values.

XIX

There can be no doubt that bad conscience is a sickness, but so, in a sense, is pregnancy. We shall presently describe the conditions which carried that "sickness" to its highest and most terrible peak. But first let us return for a moment to an earlier consideration. The civil-law relationship of debtor to creditor has been projected into yet another context, where we find it even more difficult to understand today, namely into the relationship between living men and their forebears. Among primitive tribes, each new generation feels toward the preceding ones, and especially toward the original founders of the tribe, a *juridical* obligation (rather than an *emotional* obligation, which seems to be of relatively recent origin). Early societies were convinced that their continuance was guaranteed solely by the sacrifices and achievements of their ancestors and that these sacrifices and achievements required to be paid back. Thus a debt was acknowledged which continued to increase, since the ancestors, surviving as powerful spirits, did not cease to provide the tribe with new benefits out of their store. Gratuitously? But nothing was gratuitous in those crude and "insensitive" times. Then how could they be repaid? By burnt offerings (to provide them with food), by rituals, shrines, customs, but above all, by obedience—for all rites, having been established by the forebears, were also permanently enjoined by them. But could they ever be *fully* repaid? An anxious doubt remained and grew steadily, and every so often there occurred some major act of "redemption," some gigantic repayment of the creditor (the famous sacrifice of the first-born, for example; in any case blood, human blood). Given this primitive logic, the fear of the ancestor and his power and the consciousness of indebtedness increase in direct proportion as the power of the tribe itself increases, as it becomes more successful in battle, independent, respected and feared. Never the other way round. Every step leading to the degeneration of the tribe, every setback, every sign of imminent dissolution, tends to diminish the fear of the ancestral spirits, to make them seem of less account, less wise, less provident, less powerful. Following this kind of logic to its natural term, we arrive at a situation in which the ancestors of the most powerful tribes have become so fearful to the imagination that they have receded at last into a numinous shadow: the ancestor becomes a god. Perhaps this is the way all gods have arisen, out of *fear*. . . . And if anyone should find it necessary to add, "But also out of piety," his claim would scarcely be justified for the longest and earliest period of the human race. But it would certainly hold true for that intermediate period during which the noble clans emerged, of whom it may justly be said that they paid back their ancestors (heroes or gods) with interest all those noble properties which had since come to reside abundantly in themselves. We shall have an opportunity later on of dealing with this "ennoblement" of the ancestral spirits (which is not the same thing as their "consecration"), but first, let us bring to a conclusion the story of man's consciousness of guilt.

XX

Man's firm belief that he was indebted to the gods did not cease with the decline of tribal organization. Just as man has inherited from the blood aristocracies the concepts *good* and *bad*, together with the psychological penchant for hierarchies, so he has inherited from the tribes, together with the tribal gods, a burden of outstanding debt and the desire to make final restitution. (The bridge is provided by those large populations of slaves and serfs, who, either perforce or through servile mimicry, had adopted the cults of their overlords. The heritage spreads out from them in all directions.) The sense of indebtedness to the gods continued to grow through the centuries, keeping pace with the evolution of man's concept of the deity. (The endless tale of ethnic struggle, triumph, reconciliation, and fusion, in short, whatever precedes the final hierarchy of racial strains in some great synthesis, is mirrored in the welter of divine genealogies and legends dealing with divine battles, victories, and reconciliations. Every progress toward universal empire has also been a progress toward a universal pantheon. Despotism, by overcoming the independent nobles, always prepares the way for some form of monotheism.) The advent of the Christian god, the "highest potency" god yet conceived by man, has been accompanied by the widest dissemination of the sense of indebtedness, guilt. If we are right in assuming that we have now entered upon the inverse development, it stands to reason that the steady decline of belief in a Christian god should entail a commensurate decline in man's guilt consciousness. It also stands to reason— doesn't it?—that a complete and definite victory of atheism might deliver mankind altogether from its feeling of being indebted to its beginnings, its *causa prima*. Atheism and a kind of "second innocence" go together.

XXI

So much, for the moment, about the connection of "guilt" and "duty" with religious presuppositions. I have deliberately left on one side the "moralization" of these terms (their pushing back into conscience, the association of the notion of bad conscience with a deity), and even wrote at the end of the last paragraph as though such a moralization had never taken place; as though with the notion of a divine creditor falling into disuse those notions too were doomed. Unfortunately this is far from being the case. The modern moralization of the ideas of guilt and duty—their relegation to a purely subjecive "bad conscience"—represents a determined attempt to invert the normal order of development, or at least to stop it in its tracks. The object now is to close the prospect of final deliverance and make man's gaze rebound from an iron barrier; to force the ideas of guilt and duty to face about and fiercely turn on—whom? Obviously on the "debtor," first of all, who, infested and eaten away by bad conscience, which spreads like a polyp, comes to view his debt as unredeemable by any act of atonement (the notion of "eternal penance"). But eventually the "creditor" too is turned on in the same fashion. Now the curse falls upon man's *causa prima* ("Adam," "original sin," the "bondage of the will"); or upon nature, which gave birth to man and which is now made the repository of the evil principle (nature as the instrument of the devil); or upon universal existence, which now appears as absolute non-value (nihilstic turning away from life, a longing for nothingness or for life's "opposite," for a different sort of "being"—Buddhism, etc.). Then suddenly we come face to face with that paradoxical and ghastly expedient which brought temporary relief to tortured humanity, that most brilliant stroke of Christianity: God's sacrifice of himself for man. God makes himself the ransom for what could not otherwise be ransomed; God alone has power to absolve us of a debt we can no longer discharge; the creditor offers himself as a sacrifice for his debtor out of sheer love (can you believe it?), out of love for his debtor. . . .

XXII

By now the reader will have guessed what has really been happening behind all these façades. Man, with his need for self-torture, his sublimated cruelty resulting from the cooping up of his animal nature within a polity, invented bad conscience in order to hurt himself, after the blocking of the more natural outlet of his cruelty. Then this guilt-ridden man seized upon religion in order to exacerbate his self-torment to the utmost. The thought of being in God's debt became his new instrument of torture. He focused in God the last of the opposites he could find to his true and inveterate animal instincts, making these a sin against God (hostility, rebellion against the "Lord," the "Father," the "Creator"). He stretched himself upon the contradiction "God" and "Devil" as on a rack. He projected all his denials of self, nature, naturalness out of himself as affirmations, as true being, embodiment, reality, as God (the divine Judge and Executioner), as transcendence, as eternity, as endless torture, as hell, as the infinitude of guilt and punishment. In such psychological cruelty we see an insanity of the *will* that is without parallel: man's will to find himself guilty, and unredeemably so; his will to believe that he might be punished to all eternity without ever expunging his guilt; his will to poison the very foundation of things with the problem of guilt and punishment and thus to cut off once and for all his escape from this labyrinth of obsession; his will to erect an ideal (God's holiness) in order to assure himself of his own absolute unworthiness. What a mad, unhappy animal is man! What strange notions occur to him; what perversities, what paroxysms of nonsense, what bestialities of idea burst from him, the moment he is prevented ever so little from being a beast of action! ... All this is exceedingly curious and interesting, but dyed with such a dark, somber, enervating sadness that one must resolutely tear away one's gaze. Here, no doubt, is sickness, the most terrible sickness that has wasted man thus far. And if one is still able to hear—but how few these days have ears to hear it?—in this night of torment and absurdity the cry *love* ring out, the cry of rapt longing, of redemption in love, he must turn away with a shudder of invincible horror. . . . Man harbors too much horror; the earth has been a lunatic asylum for too long.

"Reason" in Philosophy*

1

You ask me which of the philosophers' traits are really idiosyncrasies? For example, their lack of historical sense, their hatred of the very idea of becoming, their Egypticism. They think that they show their *respect* for a subject when they de-historicize it, *sub specie aeterni*—when they turn it into a mummy. All that philosophers have handled for thousands of years have been concept-mummies; nothing real escaped their grasp alive. When these honorable idolaters of concepts worship something, they kill it and stuff it; they threaten the life of everything they worship. Death, change, old age, as well as procreation and growth, are to their minds objections—even refutations. Whatever has being does not become; whatever becomes does not have being. Now they all believe, desperately even, in what has being. But since they never grasp it, they seek for reasons why it is kept from them. "There must be mere appearance, there must be some deception which prevents us from perceiving that which has being: where is the deceiver?"

"We have found him," they cry ecstatically; "it is the senses! These senses, which are so immoral in other ways too, deceive us concerning the *true* world. Moral: let us free ourselves from the deception of the sesnses, from becoming, from history, from lies; history is nothing but faith in the senses, faith in lies. Moral: let us say No to all who have faith in the senses, to all the rest of mankind; they are all 'mob.' Let us be philosophers! Let us be mummies! Let us represent monotono-theism by adopting the expression of a gravedigger! And above all, away with the body, this wretched *idée fixe* of the senses, disfigured by all the fallacies of logic, refuted, even impossible, although it is impudent enough to behave as if it were real!"

*From *The Twilight of the Idols*, in *The Portable Nietzsche*, trans. by Walter Kaufmann, pp. 479-484. Copyright 1954 by The Viking Press, Inc. Reprinted by permission of The Viking Press, Inc.

2

With the highest respect, I except the name of *Heraclitus*. When the rest of the philosophic folk rejected the testimony of the senses because they showed multiplicity and change, he rejected their testimony because they showed things as if they had permanence and unity. Heraclitus too did the sense an injustice. They lie neither in the way the Eleatics believed, nor as he believed—they do not lie at all. What we *make* of their testimony, that alone introduces lies; for example, the lie of unity, the lie of thinghood, of substance, of permanence. "Reason" is the cause of our falsification of the testimony of the senses. Insofar as the senses show becoming, passing away, and change, they do not lie. But Heraclitus will remain eternally right with his assertion that being is an empty fiction. The "apparent" world is the only one: the "true" world is merely added by a lie.

3

And what magnificent instruments of observation we possess in our senses! This nose, for example, of which no philosopher has yet spoken with reverence and gratitude, is actually the most delicate instrument so far at our disposal: it is able to detect minimal differences of motion which even a spectroscope cannot detect. Today we possess science precisely to the extent to which we have decided to *accept* the testimony of the senses—to the extent to which we sharpen them further, arm them, and have learned to think them through. The rest is miscarriage and not-yet-science—in other words, metaphysics, theology, psychology, epistemology—or formal science, a doctrine of signs, such as logic and that applied logic which is called mathematics. In them reality is not encountered at all, not even as a problem—no more than the question of the value of such a sign convention as logic.

4

The other idiosyncrasy of the philosophers is no less dangerous; it consists in confusing the last and the first. They place that which comes at the end—unfortunately! for it ought not to come at all!—namely, the "highest concepts," which means the most general, the emptiest concepts, the last smoke of evaporating reality, in the beginning, *as* the beginning. This again is nothing but their way of showing reverence: the higher *may* not grow out of the lower, may not have grown at all. Moral: whatever is of the first rank must be *causa sui.*[1]

1. "Self-caused."

Origin out of something else is considered an objection, a questioning
of value. All the highest values are of the first rank; all the highest
concepts, that which has being, the unconditional, the good, the true,
the perfect—all these cannot have become and must therefore be *causa
sui*. All these, moreover, cannot be unlike each other or in contradiction to each other. Thus they arrive at their stupendous concept,
"God." That which is last, thinnest, and emptiest is put first, as *the*
cause, as *ens realissimum*.[2] Why did mankind have to take seriously
the brain afflictions of sick web-spinners? They have paid dearly for
it!

5

At long last, let us contrast the very different manner in which
we shall conceive the problem of error and appearance. (I say "we"
for politeness' sake.) Formerly, alteration, change, any becoming at
all, were taken as proof of mere appearance, as an indication that there
must be something which led us astray. Today, conversely, precisely
insofar as the prejudice of reason forces us to posit unity, identity, permanence, substance, cause, thinghood, being, we see ourselves somehow caught in error, compelled into error. So certain are we, on the
basis of rigorous examination, that this is where the error lies.

It is no different in this case than with the movement of the sun:
there our eye is the constant advocate of error, here it is our language.
In its origin language belongs in the age of the most rudimentary form
of psychology. We enter a realm of crude fetishism when we summon
before consciousness the basic presuppositions of the metaphysics of
of language, in plain talk, the presuppositions of reason. Everywhere
it sees a doer and doing; it believes in will as *the* cause; it believes in the
ego, in the ego as being, in the ego as substance, and it projects this faith
in the ego-substance upon all things—only thereby does it first *create*
the concept of "thing." Everywhere "being" is projected by thought,
pushed underneath, as the cause; the concept of being follows, and is
a derivative of, the concept of ego. In the beginning there is that great
calamity of an error that the will is something which is effective, that
will is a capacity. Today we know that it is only a word.

Very much later, in a world which was in a thousand ways more
enlightened, philosophers, to their great surprise, became aware of the
sureness, the subjective certainty, in our handling of the categories of
reason: they concluded that these categories could not be derived from
anything empirical—for everything empirical plainly contradicted
them. Whence, then, were they derived?

2. "The most real being."

And in India, as in Greece, the same mistake was made: "We must once have been at home in a higher world (instead of a very much lower one, which would have been the truth); we must have been divine, *for* we have reason!" Indeed, nothing has yet possessed a more naïve power of persuasion than the error concerning being, as it has been formulated by the Eleatics, for example. After all, every word we say and every sentence speak in its favor. Even the opponents of the Eleatics still succumbed to the seduction of their concept of being: Democritus, among others, when he invented his atom. "Reason" in language—oh, what an old deceptive female she is! I am afraid we are not rid of God because we still have faith in grammar.

6

It will be appreciated if I condense so essential and so new an insight into four theses. In that way I facilitate comprehension; in that way I provoke contradiction.

First proposition. The reasons for which "this" world has been characterized as "apparent" are the very reasons which indicate its reality; any other kind of reality is absolutely indemonstrable.

Second proposition. The criteria which have been bestowed on the "true being" of things are the criteria of not-being, of *naught*; the "true world" has been constructed out of contradiction to the actual world: indeed an apparent world, insofar as it is merely a moral-optical illusion.

Third proposition. To invent fables about a world "other" than this one has no meaning at all, unless an instinct of slander, detraction, and suspicion against life has gained the upper hand in us: in that case, we avenge ourselves against life with a phantasmagoria of "another," a "better" life.

Fourth proposition. Any distinction between a "true" and an "apparent" world—whether in the Christian manner or in the manner of Kant (in the end, an underhanded Christian)—is only a suggestion of decadence, a symptom of the *decline of life*. That the artist esteems appearance higher than reality is no objection to this proposition. For "appearance" in this case means reality *once more*, only by way of selection, reinforcement, and correction. The tragic artist is no pessimist: he is precisely the one who says Yes to everything questionable, even to the terrible—he is *Dionysian*. . . .

The Error of Free Will*

7

... Today we no longer have any pity for the concept of "free will": we know only too well what it really is—the foulest of all theologians' artifices, aimed at making mankind "responsible" in their sense, that is, *dependent upon them*. Here I simply supply the psychology of all "making responsible."

Wherever responsibilities are sought, it is usually the instinct of wanting to judge and punish which is at work. Becoming has been deprived of its innocence when any being-such-and-such is traced back to will, to purposes, to acts of responsibility: the doctrine of the will has been invented essentially for the purpose of punishment, that is, because one wanted to impute guilt. The entire old psychology, the psychology of will, was conditioned by the fact that its originators, the priests at the head of ancient communities, wanted to create for themselves the right to punish—or wanted to create this right for God. Men were considered "free" so that they might be judged and punished —so that they might become *guilty*: consequently, every act had to be considered as willed, and the origin of every act had to be considered as lying within the consciousness (and thus the most fundamental counterfeit *in psychologicis* was made the principle of psychology itself).

Today, as we have entered into the reverse movement and we immoralists are trying with all our strength to take the concept of guilt and the concept of punishment out of the world again, and to cleanse psychology, history, nature, and social institutions and sanctions of them, there is in our eyes no more radical opposition than that of the theologians, who continue with the concept of a "moral world-order" to infect the innocence of becoming by means of "punishment" and "guilt." Christianity is a metaphysics of the hangman.

Ibid., pp. 499-501.

. . .

What alone can be *our* doctrine? That no one *gives* man his qualities—neither God, nor society, nor his parents and ancestors, nor he himself. (The nonsense of the last idea was taught as "intelligible freedom" by Kant—perhaps by Plato already.) No one is responsible for man's being there at all, for his being-such-and-such, or for his being in these circumstances or in this environment. The fatality of his essence is not to be disentangled from the fatality of all that has been and will be. Man is not the effect of some special purpose, of a will, and end; nor is he the object of an attempt to attain an "ideal of humanity" or an "ideal of happiness" or an "ideal of morality." It is absurd to wish to devolve one's essence on some end or other. We have invented the concept of "end": in reality there is no end.

One is necessary, one is a piece of fatefulness, one belongs to the whole, one is in the whole; there is nothing which could judge, measure, compare, or sentence our being, for that would mean judging, measuring, comparing, or sentencing the whole. But there is nothing besides the whole. That nobody is held responsible any longer, that the mode of being may not be traced back to a *causa prima*, that the world does not form a unity either as a sensorium or as "spirit"—that alone is the great liberation; with this alone is the innocence of becoming restored. The concept of "God" was until now the greatest objection to existence. We deny God, we deny the responsibility in God: only thereby do we redeem the world.

The Illusion of Moral Judgment*

1

My demand upon the philospher is known, that he take his stand *beyond* good and evil and leave the illusion of moral judgment *beneath* himself. This demand follows from an insight which I was the first to formulate: that *there are altogether no moral facts*. Moral judgments agree with religious ones in believing in realities which are no realities. Morality is merely an interpretation of certain phenomena —more precisely, a misinterpretation. Moral judgments, like religious ones, belong to a stage of ignorance at which the very concept of the real and the distinction between what is real and imaginary, are still lacking; thus "truth," at this stage, designates all sorts of things which we today call "imaginings." Moral judgments are therefore never to be taken literally: so understood, they always contain mere absurdity. Semeiotically, however, they remain invaluable: they reveal, at least for those who know, the most valuable realities of cultures and inwardnesses which did not know enough to "understand" themselves. Morality is mere sign language, mere symptomatology : one must know what it is all about to be able to profit from it.

Ibid., p. 501.

XII

MACH

Ernst Mach (1838-1916) was born in Turas, Moravia. After studying at Vienna he was appointed, in 1864, to the chair of mathematics at Graz, and three years later became professor of physics at Prague. In 1895 he was appointed to a professorship (also in physics) at Vienna, a post he held until 1901, when he was made a member of the Austrian house of peers. A prolific writer, his contributions ranged over a wide variety of subjects, which included mathematics, optics, mechanics, and psychology; Einstein paid tribute to his imagination and originality as a scientist when, in an obituary notice, he wrote that it was "not improbable that Mach would have found the Theory of Relativity if, at a time when his mind was still young, the problem of the constancy of velocity of light had agitated the physicists." It is, however, for his ideas concerning the philosophy and methodology of science, as set out in such books as *The Science of Mechanics* (1883) and *The Analysis of Sensations* (1886, expanded fifth edition 1906), that he is chiefly remembered today.

Mach's thinking was infused with a profound distrust of metaphysical notions and pretensions. His original philosophical debt was to Kant, whom he regarded as having "banished into the realm of shadows the sham ideas of the old metaphysics"; later he came to be deeply impressed by Hume's empiricist theories of knowledge and meaning. As the first group of selections printed here illustrates, he wished to insist that what he termed "sensations" constituted the fundamental elements from which our knowledge of the world and of ourselves proceeds and to which all meaningful assertions regarding matters of fact must ultimately refer. It followed, at the levels both of everyday common sense and of scientific theory and hypothesis, that the conceptual systems we employ are useful and intelligible precisely insofar as they enable us to correlate and organize, in an economical fashion, the basic sensory data, and to make valid predictions concerning phenomenal appearances and their relations. Higher-order conceptual structures and distinctions, such as those involving *mind* and *body*, must all be interpreted from this point of view; it was a gross error to hypostatize such ideas and to suppose that they stood for or designated independent entities lying above or beyond the experiential facts to which they in the last analysis owed their significance. Mach believed that it was especially important to preserve the natural sciences from mistakes and confusions of this kind. Like Berkeley before him, to whose analysis of scientific procedure his own exhibited striking resemblances, he criticized Newton for the employment of conceptions lacking in empirical content and sought to eliminate these in his own treatment of mechanics; he showed, moreover, considerable ingenuity in arguing that "auxiliary hypotheses," which scientists may find it convenient to use in order to facilitate their thinking about phenomena, need not and should not be regarded as referring to occult entities that mysteriously elude sensory observation. Mach's sensationalism has sometimes been attacked on the grounds of "psychologism": in fact, however, its affinities are more with what has come to be known as "neutral monism" than with the psychological atomism of earlier empiricists. As Mach himself was at pains to point out, the fundamental elements with which he considered scientific inquiries to be concerned were prior in status to the psychological or physical interpretations that might, in accordance with varying purposes or in the interests of presenting different types of correlation, be used to describe and explain them.

Introductory Remarks: Antimetaphysical*

1

The great results achieved by physical science in modern times—results not restricted to its own sphere but embracing that of other sciences which employ its help—have brought it about that physical ways of thinking and physical modes of procedure enjoy on all hands unwonted prominence, and that the greatest expectations are associated with their application. In keeping with this drift of modern inquiry, the physiology of the senses, gradually abandoning the method of investigating sensations in themselves followed by men like Goethe, Schopenhauer, and others, but with greatest success by Johannes Müller, has also assumed an almost exclusively physical character. This tendency must appear to us as not altogether appropriate, when we reflect that physics, despite its considerable development, nevertheless constitutes but a portion of a *larger* collective body of knowledge, and that it is unable, with its limited intellectual implements, created for limited and special purposes, to exhaust all the subject-matter in question. Without renouncing the support of physics, it is possible for the physiology of the senses, not only to pursue its own course of development, but also to afford to physical science itself powerful assistance. The following simple considerations will serve to illustrate this relation between the two.

2

Colors, sounds, temperatures, pressures, spaces, times, and so forth, are connected with one another in manifold ways; and with them are associated dispositions of mind, feelings, and volitions. Out of this fabric, that which is relatively more fixed and permanent stands prominently forth, engraves itself on the memory, and expresses itself in

*From Chap. 1 of *The Analysis of Sensations* (trans. C. M. Williams; revised by Sidney Waterlow; New York, 1959), pp. 1-37. Reprinted by permission of Dover Publications Inc.

language. Relatively greater permanency is exhibited, first, by certain complexes of colors, sounds, pressures, and so forth, functionally connected in time and space, which therefore receive special names, and are called bodies. Absolutely permanent such complexes are not.

My table is now brightly, now dimly lighted. Its temperature varies. It may receive an ink stain. One of its legs may be broken. It may be repaired, polished, and replaced part by part. But, for me, it remains the table at which I daily write.

My friend may put on a different coat. His countenance may assume a serious or a cheerful expression. His complexion, under the effects of light or emotion, may change. His shape may be altered by motion, or be definitely changed. Yet the number of the permanent features presented, compared with the number of the gradual alterations, is always so great, that the latter may be overlooked. It is the same friend with whom I take my daily walk.

My coat may receive a stain, a tear. My very manner of expressing this shows that we are concerned here with a sum-total of permanency, to which the new element is added and from which that which is lacking is subsequently taken away.

Our greater intimacy with this sum-total of permanency, and the preponderance of its importance for me as contrasted with the changeable element, impel us to the partly instinctive, partly voluntary and conscious economy of mental presentation and designation, as expressed in ordinary thought and speech. That which is presented in a single image receives a single designation, a single name.

Further, that complex of memories, moods, and feelings, joined to a particular body (the human body), which is called the "I" or "Ego," manifests itself as relatively permanent. I may be engaged upon this or that subject, I may be quiet and cheerful, excited and ill-humored. Yet, pathological cases apart, enough durable features remain to identify the ego. Of course, the ego also is only of relative permanency.

The apparent permanency of the ego consists chiefly in the single fact of its continuity, in the slowness of its changes. The many thoughts and plans of yesterday that are continued to-day, and of which our environment in waking hours incessantly reminds us (whence in dreams the ego can be very indistinct, doubled, or entirely wanting), and the little habits that are unconsciously and involuntary kept up for long periods of time, constitute the groundwork of the ego. There can hardly be greater differences in the egos of different people, than occur in the course of years in one person. When I recall to-day my early youth, I should take the boy that I then was, with the exception of a few individual features, for a different person, were it not for the existence of the chain of memories. Many an article that I myself penned twenty years ago impresses me now as something quite foreign to myself. The very gradual character of the changes of the body also contributes to the stability of the ego, but in a much less degree than people imagine. Such things are much less analysed and noticed than the intellectual and the moral ego. Personally, people know themselves very poorly. When I wrote these lines in 1886, Ribot's admirable little book, *The Diseases of Personality* (second edition, Paris, 1888, Chicago, 1895), was unknown to me. Ribot ascribes the principal rôle in preserving the continuity of the ego to the general sensibility. Generally, I am in perfect accord with his views.

The ego is as little absolutely permanent as are bodies. That which we so much dread in death, the annihilation of our permanency, actually occurs in life in abundant measure. That which is most valued by us, remains preserved in countless copies, or, in cases of exceptional excellence, is even preserved of itself. In the best human being, however, there are individual traits, the loss of which neither he himself nor others need regret. Indeed, at times, death, viewed as a liberation from individuality, may even become a pleasant thought. Such reflections of course do not make physiological death any the easier to bear.

After a first survey has been obtained, by the formation of the substance-concepts "body" and "ego" (matter and soul), the will is impelled to a more exact examination of the changes that take place in these relatively permanent existences. The element of change in bodies and the ego, is in fact, exactly what moves the will to this examination. Here the component parts of the complex are first exhibited as its properties. A fruit is sweet; but it can also be bitter. Also, other fruits may be sweet. The red color we are seeking is found in many bodies. The neighborhood of some bodies is pleasant; that of others, unpleasant. Thus, gradually, different complexes are found to be made up of common elements. The visible, the audible, the tangible, are separated from bodies. The visible is analysed into colors and into form. In the manifoldness of the colors, again, though here fewer in number, other component parts are discerned—such as the primary colors, and so forth. The complexes are disintegrated into elements, that is to say, into their ultimate component parts, which hitherto we have been unable to subdivide any further. The nature of these elements need not be discussed at present; it is possible that future investigations may throw light on it. We need not here be disturbed by the fact that it is easier for the scientist to study relations of relations of these elements than the direct relations between them.

3

The useful habit of designating such relatively permanent compounds by single names, and of apprehending them by single thoughts, without going to the trouble each time of an analysis of their component parts, is apt to come into strange conflict with the tendency to isolate the component parts. The vague image which we have of a given permanent complex, being an image which does not perceptibly change when one or another of the component parts is taken away, seems to be something which exists in itself. Inasmuch as it is possible to take away singly every constituent part without destroying the capacity of the image to stand for the totality and to be recognised again, it is imagined that it is possible to subtract *all* the parts and to have something still remaining. Thus naturally arises the philosophical notion, at first impressive, but subsequently recognized as monstrous, of a "thing-in-itself," different from its "appearance," and unknowable.

Thing, body, matter, are nothing apart from the combinations of the elements,—the colors, sounds, and so forth—nothing apart from their so-called attributes. That protean pseudo-philosophical problem of the single thing with its many attributes, arises wholly from a misinterpretation of the fact, that summary comprehension and precise analysis, although both are provisionally justifiable and for many purposes profitable, cannot be carried on simultaneously. A body is one and unchangeable only so long as it is unnecessary to consider its details. Thus both the earth and a billiard-ball are spheres, if we are willing to neglect all deviations from the spherical form, and if greater precision is not necessary. But when we are obliged to carry on investigations in orography or microscopy, both bodies cease to be spheres. . . .

5

Not only the relation of bodies to the ego, but the ego itself also, gives rise to similar pseudo-problems, the character of which may be briefly indicated as follows:

Let us denote the above-mentioned elements by the letters $A\,B\,C\ldots,\,K\,L\,M\ldots,\,\alpha\,\beta\,\gamma\ldots$ Let those complexes of colors, sounds, and so forth, commonly called bodies, be denoted, for the sake of clearness, by $A\,B\,C\ldots$; the complex, known as our own body, which is a part of the former complexes distinguished by certain peculiarities, may be called $K\,L\,M\ldots$; the complex composed of volitions, memory-images, and the rest, we shall represent by a $\alpha\,\beta\,\gamma\ldots$ Usually, now, the complex $\alpha\,\beta\,\gamma\ldots K\,L\,M\ldots$, as making up the ego, is opposed to the complex $A\,B\,C$ . . ., as making up the world of physical objects; sometimes also, $\alpha\,\beta\,\gamma$ . . . is viewed as ego, and $K\,L\,M$ . . . $A\,B\,C$ . . . as world of physical objects. Now, at first blush, $A\,B\,C$ . . . appears independent of the ego, and opposed to it as a separate existence. But this independence is only relative, and gives way upon closer inspection. Much, it is true, *may* change in the complex $\alpha\,\beta\,\gamma$ . . . without much perceptible change being induced in $A\,B\,C$ . . .; and *vice versa*. But many changes in $\alpha\,\beta\,\gamma$ . . . do pass, by way of changes in $K\,L\,M$ . . ., to $A\,B\,C$ . . .; and *vice versa*. (As, for example, when powerful ideas burst forth into acts, or when our environment induces noticeable changes in our body.) At the same time the group $K\,L\,M$ . . . appears to be more intimately connected with $\alpha\,\beta\,\gamma$ . . . and with $A\,B\,C$ . . ., than the latter with one another; and their relations find their expression in common thought and speech.

Precisely viewed, however, it appears that the group $A\,B\,C$ . . . is always codetermined by $K\,L\,M$. A cube when seen close at hand, looks large; when seen at a distance, small; its appearance to the right eye differs from its appearance to the left; sometimes it appears double; with closed eyes it is invisible. The properties of one and the same body, therefore, appear modified by our own body; they appear conditioned by it. But where, now, is that *same* body, which appears so *different?* All that can be said is, that with different $K\,L\,M$ different $A\,B\,C$ . . . are associated.

A common and popular way of thinking and speaking is to contrast "appearance" with "reality." A pencil held in front of us in the air is seen by us as straight; dip it into the water, and we see it crooked. In the latter case we say that the pencil *appears* crooked, but is in *reality* straight. But what justifies us in declaring one fact rather than another to be the reality, and degrading the other to the level of appearance? In both cases we have to do with facts which present us with different combinations of the elements, combinations which in the two cases are differently conditioned. Precisely because of its environment the pencil dipped in water is optically crooked; but it is tactually and metrically straight. An image in a concave or flat mirror is *only* visible, whereas under other and ordinary circumstances a tangible body as well corresponds to the visible image. A bright surface is brighter beside a dark surface than beside one brighter than itself. To be sure, our expectation is deceived when, not paying sufficient attention to the conditions, and substituting for one another different cases of the combination, we fall into the natural error of expecting what we are accustomed to, although the case may be an unusual one. The facts are not to blame for that. In these cases, to speak of "appearance" may have a practical meaning, but cannot have a scientific meaning. Similarly, the question which is often asked, whether the world is real or whether we merely dream it, is devoid of all scientific meaning. Even the wildest dream is a fact as much as any other. If our dreams were more regular, more connected, more stable, they would also have more practical importance for us. In our waking hours the relations of the elements to one another are immensely amplified in comparison with what they were in our dreams. We recognize the dream for what it is. When the process is reversed, the field of psychic vision is narrowed; the contrast is almost entirely lacking. Where there is no contrast, the distinction between dream and waking, between appearance and reality, is quite otiose and worthless.

The popular notion of an antithesis between appearance and reality has exercised a very powerful influence on scientific and philosophical thought. We see this, for example, in Plato's pregnant and poetical fiction of the Cave, in which, with our backs turned towards the fire, we observe merely the shadows of what passes (*Republic*, vii. 1). But this conception was not thought out to its final consequences, with the result that it has had an unfortunate influence on our ideas about the universe. The universe, of which nevertheless we are a part, became completely separated from us, and was removed an infinite distance away. Similarly, many a young man, hearing for the first time of the refraction of stellar light, has thought that doubt was cast on the whole of astronomy, whereas nothing is required but an easily effected and unimportant correction to put everything right again.

6

We see an object having a point S. If we touch S, that is, bring it into connexion with our body, we receive a prick. We can see S, without feeling the prick. But as soon as we feel the prick we find S on the skin. The visible point, therefore, is a permanent nucleus, to which the prick is annexed, according to circumstances, as something accidental. From the frequency of analogous occurrences we ultimately accustom ourselves to regard all properties of bodies as "effects" proceeding from permanent nuclei and conveyed to the ego through the medium of the body; which effects we call sensations. By this operation, however, these nuclei are deprived of their entire sensory content, and converted into mere mental symbols. The assertion, then, is correct that the world consists only of our sensations. In which case we have knowledge *only* of sensations, and the assumption of the nuclei referred to, or of a reciprocal action between them, from which sensations proceed, turns out to be quite idle and superfluous. Such a view can only suit with a half-hearted realism or a half-hearted philosophical criticism.

7

Ordinarily the complex $\alpha \beta \gamma \ldots K L M \ldots$ is contrasted as ego with the complex $A B C \ldots$ At first only those elements of $A B C \ldots$ that more strongly alter $\alpha \beta \gamma \ldots$, as a prick, a pain, are wont to be thought of as comprised in the ego. Afterwards, however, through observations of the kind just referred to, it appears that the right to annex $A B C \ldots$ to the ego nowhere ceases. In conformity with this view the ego can be so extended as ultimately to embrace the entire world. The ego is not sharply marked off, its limits are very indefinite and arbitrarily displaceable. Only by failing to observe this fact, and by unconsciously narrowing those limits, while at the same time we enlarge them, arise, in the conflict of points of view, the metaphysical difficulties met with in this connexion.

As soon as we have perceived that the supposed unities "body" and "ego" are only makeshifts, designed for provisional orientation and for definite practical ends (so that we take hold of bodies, protect ourselves against pain, and so forth), we find ourselves obliged, in many more advanced scientific investigations, to abandon them as insufficient and inappropriate. The antithesis between ego and world, between sensation (appearance) and thing, then vanishes, and we have simply to deal with the connexion of the elements $\alpha \beta \gamma \ldots A B C \ldots K L M \ldots$, of which this antithesis was only a partially appropriate and imperfect expression. This connexion is nothing more or less than the combination of the above-mentioned elements with other similar elements (time and space). Science has simply to accept this connexion, and to get its bearings in it, without at once wanting to explain its existence.

On a superficial examination the complex $\alpha \beta \gamma \ldots$ appears to be made up of much more evanescent elements than $A B C \ldots$ and $K L M \ldots$, in which last the elements seem to be connected with greater stability and in a more permanent manner (being joined to solid nuclei as it were). Although on closer inspection the elements of all complexes prove to be homogeneous, yet even when this has been recognized, the earlier notion of an antithesis of body and spirit easily slips in again. The philosophical spiritualist is often sensible of the difficulty of imparting the needed solidity to his mind-created world of bodies; the materialist is at a loss when required to endow the world of matter with sensation. The monistic point of view, which reflexion has evolved, is easily clouded by our older and more powerful instinctive notions.

8

The difficulty referred to is particularly felt when we consider the following case. In the complex $A B C \ldots$, which we have called the world of matter, we find as parts, not only our own body $K L M \ldots$, but also the bodies of other persons (or animals) $K' L' M'$ $K'' L'' M''$ $\ldots$, to which, by analogy, we imagine other $\alpha' \beta' \gamma' \ldots$, $\alpha'' \beta'' \gamma''$ $\ldots$, annexed, similar to $\alpha \beta \gamma \ldots$ So long as we deal with $K' L' M'$ $\ldots$, we find ourselves in a thoroughly familiar province which is at every point accessible to our senses. When, however, we inquire after the sensations or feelings belonging to the body $K' L' M' \ldots$, we no longer find these in the province of sense: we add them in thought. Not only is the domain which we now enter far less familiar to us, but the transition into it is also relatively unsafe. We have the feeling as if we were plunging into an abyss. Persons who adopt this way of thinking only, will never thoroughly rid themselves of that sense of insecurity, which is a very fertile source of illusory problems.

But we are not restricted to this course. Let us consider, first, the reciprocal relations of the elements of the complex $A B C \ldots$, without regarding $K L M \ldots$ (our body). All physical investigations are of this sort. A white ball falls upon a bell; a sound is heard. The ball turns yellow before a sodium lamp, red before a lithium lamp. Here the elements $(A B C \ldots)$ appear to be connected only with one another and to be independent of our body $(K L M \ldots)$. But if we take santonine, the ball again turns yellow. If we press one eye to the side, we see two balls. If we close our eyes entirely, there is no ball there at all. If we sever the auditory nerve, no sound is heard. The elements $A B C \ldots$, therefore, are not only connected with one another, but also with $K L M$. To this extent, and to this extent *only*, do we call $A B C \ldots$ *sensations*, and regard $A B C$ as belonging to the ego. In what follows, wherever the reader finds the terms "Sensation," "Sensation-complex," used alongside of or instead of the expressions "element," "complex of elements," it must be borne in mind that it is *only* in the connexion and relation in question, *only* in their functional dependence, that the elements are sensations. In another functional relation they are at the same time physical objects. We only use the additional term "sensations" to describe the elements, because most people are much more familiar with the elements in question *as* sensations (colors, sounds, pressures, spaces, times, etc.), while according to the popular conception it is particles of mass that are considered as physical elements, to which the elements, in the sense here used, are attached as "properties" or "effects."

In this way, accordingly, we do not find the gap between bodies and sensations above described, between what is without and what is within, between the material world and the spiritual world. All elements $A\,B\,C\ldots,\,K\,L\,M\ldots$, constitute a *single* coherent mass only, in which, when any one element is disturbed, *all* is put in motion; except that a disturbance in $K\,L\,M\ldots$ has a more extensive and profound action than one in $A\,B\,C\ldots$ A magnet in our neighborhood disturbs the particles of iron near it; a falling boulder shakes the earth; but the severing of a nerve sets in motion the *whole* system of elements. Quite involuntarily does this relation of things suggest the picture of a viscous mass, at certain places (as in the ego) more firmly coherent than in others. I have often made use of this image in lectures.

9

Thus the great gulf between physical and psychological research persists only when we acquiesce in our habitual stereotyped conceptions. A color is a physical object as soon as we consider its dependence, for instance, upon its luminous source, upon other colors, upon temperatures, upon spaces, and so forth. When we consider, however, its dependence upon the retina (the elements $K\,L\,M\ldots$), it is a psychological object, a sensation. Not the subject-matter, but the direction of our investigation, is different in the two domains. . . .

11

Reference has already been made to the different character of the groups of elements denoted by $A\,B\,C\ldots$ and $\alpha\,\beta\,\gamma\ldots$ As a matter of fact, when we see a green tree before us, or remember a green tree, that is, represent a green tree to ourselves. we are perfectly aware of the difference of the two cases. The represented tree has a much less determinate, a much more changeable form; its green is much paler and more evanescent; and, what is of especial note, it plainly appears in a different domain. A movement that we will to execute is never more than a represented movement, and appears in a different domain from that of the executed movement, which always takes place when the image is vivid enough. Now the statement that the elements A and α appear in different domains, means, if we go to the bottom of it, simply this, that these elements are united with different other elements. Thus far, therefore, the fundamental constituents of $ABC\ldots$, $\alpha\,\beta\,\gamma\ldots$ would seem to be *the same* (colors, sounds, spaces, times, motor sensations . . .), and only the character of their connexion different.

Ordinarily pleasure and pain are regarded as different from sensations. Yet not only tactual sensations, but all other kinds of sensations, may pass gradually into pleasure and pain. Pleasure and pain also may be justly termed sensations. Only they are not so well analysed and so familiar, nor, perhaps, limited to so few organs as the common sensations. In fact, sensations of pleasure and pain, however faint they may be, really constitute an essential part of the content of all so-called emotions. Any additional element that emerges into consciousness when we are under the influence of emotions may be described as more or less diffused and not sharply localized sensations. William James, and after him Théodule Ribot, have investigated the physiological mechanism of the emotions: they hold that what is essential is purposive tendencies of the body to action—tendencies which correspond to circumstances and are expressed in the organism. Only a part of these emerges into consciousness. We are sad because we shed tears, and not *vice versa,* says James. And Ribot justly observes that a cause of the backward state of our knowledge of the emotions is that we have always confined our observation to so much of these physiological processes as emerges into consciousness. At the same time he goes too far when he maintains that everything psychical is merely *"surajouté"* to the physical, and that it is only the physical that produces effects. For us this distinction is non-existent.

Thus, perceptions, presentations, volitions, and emotions, in short the whole inner and outer world, are put together, in combinations of varying evanescence and permanence, out of a small number of homogeneous elements. Usually, these elements are called sensations. But as vestiges of a one-sided theory inhere in that term, we prefer to speak simply of elements, as we have already done. The aim of all research is to ascertain the mode of connexion of these elements. If it proves impossible to solve the problem by assuming *one* set of such elements, then more than one will have to be assumed. But for the questions under discussion it would be improper to begin by making complicated assumptions in advance.

12

That is this complex of elements, which fundamentally is only one, the boundaries of bodies and of the ego do not admit of being established in a manner definite and sufficient for all cases, has already been remarked. To bring together elements that are most intimately connected with pleasure and pain into one ideal mental-economical unity, the ego; this is a task of the highest importance for the intellect working in the service of the pain-avoiding, pleasure-seeking will. The delimitation of the ego, therefore, is instinctively effected, is rendered familiar, and possibly becomes fixed through heredity. Owing to their high practical importance, not only for the individual, but for the entire species, the composites "ego" and "body' instinctively make good their claims, and assert themselves with elementary force. In special cases, however, in which practical ends are not concerned, but where knowledge is an end in itself, the delimitation in question may prove to be insufficient, obstructive, and untenable.

The primary fact is not the ego, but the elements (sensations). What was said on p. 378 as to the term "sensation" must be borne in mind. The elements constitute the I. *I* have the sensation green, signifies that the element green occurs in a given complex of other elements (sensations, memories). When *I* cease to have the sensation green, when *I* die, then the elements no longer occur in the ordinary, familiar association. That is all. Only an ideal mental-economical unity, not a real unity, has ceased to exist. . . .

The ego must be given up. It is partly the perception of this fact, partly the fear of it, that has given rise to the many extravagances of pessimism and optimism, and to numerous religious, ascetic, and philosophical absurdities. In the long run we shall not be able to close our eyes to this simple truth, which is the immediate outcome of psychological analysis. We shall then no longer place so high a value upon the ego, which even during the individual life greatly changes, and which, in sleep or during absorption in some idea, just in our very happiest moments, may be partially or wholly absent. We shall then be willing to renounce individual immortality, and not place more value upon the subsidiary elements than upon the principal ones. In this way we shall arrive at a freer and more enlightened view of life, which will preclude the disregard of other egos and the overestimation of our own. The ethical ideal founded on this view of life will be equally far removed from the ideal of the ascetic, which is not biologically tenable for whoever practises it, and vanishes at once with his disappearance, and from the ideal of an overweening Nietzschean "superman," who cannot, and I hope will not, be tolerated by his fellow-men.

If a knowledge of the connexion of the elements (sensations) does not suffice us, and we ask, *Who* possesses this connexion of sensations, *Who* experiences it? then we have succumbed to the habit of subsuming every element (every sensation) under some unanalysed complex, and we are falling back perceptibly upon an older, lower, and more limited point of view. It is often pointed out, that a psychical ex-

perience which is not the experience of a determinate subject is unthinkable, and it is held that in this way the essential part played
by the unity of consciousness has been demonstrated. But the Ego-
consciousness can be of many different degrees and composed of a
multiplicity of chance memories. One might just as well say that a
physical process which does not take place in some environment or
other, or at least somewhere in the universe, is unthinkable. In both
cases, in order to make a beginning with our investigation, we must
be allowed to abstract from the environment, which, as regards its
influence, may be very different in different cases, and in special cases
may shrink to a minimum. Consider the sensations of the lower animals, to which a subject with definite features can hardly be ascribed.
It is out of sensations that the subject is built up, and, once built up,
no doubt the subject reacts in turn on the sensations.

The habit of treating the unanalysed ego complex as an indis-
cerptible unity frequently assumes in science remarkable forms. First,
the nervous system is separated from the body as the seat of the sensations. In the nervous system again, the brain is selected as the organ
best fitted for this end, and finally, to save the supposed psychical unity,
a *point* is sought in the brain as the seat of the soul. But such crude conceptions are hardly fit even to foreshadow the roughest outlines of
what future research will do for the connexion of the physical and the
psychical. The fact that the different organs and parts of the nervous
system are physically connected with, and can be readily excited by,
one another, is probably at the bottom of the notion of "psychical
unity."

I once heard the question seriously discussed, "How the perception of a large tree could find room in the little head of a man?" Now,
although this "problem" is no problem, yet it renders us vividly sensible
of the absurdity that can be committed by thinking sensations spatially
into the brain. When I speak of the sensation of another person, those
sensations are, of course, not exhibited in my optical or physical space;
they are mentally added, and I conceive them causally, not spatially,
attached to the brain observed, or rather, functionally presented. When
I speak of my own sensations, these sensations do not exist spatially in
my head, but rather my "head" shares with them the same spatial
field. . . .

The unity of consciousness is not an argument in point. Since the
apparent antithesis between the real world and the world given through
the senses lies entirely in our mode of view, and no actual gulf exists
between them, a complicated and variously interconnected content

of consciousness is no more difficult to understand than is the complicated interconnexion of the world.

If we regard the ego as a real unity, we become involved in the following dilemma : either we must set over against the ego a world of unknowable entities (which would be quite idle and purposeless), or we must regard the whole world, the egos of other people included, as comprised in our own ego (a proposition to which it is difficult to yield serious assent).

But if we take the ego simply as a practical unity, put together for purposes of provisional survey, or as a more strongly cohering group of elements, less strongly connected with other groups of this kind, questions like those above discussed will not arise, and research will have an unobstructed future.

In his philosophical notes Lichtenberg says: "We become conscious of certain presentations that are not dependent upon us; of others that we at least think are dependent upon us. Where is the border-line? We know only the existence of our sensations, presentations, and thoughts. We should say, *It thinks*, just as we say, *It lightens*. It is going too far to say *cogito*, if we translate *cogito* by *I think*. The assumption, or postulation, of the ego is a mere practical necessity." Though the method by which Lichtenberg arrived at this result is somewhat different from ours, we must nevertheless give our full assent to his conclusion.

13

Bodies do not produce sensations, but complexes of elements (complexes of sensations) make up bodies. If, to the physicist, bodies appear the real, abiding existences, whilst the "elements" are regarded merely as their evanescent, transitory appearance, the physicist forgets, in the assumption of such a view, that all bodies are but thought-symbols for complexes of elements (complexes of sensations). Here, too, the elements in question form the real, immediate, and ultimate foundation, which it is the task of physiologico-physical research to investigate. By the recognition of this fact, many points of physiology and physics assume more distinct and more economical forms, and many spurious problems are disposed of.

For us, therefore, the world does not consist of mysterious entities, which by their interaction with another, equally mysterious entity, the ego, produce sensations, which alone are accessible. For us, colors, sounds, spaces, times, ... are provisionally the ultimate elements, whose given connexion it is our business to investigate. It is precisely in this that the exploration of reality consists. In this investigation we must not allow ourselves to be impeded by such abridgments and delimitations as body, ego, matter, spirit, etc., which have been formed for special, practical purposes and with wholly provisional and limited ends in view. On the contrary, the fittest forms of thought must be created in and by that research itself, just as is done in every special science. In place of the traditional, instinctive ways of thought, a freer, fresher view, conforming to developed experience, and reaching out beyond the requirements of practical life, must be substituted throughout.

14

Science always has its origin in the adaptation of thought to some definite field of experience. The results of the adaptation are thought-elements, which are able to represent the whole field. The outcome, of course, is different, according to the character and extent of the field. If the field of experience is enlarged, or if several fields heretofore disconnected are united, the traditional, familiar thought-elements no longer suffice for the extended field. In the struggle of acquired habit with the effort after adaptation, problems arise, which disappear when the adaptation is perfected, to make room for others which have arisen meanwhile.

To the physicist, *qua* physicist, the idea of "body" is productive of a real facilitation of view, and is not the cause of disturbance. So, also, the person with purely practical aims, is materially supported by the idea of the *I* or ego. For, unquestionably, every form of thought that has been designedly or undesignedly constructed for a given purpose, possesses for that purpose a *permanent* value. When, however, physics and psychology meet, the ideas held in the one domain prove to be untenable in the other. From the attempt at mutual adaptation arise the various atomic and monadistic theories—which, however, never attain their end. If we regard sensations, in the sense above defined (p. 375), as the elements of the world, the problems referred to appear to be disposed of in all essentials, and the first and most important adaptation to be consequently effected. This fundamental view (without any pretension to being a philosophy for all eternity) can at present be adhered to in all fields of experience; it is consequently the one that accommodates itself with the least expenditure of energy, that is, more economically than any other, to the present temporary collective state of knowledge. Furthermore, in the consciousness of its purely economical function, this fundamental view is eminently tolerant. It does not obtrude itself into fields in which the current conceptions are still adequate. It is also ever ready, upon subsequent extensions of the field of experience, to give way before a better conception. . . .

It may easily become a disturbing element in unprejudiced scientific theorizing when a conception which is adapted to a particular and strictly limited purpose is promoted in advance to be the foundation of *all* investigation. This happens, for example, when all experiences are regarded as "effects" of an external world extending into consciousness. This conception gives us a tangle of metaphysical difficulties which it seems impossible to unravel. But the spectre vanishes at once when we look at the matter as it were in a mathematical light, and make it clear to ourselves that all that is valuable to us is the discovery of *functional relations,* and that what we want to know is merely the dependence of experiences on one another. It then becomes obvious that the reference to unknown fundamental variables which are not given (things-in-themselves) is purely fictitious and superfluous. But even when we allow this fiction, uneconomical though it be, to stand at first, we can still easily distinguish different classes of the mutual dependence of the elements of "the facts of consciousness"; and this alone is important for us. . . .

The biological task of science is to provide the fully developed human individual with as perfect a means of orientating himself as possible. No other scientific ideal can be realized, and any other must be meaningless.

The philosophical point of view of the average man—if that term may be applied to his naïve realism—has a claim to the highest consideration. It has arisen in the process of immeasurable time without the intentional assistance of man. It is a product of nature, and is preserved by nature. Everything that philosophy has accomplished—though we may admit the biological justification of every advance, nay, of every error—is, as compared with it, but an insignificant and ephemeral product of art. The fact is, every thinker, every philosopher, the moment he is forced to abandon his one-sided intellectual occupation by practical necessity, immediately returns to the general point of view of mankind. Professor X., who theoretically believes himself to be a solipsist, is certainly not one in practice when he has to thank a Minister of State for a decoration conferred upon him, or when he lectures to an audience. The Pyrrhonist who is cudgelled in Molière's *Le Mariage Forcé*, does not go on saying "Il me semble que vous me battez," but takes his beating as really received.

Nor is it the purpose of these "introductory remarks" to discredit the standpoint of the plain man. The task which we have set ourselves is simply to show why and for what purpose we hold that standpoint during most of our lives, and why and for what purpose we are provisionally obliged to abandon it. No point of view has absolute, permanent validity. Each has importance only for some given end.

Newton's Views of Time, Space, and Motion*

1. In a scholium which he appends immediately to his definitions, Newton presents his views regarding time and space—views which we shall now proceed to examine more in detail. We shall literally cite, to this end, only the passages that are absolutely necessary to the characterisation of Newton's views.

"So far, my object has been to explain the senses in which certain words little known are to be used in the sequel. Time, space, place, and motion, being words well known to everybody, I do not define. Yet it is to be remarked, that the vulgar conceive these quantities only in their relation to sensible objects. And hence certain prejudices with respect to them have arisen, to remove which it will be convenient to distinguish them into absolute and relative, true and apparent, mathematical and common, respectively.

"I. Absolute, true, and mathematical time, of itself, and by its own nature, flows uniformly on, without regard to anything external. It is also called *duration*.

"Relative, apparent, and common time, is some sensible and external measure of absolute time (duration), estimated by the motions of bodies, whether accurate or inequable, and is commonly employed in place of true time; as an hour, a day, a month, a year . . .

"The natural days, which, commonly, for the purpose of the measurement of time, are held as equal, are in reality unequal. Astronomers correct this inequality, in order that they may measure by a truer time the celestial motions. It may be that there is no equable motion, by which time can accurately be measured. All motions can be accelerated and retarded. But the flow of *absolute* time cannot be changed. Duration, or the persistent existence of things, is always the same, whether motions be swift or slow or null."

*From *The Science of Mechanics* (trans. T. J. McCormack; Chicago, Open Court Publishing Company, 1902), pp. 222-232.

2. It would appear as though Newton in the remarks here cited still stood under the influence of the mediaeval philosophy, as though he had grown unfaithful to his resolve to investigate only actual facts. When we say a thing A changes with the time, we mean simply that the conditions that determine a thing A depend on the conditions that determine another thing B. The vibrations of a pendulum take place *in time* when its excursion *depends* on the position of the earth. Since, however, in the observation of the pendulum, we are not under the necessity of taking into account its dependence on the position of the earth, but may compare it with any other thing (the conditions of which of course also depend on the position of the earth), the illusory notion easily arises that *all* the things with which we compare it are unessential. Nay, we may, in attending to the motion of a pendulum, neglect entirely other external things, and find that for every position of it our thoughts and sensations are different. Time, accordingly, appears to be some particular and independent thing, on the progress of which the position of the pendulum depends, while the things that we resort to for comparison and choose at random appear to play a wholly collateral part. But we must not forget that all things in the world are connected with one another and depend on one another, and that we ourselves and all our thoughts are also a part of nature. It is utterly beyond our power to *measure* the changes of things by *time*. Quite the contrary, time is an abstraction, at which we arrive by means of the changes of things; made because we are not restricted to any one *definite* measure, all being interconnected. A motion is termed uniform in which equal increments of space described correspond to equal increments of space described by some motion with which we form a comparison, as the rotation of the earth. A motion may, with respect to another motion, be uniform. But the question whether a motion is *in itself* uniform, is senseless. With just as little justice, also, may we speak of an "absolute time"—*of a time independent of change*. This absolute time can be measured by comparison with no motion; it has therefore neither a practical nor a scientific value; and no one is justified in saying that he knows aught about it. It is an idle metaphysical conception. . . .

3. Views similar to those concerning time, are developed by Newton with respect to space and motion. We extract here a few passages which characterise his position.

"II. Absolute space, in its own nature and without regard to anything external, always remains similar and immovable.

"Relative space is some movable dimension or measure of absolute space, which our senses determine by its position with respect to other bodies, and which is commonly taken for immovable [absolute] space. . . .

"IV. Absolute motion is the translation of a body from one absolute place[1] to another absolute place; and relative motion, the translation from one relative place to another relative place. . . .

". . . And thus we use, in common affairs, instead of *absolute* places and motions, *relative* ones; and that without any inconvenience. But in physical disquisitions, we should abstract from the senses. For it may be that there is no body really at rest, to which the places and motions of others can be referred. . . .

"The effects by which absolute and relative motions are distinguished from one another, are centrifugal forces, or those forces in circular motion which produce a tendency of recession from the axis. For in a circular motion which is purely relative no such forces exist; but in a true and absolute circular motion they do exist, and are greater or less according to the quantity of the [absolute] motion. . . ."

4. It is scarcely necessary to remark that in the reflections here presented Newton has again acted contrary to his expressed intention only to investigate *actual facts*. No one is competent to predicate things about absolute space and absolute motion; they are pure things of thought, pure mental constructs, that cannot be produced in experience. All our principles of mechanics are, as we have shown in detail, experimental knowledge concerning the relative positions and motions of bodies. Even in the provinces in which they are now recognised as valid, they could not, and were not, admitted without previously being subjected to experimental tests. No one is warranted in extending these principles beyond the boundaries of experience. In fact, such an extension is meaningless, as no one possesses the requisite knowledge to make use of it.

Let us look at the matter in detail. When we say that a body K alters its direction and velocity solely through the influence of another body K', we have asserted a conception that it is impossible to come at unless other bodies A, B, C . . . . are present with reference to which the motion of the body K has been estimated. In reality, therefore, we are simply cognisant of a relation of the body K to A, B, C . . . . If now we suddenly neglect A, B, C . . . . and attempt to speak of the deportment of the body K in absolute space, we implicate ourselves in a twofold error. In the first place, we cannot know how K would act in the absence of A, B, C . . . .; and in the second place, every means would be wanting of forming a judgment of the behaviour of

1. The place, or *locus* of a body, according to Newton, is not its position, but the *part of space* which it occupies. It is either absolute or relative.—*Trans.*

K and of putting to the test what we had predicated,—which latter therefore would be bereft of all scientific significance.

5. Let us now examine the point on which Newton, apparently with sound reasons, rests his distinction of absolute and relative motion. If the earth is affected with an *absolute* rotation about its axis, centrifugal forces are set up in the earth: it assumes an oblate form, the acceleration of gravity is diminished at the equator, the plane of Foucault's pendulum rotates, and so on. All these phenomena disappear if the earth is at rest and the other heavenly bodies are affected with absolute motion round it, such that the same *relative* rotation is produced. This is, indeed, the case, if we start *ab initio* from the idea of absolute space. But if we take our stand on the basis of facts, we shall find we have knowledge only of *relative* spaces and motions. *Relatively*, not considering the unknown and neglected medium of space, the motions of the universe are the same whether we adopt the Ptolemaic or the Copernican mode of view. Both views are, indeed, equally *correct;* only the latter is more simple and more *practical.* The universe is not *twice* given, with an earth at rest and an earth in motion; but only *once*, with its *relative* motions, alone determinable. It is, accordingly, not permitted us to say how things would be if the earth did not rotate. We may interpret the one case that is given us, in different ways. If, however, we so interpret it that we come into conflict with experience, our interpretation is simply wrong. The principles of mechanics can, indeed, be so conceived, that even for relative rotations centrifugal forces arise. . . .

The Economy of Science*

1. It is the object of science to replace, or *save*, experiences, by the reproduction and anticipation of facts in thought. Memory is handier than experience, and often answers the same purpose. This economical office of science, which fills its whole life, is apparent at first glance; and with its full recognition all mysticism in science disappears.

Science is communicated by instruction, in order that one man may profit by the experience of another and be spared the trouble of accumulating it for himself; and thus, to spare posterity, the experiences of whole generations are stored up in libraries.

Language, the instrument of this communication, is itself an economical contrivance. Experiences are analysed, or broken up, into simpler and more familiar experiences, and then symbolised at some sacrifice of precision. The symbols of speech are as yet restricted in their use within national boundaries, and doubtless will long remain so. But written language is gradually being metamorphosed into an ideal universal character. It is certainly no longer a mere transcript of speech. Numerals, algebraic signs, chemical symbols, musical notes, phonetic alphabets, may be regarded as parts already formed of this universal character of the future; they are, to some extent, decidedly conceptual, and of almost general international use. The analysis of colors, physical and physiological, is already far enough advanced to render an international system of color-signs perfectly practical. In Chinese writing, we have an actual example of a true ideographic language, pronounced diversely in different provinces, yet everywhere carrying the same meaning. Were the system and its signs only of a simpler character, the use of Chinese writing might become universal. The dropping of unmeaning and needless accidents of grammar, as English mostly drops them, would be quite requisite to the adoption of such a system. But universality would not be the sole merit of such a

Ibid., pp. 481-494.

character; since to read it would be to understand it. Our children often read what they do not understand; but that which a Chinaman cannot understand, he is precluded from reading.

2. In the reproduction of facts in thought, we never reproduce the facts in full, but only that side of them which is important to us, moved to this directly or indirectly by a practical interest. Our reproductions are invariably abstractions. Here again is an economical tendency.

Nature is composed of sensations as its elements. Primitive man, however, first picks out certain compounds of these elements—those namely that are relatively permanent and of greater importance to him. The first and oldest words are names of "things." Even here, there is an abstractive process, an abstraction from the surroundings of the things, and from the continual small changes which these compound sensations undergo, which being practically unimportant are not noticed. No inalterable thing exists. The thing is an abstraction, the name a symbol, for a compound of elements from whose changes we abstract. The reason we assign a single word to a whole compound is that we need to suggest all the constituent sensations at once. When, later, we come to remark the changeableness, we cannot at the same time hold fast to the idea of the thing's permanence, unless we have recourse to the conception of a thing-in-itself, or other such like absurdity. Sensations are not signs of things; but, on the contrary, a thing is a thought-symbol for a compound sensation of relative fixedness. Properly speaking the world is not composed of "things" as its elements, but of colors, tones, pressures, spaces, times, in short what we ordinarily call individual sensations.

The whole operation is a mere affair of economy. In the reproduction of facts, we begin with the more durable and familiar compounds, and supplement these later with the unusual by way of corrections. Thus, we speak of a perforated cylinder, of a cube with beveled edges, expressions involving contradictions, unless we accept the view here taken. All judgments are such amplifications and corrections of ideas already admitted.

3. In speaking of cause and effect we arbitrarily give relief to those elements to whose connection we have to attend in the reproduction of a fact in the respect in which it is important to us. There is no cause nor effect in nature; nature has but an individual existence; nature simply *is*. Recurrences of like cases in which A is always connected with B, that is, like results under like circumstances, that is again, the essence of the connection of cause and effect, exist but in the abstraction which we perform for the purpose of mentally reproducing the

facts. Let a fact become familiar, and we no longer require this putting into relief of its connecting marks, our attention is no longer attracted to the new and surprising, and we cease to speak of cause and effect. Heat is said to be the cause of the tension of steam; but when the phenomenon becomes familiar we think of the steam at once with the tension proper to its temperature. Acid is said to be the cause of the reddening of tincture of litmus; but later we think of the reddening as a property of the acid.

Hume first propounded the question, How can a thing A act on another thing B? Hume, in fact, rejects causality and recognises only a wonted succession in time. Kant correctly remarked that a *necessary* connection between A and B could not be disclosed by simple observation. He assumes an innate idea or category of the mind, a *Verstandesbegriff*, under which the cases of experience are subsumed. Schopenhauer, who adopts substantially the same position, distinguishes four forms of the "principle of sufficient reason"—the logical, physical, and mathematical form, and the law of motivation. But these forms differ only as regards the matter to which they are applied, which may belong either to outward or inward experience.

The natural and common-sense explanation is apparently this. The ideas of cause and effect originally sprang from an endeavor to reproduce facts in thought. At first, the connection of A and B, of C and D, of E and F, and so forth, is regarded as familiar. But after a greater range of experience is acquired and a connection between M and N is observed, it often turns out that we recognise M as *made up of* A, C, E, and N of B, D, F, the connection of which was before a *familiar* fact and accordingly possesses with us a higher authority. This explains why a person of experience regards a new event with different eyes than the novice. The new experience is illuminated by the mass of old experience. As a fact, then, there really does exist in the mind an "idea" under which fresh experiences are subsumed; but that idea has itself been developed from experience. The notion of the *necessity* of the causal connection is probably created by our voluntary movements in the world and by the changes which these indirectly produce, as Hume supposed but Schopenhauer contested. Much of the authority of the ideas of cause and effect is due to the fact that they are developed *instinctively* and involuntarily, and that we are distinctly sensible of having personally contributed nothing to their formation. We may, indeed, say, that our sense of causality is not acquired by the individual, but has been perfected in the development of the race. Cause and effect, therefore, are things of thought, having an economical office. It cannot be said *why* they arise. For it is precisely by the abstraction of uniformities that we know the question "why." . . .

4. In the details of science, its economical character is still more apparent. The so-called descriptive sciences must chiefly remain content with reconstructing individual facts. Where it is possible, the common features of many facts are once for all placed in relief. But in sciences that are more highly developed, rules for the reconstruction of great numbers of facts may be embodied in a *single* expression. Thus, instead of noting individual cases of light-refraction, we can mentally reconstruct all present and future cases, if we know that the incident ray, the refracted ray, and the perpendicular lie in the same plane and that $\sin \alpha / \sin \beta = n$. Here, instead of the numberless cases of refraction in different combinations of matter and under all different angles of incidence, we have simply to note the rule above stated and the values of n,—which is much easier. The economical purpose is here unmistakable. In nature there is no *law* of refraction, only different cases of refraction. The law of refraction is a concise compendious rule, devised by us for the mental reconstruction of a fact, and only for its reconstruction in part, that is, on its geometrical side. . . .

7. The function of science, as we take it, is to replace experience. Thus, on the one hand, science must remain in the province of experience, but, on the other, must hasten beyond it, constantly expecting confirmation, constantly expecting the reverse. Where neither confirmation nor refutation is possible, science is not concerned. Science acts and only acts in the domain of *uncompleted* experience. Exemplars of such branches of science are the theories of elasticity and of the conduction of heat, both of which ascribe to the smallest particles of matter only such properties as observation supplies in the study of the larger portions. The comparison of theory and experience may be farther and farther extended, as our means of observation increase in refinement.

Experience alone, without the ideas that are associated with it, would forever remain strange to us. Those ideas that hold good throughout the widest domains of research and that supplement the greatest amount of experience, are the *most scientific*. The principle of continuity, the use of which everywhere pervades modern inquiry, simply prescribes a mode of conception which conduces in the highest degree to the economy of thought.

8. If a long elastic rod be fastened in a vise, the rod may be made to execute slow vibrations. These are directly observable, can be seen, touched, and graphically recorded. If the rod be shortened, the vibrations will increase in rapidity and cannot be directly seen; the

rod will present to the sight a blurred image. This is a new phenomenon. But the sensation of touch is still like that of the previous case; we can still make the rod record its movements; and if we mentally retain the *conception* of vibrations, we can still anticipate the results of experiments. On further shortening the rod the sensation of touch is altered; the rod begins to sound; again a new phenomenon is presented. But the phenomena do not all change at once; only this or that phenomenon changes; consequently the accompanying notion of vibration, which is not confined to any single one, is still serviceable, still economical. Even when the sound has reached so high a pitch and the vibrations have become so small that the previous means of observation are not of avail, we still *advantageously* imagine the sounding rod to perform vibrations, and can predict the vibrations of the dark lines in the spectrum of the polarised light of a rod of glass. If on the rod being further shortened *all* the phenomena suddenly passed into *new* phenomena, the conception of vibration would no longer be serviceable because it would no longer afford us a means of supplementing the new experiences by the previous ones.

When we mentally add to these actions of a human being which we can perceive, sensations and ideas like our own which we cannot perceive, the object of the idea we so form is economical. The idea makes experience intelligible to us; it supplements and supplants experience. This idea is not regarded as a great scientific discovery, only because its formation is so natural that every child conceives it. Now, this is exactly what we do when we imagine a moving body which has just disappeared behind a pillar, or a comet at the moment invisible, as continuing its motion and retaining its previously observed properties. We do this that we may not be surprised by its reappearance. We fill out the gaps in experience by the idea that experience suggests.

9. Yet not all the prevalent scientific theories originated so naturally and artlessly. Thus, chemical, electrical, and optical phenomena are explained by atoms. But the mental artifice atom was not formed by the principle of continuity; on the contrary, it is a product especially devised for the purpose in view. Atoms cannot be perceived by the senses; like all substances, they are things of thought. Furthermore, the atoms are invested with properties that absolutely contradict the attributes hitherto observed in bodies. However well fitted atomic theories may be to reproduce certain groups of facts, the physical inquirer who has laid to heart Newton's rules will only admit those theories as *provisional* helps, and will strive to attain, in some more natural way, a satisfactory substitute.

The atomic theory plays a part in physics similar to that of certain auxiliary concepts in mathematics; it is a mathematical *model* for facilitating the mental reproduction of facts. Although we represent vibrations by the harmonic formula, the phenomena of cooling by exponentials, falls by squares of times, etc., no one will fancy that vibrations *in themselves* have anything to do with the circular functions, or the motion of falling bodies with squares. It has simply been observed that the relations between the quantities investigated were similar to certain relations obtaining between familiar mathematical functions, and these *more familiar* ideas are employed as an easy means of supplementing experience. Natural phenomena whose relations are not similar to those of functions with which we are familiar, are at present very difficult to reconstruct. But the progress of mathematics may facilitate the matter.

As mathematical helps of this kind, spaces of more than three dimensions may be used, as I have elsewhere shown. But it is not necessary to regard these, on this account, as anything more than mental artifices.

This is the case, too, with *all* hypotheses formed for the explanation of new phenomena. Our conceptions of electricity fit in at once with the electrical phenomena, and take almost spontaneously the familiar course, the moment we note that things take place as if attracting and repelling fluids moved on the surface of the conductors. But these mental expedients have nothing whatever to do with the phenomenon *itself*.

Mechanics and Physics*

1. Purely mechanical phenomena do not exist. The production of mutual accelerations in masses is, to all appearances, a purely dynamical phenomenon. But with these dynamical results are always associated thermal, magnetic, electrical, and chemical phenomena, and the former are always modified in proportion as the latter are asserted. On the other hand, thermal, magnetic, electrical, and chemical conditions also can produce motions. Purely mechanical phenomena, accordingly, are abstractions, made, either intentionally or from necessity, for facilitating our comprehension of things. The same thing is true of the other classes of physical phenomena. Every event belongs, in a strict sense, to all the departments of physics, the latter being separated only by an artificial classification, which is partly conventional, partly physiological, and partly historical.

2. The view that makes mechanics the basis of the remaining branches of physics, and explains all physical phenomena by mechanical ideas, is in our judgment a prejudice. Knowledge which is historically first, is not necessarily the foundation of all that is subsequently gained. As more and more facts are discovered and classified, entirely new ideas of general scope can be formed. We have no means of knowing, as yet, which of the physical phenomena go *deepest,* whether the mechanical phenomena are perhaps not the most superficial of all, or whether all do not go *equally deep.* Even in mechanics we no longer regard the oldest law, the law of the lever, as the foundation of all the other principles.

The mechanical theory of nature, is, undoubtedly, in an historical view, both intelligible and pardonable; and it may also, for a time, have been of much value. But, upon the whole, it is an artificial conception. Faithful adherence to the method that led the greatest investigators of nature, Galileo, Newton, Sadi Carnot, Faraday, and J. R. Mayer, to their great results, restricts physics to the expression of *actual facts,*

Ibid., pp. 495-498.

and forbids the construction of hypotheses behind the facts, where
nothing tangible and verifiable is found. If this is done, only the simple
connection of the motions of masses, of changes of temperature, of
changes in the values of the potential function, of chemical changes,
and so forth is to be ascertained, and nothing is to be imagined along
with these elements except the physical attributes or characteristics
directly or indirectly given by observation.

  This idea was elsewhere developed by the author with respect
to the phenomena of heat, and indicated, in the same place, with
respect to electricity. All hypotheses of fluids or media are eliminated
from the theory of electricity as entirely superfluous, when we reflect
that electrical conditions are all given by the values of the potential
function V and the dielectric constants. If we assume the differences
of the values of V to be measured (on the electrometer) by the forces,
and regard V and not the quantity of electricity Q as the primary
notion, or measurable physical attribute, we shall have, for any simple
insulator, for our quantity of electricity

$$Q = \frac{-1}{4\pi} \int \left(\frac{d^2 V}{dx^2} + \frac{d^2 V}{dy^2} + \frac{d^2 V}{dz^2} \right) dv,$$

(where x, y, z denote the coordinates and dv the element of volume),
and for our potential

$$W = \frac{-1}{8\pi} \int V \left(\frac{d^2 V}{dx^2} + \frac{d^2 V}{dy^2} + \frac{d^2 V}{dz^2} \right) dv.$$

Here Q and W appear as derived notions, in which no conception of
fluid or medium is contained. If we work over in a similar manner the
entire domain of physics, we shall restrict ourselves wholly to the
quantitative conceptual expression of actual facts. All superfluous and
futile notions are eliminated, and the imaginary problems to which
they have given rise forestalled.

  The removal of notions whose foundations are historical, conventional, or accidental, can best be furthered by a comparison of the
conceptions obtaining in the different departments, and by finding
for the conceptions of every department the corresponding conceptions of others. We discover, thus, that temperatures and potential
functions correspond to the velocities of mass-motions. A single
velocity-value, a single temperature-value, or a single value of potential
function, never changes *alone*. But whilst in the case of velocities and
potential functions, so far as we yet know, only differences come into
consideration, the significance of temperature is not only contained in

its difference with respect to other temperatures. Thermal capacities correspond to masses, the potential of an electric charge to quantity of heat, quantity of electricity to entropy, and so on. The pursuit of such resemblances and differences lays the foundation of a *comparative physics*, which shall ultimately render possible the concise expression of extensive groups of facts, without *arbitrary* additions. We shall then possess a homogeneous physics, unmingled with artificial atomic theories.

It will also be perceived, that a real *economy* of scientific thought cannot be attained by mechanical hypotheses. Even if an hypothesis were fully competent to reproduce a given department of natural phenomena, say, the phenomena of heat, we should, by accepting it, only substitute for the actual relations between the mechanical and thermal processes, the hypothesis. The real fundamental facts are replaced by an equally large number of hypotheses, which is certainly no gain. Once an hypothesis has facilitated, as best it can, our view of new facts, by the substitution of more familiar ideas, its powers are exhausted. We err when we expect more enlightenment from an hypothesis than from the facts themselves.

Mechanics and Physiology*

1. All science has its origin in the needs of life. However minutely it may be subdivided by particular vocations or by the restricted tempers and capacities of those who foster it, each branch can attain its full and best development only by a living connection with *the whole*. Through such a union alone can it approach its true maturity, and be insured against lop-sided and monstrous growths.

The division of labor, the restriction of individual inquirers to limited provinces, the investigation of those provinces as a life-work, are the fundamental conditions of a fruitful development of science. Only by such specialisation and restriction of work can the economical instruments of thought requisite for the mastery of a special field be perfected. But just here lies a danger—the danger of our overestimating the instruments, with which we are so constantly employed, or even of regarding them as the objective point of science.

2. Now, such a state of affairs has, in our opinion, actually been produced by the disproportionate formal development of physics. The majority of natural inquirers ascribe to the intellectual implements of physics, to the concepts mass, force, atom, and so forth, whose sole office is to revive economically arranged experiences, a reality beyond and independent of thought. Not only so, but it has even been held that these forces and masses are the real objects of inquiry, and, if once they were fully explored, all the rest would follow from the equilibrium and motion of these masses. A person who knew the world only through the theatre, if brought behind the scenes and permitted to view the mechanism of the stage's action, might possibly believe that the real world also was in need of a machine-room, and that if this were once thoroughly explored, we should know all. Similarly, we, too, should beware lest the *intellectual* machinery, employed in the representation of the world on *the stage of thought*, be regarded as the basis of the real world.

*Ibid., pp. 504-507.

398

3. A philosophy is involved in any correct view of the relations
of special knowledge to the great body of knowledge at large,—a
philosophy that must be demanded of every special investigator. The
lack of it is asserted in the formulation of imaginary problems, in the
very enunciation of which, whether regarded as soluble or insoluble,
flagrant absurdity is involved. Such an overestimation of physics, in contrast to physiology, such a mistaken conception of the true
relations of the two sciences, is displayed in the inquiry whether it is
possible to *explain* feelings by the motions of atoms?

Let us seek the conditions that could have impelled the mind
to formulate so curious a question. We find in the first place that
greater *confidence* is placed in our experiences concerning relations of
time and space; that we attribute to them a more objective, a more
real character than to our experiences of colors, sounds, temperatures,
and so forth. Yet, if we investigate the matter accurately, we must
surely admit that our sensations of time and space are just as much
sensations as are our sensations of colors, sounds, and odors, only that
in our knowledge of the former we are surer and clearer than in that
of the latter. Space and time are well-ordered systems of sets of sensations. The quantities stated in mechanical equations are simply ordinal
symbols, representing those members of these sets that are to be mentally isolated and emphasised. The equations express the form of
interdependence of these ordinal symbols.

A body is a relatively constant sum of touch and sight sensations
associated with the same space and time sensations. Mechanical principles, like that, for instance, of the mutually induced accelerations of
two masses, give, either directly or indirectly, only some combination
of touch, sight, light, and time sensations. They possess intelligible
meaning only by virtue of the sensations they involve, the contents of
which may of course be very complicated.

It would be equivalent, accordingly, to explaining the more
simple and immediate by the more complicated and remote, if we
were to attempt to derive sensations from the motions of masses, wholly
aside from the consideration that the notions of mechanics are economical implements or expedients perfected to represent *mechanical* and
not physiological or *psychological* facts. If the *means* and *aims* of
research were properly distinguished, and our expositions were restricted to the presentation of *actual facts*, false problems of this kind
could not arise.

4. All physical knowledge can only mentally represent and anticipate compounds of those elements we call sensations. It is concerned
with the connection of these elements. Such an element, say the heat

of a body A, is connected, not only with other elements, say with such whose aggregate makes up the flame B, but also with the aggregate of certain elements of our body, say with the aggregate of the elements of a nerve N. As simple object and element N is not essentially, but only conventionally, different from A and B. The connection of A and B is a problem of *physics*, that of A and N a problem of *physiology*. Neither is alone existent; both exist at once. Only provisionally can we neglect either. Processes, thus, that in appearance are purely mechanical, are, in addition to their evident mechanical features, always physiological, and, consequently, also electrical, chemical, and so forth. The science of mechanics does not comprise the foundations, no, nor even a part of the world, but only an *aspect* of it.

BRADLEY

FRANCIS HERBERT BRADLEY (1846-1924) was born in London, the son of a clergyman and the younger brother of the literary critic A. C. Bradley. After studying as an undergraduate at University College, Oxford, he was elected to a fellowship at Merton College in 1870, a position he continued to hold until his death; it carried with it no teaching or lecturing obligations and left him complete freedom to devote his life to writing. Partly, perhaps, because of a kidney disease which afflicted him in 1871 and from which he never fully recovered, Bradley was always something of a recluse; his personal contacts were few, and when not in Oxford he tended to spend much of his time abroad. In political outlook he was conservative, contemptuous of egalitarian and pacifist sentiments and hostile to Gladstonian Liberalism: there was, however, nothing illiberal in his attitude to the free expression of thought and opinion, and he opposed censorship in the field of literature and the arts.

Despite the brilliance and edge of Bradley's literary style, the thought he employs it to expound is often hard to follow. Unlike many of his British contemporaries, he had read and admired Hegel; and although the extent of Hegel's influence upon his mature development has been exaggerated, a reader trying to unravel the abstract complexities of some of Bradley's arguments may at times be reminded of the dialectical convolutions characteristic of the German thinker. Yet behind such obscurities there nonetheless lurked a mind of great penetration and power, adept at discerning problems to which other thinkers had been blind.

Bradley was from the beginning an opponent of utilitarian and empiricist trends in English philosophy, and particularly of their chief nineteenth-century representative, John Stuart Mill. Thus in his first book, *Ethical Studies* (1876), he took as his main target the utilitarian theory of morality, together with the empiricist conception of the mind, which he conceived to be an essential component of that theory. And in his subsequent works—*The Principles of Logic* (1883), *Appearance and Reality* (1893) and *Essays in Truth and Reality* (1914)—the area of attack was widened to cover empiricist doctrines of logic and knowledge. It is clear, however, that, as Bradley proceeds, his intention is not confined to undermining the presuppositions of a particular philosophical tradition; he wishes also to put in question the categories which underlie what might be called the everyday or "commonsense" conception of the world.

There are already clear intimations of this in *The Principles of Logic*. Throughout that book Bradley was certainly in part concerned to demolish various fundamental empiricist dogmas. Thus he begins by claiming that empiricists have fatally confused the provinces of logic and psychology: "In England we have lived too long in the psychological attitude." Psychological questions concerning the origin and association of ideas must, in other words, be distinguished from problems concerning the nature of concepts as these function in thought and judgment; it is the use made of ideas to refer symbolically to objects, the dimension of meaning that belongs to them as signs that point beyond themselves, which is of importance to the logician, and not their character as self-sufficient psychical events. Such points led Bradley to draw certain conclusions regarding the nature of thought, one being that our ordinary categorical judgments, and (in particular) singular statements of fact, do not possess the clearcut unambiguous reference to the world we normally ascribe to them. Owing to the generality that necessarily characterizes the symbolism we employ, a gap seems to open between the descriptions by which we seek to capture particular facts and those facts themselves; in the end, Bradley goes on to propose, we must give up the conception of the isolated particular and instead understand every judgment as making an implicit reference to reality as a whole. A brief section of one of the discussions on this theme is presented in the second of the selections from Bradley's *Logic* reprinted here.

Unlike Hegel, Bradley thought that logical matters could be examined without necessarily bringing in metaphysics. Even so, many of the suggestions adumbrated in *The Principles of Logic* reappear in his avowedly metaphysical work, *Appearance and Reality*. In the former book it is argued, from a number of different directions, that the generality and artificiality of thought—the abstractions with which it operates, the divisions it seeks to impose—put in doubt the notion that it can ever be finally adequate to the reality it attempts to identify and portray: "it is a very common and ruinous superstition to suppose that . . . whenever we distinguish, we have at once to do with divisible existence."* In *Appearance and Reality* these ideas are taken up and developed in the direction of showing that the world cannot be, ultimately, what our everyday and scientific modes of characterizing it would suggest. We are accustomed, for instance, to approach experience through the notion of a thing and its qualities—a notion that underlies the subject-predicate form in which our judgments tend to be framed; again, we habitually think of things and qualities as standing in determinate relations to one another. In two condensed chapters, comprised in the first pair of our selections from *Appearance and Reality*, Bradley subjects these ideas to a destructive analysis designed to exhibit their philosophical inadequacy.† Subsequently he goes on to condemn a host of other fundamental commonsense categories: time, space, causation, the self. Each is similarly infected with confusion and incoherence; each gives "appearance, and not truth."

It might be supposed that, in rejecting ordinary thought with its "ma-chinery of terms and relations," Bradley had precluded the possibility of providing any positive account of reality as truly understood. As, however, the concluding selections show, this was not his view; the second, and by far the longer, part of the book is largely concerned with explicating what he termed "the Absolute," this being regarded as a harmonious, unitary, supra-relational system wherein all appearances were included and reconciled, and the external divisions introduced by discursive thinking overcome. Even thought itself, it is argued, would be absorbed within this all-embracing whole, reaching a consummation that could at the same time be said to involve its extinction. Whatever difficulties may attach to Bradley's account (and they are many) it seems at least clear that the view, associated with Hegel, that thought alone constitutes the inner essence of reality is not one properly attributable to the English philosopher.

The Principles of Logic, Second Edition, Vol. I, p. 95.

†Bradley's treatment of relations, of which the chapters reproduced in this volume are only a sample, was extremely complex and of great historical importance: Russell's doctrine of logical atomism, for instance, was developed in explicit opposition to it. For a fuller understanding of its nature, Appendix B to the Second Edition of *Appearance and Reality* is worth consulting, together with the unfinished paper on relations included in the posthumously published *Collected Essays*, Vol. II.

Logic and Psychology*

1. It is impossible, before we have studied Logic, to know at what point our study should begin. And, after we have studied it, our uncertainty may remain. In the absence of any accepted order I shall offer no apology for beginning with Judgment. If we incur the reproach of starting in the middle, we may at least hope to touch the centre of the subject. . . .

Judgment presents problems of a serious nature to both psychology and metaphysics. Its relation to other psychical phenomena, their entangled development from the primary basis of soul-life, and the implication of the volitional with the intellectual side of our nature on the one hand, and on the other hand the difference of subject and object, and the question as to the existence of any mental activity, may be indicated as we pass. But it will be our object, so far as is possible, to avoid these problems. We do not mainly want to ask, How does judgment stand to other psychical states, and in ultimate reality what must be said of it. Our desire is to take it, so far as we can, as a given mental function; to discover the general character which it bears, and further to fix the more special sense in which we are to use it.

2. I shall pass to the latter task at once. Judgment, in the strict sense, does not exist where there exists no knowledge of truth and falsehood; and, since truth and falsehood depend on the relation of our ideas to reality, you can not have judgment proper without ideas. And perhaps thus much is obvious. But the point I am going on to, is not so obvious. Not only are we unable to judge before we use ideas, but, strictly speaking, we can not judge till we use them *as* ideas. We must have become aware that they are not realities, that they are *mere* ideas, signs of an existence other than themselves. Ideas are not ideas until they are symbols, and, before we use symbols, we can not judge.

*From Chap. 1, Vol. I, of *The Principles of Logic* (London, 1922), pp. 1-10. By permission of the Clarendon Press, Oxford.

3. We are used to the saying, "This is nothing real, it is a mere idea." And we reply that an idea, within my head, and as a state of my mind, is as stubborn a fact as any outward object. The answer is well-nigh as familiar as the saying, and my complaint is that in the end it grows much too familiar. In England at all events we have lived too long in the psychological attitude. We take it for granted and as a matter of course that, like sensations and emotions, ideas are phenomena. And, considering these phenomena as psychical facts, we have tried (with what success I will not ask) to distinguish between ideas and sensations. But, intent on this, we have as good as forgotten the way in which logic uses ideas. We have not seen that in judgment no fact ever *is* just that which it *means*, or can mean what it is; and we have not learnt that, wherever we have truth or falsehood, it is the signification we use, and not the existence. We never assert the fact in our heads, but something else which that fact stands for. And if an idea *were* treated as a psychical reality, if it were taken by itself as an actual phenomenon, then it would not represent either truth or falsehood. When we use it in judgment, it must be referred away from itself. If it is not the idea *of* some existence, then, despite its own emphatic actuality, its content remains but "a mere idea." It is a something which, in relation to the reality we mean, is nothing at all.

4. For logical purposes ideas are symbols, and they are nothing but symbols. And, at the risk of common-place, before I go on, I must try to say what a symbol is.

In all that is we can distinguish two sides, (i) existence and (ii) content. In other words we perceive both *that* it is and *what* it is. But in anything that is a symbol we have also a third side, its significa-tion, or that which it *means*. We need not dwell on the two first aspects, for we are not concerned with the metaphysical problems which they involve. For a fact to exist, we shall agree, it must be something. It is not real unless it has a character which is different or distinguishable from that of other facts. And this, which makes it what it is, we call its content. We may take as an instance any common perception. The complex of qualities and relations it contains, makes up its content, or that which it is; and, while recognizing this, we recognize also, and in addition, *that* it is. Every kind of fact must possess these two sides of existence and content, and we propose to say no more about them here.

But there is a class of facts which possess another and additional third side. They have a meaning; and by a sign we understand any sort of fact which is used with a meaning. The meaning may be part of the original content, or it may have been discovered and even added

by a further extension. Still this makes no difference. Take anything
which can stand for anything else, and you have a sign. Besides its own
private existence and content, it has this third aspect. Thus every
flower exists and has its own qualities, but not all have a meaning.
Some signify nothing, while others stand generally for the kind which
they represent, while others again go on to remind us of hope or love.
But the flower can never itself *be* what it *means*.

A symbol is a fact which stands for something else, and by this,
we may say, it both loses and gains, is degraded and exalted. In its use
as a symbol it forgoes individuality, and self-existence. It is not the
main point that *this* rose or forget-me-not, and none other, has been
chosen. We give it, or we take it, for the sake of its meaning; and that
may prove true or false long after the flower has perished. The word
dies as it is spoken, but the particular sound of the mere pulsa-
tion was nothing to our minds. Its existence was lost in the speech
and the significance. The paper and the ink are facts unique and
with definite qualities. They are the same in all points with none other
in the world. But, in reading, we apprehend not paper or ink, but what
they represent; and, so long as only they stand for this, their private
existence is a matter of indifference. A fact taken as a symbol ceases
so far to be fact. It no longer can be said to exist for its own sake, its
individuality is lost in its universal meaning. It is no more a substantive,
but becomes the adjective that holds of another. But, on the other
hand, the change is not all loss. By merging its own quality in a wider
meaning, it can pass beyond itself and stand for others. It gains admission and influence in a world which it otherwise could not enter.
The paper and ink cut the throats of men, and the sound of a breath
may shake the world.

We may state the sum briefly. A sign is any fact that has a meaning,
and meaning consists of a part of the content (original or acquired),
cut off, fixed by the mind, and considered apart from the existence
of the sign. . . .[1]

6. We might say that, in the end, there are no signs save ideas,
but what I here wish to insist on, is that, for logic at least, all ideas are
signs. Each we know exists as a psychical fact, and with particular
qualities and relations. It has its speciality as an event in my mind. It

---

1. It would not be correct to add, "and referred away to another real subject";
for where we think without judging, and where we deny, that description would
not be applicable. Nor is it the same thing to have an idea, and to judge it possible.
To think of a chimæra is to think of it as real, but not to judge it even possible. And
it is not until we have found that all meaning must be adjectival, that with every
idea we have even the suggestion of a real subject other than itself.

is a hard individual, so unique that it not only differs from all others, but even from itself at subsequent moments. And this character it must bear when confined to the two aspects of existence and content. But just so long as, and because, it keeps to this character, it is for logic no idea at all. It becomes one first when it begins to exist for the sake of its meaning. And its meaning, we may repeat, is a part of the content, used without regard to the rest, or the existence. I have the "idea" of a horse, and that is a fact in my mind, existing in relation with the congeries of sensations and emotions and feelings, which make my momentary state. It has again particular traits of its own, which may be difficult to seize, but which, we are bound to suppose, are present. It is doubtless unique, the same with no other, nor yet with itself, but alone in the world of its fleeting moment. But, for logic, and in a matter of truth and falsehood, the case is quite changed. The "idea" has here become an universal, since everything else is subordinate to the meaning. That connection of attributes we recognize as horse, is one part of the content of the unique horse-image, and this fragmentary part of the psychical event is all that in logic we know of or care for. Using this we treat the rest as husk and dross, which matters nothing to us, and makes no difference to the rest. The "idea," if that is the psychical state, is in logic a symbol. But it is better to say, the idea *is* the meaning, for existence and unessential content are wholly discarded. The idea, in the sense of mental image, is a sign of the idea in the sense of meaning.

7. These two senses of idea, as the symbol and the symbolized, the image and its meaning, are of course known to all of us. But the reason why I dwell on this obvious distinction, is that in much of our thinking it is systematically disregarded. "How can any one," we are asked, "be so foolish as to think that ideas are universal, when every single idea can be seen to be particular, or talk of an idea which remains the same, when the actual idea at each moment varies, and we have in fact not one identical but many similars?" But how can any one, we feel tempted to reply, suppose that these obvious objections are unknown to us? When I talk of an idea which is the same amid change, I do not speak of that psychical event which is in ceaseless flux, but of one portion of the content which the mind has fixed, and which is not in any sense an event in time. I am talking of the meaning, not the series of symbols, the gold, so to speak, not the fleeting series of transitory notes. The belief in universal ideas does not involve the conviction that abstractions exist, even as facts in my head. The mental event is unique and particular, but the meaning in its use is cut off from the existence, and from the rest of the fluctuating content. It loses its

relation to the particular symbol; it stands as an adjective, to be referred to some subject, but indifferent in itself to every special subject.

The ambiguity of "idea" may be exhibited thus. *Thesis,* On the one hand no possible idea can be that which it means. *Antithesis,* On the other hand no idea is anything but just what it means. In the thesis the idea is the psychical image; in the antithesis the idea is the logical signification. In the first it is the whole sign, but in the second it is nothing but the symbolized. In the sequel I intend to use idea mainly in the sense of *meaning.*[2]

8. For logical purposes the psychological distinction of idea and sensation may be said to be irrelevant, while the distinction of idea and fact is vital. The image, or psychological idea, is for logic nothing but a sensible reality. It is on a level with the mere sensations of the senses. For both are facts and neither is a meaning. Neither is cut from a mutilated presentation, and fixed as a connection. Neither is indifferent to its place in the stream of psychical events, its time and relations to the presented congeries. Neither is an adjective to be referred from its existence, to live on strange soils, under other skies and through changing seasons. The lives of both are so entangled with their environment, so one with their setting of sensuous particulars, that their character is destroyed if but one thread is broken. Fleeting and self-destructive as is their very endurance, wholly delusive their supposed individuality, misleading and deceptive their claim to reality, yet in some sense and somehow they *are.* They have existence; they are not thought but given. But an idea, if we use idea of the meaning, is neither given nor presented but is taken. It can not as such exist. It can not ever be an event, with a place in the series of time or space. It can be a fact no more inside our heads than it can outside them. And, if you take this mere idea by itself, it is an adjective divorced, a parasite cut loose, a spirit without a body seeking rest in another, an abstraction from the concrete, a mere possibility which by itself *is* nothing.

2. There are psychological difficulties as to universal ideas, and we feel them more, the more abstract the ideas become. The existence and the amount, of the particular imagery or sensuous environment, give rise to questions. But these questions need not be considered here for they have no logical importance whatever. I assume, after Berkeley, that the mental fact contains always an irrelevant sensuous setting, however hard it may be to bring this always to consciousness. But I must repeat that this is not a vital question. It is a mistake in principle to try to defend the reality of universals by an attempt to show them as psychical events existing in one moment. For if the universal we use in logic had actual existence as a fact in my mind, at all events I could not *use* it as that fact. You must at any rate abstract from the existence and external relations, and how much further the abstraction is to go seems hardly an important or vital issue.

9. These paradoxical shadows and ghosts of fact are the ideas we spoke of, when we said, Without ideas no judgment; and, before we proceed, we may try to show briefly that in predication we do not *use* the mental fact, but only the meaning. The full evidence for this truth must however be sought in the whole of what follows.

(i) In the first place it is clear that the idea, which we use as the predicate of a judgment, is not my mental state as such. "The whale is a mammal" does not qualify real whales by my mammal-image. For that belongs to me, and is an event in my history; and, unless I am Jonah, it can not enter into an actual whale. We need not dwell on this point, for the absurdity is patent. If I am asked, Have you got the idea of a sea-serpent? I answer, Yes. And again, if I am asked, But do you believe in it, Is there a sea-serpent? I understand the difference. The enquiry is not made about my psychical fact. No one wishes to know if *that* exists outside of my head; and still less to know if it really exists inside. For the latter is assumed, and we can not doubt it. In short the contention that in judgment the idea is my own state as such, would be simply preposterous.

(ii) But is it possible, secondly, that the idea should be the image, not indeed as my private psychical event, but still as regards the whole content of that image? We have a mental fact, the idea of mammal. Admit first that, as it exists and inhabits my world, we do not predicate it. Is there another possibility? The idea perhaps might be used apart from its own existence, and in abstraction from its relations to my psychical phenomena, and yet it might keep, without any deduction, its own internal content. The "mammal" in my head is, we know, not bare mammal, but is clothed with particulars and qualified by characters other than mammality; and these may vary with the various appearances of the image. And we may ask, Is this *whole* image used in judgment? Is *this* the meaning? But the answer must be negative.

We have ideas of redness, of a foul smell, of a horse, and of death; and, as we call them up more or less distinctly, there is a kind of redness, a sort of offensiveness, some image of a horse, and some appearance of mortality, which rises before us. And should we be asked, Are roses red? Has coal gas a foul smell? Is that white beast a horse? Is it true that he is dead? we should answer, Yes, our ideas are all true, and are attributed to the reality. But the idea of redness may have been that of a lobster, of a smell that of castor-oil, the imaged horse may have been a black horse, and death perhaps a withered flower. And *these* ideas are *not* true, nor did we apply them. What we really applied was that part of their content which our minds had fixed as the general meaning.

It may be desirable (as in various senses various writers have told us) that the predicate should be determinate, but in practice this need can not always be satisfied. I may surely judge that a berry is poisonous, though in what way I know not, and though "poisonous" implies some traits which I do not attribute to *this* poison. I surely may believe that AB is bad, though I do not know his vices, and have images which are probably quite inapplicable. I may be sure that a book is bound in leather or in cloth, though the sort of leather or cloth I must imagine I can not say exists. The details I have never known, or at any rate, have forgotten them. But of the universal meaning I am absolutely sure, and it is this which I predicate.

The extreme importance of these obvious distinctions must excuse the inordinate space I allot to them. Our whole theory of judgment will support and exemplify them; but I will add yet a few more trivial illustrations. In denying that iron is yellow, do I say that it is not yellow like gold, or topaze, or do I say that it is not any kind of yellow? When I assert, "It is a man or a woman or a child," am I reasonably answered by, "There are other possibilities. It may be an Indian or a girl"? When I ask, Is he ill? do I naturally look for "Oh no, he has cholera"? Is the effect of, "If he has left me then I am undone," removed by "Be happy, it was by the coach that he deserted you"?

The idea in judgment is the universal meaning; it is not ever the occasional imagery, and still less can it be the whole psychical event.

Judgment and Fact*

... A judgment, we assume naturally, says something about some fact or reality. If we asserted or denied about anything else, our judgment would seem to be a frivolous pretence. We not only must say something, but it must also be about something actual that we say it. For consider; a judgment must be true or false, and its truth or falsehood cannot lie in itself. They involve a reference to a something beyond. And this, about which or of which we judge, if it is not fact, what else can it be? ...

4. The contrast and comparison of reality and truth no doubt involve very ultimate principles. To enquire what is fact, is to enter at once on a journey into metaphysics, the end of which might not soon be attained. For our present purpose we must answer the question from a level not much above that of common sense. And the account which represents the ordinary view, and in which perhaps we may most of us agree, is something of this sort.

The real is that which is known in presentation or intuitive knowledge. It is what we encounter in feeling or perception. Again it is that which appears in the series of events that occur in space and time. It is that once more which resists our wills: a thing is real, if it exercises any kind of force or compulsion, or exhibits necessity. It is briefly what acts and maintains itself in existence. And this last feature seems connected with former ones. We know of no action, unless it shows itself by altering the series of either space or time, or both together; and again perhaps there is nothing which appears unless it acts. But the simplest account, in which the others possibly are all summed up, is given in the words, The real is self-existent. And we may put this otherwise by saying, The real is what is individual.

It is the business of metaphysics to subject these ideas to a systematic examination. We must content ourselves here with taking them on

*Ibid., Chap. 2, pp. 40-49.

trust, and will pause merely to point out a common misunderstanding. It is a mistake to suppose that "The real is individual" means either that the real is abstractly simple, or is merely particular. Internal diversity does not exclude individuality, and still less is a thing made self-existent by standing in a relation of exclusion to others. Metaphysics can prove that, in this sense, the particular is furthest removed from self-existence. . . .

5. Such, we may say, are some of the points which constitute reality. And truth has not one of them. It exists, as such, in the world of ideas. And ideas, we have seen, are merely symbols. They are general and adjectival, not substantive and individual. Their essence lies within their meaning and beyond their existence. The idea is the fact with its existence diregarded, and its content mutilated. It is but a portion of the actual content cut off from its reality, and used with a reference to something else. No idea can be real.

If judgment is the synthesis of two ideas, then truth consists in the junction of unreals. When I say, Gold is yellow, then certainly some fact is present to my mind. But universal gold and universal yellowness are not realities, and, on the other hand, what *images* of yellow and gold I actually possess, though as psychical facts they have real existence, are unfortunately not the facts about which I desired to say anything. We have seen (Chap I.) that I do *not* mean, This image of gold is in my mind joined psychically with this other image of yellow. I mean that, quite apart from my mental facts, gold in general has a certain kind of colour. I strip away certain parts from the mental facts, and, combining these adjectival remnants, I call the synthesis truth.

But reality is not a connection of adjectives, nor can it so be represented. Its essence is to be substantial and individual. But can we reach self-existence and individual character by manipulating adjectives and putting universals together? If not, the fact is not given *directly* in any truth whatsoever. It can never be stated categorically. And yet, because adjectives depend upon substantives, the substantive is implied. Truth will then refer to fact *indirectly*. The adjectives of truth presuppose a reality, and in this sense all judgment will rest on a supposal. It is all hypothetical: itself will confess that what directly it deals with, is unreal.

6. More ordinary considerations might perhaps have led us to anticipate this result. The common-sense view of facts outside us passing over into the form of truth within us, or copying themselves in a faithful mirror, is shaken and perplexed by the simplest enquiries.

What fact is asserted in negative judgments? Has every negation I choose to invent a real counterpart in the world of things? Does *any* logical negation, as such, correspond to fact? Consider again hypothetical judgments. *If* something is, *then* something else follows, but should neither exist, would the statement be false? It seems just as true without facts as with them, and, if so, what fact can it possibly assert? The disjunctive judgment will again perplex us. "A is *b* or *c*" must be true or false, but how in the world can a *fact* exist as that strange ambiguity "*b* or *c?*" We shall hardly find the flesh and blood alternative which answers to our "or."

If we think these puzzles too technical or sought out, let us take more obvious ones. Have the past and the future we talk of so freely any real existence? Or let us try a mere ordinary categorical affirmative judgment, "Animals are mortal." This seems at first to keep close to reality: the junction of facts seems quite the same as the junction of ideas. But the experience we have gained may warn us that, if ideas are adjectives, this can not be the case. If we are unconvinced, let us go on to examine. "Animals" seems perhaps to answer to a fact, since all the animals who exist are real. But in "Animals are mortal," is it only the animals now existing that we speak of? Do we not mean to say that the animal born hereafter will certainly die? The complete collection of real things is of course the same fact as the real things themselves, but a difficulty arises as to future individuals. And, apart from that, we scarcely in general have in our minds a complete collection. We *mean*, "Whatever is an animal will die," but that is the same as *If* anything is an animal *then* it is mortal. The assertion really is about mere hypothesis; it is not about fact.

In universal judgments we may sometimes understand that the synthesis of adjectives, which the judgment expresses, is really found in actual existence. But the judgment does not say this. It is merely a private supposition of our own. It arises partly from the nature of the case, and partly again from our bad logical tradition. The fact that most adjectives we conjoin in judgment can be taken as the adjectives of existing things, leads us naturally to expect that this will always be the case. And, in the second place, a constant ambiguity arises from the use of "all" in the subject. We write the universal in the form "All animals," and then take it to mean each actual animal, or the real sum of existing animals. But this would be no more an universal judgment than "A B and C, are severally mortal." And we *mean* nothing like this. In saying "All animals," if we think of a collection, we never for a moment imagine it complete; we mean also "Whatever besides may be animal must be mortal too." In universal judgments we never mean "all." What we mean is "any," and "whatever," and "whenever." But these involve "if."

We may see this most easily by a simple observation. If actual existence were really asserted, the judgment would be false if the existence failed. And this is not the case. It would be a hazardous assertion that, supposing all animal life had ceased, mortality would at once be predicated falsely, and, with the re-appearance of animal existence, would again become true. But cases exist where no doubt is possible. "All persons found trespassing on this ground will be prosecuted," is too often a prophecy, as well as a promise. But it is not meant to foretell, and, though no one trespasses, the statement may be true. "All triangles have their angles equal to two right angles" would hardly be false if there were no triangles. And, if this seems strange, take the case of a chiliagon. Would statements about chiliagons cease to be true, if no one at the moment were thinking of a chiliagon? We can hardly say that, and yet where would any chiliagons exist? There surely must be scientific propositions, which unite ideas not demonstrable at the moment in actual existence. But can we maintain that, if the sciences which produce these became non-existent, these judgments would have *ipso facto* become false, as well as unreal?

The universal judgment is thus always hypothetical. It says *"Given* one thing you will *then* have another," and it says no more. No truth can state fact.

7. This result is however not easy to put up with. For, if the truth is such, then all truths, it would seem, are no better than false. We can not so give up the categorical judgment, for, if that is lost, then everything fails. Let us make a search and keep to this question, Is there nowhere to be found a categorical judgment? And it seems we can find one. Universal judgments were merely hypothetical, because they stated, not individual substantives, but connections of adjectives. But in singular judgments the case is otherwise. Where the subject, of which you affirm categorically, is one individual, or a set of individuals, your truth expresses fact. There is here no mere adjective and no hypothesis.

These judgments are divisible into three great classes. And the distinction will hereafter be of great importance. (i) We have first those judgments which make an assertion about that which I now perceive, or feel, or about some portion of it. "I have a toothache," "There is a wolf," "That bough is broken." In these we simply analyze the given, and may therefore call them by the name of *Analytic judgments of sense.*[3] Then (ii) we have *Synthetic judgments of sense,* which state either some fact of time or space, or again some quality of the matter given, which I do not here and now directly perceive. "This road leads to London," "Yesterday it rained," "Tomorrow there will be full moon." They are synthetic because they extend the given through an ideal construction, and they all, as we shall see, involve an inference. The third class (iii), on the other hand, have to do with a reality which is never a sensible event in time. "God is a spirit," "The soul is a substance." We may think what we like of the validity of these judgments, and may or may not decline to recognize them in metaphysics. But in logic they certainly must have a place.

8. But, if judgment is the union of two ideas, we have not so escaped. And this is a point we should clearly recognize. Ideas are universal, and, no matter what it is that we try to say and dimly mean, what we really express and succeed in asserting, is nothing individual. For take the analytic judgment of sense. The fact given us is singular, it is quite unique; but our terms are all general, and state a truth which may apply as well to many other cases. In "I have a toothache" both the I and the toothache are mere generalities. The *actual* toothache is not any other toothache, and the *actual* I is myself as having this very toothache. But the truth I assert has been and will be true of all other toothaches of my altering self. Nay "I have a toothache," is as true of another's toothache as of my own, and may be met by the assertion, "Not so but *I* have one." It is in vain that we add to the original assertion "this," "here," and "now," for they are all universals. They are symbols whose meaning extends to and covers innumerable instances.

Thus the judgment will be true of any case whatsoever of a certain sort; but, if so, it can not be true of the reality; for that is unique, and is a fact, not a sort. "That bough is broken," but so are many others, and we do not say which. "This road leads to London" may be said just as well of a hundred others roads. "To-morrow it will be full moon," does not tell us what to-morrow. Hereafter it will constantly be true that, on the day after this day, there will be a full moon. And so, failing in all cases to state the actual fact, we state something else instead. What is true of all does not express this one. The assertion sticks for ever in the adjectives; it does not reach the substantive. And adjectives unsupported float in the air: their junction with reality is supposed and

3. These analytic and synthetic judgments must not for one moment be confounded with Kant's. Every possible judgment, we shall see hereafter, is both analytic and synthetic. Most, if not all, judgments of sense are synthetic in the sense of transcending the given.

not asserted. So long as judgments are confined to ideas, their reference to fact is a mere implication. It is presupposed outside the
assertion, which is not strictly true until we qualify it by a suppressed
condition. As it stands, it both fails as a singular proposition, and is
false if you take it as a strict universal. . . .

Substantive and Adjective*

...We find the world's contents grouped into things and their qualities. The substantive and adjective is a time-honoured distinction and arrangement of facts, with a view to understand them and to arrive at reality. I must briefly point out the failure of this method, if regarded as a serious attempt at theory.

We may take the familiar instance of a lump of sugar. This is a thing, and it has properties, adjectives which qualify it. It is, for example, white, and hard, and sweet. The sugar, we say, *is* all that; but what the *is* can really mean seems doubtful. A thing is not any one of its qualities, if you take that quality by itself; if "sweet" were the same as "simply sweet", the thing would clearly be not sweet. And again, in so far as sugar is sweet it is not white or hard; for these properties are all distinct. Nor, again, can the thing be all its properties, if you take them each severally. Sugar is obviously not mere whiteness, mere hardness, and mere sweetness; for its reality lies somehow in its unity. But if, on the other hand, we inquire what there can be in the thing beside its several qualities, we are baffled once more. We can discover no real unity existing outside these qualities, or, again, existing within them.

But it is our emphasis, perhaps, on the aspect of unity which has caused this confusion. Sugar is, of course, not the mere plurality of its different adjectives; but why should it be more than its properties in relation? When "white", "hard", "sweet", and the rest coexist in a certain way, that is surely the secret of the thing. The qualities are, and are in relation. But here, as before, when we leave phrases we wander among puzzles. "Sweet", "white", and "hard" seem now the subjects about which we are saying something. We certainly do not predicate one of the other; for, if we attempt to identify them, they at once resist. They are in this wholly incompatible, and, so far, quite contrary.

*From Book I, Chap. 2 of *Appearance and Reality*, Oxford, 1930, pp. 16-20. By permission of the Clarendon Press, Oxford.

Apparently, then, a relation is to be asserted of each. One quality, *A*, is in relation with another quality, *B*. But what are we to understand here by *is*? We do not mean that "in relation with *B*" is *A*, and yet we assert that *A* is "in relation with *B*". In the same way *C* is called "before *D*", and *E* is spoken of as *being* "to the right of *F*". We say all this, but from the interpretation, then "before *D*" *is C*, and "to the right of *F*" *is E*, we recoil in horror. No, we should reply, the relation is not identical with the thing. It is only a sort of attribute which inheres or belongs. The word to use, when we are pressed, should not be *is*, but only *has*. But this reply comes to very little. The whole question is evidently as to the meaning of *has*; and, apart from metaphors not taken seriously, there appears really to be no answer. And we seem unable to clear ourselves from the old dilemma, If you predicate what is different, you ascribe to the subject what it is *not*; and if you predicate what is *not* different, you say nothing at all.

Driven forward, we must attempt to modify our statement. We must assert the relation now, not of one term, but of both. *A* and *B* are identical in such a point, and in such another point they differ; or, again, they are so situated in space or in time. And thus we avoid *is*, and keep to *are*. But, seriously, that does not look like the explanation of a difficulty; it looks more like trifling with phrases. For, if you mean that *A* and *B*, taken each severally, even "have" this relation, you are asserting what is false. But if you mean that *A* and *B* in such a relation are so related, you appear to mean nothing. For here, as before, if the predicate makes no difference, it is idle; but, if it makes the subject other than it is, it is false.

But let us attempt another exist from this bewildering circle. Let us abstain from making the relation an attribute of the related, and let us make it more or less independent. "There is a relation *C*, in which *A* and *B* stand; and it appears with both of them." But here again we have made no progress. The relation *C* has been admitted different from *A* and *B*, and no longer is predicated of them. Something, however, seems to be said of this relation *C*, and said, again, of *A* and *B*. And this something is not to be the ascription of one to the other. If so, it would appear to be another relation, *D*, in which *C*, on one side, and, on the other side, *A* and *B*, stand. But such a makeshift leads at once to the infinite process. The new relation *D* can be predicated in no way of *C*, or of *A* and *B;* and hence we must have recourse to a fresh relation, *E*, which comes between *D* and whatever we had before. But this must lead to another, *F;* and so on, indefinitely. Thus the problem is not solved by taking relations as independently real. For, if so, the qualities and their relation fall entirely apart, and then we have said nothing. Or we have to make a new relation between the old relation and the terms which, when it is made, does not help us. It either demands a new relation, and so on without end, or it leaves us where we were, entangled in difficulties.

The attempt to resolve the thing into properties, each a real thing, taken somehow together with independent relations, has proved an obvious failure. And we are forced to see, when we reflect, that a relation standing alongside of its terms is a delusion. It it is to be real, it must be so somehow at the expense of the terms, or, at least, must be something which appears in them or to which they belong. A relation between A and B implies really a substantial foundation within them. This foundation, if we say that A is like to B, is the identity X which holds these differences together. And so with space and time—everywhere there must be a whole embracing what is related, or there would be no differences and no relation. It seems as if a reality possessed differences, A and B, incompatible with one another and also with itself. And so in order, without contradiction, to retain its various properties, this whole consents to wear the form of relations between them. And this is why qualities are found to be some incompatible and some compatible. They are all different, and, on the other hand, because belonging to one whole, are all forced to come together. And it is only where they come together distantly by the help of a relation, that they cease to conflict. On the other hand, where a thing fails to set up a relation between its properties, they are contrary at once. Thus colours and smells live together at peace in the reality; for the thing divides itself, and so leaves them merely side by side within itself. But colour collides with colour, because their special identity drives them together. And here again, if the identity becomes relational by help of space, they are outside one another, and are peaceful once more. The "contrary", in short, consists of differences possessed by that which cannot find the relation which serves to couple them apart. It is marriage attempted without a *modus vivendi*. But where the whole, relaxing its unity, takes the form of an arrangement, there is co-existence with concord.

I have set out the above mainly because of the light which it throws upon the nature of the "contrary". It affords no solution of our problem of inherence. It tells us how we are forced to arrange things in a certain manner, but it does not justify that arrangement. The thing avoids contradiction by its disappearance into relations, and by its admission of the adjectives to a standing of their own. But it avoids contradiction by a kind of suicide. It can give no rational account of the relations and the terms which it adopts, and it cannot recover the real unity, without which it is nothing. The whole device is a clear makeshift. It consists in saying to the outside world, "I am the owner of these my adjectives", and to the properties, "I am but a relation, which leaves you your liberty". And to itself and for itself it is the futile pretence to have both characters at once. Such an arrangement may work, but the theoretical problem is not solved.

The immediate unity, in which facts come to us, has been broken up by experience, and later by reflection. The thing with its adjectives is a device for enjoying at once both variety and concord. But the distinctions, once made, fall apart from the thing, and away from one another. And our attempt to understand their relations brought us round merely to a unity, which confesses itself a pretence, or else falls back upon the old undivided substance, which admits of no relations. We shall see the hopelessness of its dilemma more clearly when we have examined how relation stands to quality. But this demands another chapter.

I will, in conclusion, dispose very briefly of a possible suggestion. The distinctions taken in the thing are to be held only, it may be urged, as the ways in which *we* regard it. The thing itself maintains its unity, and the aspects of adjective and substantive are only *our* points of view. Hence they do no injury to the real. But this defence is futile, since the question is how without error we may think of reality. If then your collection of points of view is a defensible way of so thinking, by all means apply it to the thing, and make an end of our puzzle. Otherwise the thing, without the points of view, appears to have no character at all, and they, without the thing, to possess no reality—even if they could be made compatible among themselves, the one with the other. In short, this distinction, drawn between the fact and our manner of regarding it, only serves to double the original confusion. There will now be an inconsistency in my mind as well as in the thing; and, far from helping, the one will but aggravate the other.

Relation and Quality*

It must have become evident that the problem, discussed in the last chapter, really turns on the respective natures of quality and relation. And the reader may have anticipated the conclusion we are now to reach. The arrangement of given facts into relations and qualities may be necessary in practice, but it is theoretically unintelligible. The reality, so characterized, is not true reality, but is appearance.

And it can hardly be maintained that this character calls for no understanding—that it is a unique way of being which the reality possesses, and which we have got merely to receive. For it most evidently has ceased to be something quite immediate. It contains aspects now distinguished and taken as differences, and which tend, so far as we see, to a further separation. And, if the reality really has a way of uniting these in harmony, that way assuredly is not manifest at first sight. On our own side those distinctions which even consciously we make may possibly in some way give the truth about reality. But, so long as we fail to justify them and to make them intelligible to ourselves, we are bound, so far, to set them down as mere appearance.

The object of this chapter is to show that the very essence of these ideas is infected and contradicts itself. Our conclusion briefly will be this. Relation presupposes quality, and quality relation. Each can be something neither together with, nor apart from, the other; and the vicious circle in which they turn is not the truth about reality.

1. Qualities are nothing without relations. In trying to exhibit the truth of this statement, I will lay no weight on a considerable mass of evidence. This, furnished by psychology, would attempt to show how qualities are variable by changes of relation. The differences we perceive in many cases seem to have been so created. But I will not appeal to such an argument, since I do not see that it could prove wholly the non-existence of original and independent qualities. And the line of proof through the necessity of contrast for perception has,

*Ibid., Chap. 3, pp. 21-29.

in my opinion, been carried beyond logical limits. Hence, though these considerations have without doubt an important bearing on our problem, I prefer here to disregard them. And I do not think that they are necessary.

We may proceed better to our conclusion in the following way. You can never, we may argue, find the qualities without relations. Whenever you take them so, they are made so, and continue so, by an operation which itself implies relation. Their plurality gets for us all its meaning through relations; and to suppose it otherwise in reality is wholly indefensible. I will draw this out in greater detail.

To find qualities without relations is surely impossible. In the field of consciousness, even when we abstract from the relations of identity and difference, they are never independent. One is together with, and related to, one other, at the least—in fact, always to more than one. Nor will an appeal to a lower and undistinguished state of mind, where in one feeling are many aspects, assist us in any way. I admit the existence of such states without any relation, but I wholly deny there the presence of qualities. For if these felt aspects, while merely felt, are to be called qualities proper, they are so only for the observation of an outside observer. And then for him they are given *as* aspects—that is, together with relations. In short, if you go back to mere unbroken feeling, you have no relations and no qualities. But if you come to what is distinct, you get relations at once.

I presume we shall be answered in this way. Even though, we shall be told, qualities proper cannot be discovered apart from relations, that is no real disproof of their separate existence. For we are well able to distinguish them and to consider them by themselves. And for this perception certainly an operation of our minds is required. So far, therefore, as you say, what is different must be distinct, and, in consequence, related. But this relation does not really belong to the reality. The relation has existence only for us, and as a way of our getting to know. But the distinction, for all that, is based upon differences in the actual; and these remain when our relations have fallen away or have been removed.

But such an answer depends on the separation of product from process, and this separation seems indefensible. The qualities, as distinct, are always made so by an action which is admitted to imply relation. They are made so, and, what is more, they are emphatically kept so. And you cannot ever get your product standing apart from its process. Will you say, the process is not essential? But that is a conclusion to be proved, and it is monstrous to assume it. Will you try to prove it by analogy? It is possible for many purposes to accept and employ the existence of processes and relations which do not affect specially the inner nature of objects. But the very possibility of so distinguishing in the end between inner and outer, and of setting up the inner as absolutely independent of all relation, is here in question. Mental operations such as comparison, which presuppose in the compared qualities already existing, could in no case prove that these qualities depend on no relations at all. But I cannot believe that this is a matter to be decided by analogy, for the whole case is briefly this. There is an operation which, removing one part of what is given, presents the other part in abstraction. This result is never to be found anywhere apart from a persisting abstraction. And, if we have no further information, I can find no excuse for setting up the result as being fact without the process. The burden lies wholly on the assertor, and he fails entirely to support it. The argument that in perception one quality must be given first and before others, and therefore cannot be relative, is hardly worth mentioning. What is more natural than for qualities always to have come to us in some conjunction, and never alone?

We may go further. Not only is the ignoring of the process a thing quite indefensible—even if it blundered into truth—but there is evidence that it gives falsehood. For the result bears internally the character of the process. The manyness of the qualities cannot, in short, be reconciled with their simplicity. Their plurality depends on relation, and, without that relation, they are not distinct. But, if not distinct, then not different, and therefore not qualities.

I am not urging that quality without difference is in every sense impossible. For all I know, creatures may exist whose life consists, for themselves, in one unbroken simple feeling; and the arguments urged against such a possibility in my judgement come short. And, if you want to call this feeling a quality, by all means gratify your desire. But then remember that the whole point is quite irrelevant. For no one is contending whether the universe is or is not a quality in this sense; but the question is entirely as to qualities. And a universe confined to one feeling would not only not be qualities, but it would fail even to be one quality, as different from others and as distinct from relations. Our question is really whether relation is essential to differences.

We have seen that in fact the two are never found apart. We have seen that the separation by abstraction is no proof of real separateness. And now we have to urge, in short, that any separateness implies separation, and so relation, and is therefore, when made absolute, a self-discrepancy. For consider, the qualities A and B are to be different from each other; and, if so, that difference must fall somewhere. If it falls, in any degree or to any extent, outside *A* or *B*, we have relation at once. But, on the other hand, how can difference and otherness fall inside? If we have in *A* any such otherness, then inside *A* we must distinguish its own quality and its otherness. And if so, then the unsolved problem breaks out inside each quality, and separates each into two qualities in relation. In brief, diversity without relation seems a word without meaning. And it is no answer to urge that plurality proper is not in question here. I am convinced of the opposite, but by all means, if you will, let us confine ourselves to distinctness and difference. I rest my argument upon this, that if there are no differences, there are no qualities, since all must fall into one. But, if there is any difference, then that implies a relation. Without a relation it has no meaning; it is a mere word, and not a thought; and no one would take it for a thought if he did not, in spite of his protests, import relation into it. And this is the point on which all seems to turn, It is possible to think of qualities without thinking of distinct characters? Is it possible to think of these without some relation between them, either explicit, or else unconsciously supplied by the mind that tries only to apprehend? Have qualities without relation any meaning for thought? For myself, I am sure that they have none.

And I find a confirmation in the issue of the most thorough attempt to build a system on this ground. There it is not too much to say that all the content of the universe becomes something very like an impossible illusion. The Reals are secluded and simple, simple beyond belief if they never suspect that they are not so. But our fruitful life, on the other hand, seems due to their persistence in imaginary recovery from unimaginable perversion. And they remain guiltless of all real share in these ambiguous connexions, which seem to make the world. They are above it, and fixed like stars in the firmament—if there only were a firmanent.

2. We have found that qualities, taken without relations, have no intelligible meaning. Unfortunately, taken together with them, they are equally unintelligible. They cannot, in the first place, be wholly resolved into the relations. You may urge, indeed, that without distinction no difference is left; but, for all that, the differences will not disappear into the distinction. They must come to it, more or less, and they cannot wholly be made by it. I still insist that for thought what is not relative is nothing. But I urge, on the other hand, that nothings cannot be related, and that to turn qualities in relation into mere relations is impossible. Since the fact seems constituted by both, you may urge, if you please, that either one of them constitutes it. But if

you mean that the other is not wanted, and that relations can somehow make the terms upon which they seem to stand, then, for my mind,
your meaning is quite unintelligible. So far as I can see, relations must
depend upon terms, just as much as terms upon relations. And the
partial failure, now manifest, of the Dialectic Method seems connected
with some misapprehension on this point.

Hence the qualities must be, and must *also* be related. But there
is hence a diversity which falls inside each quality. Each has a double
character, as both supporting and as being made by the relation. It
may be taken as at once condition and result, and the question is as
to how it can combine this variety. For it must combine the diversity,
and yet it fails to do so. A is both made, and is not made, what it is by
relation; and these different aspects are not each the other, nor again
is either A. If we call its diverse aspects a and α, then A is partly each of
these. As a it is the difference on which distinction is based, while as α
it is the distinctness that results from connexion. A is really both somehow together as A (a—α). But (as we saw in Chapter 2) *without* the
use of a relation it is impossible to predicate this variety of A. And,
on the other hand, *with* an internal relation A's unity disappears, and
its contents are dissipated in an endless process of distinction. A at
first becomes a in relation with α, but these terms themselves fall hope-
lessly asunder. We have got, against our will, not a mere aspect, but a
new quality a, which itself stands in a relation; and hence (as we saw
before with A), its content must be manifold. As going into the relation
it itself is a^2, and as resulting from the relation it itself is α^2. And it
combines, and yet cannot combine, these adjectives. We, in brief, are
led by a principle of fission which conducts us to no end. Every quality
in relation has, in consequence, a diversity within its own nature, and
this diversity cannot immediately be asserted of the quality. Hence
the quality must exchange its unity for an internal relation. But, thus
set free, the diverse aspects, because each something in relation, must
each be something also beyond. This diversity is fatal to the internal
unity of each; and it demands a new relation, and so on without limit.
In short, qualities in a relation have turned but as unintelligible as
were qualities without one. The problem from both sides has baffled
us.

3. We may briefly reach the same dilemma from the side of relations. They are nothing intelligible, either with or without their
qualities. In the first place, a relation without terms seems mere verbi-
age; and terms appear, therefore, to be something beyond their relation. At least, for myself, a relation which somehow precipitates terms
which were not there before, or a relation which can get on somehow

without terms, and with no differences beyond the mere ends of a line of connexion, is really a phrase without meaning. It is, to my mind, a false abstraction, and a thing which loudly contradicts itself; and I fear that I am obliged to leave the matter so. As I am left without information, and can discover with my own ears no trace of harmony, I am forced to conclude to a partial deafness in others. And hence a relation, we must say, without qualities is nothing.

But how the relation can stand to the qualities is, on the other side, unintelligible. If it is nothing to the qualities, then they are not related at all; and, if so, as we saw, they have ceased to be qualities, and their relation is a nonentity. But if it is to be something to them, then clearly we now shall require a *new* connecting relation. For the relation hardly can be the mere adjective of one or both of its terms; or, at least, as such it seems indefensible.[1] And, being something itself, if it does not itself bear a relation to the terms, in what intelligible way will it succeed in being anything to them? But here again we are hurried off into the eddy of a hopeless process, since we are forced to go on finding new relations without end. The links are united by a link, and this bond of union is a link which also has two ends; and these require each a fresh link to connect them with the old. The problem is to find how the relation can stand to its qualities; and this problem is insoluble. If you take the connexion as a solid thing, you have got to show, and you cannot show, how the other solids are joined to it. And, if you take it as a kind of medium or unsubstantial atmosphere, it is a connexion no longer. You find, in this case, that the whole question of the relation of the qualities (for they certainly in some ways *are* related) arises now outside it, in precisely the same form as before. The original relation, in short, has become a nonentity, but, in becoming this, it has removed no element of the problem.

I will bring this chapter to an end. It would be easy, and yet profitless, to spin out its argument with ramifications and refinements. And for me to attempt to anticipate the reader's objections would probably be useless. I have stated the case, and I must leave it. The conclusion to which I am brought is that a relational way of thought— any one that moves by the machinery of terms and relations—must give appearance, and not truth. It is a makeshift, a device, a mere

1. The relation is not the adjective of one term, for, if so, it does not relate. Nor for the same reason is it the adjective of each term taken apart, for then again there is no relation between them. Nor is the relation their common property, for then what keeps them apart? They are now not two terms at all, because not separate. And within this new whole, in any case, the problem of inherence would break out in an aggravated form. But it seems unnecessary to work this all out in detail.

practical compromise, most necessary, but in the end most indefensible. We have to take reality as many, and to take it as one, and to avoid contradiction. We want to divide it, or to take it, when we please, as indivisible; to go as far as we desire in either of these directions, and to stop when that suits us. And we succeed, but succeed merely by shutting the eye, which if left open would condemn us; or by a perpetual oscillation and a shifting of the ground, so as to turn our back upon the aspect we desire to ignore. But when these inconsistencies are forced together, as in metaphysics they must be, the result is an open and staring discrepancy. And we cannot attribute this to reality; while, if we try to take it on ourselves, we have changed one evil for two. Our intellect, then, has been condemned to confusion and bankruptcy, and the reality has been left 'outside uncomprehended. Or rather, what is worse, it has been stripped bare of all distinction and quality. It is left naked and without a character, and we are covered with confusion.

The reader who has followed and has grasped the principle of this chapter, will have little need to spend his time upon those which succeed it. He will have seen that our experience, where relational, is not true; and he will have condemned, almost without a hearing, the great mass of phenomena.

The General Nature of Reality*

The result of our First Book has been mainly negative. We have taken up a number of ways of regarding reality, and we have found that they all are vitiated by self-discrepancy. The reality can accept not one of these predicates, at least in the character in which so far they have come. We certainly ended with a reflection which promised something positive. Whatever is rejected as appearance is, for that very reason, no mere nonentity. It cannot bodily be shelved and merely got rid of, and, therefore, since it must fall somewhere, it must belong to reality. To take it as existing somehow and somewhere in the unreal, would surely be quite meaningless. For reality must own and cannot be less than appearance, and that is the one positive result which, so far, we have reached. But as to the character which, otherwise, the real possesses, we at present know nothing; and a further knowledge is what we must aim at through the remainder of our search. . . .

At the beginning of our inquiry into the nature of the real we encounter, of course, a general doubt or denial. To know the truth, we shall be told, is impossible, or is, at all events, wholly impracticable. We cannot have positive knowledge about first principles; and, if we could possess it, we should not know when actually we had got it. What is denied is, in short, the existence of a criterion. I shall, later on, in Chapter 27, have to deal more fully with the objections of a thorough-going scepticism, and I will here confine myself to what seems requisite for the present.

Is there an absolute criterion? This question, to my mind, is answered by a second question: How otherwise should we be able to say anything at all about appearance? For through the last Book, the reader will remember, we were for the most part criticizing. We were judging phenomena and were condemning them, and throughout we proceeded as if the self-contradictory could not be real. But this was surely to have and to apply an absolute criterion. For consider: you can scarcely propose to be quite passive when presented with state-

---

*Ibid., Book II, Chaps. 13-14, pp. 119-129.

ments about reality. You can hardly take the position of admitting any and every nonsense to be truth, truth absolute and entire, at least so far as you know. For, if you think at all so as to discriminate between truth and falsehood, you will find that you cannot accept open self-contradiction. Hence to think is to judge, and to judge is to criticize, and to criticize is to use a criterion of reality. And surely to doubt this would be mere blindness or confused self-deception. But, if so, it is clear that, in rejecting the inconsistent as appearance, we are applying a positive knowledge of the ultimate nature of things. Ultimate reality is such that it does not contradict itself; here is an absolute criterion. And it is proved absolute by the fact that, either in endeavouring to deny it, or even in attempting to doubt it, we tacitly assume its validity. . . .

Thus we possess a criterion, and our criterion is supreme. I do not mean to deny that we might have several standards, giving us sundry pieces of information about the nature of things. But, be that as it may, we still have an over-ruling test of truth, and the various standards (if they exist) are certainly subordinate. This at once becomes evident, for we cannot refuse to bring such standards together, and to ask if they agree. Or, at least, if a doubt is suggested as to their consistency, each with itself and with the rest, we are compelled, so to speak, to assume jurisdiction. And if they were guilty of self-contradiction, when examined or compared, we should condemn them as appearance. But we could not do that if they were not subject all to one tribunal. And hence, as we find nothing not subordinate to the test of self-consistency, we are forced to set that down as supreme and absolute.

But it may be said that this supplies us with no real information. If we think, then certainly we are not allowed to be inconsistent, and it is admitted that this test is unconditional and absolute. But it will be urged that, for knowledge about any matter, we require something more than a bare negation. The ultimate reality (we are agreed) does not permit self-contradiction, but a prohibition or an absence (we shall be told) by itself does not amount to positive knowledge. The denial of inconsistency, therefore, does not predicate any positive quality. But such an objection is untenable. It may go so far as to assert that a bare denial is possible, that we may reject a predicate though we stand on no positive basis, and though there is nothing special which serves to reject. This error has been refuted in my *Principles of Logic* (Book I, Chapter iii), and I do not propose to discuss it here. I will pass to another sense in which the objection may seem more plausible. The criterion, it may be urged, in itself is doubtless positive; but, for our knowledge and in effect, is merely negative.

And it gives us therefore no information at all about reality, for, although knowledge is there, it cannot be brought out. The criterion is a basis, which serves as the foundation of denial; but, since this basis cannot be exposed, we are but able to stand on it and unable to see it. And it hence, in effect, tells us nothing, though there are assertions which it does not allow us to venture on. This objection, when stated in such a form, may seem plausible, and there is a sense in which I am prepared to admit that it is valid. If by the nature of reality we understand its full nature, I am not contending that this in a complete form is knowable. But that is very far from being the point here at issue. For the objection denies that we have a standard which gives *any* positive knowledge, *any* information, complete or incomplete, about the genuine reality. And this denial assuredly is mistaken.

The objection admits that we know what reality *does*, but it refuses to allow us any understanding of what reality *is*. The standard (it is agreed) both exists and possesses a positive character, and it is agreed that this character rejects inconsistency. It is admitted that we know this, and the point at issue is whether such knowledge supplies any positive information. And to my mind this question seems not hard to answer. For I cannot see how, when I observe a thing at work, I am to stand there and to insist that I know nothing of its nature. I fail to perceive how a function is nothing at all, or how it does not positively qualify that to which I attribute it. To know only so much, I admit, may very possibly be useless; it may leave us without the information which we desire most to obtain; but, for all that, it is not total ignorance.

Our standard denies inconsistency, and therefore asserts consistency. If we can be sure that the inconsistent is unreal, we must, logically, be just as sure that the reality is consistent. The question is solely as to the meaning to be given to consistency. We have now seen that it is not the bare exclusion of discord, for that is merely our abstraction, and is otherwise nothing. And our result, so far, is this. Reality is known to possess a positive character, but this character is at present determined only as that which excludes contradiction.

But we may make a further advance. We saw (in the preceding chapter*) that all appearance must belong to reality. For what appears is, and whatever is cannot fall outside the real. And we may now combine this result with the conclusion just reached. We may say that everything, which appears, is somehow real in such a way as to be self-consistent. The character of the real is to possess everything phenomenal in a harmonious form.

*Book I, Chap. 12.

I will repeat the same truth in other words. Reality is one in this sense that it has a positive nature exclusive of discord, a nature which must hold throughout everything that is to be real. Its diversity can be diverse only so far as not to clash, and what seems otherwise anywhere cannot be real. And, from the other side, everything which appears must be real. Appearance must belong to reality, and it must therefore be concordant and other than it seems. The bewildering mass of phenomenal diversity must hence somehow be at unity and self-consistent; for it cannot be elsewhere than in reality, and reality excludes discord. Or again we may put it so: the real is individual. It is one in the sense that its positive character embraces all differences in an inclusive harmony. And this knowledge, poor as it may be, is certainly more than bare negation or simple ignorance. So far as it goes, it gives us positive news about absolute reality.

Let us try to carry this conclusion a step further on. We know that the real is one; but its oneness so far, is ambiguous. Is it one system, possessing diversity as an adjective; or is its consistency, on the other hand, an attribute of independent realities? We have to ask, in short, if a plurality of reals is possible, and if these can merely coexist so as not to be discrepant? Such a plurality would mean a number of beings not dependent on each other. On the one hand they would possess somehow the phenomenal diversity, for that possession, we have seen, is essential. And, on the other hand, they would be free from external disturbance and from inner discrepancy. After the inquiries of our First Book the possibility of such reals hardly calls for discussion. For the internal states of each give rise to hopeless difficulties. And, in the second place, the plurality of the reals cannot be reconciled with their independence. I will briefly resume the arguments which force us to this latter result.

If the Many are supposed to be without internal quality, each would forthwith become nothing, and we must therefore take each as being internally somewhat. And if they are to be plural, they must be a diversity somehow coexisting together. Any attempt again to take their togetherness as unessential seems to end in the unmeaning. We have no knowledge of a plural diversity, nor can we attach any sense to it, if we do not have it somehow as one. And, if we abstract from this unity, we have also therewith abstracted from the plurality, and are left with mere being.

Can we then have a plurality of independent reals which merely coexist? No, for absolute independence and coexistence are incompatible. Absolute independence is an idea which consists merely in one-sided abstraction. It is made by an attempted division of the aspect of several existence from the aspect of relatedness; and these aspects, whether in fact or thought, are really indivisible. . . .

Our result so far is this. Everything phenomenal is somehow real; and the absolute must at least be as rich as the relative. And, further, the Absolute is not many; there are no independent reals. The universe is one in this sense that its differences exist harmoniously within one whole, beyond which there is nothing. Hence the Absolute is, so far, an individual and a system, but, if we stop here, it remains but formal and abstract. Can we then, the question is, say anything about the concrete nature of the system?

Certainly, I think, this is possible. When we ask as to the matter which fills up the empty outline, we can reply in one word, that this matter is experience. And experience means something much the same as given and present fact. We perceive, on reflection, that to be real, or even barely to exist, must be to fall within sentience. Sentient experience, in short, is reality, and what is not this is not real. We may say, in other words, that there is no being or fact outside of that which is commonly called psychical existence. Feeling, thought, and volition (any groups under which we class psychical phenomena) are all the material of existence, and there is no other material, actual or even possible. This result in its general form seems evident at once; and, however serious a step we now seem to have taken, there would be no advantage at this point in discussing it at length. For the test in the main lies ready to our hand, and the decision rests on the manner in which it is applied. I will state the case briefly thus. Find any piece of existence, take up anything that any one could possibly call a fact, or could in any sense assert to have being, and then judge if it does not consist in sentient experience. Try to discover any sense in which you can still continue to speak of it, when all perception and feeling have been removed; or point out any fragment of its matter, any aspect of its being, which is not derived from and is not still relative to this source. When the experiment is made strictly, I can myself conceive of nothing else than the experienced. Anything, in no sense felt or perceived, becomes to me quite unmeaning. And as I cannot try to think of it without realizing either that I am not thinking at all, or that I am thinking of it against my will as being experienced, I am driven to the conclusion that for me experience is the same as reality. The fact that falls elsewhere seems, in my mind, to be a mere word and a failure, or else an attempt at self-contradiction. It is a vicious abstraction whose existence is meaningless nonsense, and is therefore not possible.

This conclusion is open, of course, to grave objection, and must in its consequences give rise to serious difficulties. I will not attempt to anticipate the discussion of these, but before passing on, will try to obviate a dangerous mistake. For, in asserting that the real is nothing but experience, I may be understood to endorse a common error. I may be taken first to divide the percipient subject from the universe; and then, resting on that subject, as on a thing actual by itself, I may be supposed to urge that it cannot transcend its own states. Such an argument would lead to impossible results, and would stand on a foundation of faulty abstraction. To set up the subject as real independently of the whole, and to make the whole into experience in the sense of an adjective of that subject, seems to me indefensible. And when I contend that reality must be sentient, my conclusion almost consists in the denial of this fundamental error. For if, seeking for reality, we go to experience, what we certainly do *not* find is a subject or an object, or indeed any other thing whatever, standing separate and on its own bottom. What we discover rather is a whole in which distinctions can be made, but in which divisions do not exist. And this is the point on which I insist, and it is the very ground on which I stand, when I urge that reality is sentient experience. I mean that to be real is to be indissolubly one thing with sentience. It is to be something which comes as a feature and aspect within one whole of feeling, something which, except as an integral element of such sentience, has no meaning at all. And what I repudiate is the separation of feeling from the felt, or of the desired from desire, or of what is thought from thinking, or the division—I might add—of anything from anything else. Nothing is ever so presented as real by itself, or can be argued so to exist without demonstrable fallacy. And in asserting that the reality is experience, I rest throughout on this foundation. You cannot find fact unless in unity with sentience, and one cannot in the end be divided from the other, either actually or in idea. But to be utterly indivisible from feeling or perception, to be an integral element in a whole which is experienced, this surely is itself to *be* experience. Being and reality are, in brief, one thing with sentience; they can neither be opposed to, nor even in the end distinguished from it.

I am well aware that this statement stands in need of explanation and defence. This will, I hope, be supplied by succeeding chapters, and I think it better for the present to attempt to go forward. Our conclusion, so far, will be this, that the Absolute is one system, and that its contents are nothing but sentient experience. It will hence be a single and all-inclusive experience, which embraces every partial diversity in concord. For it cannot be less than appearance, and hence no feeling or thought, of any kind, can fall outside its limits. And if it is more than any feeling or thought which we know, it must still remain more of the same nature. It cannot pass into another region beyond what falls under the general head of sentience. For to assert that possibility would be in the end to use words without a meaning. We can entertain no such suggestion except as self-contradictory, and as therefore impossible. . . .

Thought and Reality*

In the present chapter I will try to state briefly the main essence of thought, and to justify its distinction from actual existence. It is only by misunderstanding that we find difficulty in taking thought to be something less than reality.

If we take up anything considered real, no matter what it is, we find in it two aspects. There are always two things we can say about it; and, if we cannot say both, we have not got reality. There is a "what" and a "that", an existence and a content, and the two are inseparable. That anything should be, and should yet be nothing in particular, or that a quality should not qualify and give a character to anything, is obviously impossible. If we try to get the "that" by itself, we do not get it, for either we have it qualified, or else we fail utterly. If we try to get the "what" by itself, we find at once that it is not all. It points to something beyond, and cannot exist by itself and as a bare adjective. Neither of these aspects, if you isolate it, can be taken as real, or indeed in that case is itself any longer. They are distinguishable only and are not divisible.

And yet thought seems essentially to consist in their division. For thought is clearly, to some extent at least, ideal. Without an idea there is no thinking, and an idea implies the separation of content from existence. It is a "what" which, so far as it is a mere idea, clearly *is* not, and if it also *were*, could, so far, not be called ideal. For ideality lies in the disjoining of quality from being. Hence the common view, which identifies image and idea, is fundamentally in error. For an image is a fact, just as real as any sensation; it is merely a fact of another kind and it is not one whit more ideal. But an idea is any part of the content of a fact so far as that works out of immediate unity with its existence. And an idea's factual existence may consist in a sensation or perception, just as well as in an image. The main

*Ibid., Chap. 15, pp. 143-152.

point and the essence is that some feature in the "what" of a given fact should be alienated from its "that" so far as to work beyond it, or at all events loose from it. Such a movement is ideality, and, where it is absent, there is nothing ideal.

We can understand this most clearly if we consider the nature of judgement, for there we find thought in its completed form. In judgement an idea is predicated of a reality. Now, in the first place, what is predicated is not a mental image. It is not a fact inside my head which the judgement wishes to attach to another fact outside. The predicate is a mere "what", a mere feature of content, which is used to qualify further the "that" of the subject. And this predicate is divorced from its physical existence in my head, and is used without any regard to its being there. When I say "this horse is a mammal", it is surely absurd to suppose that I am harnessing my mental state to the beast between the shafts. Judgement adds an adjective to reality, and this adjective is an idea, because it is a quality made loose from its own existence, and is working free from its implication with that. And, even when a fact is merely analysed—when the predicate appears not to go beyond its own subject, or to have been imported divorced from another fact outside—our account still holds good. For here obviously our synthesis is a reunion of the distinguished, and it implies a separation, which, though it is overridden, is never unmade. The predicate is a content which has been made loose from its own immediate existence and is used in divorce from that first unity. And, again, as predicated, it is applied without regard to its own being as abstracted and in my head. If this were not so, there would be no judgement; for neither distinction nor predication would have taken place. But again, if it is so, then once more here we discover an idea.

And in the second place, when we turn to the subject of the judgement, we clearly find the other aspect, in other words, the "that". Just as in "this horse is a mammal" the predicate was *not* a fact, so most assuredly the subject is an actual existence. And the same thing holds good with every judgement. No one ever *means* to assert about anything but reality, or to do anything but qualify a "that" by a "what". And, without dwelling on a point which I have worked out elsewhere, I will notice a source of possible mistake. "The subject, at all events," I may be told, "is in no case a *mere* 'that'. It is never bare reality, or existence without character." And to this I fully assent. I agree that the subject which we *mean*—even before the judgement is complete, and while still we are holding its elements apart—is more than a mere "that". But then this is not the point. The point is whether with every judgement we do not find an aspect of existence, absent from the predicate but present in the subject, and whether in the synthesis of these aspects we have not got the essence of judgement. And for myself I see no way of avoiding this conclusion. Judgement is essentially the re-union of two sides, "what" and "that", provisionally estranged. But it is the alienation of these aspects in which thought's ideality consists.

Truth is the object of thinking, and the aim of truth is to qualify existence ideally. Its end, that is, is to give a character to reality in which it can rest. Truth is the predication of such content as, when predictated, is harmonious, and removes inconsistency and with it un-rest. And because the given reality is never consistent, thought is com-pelled to take the road of indefinite expansion. If thought were success-ful, it would have a predicate consistent in itself and agreeing entirely with the subject. But on the other hand, the predicate must be always ideal. It must, that is, be a "what" not in unity with its own "that", and therefore, in and by itself, devoid of existence. Hence, so far as in thought this alienation is not made good, thought can never be more than merely ideal.

I shall very soon proceed to dwell on this last consideration, but will first of all call attention to a most important point. There exists a notion that ideality is something outside of facts, something imported into them, or imposed as a sort of layer above them; and we talk as if facts, when let alone, were in no sense ideal. But any such notion is illusory. For facts which are not ideal, and which show no looseness of content from existence, seem hardly actual. They would be found, if anywhere, in feelings without internal lapse, and with a content wholly single. But if we keep to fact which is given, this changes in our hands, and it compels us to perceive inconsistency of content. And then this content cannot be referred merely to its given "that", but is forced beyond it, and is made to qualify something outside. But, if so, in the simplest change we have at once ideality—the use of content in separation from its actual existence. Indeed, in Chapters 9 and 10 we have already seen how this is necessary. For the content of the given is for ever relative to something not given, and the nature of its "what" is hence essentially to transcend its "that". This we may call the ideality of the given finite. It is not manufactured by thought, but thought itself is its development and product. The essential nature of the finite is that everywhere, as it presents itself, its character should slide beyond the limits of its existence.

And truth, as we have seen, is the effort to heal this disease, as it were, homoeopathically. Thought has to accept, without reserve, the ideality of the "given", its want of consistency and its self-transcendence. And by pushing this self-transcendence to the uttermost point, thought attempts to find there consummation and rest. The subject, on the one hand, is expanded until it is no longer what is given. It becomes the whole universe, which presents itself and which appears in each given moment with but part of its reality. It grows into an all-inclusive whole, existing somewhere and somehow, if we only could perceive it. But on the other hand, in qualifying this reality, thought consents to a partial abnegation. It has to recognize the division of the "what" from the "that", and it cannot so join these aspects as to get rid of mere ideas and arrive at actual reality. For it is in and by ideas only that thought moves and has life. The content it applies to the reality has, as applied, no genuine existence. It is an adjective divorced from its "that", and never in judgement, even when the judgement is complete, restored to solid unity. Thus the truth belongs to existence, but it does not as such exist. It is a character which indeed reality possesses, but a character which, as truth and as ideal, has been set loose from existence; and it is never rejoined to it in such a way as to come together singly and *make* fact. Hence, truth shows a dissection and never an actual life. Its predicate can never be equivalent to its subject. And if it became so, and if its adjectives could be at once self-consistent and re-welded to existence, it would not be truth any longer. It would have then passed into another and a higher reality.

And I will now deal with the misapprehension to which I referred, and the consideration of which may, I trust, help us forward.

There is an erroneous idea that, if reality is more than thought, thought itself is, at least, quite unable to say so. To assert the existence of anything in any sense beyond thought suggests, to some minds, the doctrine of the Thing-in-itself. And of the Thing-in-itself we know ... that if it existed we could not know of it; and, again, so far as we know of it, we know that it does not exist. The attempt to apprehend this Other in succeeding would be suicide, and in suicide could not reach anything beyond total failure. Now, though I have urged this result, I wish to keep it within rational limits, and I dissent wholly from the corollary that nothing more than thought exists. But to think of anything which can exist quite outside of thought I agree is impossible. If thought is one element in a whole, you cannot argue from this ground that the remainder of such a whole must stand apart and independent. From this ground, in short, you can make no inference to a Thing-in-itself. And there is no impossibility in thought's existing as an element, and no self-contradiction in its own judgement that it is less than the universe.

We have seen that anything real has two aspects, existence and character, and that thought always must work within this distinction. Thought, in its actual processes and results, cannot transcend the dualism of the "that" and the "what". I do not mean that in no sense is thought beyond this dualism, or that thought is satisfied with it and has no desire for something better. But taking judgement to be completed thought, I mean that in no judgement are the subject and predicate the same. In every judgement the genuine subject is reality, which goes beyond the predicate and of which the predicate is an adjective. And I would urge first that, in desiring to transcend this distinction, thought is aiming at suicide. We have seen that in judgement we find always the distinction of fact and truth, of idea and reality. Truth and thought are not the thing itself, but are of it and about it. Thought predicates an ideal content of a subject, which idea is not the same as fact, for in it existence and meaning are necessarily divorced. And the subject, again, is neither the mere "what" of the predicate, nor is it any other mere "what". Nor, even if it is proposed to take up a whole with both its aspects, and to predicate the ideal character of its own proper subject, will that proposal assist us. For if the subject is the same as the predicate, why trouble oneself to judge? But if it is not the same, then what is it, and how is it different? Either then there is no judgement at all, and but a pretence of thinking without thought, or there is a judgement, but its subject is more than the predicate, and is a "that" beyond a mere "what". The subject, I would repeat, is never mere reality, or bare existence without character. The subject, doubtless, has unspecified content which is not stated in the predicate. For judgement is the differentiation of a complex whole, and hence always is analysis and synthesis in one. It separates an element from, and restores it to, the concrete basis; and this basis of necessity is richer than the mere element by itself. But then this is not the question which concerns us here. That question is whether, in any judgement which really says anything, there is not in the subject an aspect of existence which is absent from the bare predicate. And it seems clear that this question must be answered in the affirmative. And if it is urged that the subject itself, being in thought, can therefore not fall beyond, I must ask for more accuracy; for "partly beyond" appears compatible with "partly within". And, leaving prepositions to themselves, I must recall the real issue. For I do not deny that reality is an object of thought; I deny that it is barely and merely so. If you rest here on a distinction between thought and

its object, that opens up a further question to which I shall return
... But if you admit that in asserting reality to fall within
thought, you meant that in reality there is nothing beyond what is
made thought's object, your position is untenable. Reflect upon any
judgement as long as you please, operate upon the subject of it to any
extent which you desire, but then (when you have finished) make an
actual judgement. And when that is made, see if you do not discover,
beyond the content of your thought, a subject of which it is true, and
which it does not comprehend. You will find that the object of thought
in the end must be ideal, and that there is no idea which, as such, contains its own existence. The "that" of the actual subject will for ever
give a something which is not a mere idea, something which is different
from any truth, something which makes such a difference to your
thinking, that without it you have not even thought completely.

"But", it may be answered, "the thought you speak of is thought
that is not perfect. Where thought is perfect there is no discrepancy
between the subject and predicate. A harmonious system of content
predicating itself, a subject self-conscious in that system of content,
this is what thought should mean. And here the division of existence
and character is quite healed up. If such completion is not actual,
it is possible, and the possibility is enough." But it is not even possible,
I must persist, if it really is unmeaning. And once more I must urge
the former dilemma. If there is no judgement, there is no thought;
and if there is no difference, there is no judgement, nor any self-
consciousness. But if, on the other hand, there is a difference, then the
subject is beyond the predicated content.

Still a mere denial, I admit, is not quite satisfactory. Let us then
suppose that the dualism inherent in thought has been transcended.
Let us assume that existence is no longer different from truth, and let
us see where this takes us. It takes us straight to thought's suicide. A
system of content is going to swallow up our reality; but in our reality
we have the fact of sensible experience, immediate presentation with
its colouring of pleasure and pain. Now I presume there is no question
of conjuring this fact away; but how it is to be exhibited as an element
in a system of thought-content, is a problem not soluble. Thought is
relational and discursive, and, if it ceases to be this, it commits suicide;
and yet, if it remains thus, how does it contain immediate presentation?
Let us suppose the impossible accomplished; let us imagine a harmonious system of ideal contents united by relations, and reflecting
itself in self-conscious harmony. This is to be reality, all reality; and
there is nothing outside it. The delights and pains of the flesh, the

agonies and raptures of the soul, these are fragmentary meteors fallen
from thought's harmonious system. But these burning experiences—
how in any sense can they be mere pieces of thought's heaven? For,
if the fall is real, there is a world outside thought's region, and
if the fall is apparent, then human error itself is not included
there. Heaven, in brief, must either not be heaven, or else not
all reality. Without a metaphor, feeling belongs to perfect thought,
or it does not. If it does not, there is at once a side of existence beyond
thought. But if it does belong, then thought is different from thought
discursive and relational. To make it include immediate experience,
its character must be transformed. It must cease to predicate, it must get
beyond mere relations, it must reach something other than truth.
Thought, in a word, must have been absorbed into a fuller experience.
Now such an experience may be called thought, if you choose to use
that word. But if any one else prefers another term, such as feeling or
will, he would be equally justified. For the result is a whole state which
both includes and goes beyond each element; and to speak of it as
simply one of them seems playing with phrases. For (I must repeat it)
when thought begins to be more than relational, it ceases to be mere
thinking. A basis, from which the relation is thrown out and into
which it returns, is something not exhausted by that relation. It will,
in short, be an existence which is not mere truth. Thus, in reaching a
whole which can contain every aspect within it, thought must absorb
what divides it from feeling and will. But when these all have come
together, then, since none of them can perish, they must be merged
in a whole in which they are harmonious. But that whole assuredly is
not simply *one* of its aspects. And the question is *not* whether the universe is in any sense intelligible. The question is whether, if you
thought it and understood it, there would be no difference left between your thought and the thing. And, supposing that to have happened, the question is then whether thought has not changed its
nature.

Let us try to realize more distinctly what this supposed consummation would involve. Since both truth and fact are to be there,
nothing must be lost, and in the Absolute we must keep every item
of our experience. We cannot have less, but, on the other hand,
we may have much more; and this more may so supplement the elements of our actual experience that in the whole they may become
transformed. But to reach a mode of apprehension, which is quite
identical with reality, surely predicate and subject, and subject and
object, and in short the whole relational form, must be merged. The
Absolute does not want, I presume, to make eyes at itself in a mirror,

or, like a squirrel in a cage, to revolve the circle of its perfections. Such processes must be dissolved in something not poorer but richer than themselves. And feeling and will must also be transmuted in this whole, into which thought has entered. Such a whole state would possess in a superior form that immediacy which we find (more or less) in feeling; and in this whole all divisions would be healed up. It would be experience entire, containing all elements in harmony. Thought would be present as a higher intuition; will would be there where the ideal had become reality; and beauty and pleasure and feeling would live on in this total fulfilment. Every flame of passion, chaste or sensual, would still burn in the Absolute unquenched and unabridged, a note absorbed in the harmony of its higher bliss. We cannot imagine, I admit, how in detail this can be. But if truth and fact are to be one, then in some such way thought must reach its consummation. But in that consummation thought has certainly been so transformed, that to go on calling it thought seems indefensible. . . .

BIBLIOGRAPHY

I. GENERAL SURVEYS

Adamson, R., *The Development of Modern Philosophy*, London, 1903. Still a useful survey of nineteenth-century speculative thought.

Aiken, H. D., *The Age of Ideology*, New York, 1956 (paperback). Selections from major figures with helpful introductory essays.

Barrett, W., *Irrational Man*, New York, 1958.

Blackham, H. J., *Six Existentialist Thinkers*, London, 1951; New York, 1952 (paperback). Contains chapters on Kierkegaard and Nietzsche.

Copleston, F. C., *A History of Philosophy*, Vol. VII (*Fichte to Nietzsche*) and Vol. VIII (*Bentham to Russell*), London, 1963, 1966. Lucid accounts of major thinkers and trends.

Ewing, A. C. (ed.), *The Idealist Tradition*, New York, 1957. A selection of readings from Idealist philosophers, with introduction and commentaries.

———, *Idealism, A Critical Survey*, London, 1936.

Halévy, E., *The Growth of Philosophic Radicalism*, trans. M. Morris, London, 1928.

Hartmann, N., *Die Philosophie des deutschen Idealismus*, 2d ed., Berlin, 1960.

Hayek, F. A., *The Counter-Revolution of Science*, New York, 1952.

Hook, S., *From Hegel to Marx*, New York, 1935.

Kroner, R., *Von Kant bis Hegel*, 2 vols., Tübingen, 1921-4.

Löwith, K., *From Hegel to Nietzsche*, trans. D. E. Green, London, 1965.

MacIntyre, A., *A Short History of Ethics*, New York, 1966, Chaps. 14-17.

Marcuse, H., *Reason and Revolution*, London, 1941; 2d ed. with Supplementary Chapter, 1955.

O'Connor, D. J. (ed.), *A Critical History of Western Philosophy*, London & New York, 1964. This volume includes essays by contemporary philosophers on a number of leading nineteenth-century figures.

Oesterreich, T. K. *Die deutsche Philosophie des XIX Jahrhunderts*, Berlin, 1923.

Passmore, J., *A Hundred Years of Philosophy*, London, 1957. An excellent brief history of developments in philosophy from the middle of the nineteenth century until the present day.

Plamenatz, J. P., *Man and Society*, Vol. II, London, 1963.

Popper, K. R., *The Open Society and Its Enemies*, Vol. II, London, 1945.
————, *The Poverty of Historicism*, London, 1957.
Pucelle, J., *L'Idéalisme en Angleterre de Coleridge à Bradley*, Neuchâtel & Paris, 1955. A valuable survey.
Royce, J., *The Spirit of Modern Philosophy*, Boston, 1892. Includes sympathetic studies of a number of German Idealists.
Santayana, G., *Egotism in German Philosophy*, New York, 1940 (new ed.).
Watts-Cunningham, G., *The Idealistic Argument in Recent British and American Philosophy*, New York, 1933.

II. SPECIFIC PHILOSOPHERS

F. H. Bradley

(A) WORKS

Ethical Studies, 2d ed., Oxford, 1927.
Principles of Logic, 2d ed., Oxford, 1922.
Appearance and Reality, 2d ed., Oxford, 1897.
Essays on Truth and Reality, Oxford, 1914.
Collected Essays, 2 vols, Oxford, 1935.

(B) COMMENTARIES AND STUDIES

Antonelli, M. T., *La Metaphysica di F. H. Bradley*, Milan, 1952.
Church, R. W., *Bradley's Dialectic*, London, 1942.
Lofthouse, W. F., *F. H. Bradley*, London, 1949.
Muirhead, J. H., *The Platonic Tradition in Anglo-Saxon Philosophy*, London, 1931.
Pucelle, J., *L'Idéalisme en Angleterre de Coleridge à Bradley*, Neuchâtel & Paris, 1955.
Royce, J., review of *Appearance and Reality* in *The Philosophical Review*, 1894.
Russell, B., *Principles of Mathematics*, London, 1903, Chap. 26. Bradley's theory of relations is discussed.
Segerstedt, T. T., *Value and Reality in Bradley's Philosophy*, Lund, 1934.
Walsh, W. H., essay on Bradley in D. J. O'Connor, *A Critical History of Western Philosophy*, London & New York, 1964.
Wollheim, R. A., *F. H. Bradley*, Harmondsworth, 1959 (paperback). A clear and perceptive account of Bradley's metaphysic.

Auguste Comte

(A) WORKS

Cours de philosophie positive, Paris, 1830-42.
Système de politique positive, 4 vols., Paris, 1890.

(B) TRANSLATIONS

Early Essays in Social Philosophy, trans. H. D. Hudson, New York, 1911.
The Positive Philosophy of Auguste Comte, trans. H. Martineau, 2 vols., London, 1853.

BIBLIOGRAPHY

(c) COMMENTARIES AND STUDIES

Caird, E., *The Social Philosophy and Religion of Auguste Comte*, 2d ed., Glasgow, 1893.

Lévy-Bruhl, L., *La Philosophie d'Auguste Comte*, Paris, 1900; English translation, New York, 1903.

Marvin, F. S., *The Founder of Sociology*, New York, 1937.

Mill, J. S., *Auguste Comte and Positivism*, London, 1865.

Ludwig Feuerbach

(a) WORKS

Sämmtliche Werke, ed. W. Bolin and F. Jodl, 10 vols., Stuttgart, 1903-11.

(b) TRANSLATIONS

The Essence of Christianity, trans. M. Evans (George Eliot), 2d ed., London, 1881.

(c) COMMENTARIES AND STUDIES

Chamberlain, W. B., *Heaven Wasn't His Destination: The Philosophy of Ludwig Feuerbach*, London, 1941.

Engels, F., *Ludwig Feuerbach and the End of Classical German Philosophy*, Moscow, 1949.

Grégoire, F., *Aux sources de la pensée de Marx, Hegel, Feuerbach*, Louvain, 1947.

Jodl, F., *Ludwig Feuerbach*, Stuttgart, 1904.

Lévy, A., *La Philosophie de Feuerbach et son influence sur la littérature allemande*, Paris, 1904.

Löwith, K., *From Hegel to Nietzsche*, trans. D. E. Green, London, 1964.

J. G. Fichte

(a) WORKS

Sämmtliche Werke, ed. I. H. Fichte, 8 vols., Berlin, 1845-6.

Werke, ed. F. Medicus, 6 vols., Leipzig, 1908-12. This edition does not contain all Fichte's works.

Fichte und Forberg. Die philosophischen Schriften zum Atheismus-streit, ed. F. Medicus, Leipzig, 1910.

(b) TRANSLATIONS

The Science of Knowledge, trans. A. E. Kroeger, London, 1889.

The Science of Rights, trans. A. E. Kroeger, London, 1889.

The Science of Ethics, trans. A. E. Kroeger, London, 1907.

Fichte's Popular Works, trans. W. Smith, 2 vols., London, 1848.

Addresses to the German Nation, trans. R. F. Jones and G. H. Turnbull, Chicago, 1922.

(c) COMMENTARIES AND STUDIES

Adamson, R., *Fichte*, Edinburgh, 1881. A worthy, though somewhat antiquated, attempt to penetrate the obscurities of Fichte's philosophy.

Engelbrecht, H. C., J. G. *Fichte: A Study of his Political Writings, with Special Reference to His Nationalism*, New York, 1933.

Moore, G. E., review of "The Science of Ethics as Based on The Science of Knowledge," *International Journal of Ethics*, 1898.

Rickert, H., *Fichtes Atheismusstreit und die kantische Philosophie*, Berlin, 1899.

G. W. F. Hegel

(A) WORKS

Sämmtliche Werke, ed. H. Glockner, 26 vols., Stuttgart, 1951-60.

(B) TRANSLATIONS

The Phenomenology of Mind, trans. J. Baillie, London, 1931.

Encyclopedia of Philosophy, trans. and annotated by G. E. Mueller, New York, 1959.

The Science of Logic, trans. W. H. Johnston and L. G. Struthers, 2 vols., London, 1929.

The Philosophy of Right, trans. T. M. Knox, Oxford, 1942.

Lectures on the Philosophy of History, trans. J. Sibree, New York, 1944.

Lectures on the History of Philosophy, trans. E. S. Haldane and F. H. Simpson, 3 vols., London, 1892-6.

The Philosophy of Fine Art, trans. F. P. B. Osmeston, 4 vols., London, 1920.

Hegel, Selections, ed. J. Lowenberg, New York, 1929.

Hegel's Political Writings, trans. T. M. Knox, with an introductory essay by Z. A. Pelczynski, Oxford, 1964.

(c) COMMENTARIES AND STUDIES

Caird, E., *Hegel*, London & Edinburgh, 1883. Still a good introduction.

Croce, B., *What Is Living and What Is Dead in the Philosophy of Hegel*, trans. D. Ainslie, London, 1915.

Findlay, J. N., *Hegel: A Re-Examination*, London, 1958. A comprehensive, sympathetic, and reasonably clear account of Hegel's system.

Grégoire, F., *Aux sources de la pensée de Marx, Hegel, Feuerbach*, Louvain, 1947.

Hyppolite, J., *Genèse et structure de la Phénoménologie de l'Esprit de Hegel*, Paris, 1946. An important and illuminating study of Hegel's masterpiece.

Kaufmann, W., *Hegel: Reinterpretation, Texts and Commentary*, London, 1966. A well-documented account of Hegel's intellectual development which contains, among other things, a fresh translation of the famous Preface to the *Phenomenology*.

Kojève, A., *Introduction à la lecture de Hegel*, 2d ed., Paris, 1947.

Lukács, G., *Der junge Hegel. Ueber die Beziehungen von Dialektik und Oekonomie*, Berlin, 1954.

Marcuse, H., *Reason and Revolution*, London, 1941; 2d ed. with Supplementary Chapter, 1955 (Part I).

Mure, G. R. G., *The Philosophy of Hegel*, Oxford, 1965.

Stace. W. T., *The Philosophy of Hegel*, London, 1924.

Søren Kierkegaard

(A) WORKS

Samlede Vaerker, ed. A. B. Drachmann, J. L. Herberg and H. O. Lange, 14 vols., Copenhagen, 1901-6.

Critical Danish edition of Kierkegaard's *Complete Works* ed. N. Thulstrup, Copenhagen, 1951, *et seq.*

(B) TRANSLATIONS

Either/Or, trans. D. F. Swenson, L. M. Swenson, and W. Lowrie, 2 vols., Princeton, 1944; New York, 1959 (paperback).

Fear and Trembling, trans. W. Lowrie, Princeton, 1941.

Philosophical Fragments, trans. D. F. Swenson and H. V. Hong, with introduction and commentary by N. Thulstrup, Princeton, 1962.

Concluding Unscientific Postscript, trans. D. F. Swenson and W. Lowrie, Princeton, 1941.

The Sickness unto Death, trans. W. Lowrie, Princeton, 1941; New York, 1954 (paperback, with *Fear and Trembling*).

The Concept of Dread, trans. W. Lowrie, Princeton, 1944.

The Present Age, trans., with introduction, A. Dru, London, 1962 (paperback).

Journals (selections) trans. A. Dru, London & New York, 1938.

(C) COMMENTARIES AND STUDIES

Collins, J., *The Mind of Kierkegaard*, Chicago, 1953.

Grene, M., *Introduction to Existentialism*, Chicago, 1959 (paperback). Contains a brief but interesting discussion of Kierkegaard, along with other existentialist thinkers.

Lowrie, W., *Kierkegaard*, London & New York, 1938. A full and detailed biography.

Price, G., *The Narrow Pass: A Study of Kierkegaard's Concept of Man*, London, 1963. A sympathetic treatment of Kierkegaard's central themes.

Thomte, R., *Kierkegaard's Philosophy of Religion*, London & Princeton, 1948.

Wyschogrod, M., *Kierkegaard and Heidegger: the Ontology of Existence*, London, 1954.

Ernst Mach

(A) WORKS

Die Mechanik in ihrer Entwickelung, Leipzig, 1883; 4th ed. 1901.

Populärwissenschaftliche Vorlesungen, Leipzig, 1894.

Die Principien der Wärmelehre, Leipzig, 1886.

Die Analyse der Empfindungen, Jena, 1906.
Erkenntnis und Irrtum, Leipzig, 1905.

(B) TRANSLATIONS

The Science of Mechanics, trans. T. J. McCormack, 2d rev. ed., Chicago, 1902.
The Analysis of Sensations, trans. C. M. Williams, Chicago, 1914; New York, 1959 (paperback).
Space and Geometry, trans. T. J. McCormack, Chicago, 1906. This volume comprises three essays which were originally published in *The Monist,* 1901-3.

(C) COMMENTARIES AND STUDIES

Alexander, P., essay entitled "The Philosophy of Science, 1850-1910" in D. J. O'Connor, *A Critical History of Western Philosophy,* London & New York, 1964.
Buchdahl, G., "Science and Metaphysics" in *The Nature of Metaphysics,* ed. D. F. Pears, London, 1957.
Popper, K. R., "A Note on Berkeley as Precursor of Mach," *British Journal of the Philosophy of Science,* 1953.

Karl Marx

(A) WORKS

Marx-Engels, Historisch-kritische Gesamtausgabe: Werke, Schriften, Briefe, ed. D. Ryazanov and V. Adoratsky, Moscow & Berlin. This critical edition of the writings of Marx and Engels (MEGA) started appearing in 1926, but it is not yet finished, several volumes still being due.
Karl Marx-Friedrich Engels, Werke, 5 vols., Berlin, 1957-9. This edition covers writings up to 1848.

(B) TRANSLATIONS

Karl Marx: Early Writings, trans. and ed. T. B. Bottomore, London, 1963.
The Holy Family, trans. R. Dixon, Moscow, 1956.
The German Ideology, ed. S. Ryazanskaya, London, 1965.
The Poverty of Philosophy, trans. H. Quelch, Chicago, 1910.
The Communist Manifesto, ed. with introduction H. Laski, London, 1948.
The 18th Brumaire of Louis Bonaparte, trans. E. and C. Paul, London, 1926.
Capital, trans. S. Moore, E. Aveling, and E. Untermann, 3 vols., Chicago, 1906-9.
A Handbook of Marxism, ed. Emil Burns, New York & London, 1935.
Karl Marx, Selected Works, ed. C. P. Dutt, 2 vols. London & New York, 1936.
Karl Marx: Selected Writings in Sociology and Social Philosophy, ed. T. B. Bottomore and M. Rubel, London, 1956.
Karl Marx and Friedrich Engels: Basic Writings on Politics and Philosophy, ed. L. S. Feuer, New York, 1959.

(C) COMMENTARIES AND STUDIES

Acton, H. B., *The Illusion of the Epoch*, London, 1955.
Berlin, I., *Karl Marx*, London, 1939; rev. ed., 1963.
Carr, E. H., *Karl Marx: A Study in Fanaticism*, London, 1934.
Croce, B., *Historical Materialism and the Economics of Karl Marx*, trans. C. M. Meredith, Chicago, 1914.
Fromm, E., *Marx's Concept of Man*, New York, 1961.
Grégoire, F., *Aux sources de la pensée de Marx, Hegel, Feuerbach*, Louvain, 1947.
Hook, S., *Toward the Understanding of Karl Marx*, New York, 1933.
———, *From Hegel to Marx*, New York, 1936.
Hyppolite, J., *Études sur Marx et Hegel*, Paris, 1955.
Kautsky, K., *The Economic Doctrine of Karl Marx*, Berlin, 1908.
Lichtheim, G., *Marxism: An Historical and Critical Study*, London, 1961. A brilliant contribution to the field.
Marcuse, H., *Reason and Revolution*, London, 1941; 2d ed. with Supplementary Chapter, 1955 (Part II).
Plamenatz, J. P., *German Marxism and Russian Communism*, London & New York, 1954.
———, *Man and Society*, Vol. II, London, 1963.
Popper, K. R., *The Open Society and Its Enemies*, Vol. II, London, 1945.
Rubel, M., *Karl Marx: Essai de biographie intellectuelle*, Paris, 1957.
Tucker, R. C., *Philosophy and Myth in Karl Marx*, Cambridge, 1961.

John Stuart Mill

(A) WORKS

A System of Logic, 2 vols., London, 1843; 8th definitive ed. London, 1872.
Dissertations and Discussions, London, 1859.
Mill's Utilitarianism reprinted with a Study of the English Utilitarians, ed. J. P. Plamenatz, Oxford, 1949.
On Liberty, Considerations on Representative Government, ed., with introduction, R. B. McCallum, Oxford, 1946.
An Examination of Sir William Hamilton's Philosophy, London, 1865.
Autobiography, ed. H. J. Laski, London, 1952.
Three Essays on Religion, London, 1874.
John Stuart Mill's Philosophy of Scientific Method, ed. E. Nagel, New York, 1950. Selections from Mill's *System of Logic*, with valuable introduction.

(B) COMMENTARIES AND STUDIES

Anschutz, R. P., *The Philosophy of J. S. Mill*, Oxford, 1953. A sensitive discussion of Mill's thought and outlook.
Britton, K., *John Stuart Mill*, Harmondsworth, 1953 (paperback).
Jackson, R., *An Examination of the Deductive Logic of J. S. Mill*, London, 1941.
Packe, M. St. John, *The Life of John Stuart Mill*, London & New York, 1954.
Price, H. H., "Mill's View of the External World," in *Aristotelian Society Proceedings*, 1926-7.

Russell, B., *John Stuart Mill*, London, 1956. British Academy lecture.
Stephen, Leslie, *The English Utilitarians*, Vol. III, London, 1900.
Wright, G. H. von, *The Logical Problem of Induction*, Helsinki, 1941. Contains a careful analysis of Mill's experimental methods.

Friedrich Nietzsche

(A) WORKS

Gesammelte Werke, Musarionausgabe, 23 vols., Munich, 1920-9.
Werke, ed. K. Schlechta, 3 vols., Munich, 1954-6. A useful edition of Nietzsche's main writings.

(B) TRANSLATIONS

The Complete Works, ed. Oscar Levy, 18 vols., Edinburgh & London, 1909-13.
The Portable Nietzsche, trans. and ed. W. Kaufmann, New York, 1954; paperback 1956. Contains the complete *Thus Spoke Zarathustra, Twilight of the Idols, The Antichrist*, and *Nietzsche contra Wagner*.
The Birth of Tragedy and The Genealogy of Morals, trans. F. Golffing, New York, 1956 (paperback).
Beyond Good and Evil, trans. M. Cowan, Chicago, 1955 (paperback).
The Use and Abuse of History, trans. A. Collins, New York, 1949.

(C) COMMENTARIES AND STUDIES

Brinton, C., *Nietzsche*, Cambridge (Mass.) & London, 1942.
Copleston, F. C., *Friedrich Nietzsche, Philosopher of Culture*, London, 1942.
Danto, A., *Nietzsche as Philosopher*, New York, 1965. An illuminating and balanced modern study.
Kaufmann, W., *Nietzsche: Philosopher, Psychologist, Antichrist*, Princeton, 1950; New York, 1956 (paperback).
Löwith, K., *Nietzsches Philosophie der ewigen Wiederkehr des Gleichen*, Stuttgart, 1956.
Schlechta, K., *Der Fall Nietzsche*, Munich, 1959.
Vaihinger, H., *Nietzsche als Philosoph*, Berlin, 1902.

Arthur Schopenhauer

(A) WORKS

Sämmtliche Werke, ed. A. Hübscher, 2d ed., 7 vols., Wiesbaden, 1946-50.

(B) TRANSLATIONS

The World as Will and Idea, trans. R. B. Haldane and J. Kemp, 3 vols., London, 1883.
The World as Will and Representation, trans. E. F. J. Payne, 2 vols., New York, 1966.
On the Fourfold Root of the Principle of Sufficient Reason and *On the Will in Nature*, trans. K. Hillebrand, London, 1889.

The Basis of Morality, trans. A. B. Bullock, London, 1903.
Essay on the Freedom of the Will, trans. with introduction, K. Kolenda, New York, 1960.
Selected Essays of Arthur Schopenhauer, trans. E. B. Bax, London, 1891.
Schopenhauer: Essays, trans. T. Bailey Saunders, London, 1951.
The Will to Live: Selected Writings of Arthur Schopenhauer, ed. R. Taylor, New York, 1962 (paperback).

(c) COMMENTARIES AND STUDIES

Caldwell, W., *Schopenhauer's System in Its Philosophical Significance*, 2 vols., Edinburgh, 1896.
Copleston, F. C., *Arthur Schopenhauer, Philosopher of Pessimism*, London, 1946.
Fauçonnet, A., *L'ésthetique de Schopenhauer*, Paris, 1913.
Gardiner, P. L., *Schopenhauer*, Harmondsworth, 1963 (paperback).
Schneider, W., *Schopenhauer, eine Biographie*, Vienna, 1937.
Simmel, G., *Schopenhauer und Nietzsche*, Leipzig, 1907.
Taylor, R., essay on Schopenhauer in D. J. O'Connor, *A Critical History of Western Philosophy*, London & New York, 1964.
Tsanoff, R., *Schopenhauer's Criticism of Kant's Theory of Experience*, New York, 1911.
Wallace, W., *Schopenhauer*, London, 1891. A biographical study.

Max Stirner

(A) WORKS

Der Einzige und sein Eigentum, Leipzig, 1845.
Kleinere Schriften, ed. H. Mackay, Treptow-bei-Berlin, 1914.

(B) TRANSLATION

The Ego and His Own, trans. S. T. Byington, London & New York, 1913.

(c) COMMENTARIES AND STUDIES

Löwith, K., *From Hegel to Nietzsche*, trans. D. E. Green, London, 1965. Stirner's ideas are discussed, along with those of other thinkers of his period.
Marx, K., *The German Ideology*, London, 1965. Contains a protracted polemic against Stirner ("St. Max").
Mautz, K. A., *Die Philosophie M. Stirners im Gegensatz zum Hegelschen Idealismus*, Berlin, 1936.

William Whewell

(A) WORKS

The History of the Inductive Sciences, London, 1837.
The Philosophy of the Inductive Sciences, 2 vols., London, 1840; 3rd ed. (in 3 parts, *History of Scientific Ideas, Novum Organum Renovatum, On the Philosophy of Discovery*), London, 1858-60.
The Elements of Morality, 4th ed., Cambridge, 1864.

(B) COMMENTARIES AND STUDIES

Blanché, R., *Le Rationalisme de Whewell*, Paris, 1935.

Ducasse, C. J., "Whewell's Philosophy of Scientific Discovery," *The Philosophical Review*, 1951.

Mill, J. S., "Dr. Whewell on Moral Philosophy," in *Dissertations and Discussions*, Vol. 2, London, 1859.

Strong, E. W., "William Whewell and John Stuart Mill: Their Controversy about Scientific Knowledge," *Journal of the History of Ideas*, 1955.

Todhunter, T., *William Whewell*, London, 1876.

Wright, G. H. von, *The Logical Problem of Induction*, Helsinki, 1941. Whewell's criticisms of Mill's conception of scientific reasoning are discussed.

INDEX

INDEX

qualities and relations,
421ff.

reality, 297
  and appearance, 373,
    374
  nature of, 428ff.
reason:
  conception of, 76
  in contradiction with
    itself, 64
  paradox of, 295ff.
  in philosophy, 360ff.
  as "sovereign of the
    world," 10
recognition, process of, 43
Reid, Thomas, 200
relation and quality,
  421ff.
religion:
  and dogma, 3
  essence of, 239, 282
  and freedom of spirit,
    78
  life-principle of, 258
  Marx's view of, 270,
    274
  philosophy of, 250
repentance, 112, 113
representation, 96-97
Ribot, Théodule, 371,378
right and wrong, 117
Ritschl, Friedrich, 321
Russell, Bertrand, 2, 3

Saint-Simon, Louis, 9,
  13, 131
salvation, 122
Schelling, Friedrich, 4, 7,
  40
Schopenhauer, Arthur,
  12, 88ff., 338
  and Hegelianism, 88
  and "principle of suffi-
    cient reason," 391
Schwann, Theodor, 2
science:
  concept of, 67
  economy of, 389
  empirical, 70
  function of, 392
  hierarchy of, 144ff.
scientific doctrines,
  verification of, 172
self-activity, 45
"self-alienation," 8, 269
self-consciousness, 43-44,
  52ff., 78, 265ff.

self-preservation,
  instinct of, 336
self-sacrifice, 121
Seneca, 110
sensation:
  contingent, 228
  and elements, 376, 379,
    381, 390
  as independent of the
    will, 230-31
  as ingredient of the
    will, 339
  permanent possibility
    of, 232-34, 236
  and psychology, 220
sense-perception, 63
senses, deception of, 360
senses, world of the, 23, 24
skepticism, 55, 56, 58, 241
slavery, 78
Snell, Willebrord, 162
"Social Darwinism," 12n
Socrates, 291, 295, 306,
  308, 320
Sophocles, 85
Soul, the Alienated, 5B
Spencer, Herbert, 12n, 346
Spinoza, 293n, 334
spirit:
  definition of, 77
  essence of, 82, 83
  forms of, 69
  (Geist), 7, 8, 9
  idea of, 86-87
  nature of, 84
  phenomenology of, 67
  realm of, 77
spiritual world, 79,
Stewart, Dugald, 200
Stirner, Max, 251ff.
Stoicism, 53, 54, 55, 58
Stoics, 334-35
substantive and
  adjective, 417ff.
suffering, man's recogni-
  tion of, 121, 122
supersession, act of, 270
syllogism, 70, 179, 180,
  201-203
symbols, ideas as, 405, 406
system of logic, method
  in, 71

theological method, 133
thesis and antithesis, 408
thinghood (Ansichen),
  52, 267
thing-in-itself, 64-67,
  97-99,337,352,372,439

"things-in-themselves," 5
thinking, conceptual, 61
thinking, science, 62
thought:
  elements, 382
  freedom of, 54
  and reality, 436-43
  universal, 85-86
Thucydides, 85
tidology, 215, 216
time, space, and motion,
  385-88
transcendental theory, 24
truth, concept of, 64
truth, question of, 302

understanding, forms of,
  64
understanding,
  reflective, 63
unity of opposites, 73
universe, intellectual
  view of, 67-68
Unkown, definition of,
  295, 296

Veda, formula of, 121
virture, theory of, 115, 117
Vitello, Erasmus, 161

Wagner, Richard, 321
Whately, Richard, 201,202
Whewell, William, 14
  158ff., 170-72, 194-98
will:
  as act of thought, 109
  and body, 92-93
  concept of, 98
  denial of, 122, 124
  as essence of reason, 6
  freedom of, 104f., 207,
    339, 340, 341
  identity of, 93
  and intellect, 126, 128
  objectivity of, 93
  phenomena of, 100
  Schopenhauer's view
    on, 338
  as thing-in-itself, 91ff.,
    126
work, performance of, 273
worker, as slave of
  object, 274, 275

"Young Hegelians," 261,
  284-85

Zeus, 85